Play Therapy with
Traumatized Children

Play Therapy with Traumatized Children

A Prescriptive Approach

Paris Goodyear-Brown

WILEY

John Wiley & Sons, Inc.

Library of Congress Cataloging-in-Publication Data:
Goodyear-Brown, Paris.
    Play therapy with traumatized children : a prescriptive approach / Paris
Goodyear-Brown.
        p. ; cm.
Includes bibliographical references and index.
ISBN 978-0-470-39524-0 (pbk)
1. Psychic trauma in children--Treatment. 2. Play therapy. I. Title.
[DNLM: 1. Stress Disorders, Post-Traumatic--therapy. 2. Child psychology.
3. Child. 4. Nonverbal Communication. 5. Play Therapy. WM 170 G658p 2010]
    RJ506.P66G66 2010
    618.92'8521--dc22   2009017146

10 9 8 7 6 5 4 3 2

Contents

Foreword

Approximately 20 percent of children have a diagnosable mental disorder, and 10 percent of these children have extreme functional impairment. In the US these numbers translate to 11–14 million of the over 63 million children suffering significant impairment. The number of children reported to authorities for abuse and neglect has been on the rise. Over 3 million children were reported to state child abuse hotlines for maltreatment within the past few years. In 2005 alone, as monitored by the National Child Abuse and Neglect Data System, 899,000 children were reported as having been abused. Of those children, nearly 10 percent were sexually abused. Many cases are not reported, and some only come to light as the result of disclosures made by children to perceived safe and caring individuals, such as teachers, school counselors, and therapists.

A national survey in 1995 reported that 6 percent of mothers and 3 percent of fathers had admitted to physically abusing their children at least once. And up to 10 million US children are exposed to domestic violence annually. The numbers are staggering.

As child and play therapists, we are called upon to witness the children's stories of the unspeakable brutalities of humanity—violent crime, childhood physical and sexual abuse, extreme loss, and terrorism among them. Many child and play therapists are working with large numbers of children impacted by trauma from abuse, neglect, and family and community violence. About a third of the children we see meet diagnostic criteria for PTSD, with up to 50% of traumatized children suffering PTSD nationwide. We see myriad symptoms in our child and teen clients from lack of trust in family members, distrust of adults in general, feeling worthless, depressed, withdrawn, isolated, anxious, angry, defiant, and hyper-vigilant. They suffer from lack of sleep, nightmares, refusing to go to bed, along with low self-esteem, low frustration tolerance, learning problems, developmental delays, poor social skills, and difficulty self-regulating affect. Some rage against the world through anti-social and sexualized behaviors, while others withdraw into dissociation. Many of the children we work with suffer not just from a single traumatic event, rather from more complex, repeated, and prolonged abuse experiences. Often the trauma includes early or repeated breaks in attachments. The child's safety and security is severed, creating a weak emotional foundation. Such complex trauma results in long-term and pervasive emotional impairment. The child's core capacity to self-soothe, self-regulate, and connect interpersonally is shattered. The depth of severity varies depending on the developmental stage when the traumatic events occurred. Trauma—and especially complex trauma—not only impacts the child's emotional, developmental, and social functioning, but it also goes as deeply as changing the brain physiology of the child. The work by attachment and trauma researchers Bruce Perry, Dan Siegel, Bessel Van der Kolk, and Allen Shore has shown the potent negative impact of trauma on children's developing brains. The good news is that some of this damage appears to be reversible, and certain types of play are one component in helping to reverse the damage.

Many of the children we work with find they cannot or will not talk about their traumatic experiences, even in the most emotionally safe and caring of environments. Some having been warned and threatened with punishment or bodily harm to themselves, a family member, or a pet and are terrified to disclose their abuse. Others harbor horrific images from their trauma that threaten to overwhelm weak and vulnerable defenses. They fear letting the genie out of the bottle for fear it will cause a flood, annihilate the child or those they love, or remain resistant to going back in and wreaking havoc once out. Play therapy and play-based interventions allow the child a non-verbal way to communicate the pain and horrors held within. Play therapy is developmentally based, developed from solid philosophical and theoretical underpinnings, with empirically based research showing its positive impact. Play as therapy and play in therapy allows for healing to occur for children and teens.

With over 25 years of clinical work with sexually abused, neglected, and traumatized children, I have seen the therapeutic and healing power of play close up over and over again. But if ever I needed and was thankful for the healing power of play, it was just after the horrific terrorist destruction of the World Trade Center in New York City on September 11, 2001. I volunteered on weekends for five months at Kids Korner at Pier 94 in New York City. Children waited up to ten hours for their parent to navigate the huge warehouse maze of services they had to register for in order to obtain a death certificate or short-term financial or emotional support. The children were given a supportive environment filled with typical symbolic play therapy toys such as a dollhouses, figures, blocks, toy cars, planes, emergency vehicles, and arts and crafts supplies. The space was often filled with up to 40 children, and as many counselors, psychologists, and social workers skilled in the use of therapeutic play. The one-on-one time allowed for children to share their fears, questions, worries, and horrific images in silence through their play and artwork knowing a caring, empathic, and understanding adult would respond to the metaphors and symbolism expressed. These children could not turn to their grief-stricken parents who were barely managing their day-to-day activities. In those moments of play with an empathic and caring child/play therapist, healing began for them. They could begin to let go of their fears, fantasies, and debilitating images. Through play and the play materials, they could silently communicate their thoughts and feelings and know they were being heard. You could feel them let out an emotional sigh of relief from having to hold their aching hearts still. It is no different for sexually abused and traumatized children.

We enter into this profession out of a genuine and intense desire to help others in a meaningful way. Our initial training and skills become tested and strained by the burgeoning number of trauma-ridden cases coming into our offices and agencies. As we try to respond effectively, we find ourselves needing to reevaluate programmatic and clinical services, often pushed by funding resources that want to see proven efficacy in treatment. As professionals, our basic training and skills are tested and stretched to the limits and often found wanting. Over the years, my initial nondirective psychodynamic play therapy skills were tested in working with sexually abused and traumatized children. I found that "one size fits all" of treatment approach did not work. Children who did not want to reveal their abuse story or address their rage, held it inside and found lots else to play out through nondirective play. If I did not go there, they would not either. We were at a standoff. Healing was slow, if at all, in these cases.

There had to be another way. Over time, through workshops and exposure at national Association for Play Therapy conferences, the answer came by blending play therapy through a prescriptive and integrative approach. Using knowledge gained from empirical and evidence-based trauma treatment approaches, along with cognitive behavioral components—especially the creation of the child's trauma narrative—coupled with play-based techniques, deep healing could occur. It required flexibility in being grounded in and utilizing such other theoretical frameworks as attachment and cognitive-behavioral therapy, along with updates on neurobiological-psychological research on trauma. The child and teen responded to increasing their feelings vocabulary, identifying their emotional triggers, and learning ways to self-soothe and self-regulate. Role-playing through puppet play helped to desensitize the material and then master alternative strategies that could then be generalized in many settings. I learned how to use nondirective play to set the stage for a safe environment, sensitive to the child's pacing, as well as offering a release at the end of a structured directive time in dealing with highly charged feelings and material. It became a dance of learning when to be nondirective and how and when to be directive and for how long.

Parents were used in the process to help practice skills and offer a safe and soothing environment for the child. Research has recently shown that the most effective trauma treatment approaches include the parent as part of the teaching and practice of skills for the child.

But where does one find a book that can help walk us through the process of growing into and becoming a prescriptive child and play therapist? How can we find techniques that will help us work with our traumatized child and teen clients?

Happily, Paris Goodyear-Brown has created a volume that helps clinicians work in an integrative and prescriptive approach. She takes a holistic, integrated, and multi-theoretical approach in Play Therapy with Traumatized Children: A Prescriptive Approach. This book is organized in a stepwise fashion, allowing the reader to follow her thinking and approach in systematically working with traumatized clients. She teaches us a "Flexibly Sequential Play Therapy (FSPT)" model of treatment for traumatized children. This model requires a flexible and nuanced application along with the integration of nondirective and directive approaches. After a discussion of the evolution of her model and a foundational look at definitions and symptomatology as they relate to childhood trauma, she helps us understand how children can be helped to build a sense of safety and security in the playroom. Goals aimed at preparing the child for processing, such as increasing a child's positive coping, managing stress reactions, and navigating their emotional lives, set the stage for the trauma specific work. The author explicates a "Continuum of Disclosure" which allows the child to be in control in slowly opening up and exploring the trauma content. Concrete techniques and case studies are offered illustrating how to accomplish this. She then moves into how to help children utilize "Experiential Mastery Play (EMP)." It is here that children are able to use the protected play space and a variety of play tools to restore a sense of empowerment. Goodyear-Brown accomplishes this by offering the reader ways to weave skill-based work into helping the child become grounded in play and expressive mediums. As therapy moves toward reducing the toxicity of the horrific images and memories of the trauma, the child is helped to formulate his trauma narrative. The power of play and play-based techniques allows the child to tune into the sensory perceptions of the event. We are reminded by the author that a child's verbal rehearsal of his narrative over and over again, split off from his sensory perceptions of the event, does not result in relief from symptoms or allow for the integration of difficult perceptions of the experience. It is indeed the healing power of play that brings out relief and access to physiologically encoded memories.

The model is rounded out through resolution of problematic thoughts and faulty attributions and encourages the child to integrate the trauma into a positive sense of self. Throughout the book, she equips the clinician with creative, practical, and easily replicable interventions that can be utilized within the FSPT model to accomplish its goals.

The reader is guided through treatment sessions with dialogue interwoven with practical techniques and how best to implement them. At times, the rich case examples are graphic and unsettling as they deal with horrific traumatic events. And we become privy to not only the therapist's empathic responses but also to the underlying insight and thinking employed through a multi-theoretical lens. We are cautioned that it is critical to assess the child's coping strategies and environmental supports before starting the trauma work and utilizing the techniques offered. In addition, parents/caregivers as co-regulators need to be enlisted in the trauma work in order for treatment to be effective in helping the child soothe their physiology. Her discussion of the SOOTHE strategies offers a new conceptualization of ways in which parents can serve as effective co-regulators. Her chapter on "Parents as Partners" addresses the need for developmental sensitivity by the therapist in helping caregivers utilize her arsenal of techniques to unburden the client a gentle dance of attunement. First by inviting the child to respond, then acknowledging where they are, and finally helping them take the first steps as they walk together in witnessing the trauma experience.

This gem of a book ends with care taken to acknowledge the importance of the termination process. We are helped to honor the relationship and its healing components, and celebrate the child's 'graduation' from therapy.

After reading through Play Therapy with Traumatized Children: A Prescriptive Approach, I found myself, a seasoned trauma play therapist, enriched, validated, and supported on a deep level. My work is now much more informed by the poignant wisdom of the children's case studies and therapy comments and the rich compendium of creative and easy-to-implement techniques offered. So reader, sit back, relax, and prepare for a wonderful experience as you read on!

Athena A. Drewes, PSYD, RPT-S

Director of Clinical Training and APA-Accredited Internship

Astor Services for Children and Families, Poughkeepsie, NY

Preface

My first therapeutic job was as the van driver for an after-school group therapy program for at-risk children. The vast majority of the 6- to 16-year-olds came to us with extensive trauma histories. It was during this time that I learned that working with traumatized children is messy. Just when I thought I had figured out what worked with a particular child, that child would grow and change, hit a new developmental milestone, or inexplicably regress. The number of times that a child, while enjoying a seemingly peaceful drive home, would suddenly have what I scientifically term a "meltdown" in the absence of any obvious cause, taught me to respect the trauma triggers that come in all shapes and sizes. I wanted to understand how to help these children and went back to school with this goal in mind. After graduate school, I was fortunate enough to be asked to design a therapy component for the Therapeutic Preschool Program in our area. This program served 3- to 5-year-olds who had been kicked out of regular daycare programs for their extreme, often dangerous behavior. Once again, the vast majority of these children had already experienced trauma in their young lives. At the time, behavioral therapy was the primary approach taken by programs like ours, and while it was effective in managing the children's behaviors some of the time, it did not seem to meet the deeper psychological needs of our clients.

Then across my desk came the brochure for the annual international conference of the Association of Play Therapy. I went to the conference that year and sat under the teaching of Gary Landreth, Eliana Gil, Charlie Schaefer, Kevin O'Conner, and Evangeline Munns, to name a few. I fell madly in love with the field. I am repeatedly astonished at the power of play in communicating the sometimes unspeakable pain of the children that we treat. The more I was exposed to different play therapy approaches, the more I grappled with how to integrate the knowledge I was gleaning through these various theoretical and practice models. While the field is now moving towards an integration of approaches, there was a great divide at the time between nondirective and directive play therapy approaches. My natural inclination was to value the unique contributions of each approach I encountered and to experiment with the most appropriate use of each.

Historically, clinicians have defined themselves in terms of a particular theoretical model or intervention (more on this in Chapter 1). However, if we engage in rigid self-definition, we are not able to flexibly meet the unique needs of the children we serve. As I continue to wrestle with these issues in my practice, I have evolved into a prescriptive play therapist. The prescriptive approach is simply one in which play therapists, trained in a variety of theoretical paradigms and intervention models, choose which approach to use with a given client based on the client's unique presentation. The child's symptomatology, diagnosis, developmental needs, and natural leanings are matched with appropriate treatment goals and then matched to the most helpful interventions. The appropriate interventions, which may run the gambit from nondirective to directive, can then literally be prescribed at various phases of treatment, for various lengths of time, and in a flexible, clinician informed order. This approach allows us to move from an either/or way of thinking about various models of play therapy to a yes/and way of integrating the benefits of each.

Since I have always gravitated to traumatized children in my clinical work, it is only natural that I would apply this prescriptive lens to that work. In addition to this fundamental belief that we are to cull out the best of each model and use it in the service of our clients, I find great joy in taking a theoretical construct, a treatment goal, or a piece of therapeutic insight and translating it into a prop-based play therapy intervention that facilitates growth in a particular child. The techniques that I have created and shared over the years have been welcomed by both seasoned clinicians and newcomers. As I travel, speak, and write, I am humbled by the number of professionals who use these techniques and by the number of children these clinicians are helping. While practitioners often give feedback that they are inspired and energized by the practical interventions for helping traumatized children and anxious to use them in practice, they do not always have a framework for how and when in the treatment continuum to do so. The intricacies of trauma work can be overwhelming for even the most seasoned professional, and the plethora of play therapy techniques even more so. It is easy to feel adrift in a sea of interventions.

In response to this difficulty, I have designed the model explicated in this text. The model, informed by current research and 15 years of clinical experience, lays out a systematic yet flexible approach to treating traumatized children. Treatment goals are loosely organized in a sequence that aims to minimize the risks of iatrogenic effects on our clients while maximizing the power of play. When treatment goals are pursued through nondirective approaches, case vignettes of children's self-titrated healing are shared. When treatment goals are serviced through directive approaches, specific interventions are described. My hope is that this model, flexibly sequential play therapy (FSPT), will provide a detailed pathway for new clinicians and a scaffolding on which seasoned clinicians can place their most effective interventions. While any articulated model runs the risk of being used as a cookie-cutter, I have great faith in the clinical finesse of my colleagues to embrace the plasticity of the model in a way that meets the unique needs of each traumatized child that we have the honor to treat. It is with humility that I submit this text to you.

Paris Goodyear-Brown, LCSW, RPT-S

Acknowledgments

I want to begin by thanking my colleagues, especially Charles Schaefer, Eliana Gil, and Athena Drewes, who have provided mentorship and encouragement, both through their vast clinical knowledge and their practical help with the writing process. You have enriched both my personal and professional identities and I thank you.

Thanks, also, to Kathy Lebby, Teri Krull, and others at the Association for Play Therapy, who were some of the first to offer me a place to present and continue to shape the ideas comprising this book. Thanks for recognizing the promise before I did and for believing in me along the way.

I am forever grateful to my editor, Isabel Pratt, for her initial pursuit of me when I wasn't sure if I could do this and her continued help in navigating all things related to the minefield of publishing. Thanks also to the editing staff who were willing to rework deadlines when my third child arrived on the scene earlier than expected.

Thanks also to Janine Shelby, Scott Riviere, and Liana Lowenstein, my dear friends and kindred spirits, who have supported my work and expanded my ideas. Special thanks to Patti van Eys and Linda Ashford, my colleagues at Vanderbilt University, for their excellent collaboration in the creation and implementation of the SOOTHE strategies.

Finally, this book would not have been possible without the tireless support of my family: My husband, Forrest, who is my constant cheerleader, my maypole in the midst of mayhem, and my technical guru. My 8-year-old son, Sam, who called me nightly during the final push of the book to ask how many chapters I had revised that day. My bright light Madison, and my newborn, Nicholas, who grew inside me right along with this book.

Lastly, I want to thank my mom, who put food under my nose when I needed it, challenged me time and time again to get to the essence of what I really meant to say, and who wasn't above the grunt work that goes into producing a manuscript. I've said it before and I'll say it again, my cup truly runs over.

1

Introduction: Dimensions of Treatment for Traumatized Children

"It hurts inside,
it hurts inside,
it hurts inside so baaaad"

This was the sing-song refrain of Racquel, a seven-year-old little girl who had just survived a night sleeping on her front porch. She arrived at school that morning dressed in the same clothes she had worn the day before and complaining of being hungry. Her teacher reported that she was uncontrollable in the classroom, aggressively engaging her peers and disrupting the other students. She was sent to my office, where she sat down on the couch with her arms crossed over her chest and glared at me defiantly. She looked at me with hot tears held back by sheer willpower and said, "I don't want to talk about it." I explained that sometimes it was difficult to talk about feelings, but that they could get out through music or drawing. Racquel looked at me thoughtfully and then reached for the toy guitar and began to strum these words in a frenzied rhythm, repeating them over and over again until she reached a fever pitch. Then she sighed, put the guitar aside, and sat back down. The tears began to flow, and so did her tale. Mom had gone out prostituting herself in an attempt to keep the family afloat financially but had forgotten to leave a key under the mat.

The fact is that our traumatized children do hurt inside. Sometimes the hurt comes out in externalizing behavior problems. Sometimes the hurt is held close and causes a host of internalizing symptoms. Either way, child therapists become, in our use of self and the space, the strong containers who help to hold the hurt for the children we serve. This book highlights the many ways a therapist holds trauma content for a child, while navigating a developmentally sensitive, individualized course of treatment.

The Goals of This Text

The aim of this book is threefold. The first objective is to outline my approach to trauma treatment, what I have termed the flexibly sequential play therapy (FSPT) model of treatment for traumatized children. Although each child is unique, each case is different, and all require the finesse of a skilled clinician, a series of foundational treatment goals come up over and over again during a course of therapy for a traumatized child. They are:

1. Building a child's sense of safety and security within the playroom and in relation to the person of the therapist
2. Assessing and augmenting coping skills
3. Soothing the physiology
4. Using parents as partners: Ensuring that caregivers are facilitative partners in the therapy process and effective co-regulators of the child's affect
5. Increasing emotional literacy
6. Creating a coherent narrative of the trauma that integrates the linguistic narrative with somatosensory content
7. Addressing the thought life, including challenging faulty attributions and cognitive distortions while restructuring maladaptive cognitions and installing and practicing adaptive thoughts
8. Making positive meaning of the post-trauma self

In addition to these treatment goals, the rich environment of the playroom encourages two other processes that I have seen play out over and over again as children work through trauma. I have labeled the first of these the continuum of disclosure, which refers to the ways in which children self-titrate their exposure to trauma content. The second phenomenon is called

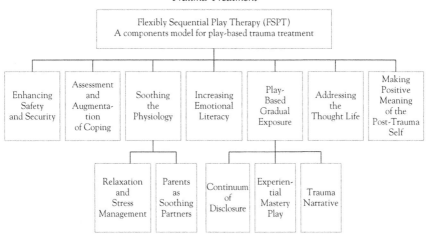

COMPONENTS OF FSPT
*Flexibly Sequential Play Therapy for
Trauma Treatment*

Figure 1.1 Components of FSPT

experiential mastery play (EMP) and refers to the myriad ways in which children use the play space and the tools of childhood to restore the sense of empowerment that posttraumatic children have often lost. These twin processes, grounded in play and expressive mediums and woven throughout the other skill-based work, are so pervasive with traumatized children that each is given its own chapter.

The FSPT model delineates specific treatment goals, delivered through a variety of specific play-based technologies and supported by an understanding of the facilitative powers of play and the therapist's use of self in the play space. The specific needs and symptom constellations of each child *require* a flexible, nuanced application of the model and also leave room for the integration of nondirective and directive approaches. The sequence is also flexible with respect to both chronological order and the length of time that is spent in the pursuit of each goal. The goals are laid down sequentially. This delineation may give the faulty impression that each goal can be fit neatly into a box and done in an ordered fashion with every client. The opposite is more likely to be true.

Although the skill sets may be introduced in a certain order, it is often the case that several goals are being pursued simultaneously. For example, although trauma narrative work is generally saved until the child has established a strong foundation of positive coping, relaxation strategies have been rehearsed, and parent support has been increased, children may begin to share trauma content spontaneously. It is the therapist's job to become a container for this content, record it in some fashion as part of the narrative, and, if necessary, invite the child back into safer territory.

The flexible nature of FSPT also allows for steps in the sequence to be skipped if the child or family already seems to have a healthy grasp of the therapeutic content that would otherwise be covered. For example, a child who enters treatment after being involved in a serious car accident may not need to progress through every step of the therapy. He may already have some of the internalized abilities that would be provided through treatment. If he has a strong, contingently responsive caregiver, he is likely to already have internal capacities for self-soothing based on a history of being soothed by the parent. Additionally, if the parent is not mired in her own trauma reaction and is functioning as a healthy support to the child, the components of treatment related to soothing the physiology and maximizing the role of the caregiver may be minimal. Through careful assessment and clinical judgment, the most salient treatment goals from the model can be mapped out on a case-by-case basis.

The application of FSPT requires breadth of knowledge and finesse with a variety of treatment technologies. Goals such as coping, emotional literacy, and cognitive restructuring require an understanding of cognitive-behavior theory (Beck, 1975, 1979, 2005) and its derivative methodologies for children and adolescents (Asarnow, Tompson, & Berk, 2005; Cohen, Deblinger, Mannarino, & Steer, 2004; Cohen, Mannarino, & Deblinger, 2006), as well as cognitive-behavioral play therapy (Knell, 1993, 1998). Soothing the physiology requires an understanding of trauma theory and developmental traumatology (Briere & Scott, 2006; Cicchetti & Tucker, 1994; DeBellis et al., 1999; DeBellis & Putnam, 1994; Perry & Azad, 1999; Solomon & Siegel, 2003), physiological stress responses (Bremner et al., 2003; DeBellis & Thomas, 2003; Van der Kolk, 1994), and the theoretical underpinnings of somatic therapies (Rothschild, 2000) and mindfulness practices (Kabat-Zinn, 1990, 2005; Segal, Williams, & Teasdale, 2002).

Maximizing the role of parents as partners in a child's trauma treatment requires an understanding of family systems theory and attachment theory and familiarization with the latest dyadic interventions, including parent-child interaction therapy (Herschell & McNeil, 2007; Urquiza & McNeil, 1996), Theraplay (Jernberg & Booth, 2001; Martin, Snow, & Sullivan, 2008; Munns, 2009), filial therapy (Guerney, 1964; Guerney, Guerney, & Andronico, 1999; VanFleet, Ryan, & Smith, 2005), child-parent psychotherapy (Lieberman,

Van Horn, & Ippen, 2005, 2006), child–parent relationship therapy (Bratton, Landreth, Kellam, & Blackard, 2006; Landreth & Bratton, 2006), and the Circle of Security Project (Cooper, Hoffman, Powell, & Marvin, 2005; Hoffman, Marvin, Cooper, & Powell, 2006; Marvin, Cooper, Hoffman, & Powell, 2002; Powell, Cooper, Hoffman, & Marvin, 2007). Although it is not necessary to be proficient in every one of the models listed here, it is essential that the modern clinician's tool kit include sound dyadic interventions and psychoeducation components for the parent.

The developmental needs of children also require that clinicians have a healthy respect for the therapeutic uses of play (Landreth, 1991; Schaefer, 1993; Schaefer & Drewes, 2009) and the effectiveness of play therapy as a treatment modality (Bratton, Ray, Rhine, & Jones, 2005; Ray, Bratton, Rhine, & Jones, 2001). Overlaying all these areas of knowledge should be a great respect for a child's individuality and a deep belief in a child's ability to heal from trauma.

The second intention behind this book is to equip clinicians with creative, practical, easily replicable interventions that can be employed to accomplish each of the goals of the FSPT model. The most common concern I hear from practitioners is that techniques and theoretical information about trauma are easy to find, but the blending of solid theoretical groundwork with techniques is more difficult. The application of specific techniques or interventions, without the proper scaffolding of a comprehensive model of treatment in which to place them, may end up producing iatrogenic effects. To this end, an explication of prop-based intervention (PBI) is made. Additionally, all the goal-directed chapters include examples of specific, prop-based play interventions that can be employed in the pursuit of that goal.

The third aim of this book is to accurately convey the myriad ways in which children eloquently articulate and begin to resolve their experiences of traumatic events through play, art, and story. This book is not limited by the form that a particular trauma might take. Case examples include clients who have experienced physical abuse, sexual abuse, domestic violence, divorce, the death of a loved one, tragic accidents, chronic illnesses, and natural disasters.

The Need for Integration

In conference settings, I am often asked, "How should we conceptualize the underlying anxiety problem in posttraumatic children? From a neurophysiological perspective? From a psychodynamic perspective? From a behavioral perspective? From a family systems perspective? From a cognitive perspective?" My answer is unabashedly, "Yes, yes, yes, yes, and yes." FSPT is both inclusive, in that it recognizes the valuable contributions of widely diverse paradigms to functional trauma treatment, and holistic, in the sense that all aspects of the child's life (developmental, social, cognitive, filial, neurobiological, etc.) must be considered when planning treatment.

An example may help to flesh out the complexities of treatment. Julie, a ten-year-old girl referred to treatment after witnessing her father violently attack her mother, is suffering from intense separation anxiety. In this case, it can be hypothesized that the avoidance of separation from mom is directly related to the trauma, because Julie had no difficulty separating from mom before the attack. Julie insists on staying in the same room with her mother, even when they are at home during the daytime. Mom is exhausted and bewildered by her daughter's behavior and vacillates between yelling at her daughter and accusing her of manipulating the situation and feeling guilty about the child's pain and enabling Julie's dependence on her. In this case, the child and parent need psychoeducation about the effects of trauma and anxiety and the best mechanisms through which to fight them. The mom needs specific training in strategies that will soothe her daughter while challenging her to push through the anxiety. The parent and child need to create a coherent narrative of the attack together and discharge the toxicity associated with that event. The child needs individualized play-based interventions that will augment her coping, equip her with relaxation strategies, and train her to "boss back" the anxiety and make strides in identifying and restructuring faulty cognitions. A process of graduated exposures will most likely have the greatest success if it is reinforced through behavioral rewards for the child. In addition to these pieces, the child may benefit from spontaneous reenactment of the trauma through the play materials in the room. Yes, yes, yes, yes, and yes.

The trend toward integration promoted by child clinicians from other professional fields is being trumpeted by play therapists as well (Gil, 2006; Kaduson, Cangelosi, & Schaefer, 1997; Shelby & Felix, 2005). Currently many theoretical orientations and working models fall within the scope of play therapy. Although each orientation has a valuable contribution to make, it is critical that clinicians select and tailor intervention models to the unique needs of each client, as opposed to championing one theoretical approach to the exclusion of others.

Clinicians have historically defined themselves in relation to their theoretical orientation. "I am a psychoanalytic therapist." "I am a cognitive-behavioral therapist." "I am a child-centered play therapist." "I am an attachment therapist." Each of these theoretical orientations birthed a host of technologies that allow for the practical application of each theory. These technologies may include a premeditated way of responding to clients, a series of intentionally designed questions aimed at exploring a particular area of a person's experience, a set of psychoeducational activities, or a succession of experiential exercises that support the model. Although all of these models have valuable contributions to make to the field of child therapy, no single therapy can claim to be the fix or the cure for every child who comes through our doors. In fact, when we as clinicians have too closely aligned ourselves with one particular mode of practice, we increase the likelihood that we will have clients whom we are unable to help. In these cases, we run the risk of eventually characterizing a clinical failure as one in which the child cannot be helped when what may be more accurate is that we have not yet found the most effective way of helping. With these dangers in mind, it is incumbent upon contemporary child therapists to be well versed in a variety of intervention models.

My own evolution as a trauma therapist may mirror the journey of many readers. I was originally trained in child-centered play therapy (CCPT) and its offshoot, filial therapy, both of which gave me a healthy respect for a nondirective approach and a child's ability to lead. There will be many examples throughout this text of the magic that can occur when a child is allowed to use play, the language of childhood, to work through her trauma experiences. I am constantly amazed at a child's ability to spontaneously go where she needs to go, eloquently describing her experiences through the play, art, and sand. I am, however, equally amazed at how a traumatic experience or maltreatment history can rob a child of this same spontaneity. Recognizing the limitations that an exclusively nondirective approach placed on my own practice, I went in search of additional tools.

Racquel, the seven-year-old girl who spent the night on the porch at the start of this chapter, moved from dysregulation to immobilization in the course of the morning. Her tightly crossed arms mirrored her tightly held control. She needed an invitation toward movement, and my offers of music, drawing, or sand play gave her options among which she could choose. The facilitative invitation, while directive in nature, opened the door for her self-directed creation of the "It hurts inside" mantra. In this case, Racquel needed help getting started.

Other aspects of trauma treatment may also require more directive intervention from the therapist. Psychoeducation related to a child's specific traumatic events and skill building in target areas can both be accomplished through the medium of play but must be intentionally pursued. In addition, some children engage in trauma reenactment play that is repetitive and aimless, often separated from any meaningful thoughts, emotions, or energized movement. Gil (2006) terms this mired play pattern stagnant posttraumatic play. The therapist's response in these situations requires a range of purposeful invitations to help the child become unstuck.

Another aspect of trauma recovery relates to the restoration of disrupted attachment relationships with caregivers. In some cases a traumatic event has compromised the parent, the child, or both parties to such an extent that they need directive help in reestablishing a relationship of coregulation. In other cases, the depth of maltreatment requires a child to develop a relationship with an entirely new caregiver. In either case, a host of directive interventions exist that purposefully facilitate these connections. Keeping in mind the variety of these needs, the FSPT model embraces both nondirective and directive approaches to treatment, promoting the flexible application of each.

In sum, the FSPT model represents a systematic integration of theoretical constructs and tools drawn from these diverse schools of thought. Nondirective approaches are used in relation to specific goals. Building safety and security in the playroom is often a child-led process that is simply reinforced by the therapist. The broad processes that I term the continuum of disclosure and experiential mastery play and certain aspects of trauma narrative work tend to be child-directed. Directive approaches are implemented to concretize or augment the work done in these categories and are the primary portals through which skill building and psychoeducation occur, both for the children and their caregivers.

The Facilitative Power of Play in FSPT

FSPT relies heavily on the therapeutic and facilitative powers of play to deliver developmentally sensitive treatment. The facilitative power of play forms the foundation for the application of all evidence-based methods delineated in the FSPT model. The integration of play into the delivery of other intervention models can maximize the developmental sensitivity of the model. For example, recent literature highlights challenges in the nuanced application of CBT for children and adolescents (Gravea & Blisset, 2004; Weisz, Southam-Gerow, & McCarty, 2001). Although CBT is the gold standard of evidence-based practice for the treatment of PTSD and depression in children and adolescents, recent concerns have been articulated related to the cognitive limitations of younger children. Children younger than eight may lack the sophisticated cognitive capabilities (processes such as metacognition) that impact the effectiveness of CBT (Holmbeck et al., 2003). According to two separate meta-analyses of CBT treatment with children and adolescents, older children benefited significantly more from treatment than younger children (Weisz, Weiss, Han, Granger, & Morton, 1995; Durlak, Fuhrman, & Lampman, 1991). The integration of play with the cognitive and behavioral information being conveyed may enhance the treatment's effectiveness. Some of the ways in which play functions as a mechanism for change in trauma treatment are listed next.

Play Counters Toxicity

Traumatic events have toxic effects on our children. Children naturally avoid exposure to noxious or overwhelming content. However, children are naturally drawn to play. Play is inherently fun and is as natural to children as breathing (Schaefer & Drewes, 2009). A child's natural inclination to play is activated in a fully equipped playroom and counters the felt toxicity of the trauma content being explored. In other words, play itself is a process that mitigates the felt potency of trauma material. Typically, children receive reinforcement through the simple pleasure of manipulating objects, creating things, using their imaginations, building relationships with others, and relieving stress.

The many therapeutic powers of play have been delineated in the literature (Schaefer, 1993, 1999; Schaefer & Drewes, 2009; Landreth, 1991, 1993). Two of these powers, the counterconditioning of negative affect and the reestablishment of a child's sense of power and control, work together to leach the toxicity out of disturbing material, affording the child a less perilous approach to the trauma content. The intrinsic enjoyment of the play counters the toxicity of the trauma content while motivating the child to stay engaged in a process that can feel overwhelming or scary.

For example, an 8-year-old girl named Clara, who had been sexually molested by two male family members, came to treatment stuck in avoidance symptoms. She became overwhelmed whenever anyone approached the subject of her sexual abuse. One day she came into the playroom and began pouring glue onto a piece of paper. She squeezed out lots of glue and said, "I don't want to touch it." I reflected her desire to avoid tactile contact with the glue and then stated, "If and when you're ready to touch the sticky stuff, you'll know." Clara looked at me briefly and then began to smear the glue around with her fingers. Eventually, her hands were covered in the sticky substance. I asked what the sticky stuff made her think of and she immediately offered the names of her two perpetrators. I reassured her that in the playroom she was in control of the sticky stuff. She continued to smear the glue around the page as she talked about the men's ejaculations and the semen that she had been forced to touch. As she talked, she was having a self-directed in vivo exposure to a trauma reminder, which enabled her to begin the process of desensitization to the traumatic event. After a few minutes, she began to paint pictures with the glue, effectively recreating the meaning of the sticky stuff as an artistic tool fully under her control.

Play as Prelinguistic Communication

One theme that runs throughout this book is the function of play as nonverbal communication. From the moment that children begin to walk and talk, grownups repeat phrases like, "Use your words!" over and over again. However, words are not the primary language of children. Children primarily communicate through their behavior and secondarily through their play. Plato wrote, "You can discover more about a person in one hour of play than in a lifetime of conversation" (*The Republic*, 360 BC). This is particularly true of our child clients.

Moreover, many of the children we see in practice have experienced prelinguistic trauma, meaning that the trauma occurred prior to the development of language. There are no words that accurately capture their experience because there were no words at the time the trauma took place. In these cases, play therapy is an optimal modality, in that it allows the child to approach the trauma through nonverbal and sensory avenues.

Children may depict aspects of the trauma through manipulation of the toys. Because prelinguistic trauma is stored mainly in the body (Rothschild, 2000), child clients may have important sensory aspects of the trauma activated by being kinesthetically involved with the tools of the playroom. Play, a positive form of coping for children, runs a course parallel to the overwhelming implicit and explicit memories of the trauma. At the intersections of the play and the trauma, the play itself acts as a grounding device for the more difficult content that may materialize.

Play as Digestive Enzyme

In each of the play-based interventions described in this book, play becomes the digestive enzyme through which the child is fully able to ingest the therapeutic content that is being conveyed. Play ensures the most potent absorption of conceptual information for children. The FSPT model, in addition to holding the child's trauma experiences, includes a focus on skill building and psychoeducation. In the same way that the absorption of certain vitamins is aided by the accompaniment of other vitamins, the digestion of psychotherapeutic content with children is aided by the accompaniment of play.

The Power of Props as Anchors for Therapeutic Learning

My approach to working with traumatized children relies heavily on props. The fully equipped playroom is filled with a variety of props that are used in the service of the children's healing. A baby doll can become a child's self-object. As the therapist bandages the baby doll, the child receives a vicarious experience of caretaking. As the child nurtures the baby doll, the child may be empowered to take care of himself. A pair of handcuffs, simply by being made available to the child, can draw out a narrative of a parent being taken to jail. The dollhouse elicits a variety of play from traumatized children and is a prop rich with possibility for exploring family dynamics or for projecting fantasies of the hoped-for family. In addition to the spontaneous child-directed use of the playroom materials, I use props as the anchors for directive interventions I have created over the years (Goodyear-Brown, 2001, 2002, 2003a, 2003b, 2005). This series of techniques evolved as an attempt to meet the treatment goals of the FSPT model while being developmentally sensitive to the most effective mechanisms for teaching.

Literature in the areas of learning styles and forms of intelligence help inform our understanding of how people learn (Fleming & Mills, 1992; Gardner,1993). According to Fleming and Mills, people develop preferences for learning that fall into the categories of visual, auditory, reading/writing, or kinesthetic. Some people, when trying to absorb information from a speaker, need to sit on the front row and have an unfettered view of the presenter. These people are visual learners. Others would prefer to read the information in book form. Another subgroup of people can easily absorb the needed information simply by listening to a recorded version of the content. These people are auditory learners. A final group of people need to have hands-on application of the material and physically practice the skills presented before they feel that they have grasped the information. These people are kinesthetic learners.

What we know about children is that they are first of all kinesthetic learners. Piaget's cognitive development stages begin with the sensorimotor phase and progress into more complex cognitive processes during developmentally sensitive time frames (Piaget, 1954). Children may also be secondarily wired for either visual or auditory learning. It makes sense, then, that the most effective delivery of new information or alternate experiences would be through all three mediums. Using a prop as the centerpiece of an intervention allows the child to access all three modes of learning. Moreover the prop provides an anchor for the therapeutic content. Additionally, when the child is given a prop that can be taken home, he receives the added benefit of having the prop function as a transitional object, a connection between the safety of the playroom and play therapist to his home environment. A prop that can be used to help practice a new skill is especially useful as it anchors the therapeutic content, serves as a transitional object, and encourages the child to engage in therapeutic homework.

I use a three-step process to design these interventions. The first step is choosing a prop. As I scan the environment for props, I am looking for two things. I assess the potential metaphorical value of the prop and, equally important, how much it might appeal to a child. These are, of course, totally subjective criteria, but the prop must meet a certain fun quotient. The best prop is one that, as soon as you show it to the child, she grabs it, says "Cool," and begins to explore. I then think about the function of the prop. What was it created to do? Once I have defined the function of the prop, I parallel this function with a similar process in therapy. Magnifying the feel goods, for example, is an intervention that I designed several years ago to help children boost self-esteem while silencing negative self-talk. One day I was walking through a toy store and I came across an elaborate set of magnifying glasses. It was just the sort of prop that would fascinate children. I then asked myself how the prop was designed to function. Obviously, a magnifying glass is meant to make something small appear to be bigger. What would I like to magnify in the children with whom I work? I would like to enhance their positive self-talk. This was the beginning of the intervention design.

These procedures for designing play-based activities, along with the theoretical constructs related to the usefulness of props (anchoring the child's learning, functioning as transitional objects, and encouraging the completion of therapeutic homework), comprise the treatment model that I have labeled prop-based intervention. PBI is the mechanism for creating the play-based technologies used in the fulfillment of each treatment goal delineated in the FSPT model.

Children are intrinsically rewarded by the manipulation of props. Attaching difficult therapeutic content to the manipulation of fun props greatly increases the child's tolerance for approaching the harder subject matter. A good example of this dynamic happened in a recent session with a ten-year-old girl. Her mother brought her in for issues related to anxiety. I asked her if she could tell me some of the thoughts that worry her. She said, "Well, when my papaw died last year, I got really scared that I might die too and I couldn't sleep. But I started reading at night, to distract myself, and now I can sleep. That's about all." This concise description of one specific problem area and its eventual resolution minimized the extent of this little girl's anxiety. Because mom had given other examples of the child's anxiety, I decided to offer her a game that would playfully invite more information while allowing a titrated approach to looking at the anxiety-provoking content.

I explained that I would hide Worry Worms around the room and that she would get to find them. She began to grin and seemed to experience immediate relief at the thought of doing something active, playful, and familiar. I also explained that for each Worry Worm she found, she would tell me one worried thought that she had. Through the game play, she was able to generate a series of twelve worried thoughts, many of which began with "What if." What if my mom dies in the night? What if my dad dies in the night? What if I drown while I'm swimming? This particular thought had assailed her all summer. She would spend the day at the pool swimming and having fun, but once she laid down in bed, she would worry about drowning. She was able to tolerate sharing these uncomfortable thoughts out loud with me because she was motivated by the challenge, reward, and fun of finding the hidden props. Although the game looked like hide-and-seek to her, it was actually a titrated set of exposures to anxiety-producing content that she completed while remaining grounded in the safety of the prop. The addition of a playful prop exponentially increased the amount of therapeutic content shared in the session.

Empowerment through the Manipulation of Playthings

For a traumatized child, the externalization of trauma-related content takes concrete form in the playthings a child uses for reenactment. As the child manipulates the smaller, controllable symbols of the larger, uncontrollable trauma, a sense of power and control can be restored. One way that the externalization process may work is that a child who has been unable or unwilling to share any details of her trauma before coming to treatment agrees to draw a picture or reveal a piece of her story through the way she uses the toys. The content left in the playroom can later be revisited or manipulated in a variety of ways.

Perpetrator Symbols and Self-Objects

Another form of externalization is when a child chooses a perpetrator symbol or a self-object. A perpetrator symbol is any miniature, puppet, art creation, or other toy that the child may choose to represent the person or people who hurt him. A child may choose one perpetrator symbol and continue to use him throughout treatment. A child might vary the symbol for the perpetrator over time or may choose two or three different symbols that remain consistent throughout treatment but represent different aspects of the perpetrator. One of the symbols most used to represent perpetrators in my playroom is the character Two-Face from Batman. This figure, as well as my two-headed dinosaurs, seems to resonate with children who have been sexually or physically abused or have had parents with extreme mood swings. The symbols depict the dual nature that is possible within the same person. Two-Face is at times a charming gentleman and at other times a monster. Children who have experienced these two persons in one are drawn to these characters.

Once a perpetrator symbol has been selected, it can then be manipulated in any number of ways that allow the child a sense of empowerment in relation to a person by whom they were disempowered. A child may choose to draw a picture of the perpetrator, then crumple it, rip it, or burn it. The child may choose a miniature and insist that it be handcuffed and put in jail. The ways in which children may deal with their perpetrator symbols in the playroom are as diverse as the children themselves. Chapter 9, "Experiential Mastery Play," gives many examples of how children contain and manipulate perpetrator symbols as one process in their healing journeys.

Self-objects are the props that children choose to represent the self. A child may choose a superhero or a wizard puppet to be the self. In these cases, the child often needs the reassurance that comes from seeing himself as invincible. Other children may choose a baby doll or other toy that speaks of their vulnerability. Children who are not ready to receive nurture directly may be able to experience it vicariously through the therapist's nurture of the self-object.

Dimensions of the Therapist's Use of Self in the Play Space

Therapist as Container

Children often carry carefully suppressed sensory information, intrusive cognitions, and overwhelming emotions related to their traumatic events. Their developing bodies and minds were not meant to contain horrifying images, disgusting smells or tastes, overwhelming sounds, and tactile sensations that accompany trauma. Children who have endured gruesome experiences quickly recognize that the details of these experiences may be overwhelming to others. Children need their immediate caregivers to remain strong, stable, and available to them for care and comfort. Therefore, children are unlikely to take the risk of sharing the ugliest parts of their trauma experiences with their day-to-day caregivers. These children sense the precarious position in which they would find themselves if they flooded the parent with detailed trauma imagery and therefore perceive the laying bare of their worst experiences as a form of self-endangerment.

However, a terrible paradox is created for the child who desperately needs the care and comfort that adults can offer but cannot share the content that will better inform those adults as to how to soothe the child.

How does the child cope with the paradox? Often the child just keeps the content inside, pressed down and under tight control. The unshared images, smells, and sensations take on an internal life of their own, using up valuable developmental energy. A good child therapist becomes a holding tank for the child, communicating that she is strong enough, safe enough, and wise enough to carry whatever information or imagery a child needs to discharge.

Sometimes the containment takes a practical form. A child may arrive in the playroom with a number of intrusive thoughts or images. The therapist may help the child create a containment device such as a worry box or a sealable physical container into which the troublesome images and thoughts can be dumped. The externalized thoughts then remain locked in the play-room when the child leaves, relieving the child of the felt burden of return-ing home with them. Each image and thought is addressed together and handled on subsequent visits to the playroom.

At other times, the containment takes the form of the therapist evenly saying, "I see what you are showing me." As the child's trauma glimpses are met with equilibrium on the part of the therapist, the child is emboldened to show more of his internal life. The unique positioning of the therapist as container helps the child bridge the gap between the burdensome inter-nal life and an externalization of the images, sensations, and stories that describe the child's trauma experiences. It begins to bring into question the previously unquestionable need to keep the content hidden. This gradual exposure process detoxifies the trauma content and allows the child to move toward integration.

Therapist as Partner in the Dance

There is a dance that children do in the midst of trauma work, a dance toward and then away from the trauma content. A wise therapist knows how to be a partner in this process. Children must have freedom in the playroom to break away from content that is becoming overwhelming for them. A sen-sitive therapist will understand these breaks as a necessary respite the child needs in order to get back to a state of internal equilibrium. I have had super-visees who, in the midst of describing a session, will say that the child had trouble staying on task and became easily distracted. Obviously, we all see children who manifest true deficits in attention. These children have short attention spans and little impulse control. However, I always explore further when a clinician characterizes the child's behavior as distractible. When the identified child has a trauma history, what is perceived as distractibility may actually be a pattern of moving away from the trauma content in order to get back to a state of internal calm. Processing trauma content can cause upset and dysregulation in even the most well-adjusted adults. With this in mind, it seems prudent to titrate the doses of a child's exposure to trauma content.

Many times the child will instinctively back away from the trauma content by moving toward a fairly innocuous activity, such as bouncing a ball or running his fingers through the sand. The child moves to a prop that will not stimulate trauma processing. Beginning clinicians often make the mistake of trying to pull a child back into the processing at this point, to "keep him on task." It has been my experience that if you allow the break from the processing and genuinely move your interest and attention to the play material in which the child has become interested, it is easier to return to the trauma content at a later time.

The therapist's response to the child's dance toward and away from the trauma content can be viewed as another form of interactional synchrony. Examples of this dance are woven throughout the text. Interactional synchrony is a concept used to describe the contingently responsive relationship between an infant and her primary caregiver. A fascinating set of experiments using a maternal still-face paradigm (SFP) have looked at the dysregulation that occurs in infants when their mothers do not respond with expected affectual responses (Haley & Stansbury, 2003; Moore & Calkins, 2004; ; Tronick, Als, Adamson, Wise, & Brazelton, 1978; Tronick & Cohn, 1989).

In a similar set of conditions, mothers were asked to play with their infants. They found that as the mother and the infant played together, the infant would intermittently turn his head to stare at the wall. Some mothers waited patiently and attentively while their babies looked away and were ready to engage the infants again when they sought out the interaction. Other mothers worked hard to immediately recapture their infants' attention. The mothers who allowed the infant to turn away were seen as more attuned to their infants. The infant's need to stare at the wall is another manifestation of the infant's attempt to calm himself. Play with mother is exciting and sometimes overwhelming for a developing infant's autonomic nervous system. The infant's choice to look away from mom allows him to unplug from the intensity of relationship, recalibrate his internal state, and then reengage with mom. A child's dance toward and away from trauma processing has a similar rhythm, and the therapist must not only recognize the dances away from the trauma but value them as a necessary part of the child's continual struggle to soothe himself while working through the trauma.

Therapist as Titration Agent

A first glance at the literature might give a false impression that a trauma narrative is something that can be explicated in a smooth, ordered way in the course of a couple of sessions. Certainly this is possible with some of the children we see, particularly if the child has experienced a single traumatic event and is living in an otherwise healthy and supportive environment. However, many of the children whom we see have a complex trauma history involving ongoing neglect or maltreatment. The narrative is never easy or uncomplicated for these children. The telling of the narrative is often sporadic and nonsequential. One part of the narrative may even seem to contradict other parts of the narrative. I have learned to take all this in stride. In fact, I have become so used to the erratic and patchy nature of the child's trauma disclosures that I have created a new way of recording the slices of narrative that they offer. I keep a variety of sticky note pads in various shapes and sizes in the office. Whenever a child verbalizes some new aspect of his trauma memory, I repeat it out loud while writing it down on a sticky note of the child's choosing. In most cases, I have previously helped the child create a rudimentary timeline. When new pieces of information are volunteered, I witness them, both verbally and in writing, and put the sticky note on their timeline. This allows for the child's experience to be contained and recorded. However, the sequencing of various pieces of information is usually left until later in treatment.

A Rationale for Flow of Goals (and Chapters) Outlined in FSPT

Having described the many foundational roles that play, play materials, and the play therapist fill in the application of the FSPT model, we now return to the flow of chapters as they reflect the flow of the FSPT model. To this end, the first goal covered in the text relates to building safety and security in the playroom and in the person of the play therapist. It is difficult to do any meaningful work related to a child's trauma experiences if the child has not developed a sense of safety in the space where the work is done and a sense of security with the chosen clinician.

The playroom may provide the first atmosphere that is safe enough for the child to risk letting the internal life be glimpsed. The four walls of the playroom and all the tools within can become a place set apart, a place where anything is possible. Wish fulfillment through fantasy is a powerful tool in healing, and the playroom provides myriad opportunities for a child to fulfill her wishes through play. The therapist's ability to assess the child's developmental level and then meet the child in developmentally appropriate ways will increase the child's sense of safety in the playroom. The therapist must communicate acceptance of the child and delight in the child as a unique individual. The play therapist who allows a child to be fully himself in the playroom helps to build a foundation of safety upon which further interventions are scaffolded. Chapter 3, "Enhancing a Child's Sense of Safety" highlights specific examples of ways in which clinicians can use the child's metaphors for safety to create an atmosphere in which the previously untouchable content can be touched.

Once safety and security have been established, a host of goals open up as potential targets for treatment. Children are usually unequipped to tackle their trauma memories at the beginning of treatment. Because looking at trauma content is stressful, it is critical to assess how a child deals with stress before inviting him to enter into content that is likely to be stressful. Coping skills include the behavioral, cognitive, and somatic ways in which a child deals with exposure to stress. Therefore, a clinician's first job after providing safety and security is to assess the child's current coping skills with a view to augmenting the positive coping and extinguishing or at least minimizing the negative coping. Chapter 4, "Assessing and Augmenting Positive Coping Strategies," includes detailed information regarding assessment and intervention around this issue.

Stress management strategies are one critical component of adaptive coping. Physiological hyperarousal often accompanies a child's reaction to trauma, and specific techniques can aid a child in physiological de-escalation. Stress inoculation techniques include deep breathing exercises, centering exercises, progressive muscle tension and relaxation, guided imagery, and biofeedback. All these activities can be delivered through play-based intervention. The use of play as the medium through which these skills are communicated and practiced ensures that the learning will be better integrated than if the skills were merely taught didactically. Chapter 5, "Soothing the Physiology," details these stress inoculation exercises.

Chapter 6, "Parents as Partners," follows directly after the chapter that focuses on the child's proficiency with self-soothing, in large part due to the fact that parents are often the initial soothing agents and coregulators of affect and arousal for their children. Sometimes the parent/child work revolves around restoring a healthy relationship of coregulation. Parent involvement can take many other forms as well. Parents often need psychoeducation about the effects of trauma on children and on the best parenting approaches for children in various stages of trauma recovery. Sometimes the focus of work is on positive enhancement of the parent/child relationship. In other cases, the therapist is fostering a healthy attachment bond between parent and child. In still other cases, the work is focused on building a coherent family narrative related to the traumatic events. Various forms of play-based intervention are described and augmented with case examples in this chapter.

One subset of positive coping involves the accurate identification and verbalization of one's feeling states. Chapter 7, "Emotional Literacy," deals with helping children understand, identify, and appropriately express their feelings. Another important subset of positive coping has to do with the successful use of social supports in both the peer and adult realms. Nonverbal play-based interventions as well as activities that promote kinesthetic engagement are covered in this chapter.

The next three chapters focus on the various ways in which children, through both nondirective and directive methods, begin to approach the trauma proper. Once children have the safety net woven from the intentional pursuit of the previous treatment goals, they often begin to tell their story in snippets. These processes are articulated in Chapter 8, "The Continuum of Disclosure." Children also face the trauma content in a more confrontational manner, allowing in vivo exposures while mastering the trauma material. Examples of this phenomenon are described in Chapter 9, "Experiential Mastery Play." Trauma often results in disjointed or episodic recollections of events. In PTSD reactions, it is posited that neurochemicals released during the body's reaction to the stress of a traumatic event may result in a blockage that keeps the linguistic narrative of events separate from important sensory information (Siegel, 2003). Until these two kinds of information are synthesized, a myriad of trauma symptoms may trouble the child. Chapter 10, "Trauma Narrative Work," demonstrates a variety of ways in which a trauma narrative may take shape and gives more thought to the question of when and how to include parents in the creation of a child's narrative.

Addressing the thought life is another important treatment goal. Although I have placed it after the trauma narrative work, that placement has more to do with the need to be sure that faulty cognitions are restructured before termination than a denial of the fact that this work may begin earlier in treatment. It is likely that a child's first look at adaptive and maladaptive thoughts will occur as part of the assessment and augmentation of coping. However, it is often challenging to unearth a child's most troublesome traumagenic thoughts early in treatment. The difficulty with approaching a child's faulty attributions or cognitive distortions early in treatment is twofold. A child may not feel safe enough to share thoughts that engender deep feelings of shame or worthlessness during the initial phase of treatment. Moreover, the child may not even be aware of their most traumagenic cognitive distortions on the front end of treatment. In the synergistic process of establishing a trauma narrative, details related to the trauma emerge that often reveal a child's misplaced blame, magical thinking, cognitive distortions, and so on. In summary, although thought life issues may be addressed throughout treatment, it is critical that a final cognitive clean-up be done before graduating a child from treatment. Specific strategies for accomplishing this goal are covered in Chapter 11, "Addressing the Child's Thought Life."

Finally, after all these goals have been successfully navigated, the child and supportive adults should celebrate the child's healing journey. The trauma needs to be given a place within a personal narrative that allows the child to have a positive experience of the post-trauma self. In addition, a meaningful goodbye should be intentionally structured by the therapist. In some cases, the meaningful goodbye with the therapist may be the first meaningful goodbye a child has experienced and is therefore valuable in its own right. Examples of a client's self-directed use of space to achieve closure, as well as practical play-based interventions to aid the process of termination, are given in Chapter 12, "Making Positive Meaning of the Post-Trauma Self."

A Final Note

Throughout this text both masculine and feminine pronouns are used to represent clients in the third person. Case examples remain true to salient case content, and the names and other inconsequential details of cases have been changed to protect the confidentiality of the families who have graciously allowed me to use their healing journeys as teaching tools for the next generation of child therapists.

CHAPTER

2

❦

Trauma Definitions
and Symptoms

"You can take the child out of the trauma, but it is much more difficult to take the trauma out of the child."
—*Ziegler, 2002, p. 40*

The word *trauma* means different things to different people. The original Greek word for *trauma* meant "physical wound." It wasn't until the late 1800s that the word gained popularity as a way of describing a psychic wound. In our contemporary lexicon, the word *trauma* is casually tossed about in reference to traffic jams and hangnails. I overhear conversations at the coffeehouse in which one young woman says to another, "I had the worst hair cut last week. It was so traumatic." The young lady in question may have felt upset that the cut was not all that she had hoped for, and yet her statement begs the question: What qualifies as trauma? A whole host of checklists exist that can be used during assessment to ascertain if a child meets criteria for posttraumatic stress disorder (PTSD), acute stress disorder, depression, generalized anxiety disorder, or any number of disorders that can be associated with posttraumatic stress.

The complexities of maltreated and neglected children make accurate diagnosis within our current diagnostic frameworks problematic. Taking these limitations into account, Van der Kolk (2005) has offered a new diagnostic label, developmental trauma disorder, that ushers in a new paradigm for understanding trauma symptoms and processes in children, particularly those with complex trauma histories. Another conceptual framework distinguishes between small *t* and large *T* traumas (Nebrosky, 2003;

Shapiro, 1995, Shapiro & Maxfield, 2003). Large *T* traumas encompass the range of events that threaten imminent harm and leave us feeling overwhelmed and immobilized. Small *t* traumas include the various events of childhood that generate feelings of anxiety, shame, guilt, and fear that did not receive a repair.

Recent advances in our understandings of trauma in children have outdistanced our current classification systems, resulting in many children being referred for treatment following a traumatic event who may not meet criteria for any of the previously mentioned disorders. They may, however, exhibit certain quirky or unusual behaviors or develop new, idiosyncratic fears that were not present before the traumatic event.

Frank Parkinson offers a characterization of trauma as "the normal reactions of normal people to events that, for them, are unusual or abnormal" (Parkinson, 2000, p. 29). This definition is helpful in depathologizing a child's response to trauma. Our bodies were not meant to contain the horrible atrocities to which we are so often exposed. For children who grow up in war-torn areas, land mines, explosive noises, and dismembered bodies are daily experiences that bring with them gruesome images, unholy smells, and terrifying sounds. Children who have survived the experience of being sexually abused by a family member have no template for making sense of the ripping pain caused to their bodies, the sticky, slippery secrecy that is often demanded, or the sense of betrayal and bewilderment that follows the event. The child who was trapped inside a burning car has no words to express the intensity of that heat, the throbbing ache of a burn, or the hideous smell of scorched flesh. The sheer force of these sensory onslaughts can overwhelm a child's burgeoning coping constructs, evolving paradigms of safety, and tremulous trust in the world around him. When a child's foundations are shaken through traumatic events, maladaptive coping patterns, traumagenic thought patterns, and a host of behavioral symptoms can result. A thorough understanding of the ways in which trauma symptoms manifest helps us identify and treat these various forms of overflow.

The conceptualization of trauma that most informs my paradigm for treatment was articulated by Beverly James (1989, p. 1). In her definition, *trauma* refers to "Overwhelming, uncontrollable events that psychologically impact victims by creating in them feelings of helplessness, vulnerability, loss of safety and loss of control."

By contrast, the markers of a healthy child include a sense of self-efficacy, a belief that he can have a positive effect on his world, and that his caregivers can be trusted to keep him safe. This paradigm is an outgrowth of early attachment behavior. When the baby comes into the world, looks up at mommy, and says "Gaga googoo," the majority of mothers beam with delight and coo back to their infants. The baby learns that he can impact his world. The thousands and thousands of these contingently responsive communications between the baby and the parent, and later between the growing child and the expanding microsystems of his daily experience, reinforce the notion that the world is a safe place and that people can be trusted. The first crisis of development is one that has been characterized as trust versus mistrust. A successful navigation of this initial stage of development results in a child's belief that the caregiver (and by extension the world) can be trusted (Erikson, 1950).

When something traumatic happens to a child, this initial belief can be shaken. Indeed, a sense of safety and security can be stripped away. In the wake of trauma, a child may be left with overwhelming feelings of disempowerment. Many of a child's posttraumatic symptoms can be conceptualized as dysfunctional attempts to regain a sense of control or safety within his environment. Therefore the initial goal of trauma treatment is to help the client regain a sense of safety and security, at least in relation to certain people and places. Specific strategies for pursuing this goal in the playroom are discussed in the next chapter.

Physical Effects of Trauma on Children

Jake, a 4-year-old freckle-faced boy, talks about his posttraumatic anxiety as a "tornado in my tummy." Traumatized children can be assailed with a whole host of psychosomatic illnesses. Trauma therapists who work in the public schools often find the school nurse to be a valuable referral source. Children who end up in the nurse's office, day after day, complaining of headaches, stomachaches, dizziness, or shortness of breath are often signaling more significant complaints. Whenever a child describes the same physical complaint consistently, the clinician should refer the child for a full medical evaluation. Occasionally, these evaluations may uncover an underlying physiological abnormality or biological problem. However, in many cases the doctor or specialist is unable to find any physiological cause for the difficulty and the disturbing complaints can be reframed as psychosomatic symptoms of trauma. Psychosomatic symptoms are the body's way of complaining about the post-traumatic stress that it is being required to contain (Rothschild, 2000; Van der Kolk, 1994, Van der Kolk et al., 1996).

Physical manifestations of anxiety can have an insidious onset. At first, a child may have a tummy ache after eating a big meal. Parents may ascribe symptoms to the most immediate antecedent event and assume that the child had too much to eat or that she overheated while running around after school. The truth may be that the end of dinner is a trauma trigger for a complex post-trauma anxiety reaction related to a pattern of abuse that occurs after the child is put to bed. A child might also complain of a head-ache after a long car drive. The parents explain the headache away as car sickness when, in fact, the unstructured time in the car may have left the child's mind free to replay the details of a traumatic event, causing a physi-ological manifestation of anxiety.

Psychosomatic symptoms can bring with them some hope for a child's recovery in that they can mark a path for exploring a child's thoughts and images related to a particular trauma. They can serve as a way in. Suzy, a 9-year-old girl, was referred for treatment after she began to complain of a racing heartbeat and shortness of breath. Her parents said that the symp-toms looked like mini panic attacks. In completing the intake, the parents gave no indication that anything particularly traumatic had occurred in the recent past. They mentioned the death of the maternal grandfather several months prior to the referral but believed that his passing had been as natural and gentle as one could hope for. He had lived a rich, full life and died of natural causes at a ripe old age.

When Suzy came into the office she described her shortness of breath as a problem that happened several times a day. I asked her what thought was going through her head when she experienced the shortness of breath. She looked startled, as if no one had asked her this before, and then she said, "That I might just stop breathing." I asked her if she'd heard of this hap-pening before. She said, "Yes. My grandpa died last summer. When I asked mom how he died, she said that he just stopped breathing in the night." She had, since her grandfather's death, translated mom's attempt at a soothing explanation into an idiosyncratic fear. The articulated fear was, *I might stop breathing in the night.* This thought, left unchecked, was becoming more and more automatic for her and triggered the physiological shortness of breath.

Whenever she began to think that she might stop breathing, her breathing began to change. The shortness of breath reinforced the irrational fear, and a vicious cycle was born.

I used a two-pronged approach to helping her fight the fear. First, we identified the irrational thought and generated replacement cognitions based on psychoeducation about how the body works and how long children usually live. Most people live to be very old before they die. So we generated replacement statements for the troublesome thoughts, *I might die; I might stop breathing*. These new thoughts included, *I'll probably live to be really old*, *My body knows just how to keep breathing*, and *My body breathes automatically for me, even when I'm asleep!* We used cognitive-behavioral play therapy interventions to install and practice the restructured cognitions. (Chapter 11, "Addressing the Child's Thought Life," gives detailed explanations of some of the most useful play therapy interventions for challenging cognitive distortions.) I also engaged Suzy in some play-based relaxation exercises. The combination of play-based somatic work and cognitive work gave her the power she needed to fight back her fears. Her psychosomatic symptoms subsided within two to three sessions. Psychosomatic symptoms often give us important feedback about the underlying problem and the best strategies for fighting it.

The Amygdala Alarm

Part of the limbic system, the amygdala consists of two lobes of almond-shaped clusters of cells located in the midbrain, one on each side of the brain (Siegel, 2003). The amygdala is implicated in the fight-or-flight response and serves as the doorkeeper of somatosensory memories related to heightened emotional experience (Schore, 2003; Rothschild, 2000). The amygdala, along with other mediating structures of the limbic system, encodes the sense memories related to intense experiences, pleasant or unpleasant, but is specialized to detect high-arousal negative stimuli (Garavan, Pendergrass, Ross, Stein, & Risinger, 2001) and novel emotional stimuli (Wright et al., 2001). You probably have some joyous memories that you relive with palpable clarity—the feel of your baby the first time he was placed in your arms, your first kiss, or the sound of applause as your name was called to receive your diploma. When we remember sensory details of terrifying events with this same level of exactitude, the results can be problematic. The amygdala is made to encode sensory data related to overwhelming, endangering events. It then scans the environment as we go about our daily lives. It kicks into high gear when it picks up a sensory detail in the environment that is similar to a detail of the previous trauma. The problem is that the amygdala, while designed to help us react quickly and thereby respond adaptively in life-threatening situations, is a sloppy encoder. Therefore, the amygdala can process a stimulus that does not indicate a threat in the here and now but is close enough to a past stimulus that was associated with imminent danger to trigger a survival response.

I explain this phenomenon to my child clients using the following scenario. I offer the child one of my toy soldiers to play with while I tell the following story. "Okay, let's pretend like this guy is serving over in Iraq. One day he goes outside to fill up his tank with gas and he hears a gun-shot—BANG!—and drops to the ground. This saves his life. He doesn't get shot because he heard the gunshot and immediately he dropped to the ground. The next day he's with another soldier and they go outside together to wash the tank. Suddenly they hear gunfire. BANG! Our soldier drops to the ground. His buddy gets a little bit hurt but he gets fixed up pretty quick. Our guy stays safe, because he dropped to the ground when he heard the gunshot. BANG! So that happens over and over again while he is in Iraq. He hears a gunshot. BANG! He drops to the ground. He hears a gunshot. BANG! He drops to the ground. When he's done with his tour of duty, he comes back home to Nashville. One day he's going shopping at Opry Mills mall. While he's walking to his car in the mall parking lot he hears a door slam. BANG! What do you think he's going to do?" Children as young as five years old will tell me that the soldier is going to drop to the ground. Through simple storytelling devices like this one, we can begin to give children a rudimentary understanding of how our bodies react to threat, how our survival responses become habituated, and how cues can sometimes be misinterpreted. This psychoeducational training can begin to help children make some sense of why they do the seemingly strange things that they sometimes do to cope with current trauma triggers.

So why does the soldier drop to the ground? His body has developed a habituated response to a certain sensory experience related to trauma. Unfortunately, because the limbic brain provides a quick and dirty inspection that sometimes yields a less than accurate classification, the BANG of the car door was close enough to the BANG of the gunshots fired in Iraq to activate the same physiological reaction. Daniel Goleman (1995) characterizes the shortcut route activated by the amygdala in such situations as an emotional hijacking. Sensory information is typically received through the thalamus and then sent to the neocortex for meaning making. However, when the incoming sensory information has indicators associated with imminent danger, the thinking brain is bypassed and information is sent directly to the centers of the brain that activate the flight, fight, or freeze response. If the neocortex had not been bypassed in the case of the Iraqi soldier, he might have had an internal monologue that sounded like this: *OK, I'm in a mall parking lot. I'm not in Iraq anymore, so that was probably a car door slamming and not a gunshot. Therefore there is no reason to drop to the ground.* However, because an emotional hijacking had already been instigated, there was no time for the monologue. The soldier was physiologically obligated to hit the dirt.

What relevance does this amygdala alarm concept have for the traumatized children we see? The implications are many. When I worked in the inner city schools, most of the children on my caseload carried complex trauma histories. These children met criteria for a host of DSM-IV diagnoses. The majority of them were also comorbidly diagnosed with learning disabilities. The double whammy of trauma symptomatology and learning differences made for a lot of acting out in the classroom. The way in which a teacher handled the child's misbehavior could heighten the child's distress or serve to de-escalate him. Teachers, administrators, and day care workers may inadvertently trigger trauma reactions in children in their care due to a lack of awareness. Even a rudimentary understanding of the neurophysiological processes that occur as traumatized children scan their environments can help clinicians advocate for appropriate interventions in children's school settings. Training on how trauma affects development and behavior in children should be required for all school personnel, with an emphasis on verbal de-escalation techniques.

When I am talking to groups of teachers about positive classroom management strategies and verbal de-escalation techniques, often a paradigm shift needs to take place. Most teachers believe that *verbal de-escalation* refers to something that can be said to a child to make her calm down, rather than the intentionally pacifying use of self. Teachers often have a false impression that de-escalation techniques are aimed at controlling the child, when in fact they are aimed at controlling the self. When a child is hyperaroused, the only components of the environment that are exclusively under our control are our own words, movements, facial expressions, and attitudes. The intentional shaping of our own responses can give the child an anchor point to use in calming down. Short of physically restraining a child, we cannot control an out-of-control child. Our job is to create an environment where a child can successfully control herself.

The intentional employment of a soft tone of voice is a key strategy in verbal de-escalation. Using a soft tone of voice exerts control over our own physiology while giving the child an anchor below his current level of escalation. I often talk with parents and teachers about also using a soft tone of face. This recommendation was born out of my exposure to a body of research exploring the effects of early experiences on a child's recognition of facial displays of emotion (Pollak & Sinha, 2002) The investigators presented a series of pictures to a group of physically abused children and a control group. They use a technology called random image structure evolution (RISE) to display a series of facial images that become less amorphous and more structured with each frame. Over and over again, the traumatized children identify the anger in the facial image earlier than the control group. Traumatized people are more sensitive to indicators of anger in facial expressions than people whose experiences fall in the normal range of development. In other studies, children with atypical emotional experiences were shown pictures of angry, happy, and neutral faces. They found that maltreated children responded differently to angry versus happy faces and with more cognitive resources. They posit that the increased attention to the angry faces represents an organized response to previous challenges in their environments. However, this over-responsiveness may lead to maladaptive interactions between traumatized children and safe caregivers (Pollak, Cicchetti, Klorman, & Brumaghim, 1997; Pollak & Tolley-Schell, 2003).

A child who has experienced many instances of physical abuse has become accustomed to a pattern of parental behavior in which the parent clenches his jaw, makes an angry face, yells, "You lazy piece of so-and-so!" and then slaps the child across the face. After several repetitions, the amygdala encodes the clenched jaw as a signal that danger is imminent. This allows the child to run and hide or avoid the worst of the slap that is coming. The problem arises when the child moves to a new environment but continues to detect imminent danger through a signal that may not, in the new milieu, represent a threat. A clenched jaw is the natural response of many people when they are frustrated. In fact, it usually signals a person's exertion of self-control. A teacher might clench her jaw when frustrated, which buys her time to regroup, take a deep breath, and use an appropriate mode of communication with a child who is acting out. The traumatized child described earlier would encode the clenched jaw itself as a danger signal and react without thinking. The child's trauma-triggered behaviors will be seen as an escalation on the child's part but may have been sparked by a behavior within the teacher's control. Intentionally softening one's face when dealing with an escalated child can remove a host of potential land-mines from the equation.

An example of the interplay between typical teacher behavior and trauma triggers follows. Johnny, an 8-year-old boy who has grown up in domestic violence and also has a learning disability, is taking a math test. He can't do the problems, so he copies the answers off a friend's paper. His teacher, Mrs. Hall, sees him cheating and calls out to him in front of the class, "Johnny, I saw you cheating on the test. Go put your paper in the trash can right now." Her first mistake is calling negative attention to him in front of his peers. He stands up and saunters over to the trash can, where he dangles the paper defiantly over the trash bin while taunting the teacher with his eyes. Mrs. Hall gets up and walks over to him, more firmly repeating the com-mand to throw the paper away. Johnny stares at her defiantly. Mrs. Hall puts her hand on his back to "help him" throw it away and he whirls around with his fist clenched and raised above his head. The teacher takes him down into a full body restraint.

This is a real case example. Johnny was suspended from school for 10 days. At a suspension addendum meeting, several administrators sat around the table and agreed to expel Johnny from school based on the school's zero tol-erance policy. It was at this point that I brought out the functional behavior assessment (FBA) that had been done at the beginning of the school year. The assessment had taken the child's trauma triggers into account and had been signed by myself, the principal, and the teacher involved. The FBA clearly stated that Johnny was not to be touched during moments of disci-pline because it often prompted an escalation in his behavior. For Johnny, touch during conflict was threatening. It held only associations to domestic violence situations that called for self-defense. Because the guidelines were in writing, the child was spared the expulsion. An understanding of this child's trauma history and his specific trauma triggers informed the param-eters of intervention set forth in the FBA.

Consider the number of possible triggers that might be activated when a teacher pulls a child out into the hallway, wags her finger at him sternly, and tells him to stop misbehaving. Dimensions of both her paraverbal and nonverbal communication may be threatening to a previously traumatized child. The very act of being separated from the other students may cause a child to go on hyperalert. The wagging finger may signal danger to the traumatized brain, the quick, intrusive movement necessitating evasion on the part of the child. The teacher's elevated pitch, tone, and volume could all be potential triggers for the child.

Most teachers would readily agree that they must use all the tools at their disposal to manage children who engage in disruptive classroom behavior. The paradigm shift is that the teachers themselves are the tools. Body language, gesture, tone, and method of approach are powerful devices that caregivers carry with them at all times. As clinicians, we must see ourselves as advocates, mediators, and educators about appropriate responses to traumatized children.

Children who have been traumatized experience dysregulation on a variety of levels. They may experience dysregulation of the hypothalamic-pituitary-adrenal (HPA) axis, hyperarousal at unexpected moments, and difficulty in their relational abilities, including extreme rages or aggressive outbursts. These children may also experience intrusive thoughts, nightmares, or flashbacks. These symptoms require a treatment focus that equips the child with stress management strategies and experiences of self-soothing and soothing by key caregivers.

Other Physical Symptoms

Other readily observable physical symptoms include excessive fatigue or excess energy. A marked change in eating habits can also be a symptom. A child's appetite may decrease dramatically. Conversely, a client might begin to eat excessively. Excessive weight gain or weight loss should be more fully explored. Regressive behavior can also occur after trauma. For the child who has been potty trained for six months or more, sudden regression can be a red flag that the child is having a traumagenic reaction.

Children who have been traumatized often have an increased sensitivity to touch. This sensitivity may be accompanied by an unconscious flinch reaction. Touches such as pats on the back may be perceived as painful. A child who is having warm lotion applied after a bath might insist that it is too cold. Sometimes a differential diagnosis must be made between issues related to sensory integration disorder and physical reactivity related to trauma.

The saying "Neurons that fire together wire together" may help us explain this phenomenon. Our neural pathways are experience-dependent. A child who has experienced rough, controlling, or punitive touch during early development will cultivate neural nets that are predisposed to encoding this information in the future. In essence, our experience-dependent neurological development sets up experiential expectancies as well (Perry, Pollard, Blakely, Baker, & Vigilante, 1995; Schore, 2003; Siegel, 2003). Decades before the recent explosion of neurobiological research, Piaget (1954) wrote about the dual processes of assimilation and accommodation. Burgeoning brain research helps us understand how repeated experiences of painful touch shape the brain to expect touch to be painful.

Experience-dependent pathways are strengthened by the aversive touch experience and shape the brain's expectancies of future touch (Schore 1998). This has powerful implications for the maltreated child. Based on his past maltreatment, he has developed neurophysiological expectations that he will be hurt again. A child who has been hurt a lot may develop a cognitive schema that, crudely put, says touch is bad. Because the child expects touch to be bad, he is likely to assimilate any future harsh touch experiences into this schema, thereby reinforcing it. It will take an intentional, prolonged, opposing responsiveness to negate this expectation. A child must receive enough new experiences of nurturing touch in safe relationships to accommodate the new information that touch can be good, helpful, and healing. Traumatized children need corrective emotional experiences and physical feedback that is antithetical to their earlier abusive experiences.

One particularly disturbing physical symptom of trauma is decreased reactivity to physical injury. Children with decreased reactivity to physical injury are some of the most concerning clients that I see. This kind of child will run on the playground, accidentally cut herself on the playground equipment, and not seem to notice that she has been hurt. When caregivers call attention to the fact that she is bleeding, this child reacts with surprise or blunted affect. This subset of traumatized children have either had so many painful physical experiences that they are desensitized to pain, or they have found a way to disconnect their minds from their bodies in order to cope. It is through the intentional nurturing care of this child's physical body that she begins to grow in awareness of her hurts. Valuing the physical body of a maltreated child by taking care of her bumps and bruises gives her permission to value herself.

In foster and adoptive families with young children, I encourage the addition of a boo-boo routine at bedtime (Jernberg and Booth, 2001; Munns, 2009). The caregiver takes time to inspect the child, looking for any bruises, cuts, or scrapes that might need attention. The caregiver has lotion, band-aids, and bandages available, depending on the intensity of the hurt. I warn parents that when they begin to take care of the hurt child's physical body, the child may swing to the other end of the pendulum. The child who previously had no awareness of his own boo-boos may begin to come constantly to a caregiver asking for band-aids. Sometimes they may not even have a visible injury. I encourage the parent to give the band-aid anyway. This solicitation of care is often the child's way of saying, "I trust you to help heal the wounds that can't be seen." The current caregiver for a maltreated child is playing catch-up for a lifetime of the child's missed opportunities to receive the message, "Your body is worth valuing." Eventually, children who get large doses of nurturing feedback for their corporeal selves will come back to a middle ground, where they only need bodily attention when there has been a real injury.

Behavioral Effects of Trauma

Nightmares and Night Terrors

Children who have experienced trauma may have a range of sleep disturbances. Nightmares are common reactions to trauma. Young children often require differential diagnoses of nightmares versus night terrors. Nightmares and nighttime fears are listed as symptoms for a variety of DSM diagnoses (Muris, Merckelbach, Ollendick, King, & Bogie, 2001) and are one of the primary intrusive symptoms of PTSD (APA, 2000; Van der Kolk, 2003). Whereas nightmares occur during rapid eye movement (REM) sleep, night terrors occur during the transitions between stages of non-REM sleep and are characterized by sudden arousal from slow-wave sleep (Mindell, 1993), usually within two hours of sleep onset (DiMario & Emery, 1987). When a child has a nightmare, he usually wakes up on his own, remembers specific content from the nightmare, and seeks out a caregiver for comfort. A child who has had a nightmare is easily soothed and typically falls back to sleep quickly.

While nightmares are unpleasant for the child experiencing them, night terrors are often most distressing for the parents.

In one study, night terrors with onset less than 3.5 years of age had a peak frequency of 1 episode per week, whereas children whose symptom onset was between 3.5 and 7.5 years reported a peak frequency of 1–2 episodes per month (DiMario & Emery, 1987).When a child has a night terror, he may sit straight up in bed and appear to be awake while screaming or crying inconsolably. A parent may mistake the child as being conscious when in fact he is deeply asleep. It can be difficult to wake a child out of a night terror and waking is not advised, as it is often difficult to soothe a child who has had a night terror interrupted. It is generally better to let the night terror run its course. Afterward, children who have experienced night terrors do not remember what they were dreaming about. Night terrors have their onset at 3.5 years of age and usually resolve on their own during adolescence. Stressful life events, fevers, and medications that affect the central nervous system are all possible causes of night terrors. One behavioral intervention used to reduce sleep terrors is scheduled awakenings thirty minutes prior to the expected onset of the sleep terror (Durand & Mindell, 1999). Children usually grow out of night terrors on their own, whereas a child who is experiencing trauma-related nightmares may continue to have them until the trauma content has been desensitized or integrated into a comprehensive trauma narrative.

One step in the process of desensitization to the nightmare might be to have the client draw a picture. The act of drawing a picture requires several processes. First, the child must get a picture in his mind's eye of the content he wishes to draw. The mind's eye view of the nightmare serves as an exposure to the scary content. The child's anxiety may be tapped. Drawing the picture requires the child to keep the nightmare in mind while engaging in the physical activity of drawing. The parallel processes of holding the image in mind while recreating it on paper encourage the mind and the body to work together to weaken the power of the nightmare. Once a drawing is complete, a child can manipulate that drawing in several different ways. This exercise affords the child an opportunity to engage in some creative problem solving and come up with a solution for the problem of the nightmare. This procedure, although applied to the content of nightmares here, is an adaptation of the experiential mastery technique (Shelby, 1997).

Imagery rehearsal treatment (Schredl, 2009), a more recent elaboration of this approach, conceptualizes the drawing of the image as a confrontation with the child's fear. The child is then asked to create a new ending that includes a personal coping strategy. Active coping strategies that include talking back to the scary image, taping up the monster's mouth, and so on are recommended above more passive endings. Over the next two weeks, the child is asked to visualize the new ending for five to ten minutes a day.

In my office we take this intervention one step further and play a game called Change the Channel. The child draws one or more replacement endings that utilize active coping strategies. The child gives each of the pictures a channel name. For example, a little girl draws a picture of herself inside a big tank running over a scary monster from her dream. She might label this picture the Squashing Channel. If she draws a second picture in which she puts on giant boots and stomps on the monster, she might label this picture the Stomping Channel. The child is given a real remote control to use as a prop during the game. I become the TV screen and hold up each of the different pictures as she calls out the names of different channels. This intervention gives the child intermittent exposures to the nightmare imagery and to the versions of "the nightmare all gone" that she has created. Moreover, the physical act of being able to press a button and change the visual reality in front of her gives the child a sense of control over the scary content. Other manipulations of the nightmare drawing might include crumpling it up and throwing it away, tearing it to shreds, or scribbling all over it. Each of these serves as a way to manifestly rid oneself of the nightmare. Other expressive arts and play interventions have been employed in the service of imagery and desensitization work around nightmares (Gil, 2006; Gordon, King, Gullone, Mursi, & Ollendick, 2007).

Penny, a 9-year-old girl, was referred for recurring nightmares. Her parents were exhausted and at their wit's end. Penny had been sleeping in their bed every night for the last several months and no one was getting a restful night's sleep. When she awoke from a nightmare, her parents would ask her what she dreamed about and she would say, "I can't talk about it." The avoidance indicated by this statement was very concerning to Penny's parents and they brought her for treatment. At our first meeting, she told me that she kept dreaming about bats getting into her bedroom and biting her. I invited her to draw a picture of the nightmare and she said it was too scary. I reflected her fear and told her that one day she would feel strong enough to look at it. She spent the rest of that session making a safe place image in the sand. When Penny walked into her second session one week later, she said, "I'm ready to draw the bats!" She drew a picture of herself in her bed and the bats all over her bed. It was indeed a scary image.

As she was drawing, I made reflections related to her color choices and highlighted her drawing abilities. I deliberately held off on responding to the content of the picture as it was being created. Penny was experiencing enough anxiety as she kept the content of her nightmare in mind to recreate it in the drawing. I chose to function as a grounding influence until she had worked through the exposure and completed the drawing. Then I prompted, "Tell me about your picture." Penny was able to tell the story of her nightmare. Her verbal description served as another method of desensitization to the content. Then I invited her to draw a picture of the bat problem all better.

Penny thought about it for awhile and then drew a picture of her house with a view from the outside. She sealed up all the windows and doors so that there was no way for the bats to gain entry into her house. I asked if she would like to show both her pictures to her mom, and she eagerly nodded. I invited mom into the room and Penny explained the pictures to her mom. I said to both of them, "Sometimes it can help kids feel better if they do something with the nightmare drawing—find some way to get rid of it." Penny and her mom put their heads together and decided to tear it into pieces while verbally bossing back the nightmare. The experiential mastery component of this activity was even more potent because it was supported by her caregiver. Penny and her mom both used the destruction of the nightmare in the playroom as a marker, a line in the sand to mark the moment in time in which they gained control over the bad dreams. We also designed a stepped positive reinforcement system that gradually moved Penny back into her own bed and allowed for the whole family to have a good night's sleep. In this way, play-based interventions can augment caregiver training and strictly behavioral approaches, which are currently endorsed as the most effective treatments for sleep disturbances in children (Gordon et al., 2007; Hiscock, 2008; Nielson & Levin, 2007; Phelps, Forbes, & Creamer, 2008; Sadeh, 2005).

Hypervigilance

Another symptom often exhibited by children after a trauma is hypervigilance. A child's response to your office setting can provide informal assessment for this symptom. For years my office was located in busy downtown

Nashville. The building was in between three busy hospitals, and sirens could be heard at regular intervals on the street far below my office window. Children who were referred for attention deficit issues, for oppositional behavior, or for help with divorce resolution issues would remain focused on their immediate play no matter what else was going on around them. Conversely, children who presented with acute or chronic trauma histories would abruptly interrupt their own play when they heard a noise. Typically their awareness of the noise preceded mine. These kids would freeze and ask, "What's that, Miss Paris? What's that? What's that siren for?" Traumatized children are always listening, always watching, and consequently exhausted by their felt need to remain on alert.

A young girl made an eloquent expression of this hypervigilance. I asked her to create a puppet to show how she had felt while her sexual abuse was occurring. She gave the puppet bloodshot eyes. When I asked her why she had chosen those eyes out of all the choices available to her, she talked about how tired her eyes would get in the middle of the night as she tried to keep them open, straining to see any shadow under her door or hear any creaking in the hallway that might signal the approach of her perpetrator.

Heightened Irritability

Another indicator that trauma may have occurred is heightened irritability. To qualify as an indication of possible trauma, the irritability must represent a substantial change from the child's previous functioning. When parents reports that their child is irritable all the time, the first question I ask is when the irritability began. If they say that the child was colicky during infancy and has always been prone to irritability, the irritability can be conceptualized as part of the child's temperament. If they characterize the child as previously easygoing and suddenly short-tempered, it is more likely that the irritation is trauma related.

Increased Reliance on Caregivers

Another post-trauma symptom is increased reliance on a caregiver. The child who was previously independent may develop a regressive dependence on the parent that includes whining, clinging behavior and difficulty with separations. In some cases, a child who used to roam the house and yard freely will insist on remaining by his parent's side. A child may become extremely upset at the thought of separating from the parent, even to go to school. Sometimes this disturbance is misunderstood as school phobia when the real culprit is trauma.

Jake, a ten-year-old boy who had just experienced the loss of his father, is a good example of this increased dependence on the caregiver. Jake's dad, a high-profile local gang leader, was shot and killed in an act of retribution from a rival gang. Other members of Jake's family were also involved in the gang. At the time that I saw Jake, he was tormented by the possibility that another family member might die a violent death. Jake was a good student and had attended class regularly before his father's shooting. He was out of school for one week while the visitation and funeral took place. The following Monday, when mom attempted to drop him off at school, he became angry and tearful and insisted that he could not go into his classroom. The school personnel were understanding and allowed him to return home with mom. The next morning a similar meltdown ensued when it came time for Jake to separate from mom. Jake became panicky when he entered the building and was unable to settle himself. He was paralyzed with anxiety and refused to even enter the school building. The school's response was cut and dried: He needed to come to school on his own, or he would be moved to the homebound program. The school characterized Jake's behavior as a manipulative attempt to get out of going to school. Jake's mom brought him for treatment after one week of this school refusal.

I worked with the school to reconceptualize Jake's school refusal as an increased post-trauma reliance on his caregiver. We then designed a classic desensitization program in which mom accompanied Jake to class and stayed with him for his whole first day back to school. The second day mom walked him into his classroom, stayed in the room for one hour, and then sat outside in the hallway in case Jake needed her for the next hour. On the third day, mom said goodbye to Jake in the lobby of the school, but spent the morning in her car just outside the school in case he needed her. In Jake's case, the horror of losing one parent understandably increased his reliance on his other primary source of comfort, his mother. A forced, prolonged separation from mom would have flooded the child and reinforced his aversion to school. Allowing him access to his attachment figure while navigating a return to his classroom through a graduated system of exposures was a more successful approach.

Avoidance

Avoidance of people, places, or things is a classic symptom of PTSD. Children who have experienced a traumatic event may avoid all reminders of that event. For example, a child who had to be rushed to the hospital following a serious car accident may ask his parent to reroute his drive to school so he doesn't have to drive by the hospital. This same request may be made in regards to the road on which the accident took place. Children who have experienced abuse may avoid contact with anyone who looks like the perpetrator. Children may also refuse to talk about what happened. The playroom affords these children a unique opportunity to begin approaching reminders of the trauma through nonverbal methods.

Repetitive Posttraumatic Play

Repetitive posttraumatic play is another symptom manifested by traumatized children (Gil, 2006; Malchiodi, 2008; Terr, 1993). When a child is using the playroom in an active, engaged, manner there is a focused energy present and a metaphoric content that takes various shapes over the course of treatment. A child who experienced violence that included exposure to blood or other bodily fluids might engage in cleansing rituals in the playroom. A child who is trying to regain a sense of power and control over an untouchable perpetrator might choose a symbol to be that perpetrator and manipulate it in a variety of ways. A child who has witnessed domestic violence might choose a large bear to represent a parent and a baby bear to be the self-object and put them both in the dollhouse. The child might place the baby bear behind some furniture, crouching and crying, while the big bear knocks over furniture in anger. The symbolic use of the toys is a symbolic reenactment of the violence. In subsequent sessions the child who is actively using the treatment milieu gives the content in shifting metaphors, through expressive arts activities and through portions of verbal narration.

The case of 6-year-old Timmy illustrates this point. Timmy was referred to me after a car accident in which 70 percent of his body was burned. Timmy's mom and dad had been taking him and his 2-year-old sister to buy school clothes when they were hit by a truck driver who had lost control of his vehicle. The truck hit the family's car and flipped it over. The car flipped several times and then caught on fire. The paramedics pulled mom and Timmy out of the car. Then the car blew up. The father and the 2-year-old sister who were still trapped inside did not survive. Both Timmy and his mother were in medically induced comas for several weeks as the surgeons performed skin grafts and dealt with the burns.

Timmy used the playroom in an active way to build a sense of safety and security. Rapport was established quickly, and we began to explore his feelings of loss, both in relation to the deaths of his dad and sister and in relation to his loss of previous functioning and body image. Finally, Timmy was dealing with feelings of loss regarding mom's previous functioning and her current limitations in caring for him as she recovered from her own injuries. Timmy embraced the relaxation strategies, developed his emotional vocabulary, and worked on a memory book to celebrate the lives of his sister and his father. During his eighth, ninth, and tenth sessions, Timmy replayed the traumatic event, showing me the position of the family car on the highway and how the eighteen-wheeler had hit it. He was eager to learn any details that he was missing from the narrative, and mom was available to help fill in any gaps in his memory. He chose rescue vehicles and had them arrive on the scene to take mom and himself to the hospital. He created another scene in which he and mom were in the hospital being taken care of. Lastly, he created a cemetery and showed me what the gravestones looked like that mark dad and sister's graves. He did all this work in a very animated fashion. By the end of the tenth session, he had created a trauma narrative that was internally coherent and shared by a supportive caregiver.

Contrast Timmy's play with that of seven-year-old Anna, who had also been in an accident involving a car and an eighteen-wheeler. Anna came into the playroom, chose a car and an eighteen-wheeler and crashed them into each other, saying, "And everybody dies." I reflected this content. She pulled the car and the eighteen-wheeler apart and crashed them into each other again, saying, "And everybody dies." I made invitations to elaborate on the story, but nothing was added. She pulled the car and the truck apart again and then, with blunted affect and a monotone voice, crashed the two cars together again, saying, "And everybody dies." The repetition of content devoid of meaningful affect and without forward movement can be conceptualized as stuck play.

Whenever a child becomes mired in a posttraumatic play sequence, more directive intervention is required. After 9/11, every major mental health organization in the country stressed the importance of limiting our children's exposure to the horrific images of the burning buildings. Clinicians advised parents and teachers to limit children's exposure to the repetitive images on television. There was clinical consensus that watching the images of the towers toppling over and over again on TV was maladaptive. Stagnant post-traumatic play is the three-dimensional version of this same dynamic. As clinicians, we have an obligation to invite children out of these stuck places.

An understanding of trauma theory makes it necessary to reevaluate a strictly nondirective approach in relation to posttraumatic play. Nondirective therapy has at its root the theoretical underpinning that children have it within themselves to heal under their own direction. The process of self-actualization is realized in the presence of the therapist, who functions as a witness to and reflector of the child's process. However, traumagenic reactions mitigate the child's normal bent toward healing. Trauma, at its root, leaves us with feelings of helplessness and vulnerability. A loss of control and a questioning of one's ability to protect oneself is at the heart of trauma. Children with post-trauma symptoms may not be able to access the parts of themselves that can promote healing on their own. They often need more directive intervention by the therapist.

In Anna's case, the initial invitation out of the stuck play pattern can be made very nonintrusively. When she comes for her next appointment, I could place rescue vehicles and a doctor's kit near the area where the child normally plays out everyone's deaths. This invitation is a gentle and a nonverbal way of communicating to Anna that help is available to her. If she doesn't take the bait, I might overtly state the dilemma that keeps being replayed by saying, "I'm noticing that the car and the truck keep running into each other over and over again and everybody dies. I wonder if there's anything we can do to help these guys so that they don't have to keep running into each other." I have been surprised at the number of times that children have generated creative solutions to the problem after they are given permission to change the play *and an invitation to do so*. If the child is still unable to move out of the stuck play pattern herself, I will offer two or three options for intervention. I might say, "Here are some ideas that might help. We could get out the traffic cop puppet and send these guys to school to learn how to drive more safely. We could take the blocks and make a median, so that when they are driving they can't run into each other anymore. Another option is to make one of them stay home for the day so that their car isn't even on the road." Normally, when I give several options even the most stuck child will choose one. The ensuing play allows the child to experience a different possibility, a different end or outcome for the play pattern.

Risk-Taking Behavior

An increase in risk-taking behavior can also be seen in some traumatized children. Lenor Terr, in her book *Too Scared to Cry* (1990), documents the kidnapping of a busload of school children in Chowchilla, California. The bus was stopped on the road and the children and driver off-loaded into vans. The kidnappers had previously buried a truck trailer underground and put the children inside. The children spent an estimated 16 hours underground in a dark, cramped room. The children believed that they were going to die. Against all odds, the children eventually dug themselves out. Lenor Terr conducted a longitudinal study looking at the play behaviors of the kidnapped children. She compared these play behaviors to those of a control group of children. One of the patterns that she found was an increase in risk-taking behavior. She describes one play sequence in which a child put a chair on top of a table, near the edge, sat down in it and then pretended to drive. The risk of the chair slipping off the table and the child being hurt was high. Children in the control group did not evidence elevated levels of risk-taking in their play.

Several hypotheses exist that can attempt to explain why traumatized children are more likely to engage in risk-taking behavior. A child who grew up in a stressful environment may have been physiologically conditioned to higher levels of cortisol stress hormones and elevations in certain neurochemicals that are released when the brain has its survival mechanisms triggered. The elevated arousal level becomes a normal state for this child.

When there is no immediately stressful event, a child may create one (through engaging in risk-taking behavior) in order to feel what he is used to feeling. Some children have experienced abuse or maltreatment that occurred in a cyclical pattern. For example, a sexually abused child may have been assaulted once and then left untouched for several weeks. Just as the child is beginning to relax and to hope that it might not happen again, it happens again. These children live in a state of constant hypervigilance, waiting and wondering when the unspeakable will happen to them once more. These children experience the lull between abusive episodes as dangerous in their own right. Some children describe an experience of relief just after the sexual act has occurred. They understand that there will be some time now before it happens again. The longer the respite from the abuse, the more certain the child becomes that the next instance is just around the corner. The child's anxiety climbs higher and higher. Eventually the thing that they most fear does happen again, reinforcing the cycle.

Let's imagine that a child who has experienced this kind of cyclical abuse is given a way out. The immediate danger is removed. Caring adults begin to tell her that she is safe now. She may or may not begin to accept this cognitively. She may or may not begin to parrot those words back to the adults around her. However, the child's physiological trauma clock may take a much longer time to reset. The child's body has stored the rhythm of abuse something like this: Bad thing happens . . . now it's over . . . safe, safe, left alone, safe . . . . it's been awhile, I better get ready . . . please, don't, please don't . . . the bad thing happens.

The child who has ostensibly been "made safe" faces a situation in which the objective reality of the rhythm of the abuse is interrupted. However, the child's body is still waiting for it. The child is used to the post-trauma lull, followed by a buildup of anxiety, followed by the bad thing happening. In lieu of the bad thing happening, this child may engage in risk-taking behavior to make the bad thing happen. It's paradoxical, but the longer the child goes without experiencing the abuse, the more sure his sympathetic and parasympathetic systems become that the event is imminent. The high anxiety that this surety creates is exhausting for the child, so he searches for a solution. The risk-taking behavior increases the likelihood that the bad thing will happen soon. Put another way, the child is waiting for the other shoe to drop, and the anxiety becomes so intense that he goes ahead and drops the other shoe himself.

I see this dynamic play out over and over again with the adolescents in my practice. A 16-year-old girl with a history of sexual abuse and exposure to domestic violence comes to counseling. She has, for the first time, an alternate voice telling her that she is worthy, beautiful, and capable. She begins to make great strides in her peer relationships. She finds and holds a job as a waitress after school. She is getting along better with her parents, who are giving her more privileges and lots of praise for her recent changes in behavior. This goes on for a month or two. Then suddenly, she doesn't show up for work for a day or two. She sneaks out of the house to meet a boy. She cheats on a test at school. These behaviors, while self-sabotaging, can be characterized as her unconscious solution to the lull in crisis and the buildup in anxiety because things have been going so well.

Cognitive Effects/Thought Life Issues

Difficulty concentrating, distractibility, and a short attention span are all symptoms that can manifest as a response to trauma. Traumagenic anxiety can look very much like traditional deficits in attention and impulse control. This crossover in symptoms can play a role in misdiagnosis. Parents may come into an initial intake and list these symptoms. When a clinician is presented with this cluster of symptoms and has no reason to suspect trauma, a diagnosis of attention-deficit/hyperactivity disorder (ADHD) is often made. Frequently children who come to my practice have previously been diagnosed with ADHD, oppositional defiant disorder (ODD), or bipolar disorder. These children have already had a variety of medication trials, none of which have significantly impacted symptom reduction. In these cases, it is important to keep the door open to the possibility of undisclosed or unprocessed trauma. The inclusion of relaxation training in the treatment plans of these complicated children can help alleviate dysregulated manifestations of anxiety that may have been improperly diagnosed.

Posttraumatic children may also develop idiosyncratic fears or specific worries that did not trouble them before the trauma. Moreover, traumatized children may perseverate on a certain aspect of the trauma or develop repetitive maladaptive thoughts in response to their traumatic events. These intrusive, repetitive thoughts can be very disturbing for children. They may be flooded by these thoughts and feel that they have no mechanism for holding them in check. A case example follows.

An eleven-year-old boy named William was sexually molested by an older boy in his neighborhood. After William told his mom, the abuse stopped. However, William began to have intrusive thoughts that engendered strong feelings of guilt. He told mom about each of the molestation incidents in detail. Then he went back and told her again. He kept repeating details in an anxious manner, asking mom, "Did I tell you that part yet? I'd feel guilty if I hadn't told you that part. Mom, I need to tell you that part again." Mom was becoming understandably weary in her constant containment role. The family was Catholic, and their spiritual traditions were an important part of their family culture. William had gone to speak with the priest and told him everything that happened. Even though the priest contained the information appropriately and did his best to help William resist self-recrimination, William went back to the priest over and over again, driven to make sure he had "confessed everything." William needed help externalizing his intrusive thoughts in order to deal with them definitively. I offered William a box to decorate as he wished (Figure 2.1).

He put a cross on the front of the box and added glitter. I laid out a variety of sticky note pads in different shapes, sizes, and colors. Over the course of two or three sessions, William wrote down every intrusive thought that he had regarding the sexually inappropriate acts he had experienced. Every time he wrote one down, he read it out loud and put it in the box (Figure 2.2).

We agreed that once it was in the box, it would not be revisited until he took it out of the box again. Writing down the substance of each thought afforded him an externalization of the troublesome content. Putting it in the box afforded him both a sense of empowerment over the material and a marker in time for when he physically put it aside. Over time we took out each thought, processed and integrated any somatosensory content that needed to be added, and stuck the sticky note onto a growing timeline of the trauma.

The purposeful coherence-building of the narrative desensitized him to the guilt and anxiety that accompanied his episodic retelling of the content. We also used play-based thought-stopping games, and cognitive restructuring

Figure 2.1 William's *Final Confession* Box

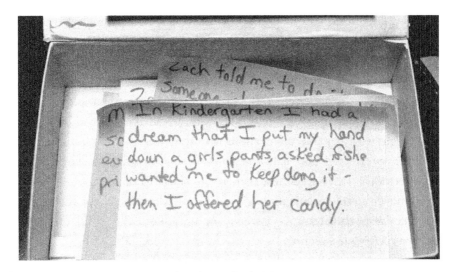

Figure 2.2 William's Intrusive Thoughts on Sticky Notes

activities to fight the irrational thoughts. Children with intrusive or repetitive maladaptive thoughts can benefit from cognitive-behavioral play therapy strategies that give the child a full-body kinesthetic experience of bossing back the troublesome thoughts while rehearsing empowering counter statements. Chapter 11, "Addressing the Child's Thought Life," offers more detail regarding these kinds of play-based interventions.

Dissociation is a symptom of trauma that can vary in degree from client to client. In general, the playroom itself serves to mitigate these tendencies in posttraumatic children. The child's body is often soothed by the play materials themselves: sifting hands through the sand, squeezing a stress ball, and painting a picture are all activities that ground the child in the here and now of the treatment milieu. The child whose body is grounded in the sifting of sand is soothing the self as he approaches the trauma content. The rhythmic play behavior soothes and mitigates the anxiety response, allowing the client a closer approach to the trauma content without having dissociative tendencies triggered. If a child becomes dissociative in the playroom, it is helpful to have premeditated ways of anchoring the child in the here and now. In all cases, I shift the focus away from the content or activity that has triggered the dissociation. I may redirect the child by picking up a superhero figure and asking the child to remind me of the character's name. I may play a game with the child in which I ask him to draw pictures of two objects in the room and have me guess what they are. A very simple grounding activity is to play I Spy. In some cases a grounding touch may help to anchor the child. However, any intervention that involves touch, even if it is a simple touch on the hand, should be agreed upon in a previous session, while the child is fully psychologically present.

Many children experience guilt as a result of their traumatic experience. Children who have survived a natural disaster may have survivor guilt. They may struggle with bewilderment about why they were spared. Children who have been maltreated may feel a sense of false responsibility. They grapple with a sense that they somehow caused the abuse to happen. Guilt may be felt whenever a child is asked to keep a secret. Whether or not the demand for secrecy was threatening, coercive, or unspoken, the child often feels guilty for keeping the secret.

Finally, posttraumatic youth may have preexisting paradigms challenged. Young people often question their values and beliefs as part of a trauma recovery process. Children and adolescents who were raised with a strong faith base, one that promotes God as a loving being who protects us and loves us, often have these beliefs thrown into chaos in the wake of interpersonal violence, natural disaster, or sexual abuse. The young person may come out the other side of trauma with a deepening of her beliefs, owning a faith that had previously been her parents'. Conversely, a client may abandon a set of beliefs that no longer fit into his worldview.

Conclusion

Understanding the myriad ways in which children manifest the symptoms of trauma can inform our choice of play-based interventions and the timing and duration given to each of the goals within the flexibly sequential play therapy model. The flexibility of the model allows for the child's most distressing symptoms to be addressed in a timely manner.

3

Enhancing a Child's Sense of Safety

Joining with the Child

The sense of safety and security that most children take for granted is often one of the first casualties in the world of the posttraumatic child. The reestablishment of a child's sense of safety should be at the forefront of your mind in treatment planning. Very little work can be done around a child's trauma issues until the client is feeling safe with you. Although safety building is a process that occurs over time, play therapists are in a unique position to use the tools of the playroom and the person of the play therapist to actively augment a child's sense of perceived safety. Although play therapists cannot ensure a child's safety in the world at large, we can communicate dual messages that the playroom is a safe place and that the play therapist is a safe person.

Initially the therapist's role is to assist the child in experiencing the playroom as a safe place. This is accomplished, in part, by clearly delineating the boundaries of the playroom. Play therapists often become active partners in the process of ridding a room of ghosts, demons, or concrete objects that represent perceived threats. We are often asked to witness a child's courageous approach toward and capture of a perpetrator symbol. The second aspect of the therapist's role is to augment the child's experience of the play therapist as a safe person. This is done in part through typical attunement processes that build rapport, but it is powerfully helped along by the child's playful placement of us in the role of protector, defender, guardian, or eradicator of evil or any other role that is needed. Our ability to correctly hear what the child is asking for and to meet that need goes a long way toward building a foundation of trust.

Verbalizations such as "This is a safe place" and "I am a safe person" may certainly need to be said but are often dismissed by maltreated children as just so many grown-up words, words devoid of any experiential meaning for the child. As in any other life arena, the child's perceptions of the therapeutic space are influenced by his experiences within the space. A playroom carefully stocked with the materials of childhood has a definite advantage over traditional offices in that the objects are immediately familiar to children. Children perceive a playroom as "their kind of space." The child's curiosity is caught, and the natural enjoyment of the toys and delight in exploring them often counters the wariness with which children can enter the room.

When a child enters the playroom, she is bringing with her all her prior experiences and a set of assumptions about how the materials can be used. Evaluating the way in which a child enters the playroom can provide a wealth of information about how the client handles new stressors. Virginia Axline articulated this phenomenon beautifully.

"When a child comes for play therapy, it is usually because some adult has either brought or sent him to the clinic for treatment. He enters into this unique experience just as he enters all new experiences—either with enthusiasm, fear, caution, resistance or any other manner that is typical of the way he reacts to new situations."

—Axline, *Play Therapy, p. 74*

Becoming a Secure Base for the Child

The careful observation of a child's first moments in the playroom can inform the therapist's approach to increasing safety for that particular child. Some children feel safest if they are given the lead and allowed to explore the playroom at their own pace and in their own timing. Children who project self-confidence, whether it be real or a facade, will often bound into the playroom, move directly to a set of toys, and begin to explore. This exploration is often accompanied by spontaneous verbalizations. This child's safety is increased by following his lead, reflecting his talk, describing his play, and generally "being with" him, being attuned to his communications in the space.

Other children will step into the room and freeze. They may put their hands in their pockets, keep their eyes downcast, and remain frozen in the center of the space, seemingly adrift at sea in this new environment. In these cases, I still begin the process of connecting with the child by reflecting the child's discomfort and giving express permission to use the space. I might say, "Sometimes it's hard to know what to do in a new place. This is your special time in the playroom. In here you can do almost anything you want to do. If there's anything you can't do, I'll let you know." If the child looks up and at the toys, I might say, "You're looking around, trying to decide what you'd like to play with." This is, however, where my methodology begins to diverge from a strictly nondirective approach. Whereas traditionally trained nondirective play therapists embrace the mantra *Follow the child's lead*," the guiding maxim that I employ is *Follow the child's need.*" (Marvin, Cooper, Hoffman, & Powell, 2002). This phrase is grounded in attachment theory and references the way in which children look to their caregivers to structure their environments and meet their needs. I am the caregiver in the dyad whenever I am alone with a child in the playroom, and in order to be contingently responsive to the child, a more directive approach may be necessary.

My first job in establishing safety for each client is to become a secure base for that child. I try to understand what a child is asking for when he comes into the playroom. A child, from the moment of his birth, is engaged in a dance with his caregivers and his environment. Children have two predominant needs: the need to explore and the need to be comforted and welcomed back when they need soothing. When a child is secure and feeling good, the child's natural drive for exploration takes over and the child moves away from the secure base parent. If the child hurts himself, doesn't feel good, or experiences something scary, he will likely return quickly to his caregiver. These two cycling needs of the developing child are succinctly delineated by the Circle of Security project (Hoffman, Marvin, Cooper, & Powell, 2006; Cooper, Hoffman, Powell, & Marvin, 2005). They have delineated an arc on the top of the circle in which the child leaves the parent to explore. While the child is exploring, the child needs the parent to (1) watch over him, (2) delight in him, (3) help him, and (4) enjoy with him. When the child needs to return to the parent, the child needs the parent to (1) protect him, (2) comfort him, (3) delight in him, and (4) organize his feelings.

Parents become a secure base for their children by accurately responding to the moment-to-moment needs of their children. This same process of attunement is imperative for child clinicians to become a secure base for the children in their care. Increasing a child's sense of perceived security in the playroom comes in large part from the therapist's ability to assess where a particular child is on the circle. Children are generally either joint attention seeking or structure seeking when they first enter the playroom. If the child is exploring the play space confidently, the play therapist can best build rapport by delighting in the child's exploration, providing joint attention, and enjoying the space with the child. However, children who have been traumatized may have been stripped of their pretrauma confidence.

A given child may enter the playroom feeling vulnerable, adrift, and in need of structure. Sometimes the most effective method for increasing a child's sense of safety in the playroom quickly is to provide additional structure. When a securely attached child is unsure of what is expected, she references her caregiver. A good caregiver recognizes that the child needs additional structure and provides it. The role of the play therapist is the same.

When a child who has been standing forlornly in the middle of the room has not responded to my nondirective bids for engagement, I offer a way out in the form of an invitation. "It looks like you are not sure what to do right now. In here, you can choose what to play with first or I can choose what we do first." The clients who have been communicating their need for additional structure usually jump at the option of having the therapist choose. I often offer a choice of two to three separate activities, one involving the sand tray, one involving the art materials, and one involving the manipulation of toys. The child, having his choice parameters safely narrowed, can usually choose between these options. The posture and affect of these structure-seeking children changes almost immediately as the therapist takes the lead. The child's closed body language opens up. A shy smile is often attempted. Tentative eye contact is made for the first time. The first spontaneous verbalizations may be produced as the child comes alongside the therapist to begin the chosen activity.

Once the initial joining process has been successfully navigated, the child's need for safety in relation to her specific trauma history may surface. This typically happens in one of two ways. A child may choose a toy that is symbolic of danger. For maltreated children, the symbol may represent a perpetrator. For children who have experienced other traumatic events, the symbol may represent the scary event itself, an intrusive thought, or even a problematic behavior. Conversely, a child may choose a toy to represent herself. For the purposes of this text, we will call the toy that the child chooses to represent herself the self-object. Much of the work involved in enhancing a child's sense of security in the playroom can be done through the therapist's intentional responses to the client's choice of perpetrator symbols and self-objects. A therapist can quickly enhance her legitimacy as a safe person for the child by facilitating a child's manipulation and containment of perpetrator symbols. Equally effective are a therapist's nurturing and protective responses to a self-object.

Therapist as Megaphone

Using a role description that I call "therapist as megaphone," I become the amplifying device for safety in whatever way the child seems to need it. As I follow the child's use of metaphor, I become aware of the child's symbolic uses of the play materials and can begin to work with the thematic content to return power to the child. The therapist can make invitations to action that will result in a child's experience of power regained in the play space. For example, a young girl who has been sexually molested chooses a two-headed dragon to represent the uncle who molested her. The two-headed dragon has become a perpetrator symbol for this client. The therapist can give express permission for the containment and manipulation of the two-headed dragon. The therapist might point out the containment devices in the room, such as the jails and handcuffs. Children are often delighted by the opportunity to lock up the perpetrator symbol in some way. In many cases the child chooses containment devices in a self-directed fashion, and the therapist has only to augment the power and control that the child has over the use of the play materials.

A 7-year-old boy named Jake lived in constant fear of being kidnapped by his dad while he was at school. Three months prior to Jake's first session with me, his father and mother had divorced. Dad had a schizophrenic break and assaulted mom in their home. Dad had been hospitalized and a restraining order had been filed. However, dad had recently been discharged and Jake felt vulnerable and unprotected. In his initial session he chose a figure to be dad and enclosed him in a miniature closet. Then he wrapped rubber bands around the closet, effectively sealing off the doorway (Figure 3.1).

Figure 3.1   Jake's Dad Sealed in the Closet

Figure 3.2   Three Layers of Containment

Jake enjoyed the process of containing his dad symbol. After he had placed the rubber bands around the closet, he moved to another part of the playroom and became engaged in another activity. However, just before the end of the session, Jake returned to the closet and moved it into the jail, effectively containing the dad behind a third layer of barrier (Figure 3.2).

Amplification of Safety by Supporting the Child's Chosen Method of Containment

A case example will help explicate this concept. The following is a transcript of an early session with Josh, a 3 ½-year-old boy who had witnessed domestic violence for the entirety of his young life. He had also been physically abused by his father on several occasions. Earlier in the session, Josh put a jail in the sand tray and placed a crab with piercing claws inside it. He chose a baby doll and put it next to the jail. Then he opened the jail, took out the crab, and pretended to have the crab bite his own nose. Then he had the crab bite the baby.

Paris: The crab is out of its cage and it bit you.
Josh: Yeah.

Josh picks up the key to the jail.

Josh: I see the key!
Paris: You see the key. You found it.
Josh: Yeah.
Paris: Now you can lock and unlock the cage.

After reflecting the child's words and describing his discovery, I amplify his sense of power by highlighting the control he can exert over the perpetrator through the key. My statement serves as an invitation to empowering action.

Josh: Yeah . . . umm . . . what am I gonna put in there?
Paris: You're looking around trying to decide what to put in the cage.

I create awareness of his decision-making process while leaving the responsibility of choosing in his hands. Josh chooses an octopus, makes it bite the baby doll, and looks at the therapist.

Paris: The octopus grabbed the baby! That baby is getting grabbed by all kinds of scary things.

The client's manipulation of this perpetrator symbol is empowering. In the real world, Josh feels helpless and paralyzed in the face of threat. Josh's greatest threat in the real world is his physically abusive father, from whose care he has recently been removed. It could be hypothesized that the octopus represents the threatening dad. Either way, Josh is significantly larger and more powerful than the symbol he has chosen.

Paris (pointing her finger at the octopus): You stop grabbing that baby!

In this moment, the therapist is actively aligning with the client against the perpetrator symbol. Josh smiles at the therapist and points to the jail, nonverbally directing the therapist to continue talking to the symbol.

Paris (talking to the octopus): "You've got to go in the cage because you bit the baby."

Josh smiles broadly and begins to put the octopus in the jail. His ability to symbolically contain the threat serves as a kind of wish fulfillment while increasing his sense of safety in the space.

Once the source of danger in the room has been identified through play, in this case the octopus, the therapist can further amplify the safety message by speaking directly to the dangerous creature. This allows the client the experience of watching the therapist stand up to the perpetrator symbol, model appropriate limit setting, and protect the child from the injustices done by the perpetrator symbol in play. All these processes, performed in the context of the play scenario, allow the therapist to align with the child against the perpetrator and therefore concretize the role of the bigger, stronger, wiser, kind helper.

Josh: Now get in there. Put him in there. Get your thing [tentacle] in there.

Josh wrestles with the tentacle as he tries to fit it into the jail.

Josh: There!

Josh smiles broadly, clearly proud of his accomplishment.

Paris (talking to Josh): There he is, all caged up. (Addressing the symbol): You're in a cage because you bit the baby.

Josh, grinning triumphantly: Yeah!

Paris, matching client's affect: Yeah! You hold the key.

Josh: Lock him up!

Paris: Lock him up. (Addressing the octopus): Now you can't get out till Josh says so.

Josh: That's it.

Josh gets an experience of being in charge of the perpetrator through play. He gets to decide when and how the dad is put away. Josh starts to open the jail.

Paris: You're gonna let him out. What if he bites again?

Josh: Then he'll go back in the cage.

Paris: Oh, I see!

Josh sits quietly looking at the octopus. Then he picks it up and holds it close to his face.

Josh: Then it's gonna bite me!

Paris: Oh, it's gonna bite you?

Josh hesitates and then has the octopus bite the baby again instead.

Paris: Oh, you changed your mind. It bit the baby again!

Josh, talking to the octopus while putting him in the cage: Go in the cage.

Paris: Gotta go in the cage again. (Addressing octopus): You don't bite the baby anymore! Babies are for keeping safe and loving.

Josh grabs a large, vicious-looking beetle.

Josh: It's gonna bite the baby . . .

Paris: That one's gonna bite the baby too?

Josh nods while grinning and has the beetle bite the baby.

Paris, addressing the beetle: You bit the baby too!

Josh, sighing: Yep. Put him in the cage.

Paris, matter-of-factly: He has to go in there too.

I am still aligning myself with the client while setting limits with the symbols of danger. The client is now trying out this new narrative in which the source of the danger does something dangerous and has consequences. Josh has certainly seen his dad engage in destructive behavior before, but with very few consequences. In the thematic material of the session, the client has the power to dispense immediate consequences to the figure and does so by placing him behind bars. Moreover, the client gets to decide the nature of the consequence and how long it lasts.

Josh: Yeah. (Josh grabs the baby doll and points to her leg). And then she has a leg ache.

A shift occurs right here in the session. After practicing this new narrative in which, within the walls of the playroom, Josh has power to stop the dangerous behavior, he experiences a restoration of power and choice and through this restoration begins to experience the playroom as a safe place. Moreover, the client has watched with delight as I have repeatedly aligned myself with him and set verbal limits with the chosen symbol. Josh had not seen his mother stand up to dad's abuse and on some level did not perceive her as truly able to protect him. Watching me stand up to his threatening symbol helps him embrace me as trustworthy and able to protect him within the confines of the playroom. Josh completes several energized cycles in which he chooses a dangerous creature, has this creature violate the limits (i.e., bite the baby, bite the boy), and then contains the creature. Through these cycles he gains experiential knowledge that he has power over the perpetrator here.

Moreover, he understands that the play therapist will support his power by aligning herself with him against the perpetrator symbol. After this foundational safety has been established, Josh shifts his focus to the baby doll's wounds. He calls the baby doll "she" and describes her wound as a leg ache.

This glimpse into the pain of another chosen symbol—in this case the baby doll—is Josh's way of saying that I passed the first safety test and can be trusted to see the victim's hurts.

In terms of Josh's chronological age, the developmental processes of individuation and separation from mom should be complete. However, because Josh experienced chronic danger for the first three years of his life, the energy that might have been used to successfully navigate the developmental milestones of separation and individuation may have been rerouted into survival mechanisms. If the individuation process was delayed, Josh may have unclear boundaries with his mom. He may continue to experience mom as an extension of the self. When he watched mom get hit by dad, he may have experienced it, to some extent, as being hit himself. Whether he perceives the baby doll as a self-object, a mother object, or a symbol that shifts to embody each at different times, the therapist's treatment of the baby doll becomes another opportunity for establishing safety. The therapist must attempt to provide help to the baby doll.

Paris: Oh . . . does she need a Band-Aid? Let me get some Band-Aids.

Therapist gets a large box of bandages.

Paris: Where should we put the Band-Aid?

Josh, pointing to the part of the leg he wants bandaged: Right here. Aw, she has a bleed.

Paris: Oh, she's bleeding!

Therapist unwraps a bandage.

Paris, speaking to the baby doll: Here we go. We're going to help you feel
    better.
Josh, smiling: She feels better.
Josh: Put this here.

Josh puts different objects in front of the jail door.

Paris: Oh, you're putting that in front of the door so he can't get out.

Josh takes the beetle out of jail, hesitates, and then puts him back.

Paris: It's hard to decide when he can come out.

Josh picks up a police car and puts it in front of the jail. Josh seems confused about where he should put the police car. He moves it restlessly around the tray.

Josh: I'll put this right here. No, I'll put him right here.
Paris: It's hard to decide where the police go too.

It is almost time to leave the session. I let him know that time is almost up for today. Josh chooses to leave the beetle locked in the jail with the police car guarding it. He takes the Band-Aid off the baby doll and leaves her "all better."

Josh's ambivalence about the role of the police is typical of children who have lived through domestic violence. Josh desperately wants someone to make daddy stop hurting mommy, but every time the police come, daddy has to go away. The police are a double-edged sword for Josh. On the one hand they represent an immediate reprieve from the danger, a short respite of peace. On the other hand this reprieve is accompanied by the loss of a needed parent. This dilemma is one faced by many child survivors of domestic violence. Josh finally chose to place the police car directly in front of the jail. The final diorama is one in which the police car is left guarding the jail and in which the perpetrator symbol is safely behind bars. This parting snapshot affords Josh a powerful external three-dimensional image that can be stored in memory as a safety reminder. Moreover, the perpetrator is doubly contained. The threatening symbol is in the jail and the jail is left inside the office, behind the closed and eventually locked door of the playroom. The dad-related anxiety that may have been previously experienced by the child as a nebulous force, a continuous hypervigilant readiness, has been given a much narrower focus in Josh's chosen symbol. Josh has a threat that can be touched, manipulated, and contained.

The simple act of identifying a perpetrator symbol and leaving it in the playroom can provide psychological relief for children. Recently a 7-year-old boy created a perpetrator symbol out of construction paper and popsicle sticks.

He named his nemesis "Mr. Bad Guy," and when he left the session he put Mr. Bad Guy in a toy safe and locked it. His mother reported that he experienced immediate relief from his nagging fears because he knew that Mr. Bad Guy was in Ms. Paris's office. When they arrived in the lobby the next week, mom reported that he was staring at the bottom of the door to the playroom. I had previously put additional weather stripping at the bottom of the door to add privacy. The little boy said to his mom, "I know why Ms. Paris put that stuff under the door!" When mom asked why, he said, "So that Mr. Bad Guy can't get out." We can give our clients the gift of a space set apart, a place where dangerous icons can be enclosed and fantasies of safety can be concretized.

In the previous play sequence with Josh and the jail, the goals of Therapist as Megaphone were accomplished. The message, "You are safe in here!" was amplified. The amplification often happens within an evolving metaphor of the child's choosing and therefore provides for endless variation.

Amplifying the Safety Message Through Physical Alignment

Sometimes the most powerful amplification of safety in the playroom occurs on a kinesthetic level, as the therapist and client act together in handling the objects in the room that evoke danger for a child. For instance, a 4-year-old boy named Taz was referred to therapy for selective mutism. The first time Taz entered the playroom he stood, stiff as a board, in the center of the room. I normalized his discomfort and reflected that he was looking around the room and not sure what to do first. He remained rooted to the spot, eyes downcast and body rigid. I continued to make an occasional reflection of the difficulty he was having adjusting to the space, "You're getting used to the room, trying to figure out what to do, looking around, checking it out." After a long pause in which we both remained silent, he looked up at me and then his eyes skittered over to the shelf with the dart guns. Cautiously he moved to the shelf and picked up my two orange dart guns. He walked over to me and put one in my hand. Then he pulled on my sleeve. I got up to go with him. He found the first dangerous creature in the room, a spider, shot it with the dart gun, and then gestured for me to do the same with mine. So we circled the room together. He would point to a scary looking creature, shoot it, and then make it clear that he wanted me to shoot it too. I would say something like, "Taz doesn't want you here, so you have to go," and then I would shoot the object with my dart gun too. He kept his body very close beside mine as we moved around the playroom, approaching the danger together. We did that over and over again for the larger part of three sessions. The more repetitions of this sequence we enacted, the more positive affect Taz showed. He began to visibly relax, made more spontaneous eye contact, and grinned from ear to ear as we rid the room of all the threats. Midway through the third session of actively making the room as safe as we possibly could, he put the dart gun down, turned around, and spoke to me.

This selectively mute child was able to overcome the anxiety that kept him silent by teaming with the therapist and experiencing mastery over the concrete dangers in the playroom in a way that he felt powerless to control in the other areas of his life. The way that we eradicated the perceived threats in the playroom served as an equipping experience for him. He now had an experience of successfully conquering his fears that could translate into how he faced perceived threats in other areas of his life. The confidence learned by being an active participant in establishing his own safety in the playroom began to generalize to both home and school. Over time, he began to take verbal risks outside the playroom and enjoyed the rewards of having his words be understood and welcomed.

Cleansing Rituals

In cases of sexual abuse, violent assaults, and serious accidents, children have been forced to come into contact with substances such as blood, semen, and other body fluids. Posttraumatic children may come to the playroom feeling contaminated or unclean. One of the child's processes for reestablishing a sense of safety and control is to engage in cleansing rituals in the playroom. This dynamic played out in the case of Eric, a 4-year-old boy, referred for treatment for extreme dysregulation. Eric's mom and dad had moved into separate homes shortly before Eric entered treatment. His father came to pick him up for visitation one day and asked if he could use the bathroom. Eric's dad locked Eric in the bathroom with him and proceeded to shoot himself in the head. When the mother was able to break into the room, she found Eric trying to clean up some of the blood and brain tissue that covered the walls and the floor.

During Eric's first session, his dysregulation was pervasive. His words were incoherent. His affect was incongruent. His body was uncoordinated. He would pick up one toy, quickly place it back on the shelf, and move to another part of the room. He had no organized play pattern and was in constant physical motion. I eventually got out the Play-Doh, intending to give him some sensory material in which to ground his current experience. He came over to the table and chose the red Play-Doh. He mushed it around and spread it over his hands. He then went to my water station and began to clean his hands. He repeated this pattern over and over. He then chose the red finger paint, mucked around in it until his hands were covered with the dripping red paint, and then raced to my water tray to clean it off. Throughout this process, I described his play behavior. "You are covering your hands in the red paint. You have so much paint on you it is dripping on your clothes and on the floor." While he was washing I reflected, "You are scrubbing and scrubbing to get all that yucky stuff off. You don't want any more sticky stuff on you." After his hands were clean, I commented, "You worked hard to get the sticky stuff off of you and now it's all gone." This verbalization reinforced the client's effectiveness at being able to make himself clean. I witnessed the process and, in this witnessing, sent a dual message that I could handle what he was showing me *and so could he.*

Eric's kinesthetic handling of the sticky red paint represented a self-directed approach to the sensory experiences he absorbed in the bathroom while dealing with the sticky remains of his father. Experienced through the play materials and witnessed by the safe, available adult Eric was able to wrestle through the sensory sensations encoded during the trauma. By degrees, Eric used less and less paint on his hands and washed for less time. Eric was working through a process of play-based in vivo exposures that resulted in his desensitization to the trauma-laden sensory content. By the end of the session, he had returned to exploring the toys. Eric chose the initial approach to his trauma, he showed the therapist the muck as he struggled to free himself from it. He chose the exposures to the sticky stuff that mimicked the blood and brain tissue of the trauma. He performed cleansing rituals with decreasing intensity. All these behaviors served to soothe and regulate him. The therapist's ability to be with the child in these metaphoric reenactments begins to build a safety scaffold for the traumatized child.

Sometimes children choose a self-object, such as a baby doll, and become very intent on dirtying the baby doll and then making it clean again. For this reason, it is important to make toy bathtubs, water, soap, and towels available to posttraumatic children in the playroom. In my office a miniature tub is often chosen for use in the sand tray. A miniature figure is often chosen as a self-object, placed in the tub, and cleansed in the make-believe water. I also have a larger tub that can fit a good-sized baby doll. Clients often fill this toy with tap water and cleanse the self-object repeatedly. Sexual abuse survivors can carry around an impression of themselves as tainted, dirty, or contaminated. Some have a desperate desire to feel clean again. The cleansing ritual work in the playroom can provide them in vivo experiences of being washed clean.

When a child begins this kind of self-directed approach to the trauma, the therapist's most effective tools for communicating safety are attunement, verbal and behavioral tracking, and containment of the content shared by the child. In Eric's case, he felt supported enough in his initial session that he continued his metaphoric communication in the next session. The next time Eric came in, he turned off all the lights in the room so that the room was pitch black. He then turned on a strobe light, which cast a frenetic pattern of light over the room. Finally, he chose a rubber mallet and began smashing the flexible play tent in the corner of the room. The atmosphere was frenzied, the scene chaotic. My impression of Eric's play was that he was giving me a snapshot of the chaotic state of his internal world since the shooting. I gave soothing reflections of his play throughout and communicated that I was not overwhelmed by what he was showing me.

Amplifying Safety by Setting Limits with the Perpetrator Symbol

In his third session, Eric chose an African-American mom figure and an African-American child figure and placed them in the middle of the room. Then he went and got the vicious, ugly, creepy, vinyl cobra puppet. It is one of the most sinister puppets in my collection. He put the puppet on his hand and projected the snake's voice. He had the puppet threaten the mom and the baby with violence and death. Based on the information that mom gave during intake, many of the snake's threats were direct reenactments of threats that dad made during the domestic-violence episodes. He said, "I'm going to kill you," and "You won't have nothin' left," and "You ain't gonna have any kids anymore," as he brought the snake physically closer and closer to the mom and baby in the middle of the room.

I tried something. I moved quickly to the mom and baby, scooped them up, and hid the two figures behind my back. Then I spoke firmly to the snake, saying, "You can't hurt them in here. I won't let you. In here these guys stay safe and you can't bother them anymore." Eric absorbed these responses, stared at me for a moment, and then, breaking into a wide grin, said enthusiastically, "Let's do that again." I chose to actively align with the child and set clear limits on the perpetrator. I stood in the role of protector and told the snake, "Not in my playroom." It is critical that the therapist be attuned to the child's signals directly after an intervention like the one described here. Many children will welcome the metaphoric rescue as a form of alignment and safety building. Some children, however, need to show you more of the traumatic reenactment without interruption. Caution and clinical judgment should inform the therapist's decision to intervene by setting metaphoric limits on the perpetrator symbol.

In this case I made the bid for protection and Eric signaled his delight by asking to play out this scenario again. After I rescued the mom and baby a second time, he asked, "Can we play it again?" My response was, "We can play it as many times as you want." Eric played it over and over again. After several repetitions he began to give me prompts of specific limits he wanted me to set with the snake. I readily obliged. Together we created an experiential rescue narrative. The kinesthetically rich play in which the narrative occurs allows for the play sequences to become potent memories that can run parallel to the memories created in Eric's recent past. In the playroom, help was always available and the father's threats were always silenced. Through the many repetitions of safe outcomes that are experienced through the metaphoric play, the client begins to build an alternative script to the one of danger that has previously been rehearsed. In the same way that sensations of helplessness and terror can be conditioned through traumatic experiences, sensations of empowerment and security can be conditioned through repetitions of energized, experiential play.

The intentional presence of the play therapist is a key ingredient in establishing a child's sense of safety and security in the playroom. Once initial safety has been established in the playroom, clients will begin testing the therapist. This has been characterized as the "testing for protection" stage (Norton, 2002). After I had been tested by Eric and proven to be a safe enough container for him, he began to show me more of his early life experience. Children often reward a therapist's initial efforts to enhance the child's felt safety in the playroom with reenactments of the traumatic events they have survived. In his fourth session, Eric chose one oversized alligator and one very small alligator and put them in the dollhouse. He hid the small alligator behind a couch and had the oversized alligator whip his tail back and forth throughout the house, knocking over furniture. While the large alligator destroyed the house, the small alligator crouched behind the couch and cried. Eric moved from amorphous expressions through Play-Doh and finger paints by degrees into more concrete manipulation of objects. Through his play in the dollhouse, Eric reenacted the destruction that often accompanied dad's violence.

The therapist's role as protector requires us to show children that we can hold for them whatever they need us to hold. It is vital that when they risk giving us a glimpse of the unthinkable, we project a steady message that communicates both "I see what you're showing me," and "I'm strong enough to contain it for you." For this very reason, when I provide training on treating sexually abused children, I have participants generate a list of all the words for sexual acts and body parts that are most disturbing to them personally. Then I give them a homework assignment that requires them to stand in front of their bathroom mirrors and repeat each word on their lists out loud until the words lose their potency. This is not done to embarrass burgeoning clinicians but to desensitize them to these loaded words so that when a child uses one while describing his own abuse, the therapist can remain fully present for the child and contain both the images and the language of what the child is communicating.

Learning to Bear It

Once the child has established a sense of the playroom as a safe place and the therapist as a safe person, it is useful to give him transitional objects that can help carry the perceived safety into other arenas. For a variety of reasons a child may experience more safety in our offices than in any other environment. It is my goal to maximize his connectedness with me outside the playroom and I use a variety of props to aid in this endeavor. If I can only be with a child an hour or two a week, I want pieces of me, through the props, to be able to go with the child throughout the rest of the week. In this way, the props become a tangible extension of the child's safe connection to the therapist and the play space that can be accessed in his other environments.

I was first introduced to the autographable bear as a novelty item that children use at the end of the school year to collect their friends' signatures.

The plain canvas that constitutes the bear's body functions much like a year-book page, encouraging children to personalize it with their own writing. My clients also write on the bears, but what we record are positive affirmations, coping statements, or the names and phone numbers of the people in a child's support network. This intervention can be a useful adjunct to a standard no-harm contract when a child presents with suicidal ideation. In cases where there is no imminent threat, the bear can serve as a visual reminder to use the adaptive coping strategy of reaching out for help when it is needed. The hurting child then has a three-dimensional nurturing symbol to remind her of all the people who are available to help. The bear serves as a tangible cue to reach out to others when she is having thoughts about hurting herself or simply needs support (Figure 3.3).

Figure 3.3   Learning to Bear It

The Intentional Construction of Safe Places

In trauma work with adults a client might say, "I wish that I could feel safe again." The therapist might respond with the question, "What would that feel like?" or the question, "What would that look like?" Adults can hold an internally generated image in mind, cognitively manipulate the image, and give detailed verbal descriptions. Children are less able to hold an image steadily in mind, particularly one that has not previously been grounded in the child's concrete world. The marvelous dimension that play therapy affords children is that as the child creates play scenarios, he instinctively shows us what safety looks like, and by showing us, he shows himself. External visual images produced kinesthetically in the playroom can be encoded and added to the child's internal repertoire of safety images.

Maltreated and neglected children have such a skewed repertoire of experiences, many of which would engender the antithesis of safe feelings, that asking them to close their eyes and imagine a safe place could have iatrogenic effects. When maltreated children close their eyes, sometimes all they can see behind their closed eyelids are disjointed flashes of trauma-specific imagery. So when I am helping a client to create a "safe place" production, whether in art, sand, or clay, I give a dual prompt: "Think of a place that you have visited where you felt really safe, *or create a place* where you could feel that way." It is important to give permission for the client to imagine or create a place. One can never assume that a client has a safe place in their current repertoire of experiences. Moreover, the many magical symbols in the playroom may tease the child's imagination into creating a place more beautiful and serene than any the client has visited in reality.

Even when we ask for a safe place image, what we may get is the starkness of the trauma replayed before our eyes. It may be that the tapes of the trauma are on a continuous loop in the mind of the child. When the child shows it to me and I become the container for it, he is able to begin to look at it differently, to see the possibility of turning it into something else. Whenever a child can show us his internal nightmares through the play materials, it opens up the possibility that those materials could be transformed into a different reality, first through the play materials and later through an internalized image of the externally altered reality.

Years ago I worked with a 13-year-old boy named Sam. Sam had a long history of maltreatment and neglect and had been placed in multiple foster homes. At the time I was refining an intervention called "postcards in motion." The first step of the intervention was to give the client a postcard-sized piece of paper and ask him to draw a picture of a place that he would like to visit, a place in which he could feel really safe and good and content. I waited patiently as Sam drew his picture and passed it across the table to me. In the middle of his postcard was a straw hut on a deserted island. From the outside this dwelling appeared to provide satisfactory protection from the elements. However, as Sam began to describe the hut, he said that it leaked, had no food, and was infested with rats (Figure 3.4).

The hut spoke of inadequate protection from the elements. The rats added overtones of danger and filth to the image. The sense of isolation, of being all alone, seemed, understandably, safer to him than being with people. As we explored the feelings this image evoked in him, it became clear that Sam simply had no accurate internal template for safety and security. His biological home had been so toxic, his placements and subsequent removals so seemingly random to him, the nurturing influences in his life so sparse, that he had no plot of historical land on which to ground a safe place image.

Another instance of a child having no internal template for safety is shown in the following case vignette. Several years ago I created an intervention, the main goal of which was to add to the internal safety imagery of traumatized

Figure 3.4   Sam's Rat-Infested Hut

children by first creating a three-dimensional safety image based on a bibliotherapy prompt. The intervention began by reading the book *Where Do
Balloons Go?* (Curtis, 2000) to a group of school-aged clients. In this fanciful
story, a little boy wonders about where balloons go when they ascend out of
sight. Some balloons go to a fancy dinner party and others go to the fair. After
reading the story, I led the children in guided imagery. I asked them to picture themselves as balloons. I helped hone the imagination by asking specific
questions about what shapes and colors they chose for their balloons. Then I
guided them through a scenario in which wind lifted them higher and higher
into the sky and gently dropped them down into a safe, wonderful place. Once
they have envisioned the balloon's destination, I gave each of them a real balloon and invited them to create sand trays that depicted their landing spots.

Derrik, a 6-year-old African-American boy who was living in domestic violence at the time, chose a round orange balloon as his self-object. Figure 3.5
shows a picture of the world in which his balloon landed.

Paris: Tell me about where your balloon landed.

Derrik: Um . . . in the middle of the Civil War to save the states—to save the
United States.

Paris: And what happened to your balloon when it landed in this war?

Figure 3.5   Civil War Sand Tray

Derrik: It got blown up.

Paris: It got blown up?

Derrik: It got torn into pieces.

Paris: It got torn into pieces. How does your balloon feel about being in the middle of the war?

Derrik: Sad and mad.

The metaphor of a civil war is an apt one for this child whose home had been ground zero for person-to-person violence. Whereas most of the children who do this intervention blow up the balloon that they choose and place it in the sand tray, Derrik left his deflated, as he himself was deflated by the constant threat of harm that pervaded his home environment. Using the balloon as a self-object allowed him a level of distance and therefore more psychological room to comment on his experience. He described himself as being torn into pieces. The therapist's job is to first witness and validate the child's experiences and then work within the metaphor of the balloon caught in a war zone to create a new, safer image to come alongside the original one.

I use two therapeutic strategies to help clients make room for safer images. First I notice, and then I invite. In this case, I would say, "I notice that the balloon lands in a place where it gets hurt. I wonder if we could find a way to keep the balloon from getting hurt." This invitation may serve to give Derrik the permission that he needs to create a new solution. If Derrik remains stuck, I might then offer a couple of options. I might say, "There are several things that we could do to help this balloon stay safe. We could make a safer place in the sand tray for the balloon to land, we could take away, some of the dangerous people who are making the war or we could make a whole new tray." Usually a client latches on to one of the invitations that have been made and changes the tray in some way that makes it feel better or safer.

A 10-year-old boy named Billy had his balloon come to a similarly violent end. Billy's description of his sand tray was as follows: "My balloon landed on top of a jail and the guy inside shot it when it was coming down" (Figure 3.6).

The safety template may also be lacking for children with histories of neglect. However, their presentation tends to be a bit different. Whereas maltreated children often include hints of imminent danger or violence in their safe place productions, neglected children often present a depleted environment. For example, a child may choose a dead tree as the only ornament in a barren landscape. A 7-year-old girl named Sally taught me about this. When given the safe place

Figure 3.6   Billy's Safe Place Jail

prompt, she stated, "I'm going to make a nice home." She proceeded to put a bed in the sand and a television. She chose a figurine of a little girl and laid it down on the bed. She added nothing else to this denuded landscape. Finally, she looked at me in resignation and sighed. Then she put a fence down the middle of the tray and she demanded of me, "You've gotta make a nice home too . . . a really good one." I understood her request as a need for template, a need for external resources to be added to her experience of "a nice home." Sally had lived in such a depleted environment she wasn't sure what would be included in a good one. I began to make a home that included food and a rocking chair, a family, and fun. I invited her to make additions to this home and she declined, but she remained very interested in what I was creating. When I was finished, she looked at the tray for a long time. Then she quietly took down the fence and moved her figurine of the little girl into the home I had created.

Children who live in poverty often respond to the invitation to create a safe place in an equally unique way. These children often have trouble limiting themselves to a certain number of play materials. If a child living in poverty creates a sand tray, he often fills it up with a plethora of symbols that represent various aspects of safety to that child. Children who live in an atmosphere of lack sometimes have trouble staying within the confines of the tray and the necessary supplies spill outside the boundaries of the tray into the surrounding area. Safety symbols that are often crowded together in the trays of these disenfranchised young people are telephones, doctor's kits, bandages, piles of food and drink, fierce animals to guard their territory, transportation for quick escape, and lots and lots of money.

In the following series of pictures, a 3½-year-old boy named Johnny articulates his current internal picture of ever-present threat and is able to morph the image into a replacement image of safety. Figure 3.7 is a family play genogram (Gil, 1994, 2006) that Johnny created during an early session. Johnny chose a cup to represent mom, the cupcake holder to represent his brother, the tiny car to be himself, and the giant spider creature to be his father. The family play genogram is a helpful tool in a number of ways. It gives glimpses into the child's perceptions of the family members and the family dynamics, and it provides identified self-objects and other objects that take on significance as they are manipulated in later play scenarios.

Looking at the image, it is clear which member of the family Johnny perceives as threatening. Johnny watched dad abuse both his mother and his older brother for the first 3 years of his life. Although the father had been physically removed from the home for 1 year at the time that this sand tray was completed, the child had not yet translated this into a sense of inner safety. The child's current internal truth was that dad was still an omnipresent danger. The shifting of the actual situation has not been enough to

Figure 3.7   Johnny's *Family Play Genogram*

Figure 3.8 Johnny's Sand Tray with Dad Removed and Rescue Vehicles Added

impact the child's daily hypervigilance. These symptoms of vigilance were the impetus for the child's referral to treatment. After Johnny completed this image, I asked him if he could change it in any way that would make it safer for the little van. Johnny thought about it for a few minutes and then changed the tray in the ways reflected in this second picture (Figure 3.8).

Johnny removed the spider creature from the tray and hemmed himself in on both sides with rescue vehicles. The kinesthetic manipulation of the scene and the physical transformation of the tray from a place of danger to a place of safety gives the child a new and different concrete truth that can become an internal safety image. Once a child has transformed a tray, I often invite the child to close his eyes and picture the new tray in his mind's eye. We repeated this process several times, with Johnny opening his eyes, absorbing more details from the external image to add to his internal visual image, and then quickly accessing the new internal image with his eyes closed.

Another example of this transformation process can be seen in the sand tray pictured in Figure 3.9. The client chose a baby doll as the identified self-object. Lined up on the other side of the tray are several symbols representing various perpetrators in the child's life.

I made the invitation to change the tray in some way that made it safer for the baby doll (Figure 3.10). He chose the giant wizard puppet and inserted it in between the baby and the perpetrators, effectively providing a protector for the baby and by extension providing a sense of protection for himself.

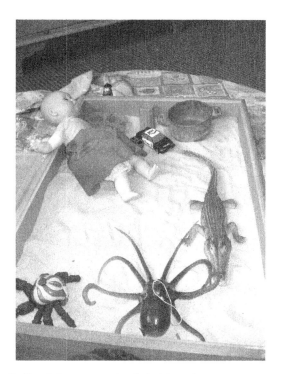

Figure 3.9 Baby Doll with Perpetrator Symbols Aligned Against Her

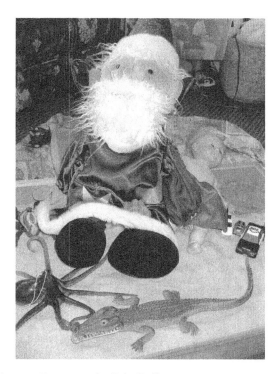

Figure 3.10 Magician Protecting the Baby Doll

75

Figure 3.11   Safe Place: Nurse's Station Filled with Trees

Figure 3.11 shows a tray created by a fifth-grade boy. His safe place sand tray is based on an actual location and is enhanced with symbols that augment his sense of security.

His safe place is the nurse's office in his inner-city school. He stressed the fact that the room is windowless. He described an ambulance parked outside the school all day every day just in case someone gets hurt and needs to be rushed to the emergency room. He added trees to the nurse's office and exchanged the chairs in the office for comfortable beds. In this way he enhanced the external soothing imagery that could then be internalized. He also mentioned police officers who walk around the school and make sure things are safe. For this young man, school is the safest place in his life.

In some cases, a child may want to feel safer but may be struggling with the feelings of guilt that surface when she rejects the perpetrator. In these cases, play therapy can offer powerful, tangible metaphors in which the rejection of the perpetrator can be worked out from a safe distance. Anna, a bright-eyed, gangly 8-year-old girl who was sexually assaulted by a 15-year-old neighbor, used the metaphor she developed through her safe place sand tray to psychologically adjust to the removal of the perpetrator from her daily experience.

Anna used to play in the backyard with her friends. One day, John, the neighbor boy, called her inside to show her something in his room. Once they were inside, he told her that he had a massage therapy exam at school and that he needed to practice. Anna, in all her innocence and inexperience, agreed to practice with him. He asked her to take her clothes off and lay on the bed and then performed sexual acts of an oral nature. She protested once or twice, but when he asked if she wanted him to fail his test, she acquiesced. This happened on four or five separate occasions. Later, John confessed his actions to a clergy person who got the authorities involved. The authorities interviewed Anna, who told them tearfully about all that had happened. John was immediately put under house arrest and was eventually transferred to a residential treatment center.

The most important part of this case, for purposes of this illustration, is that Anna was not the one to tell. John confessed on his own. Yet Anna experienced intense guilt about John's consequences. She felt responsible for what she called "the bad things that were happening to him." She became angry when her mom told her that she wouldn't have any contact with John anymore. At the same time, she became paralyzed with fear on the one occasion where she caught a glimpse of him through a car window. Anna manifested an ambivalence that many children have in relationship to their perpetrator.

Aspects of Anna's relationship with John had been fun. Memories of the few times that he had played enjoyable games of hide and seek contributed to her occasional wistfulness. She repeated over and over again that John was the one who, in her words, "told on himself." Anna viewed her mom and dad as overly harsh for not giving him a second chance. I explored this duality of emotion toward the perpetrator while providing psychoeducation about the dynamics of sexual abuse and why it was necessary for the adults to keep her safe by disallowing contact. Anna seemed to absorb the head knowledge, but she remained stuck in feelings of guilt and an insistence that he should be able to try again. It was at this impasse that I asked her to create a world in the sand tray where she could feel safe and content and happy. The world she created is pictured in Figure 3.12.

Anna described the world as "a wonderful place full of horses and special shiny rocks. I'm the horse by the golden tree. The tree gives life and food and keeps everybody warm. The tree is like God" (Figure 3.13). When I noticed out loud the black tree in the corner of the tray, she said, "That tree is always sucking the life out of everything. It's full of sadness and making everyone else mad" (Figure 3.14).

After Anna processed the tray, I asked if there was anything we could do to make the tray safer for the horse. She actively wrestled with this question. First, she moved her self-object, the horse, closer to the golden tree

Figure 3.12   Anna's Initial Safe Place Sand Tray

Figure 3.13   The *God Tree*

and said, "The horse will eat from the golden tree and get filled back up with happiness." I invited her to take the perspective of the horse (self-object) in the tray. I wondered out loud how the horse felt knowing that the black tree was still in this place. Anna looked closely at the tray for

Figure 3.14   The *Life-Sucking Tree*

Figure 3.15   The Removal of the *Life-Sucking Tree*

awhile. Then she moved a couple of animals in between her self-object and the dark tree. Finally, she looked at me and said, "He's a bad tree. He makes everyone sad. He has to go." Then she plucked the black tree out of the tray (Figure 3.15).

Anna moved the black tree all the way across the room and came back to contemplate the tray now that this constant threat had been removed. Anna smiled and said, "Now we can put more nice animals there," and she began to choose her favorite animals to fill up the empty space. After this session, Anna stopped pressing her parents to let her see John and they reported a decrease in her angry behavior toward them. Anna, through the juxtapositioning of the trees, finally gave herself permission to create a boundary between herself and John.

Conclusion

In this chapter I have described myriad ways in which the play therapist can enhance a child's sense of safety and security as a first step in trauma treatment. The thread that weaves its way through all safety enhancement work with traumatized children involves following the child's need. In the process of following the child's need, the play therapist may often follow the child's lead by reflecting, supporting, and validating the child's self-direction and choice of metaphoric content in session. It is equally likely, however, that following the child's need will require additional structure, nurture, active alignment, or role fulfillment on the part of the therapist. The therapist may be invited to serve as defender, protector, doctor, nurse, or boundary builder or to take on any one of many possible roles that facilitate the child's experiential processes. The therapist may be required to "stay close" while the child fight's his own battles or to stand in front when the child requires a hero. An accurate assessment of the child's need guides the therapist's intervention at every turn. The manipulation and containment of perpetrator symbols is also addressed as a safety-building device. Many more examples of this kind of play are given in Chapter 8, *The Continuum of Disclosure*, and Chapter 9, *Experiential Mastery Play*. Although this type of play pattern can and often will occur throughout treatment, initial containment can solidify the child's perception of the playroom as a safe place.

This chapter also sets forth examples of directive interventions that can be used in the service of enhancing a child's sense of safety. The creation of three-dimensional safe places allows the child external, kinesthetically based safety metaphors that can be transformed into internal images. The autographable bear and other transitional objects can be conceptualized as generalizing the sense of safety augmented in the playroom to other environments in the child's milieu.

4

Assessing and Augmenting Positive Coping Strategies

Assessment of Current Coping Strategies

It is important to assess a child's coping responses before any intentional processing of trauma-related content (Felix, Bond, & Shelby, 2006; Kimball, Nelson, & Politano, 1993; Shelby & Berk, 2009).

Children lack sophistication in their coping strategies because of their continually developing neurological, physiological, and relational systems and can be easily overwhelmed by traumatic events (Perry, Pollard, Blakely, Baker, & Vigilante, 1995). Young children are vulnerable to developing maladaptive coping strategies. They lack both life experience and the cognitive capacity to evaluate their own coping responses with a view toward whether or not these responses are adaptive (Baggerly, 2006). The child's eventual approach to the trauma content can be positively mitigated by helping a child augment her current positive coping skills, extinguish maladaptive coping responses, and develop new, healthy coping strategies.

Attempting to approach a client's substantive trauma history before assessing and augmenting his coping repertoire can result in iatrogenic effects. Children who overdisclose at the beginning of treatment are likely to be unprepared for the emotional reactions that follow. This early vulnerability may translate to a perception of therapy as unsafe, and the child may cope with early overdisclosure by engaging in subsequent withdrawal. A play therapist may lose important ground in the areas of trust and rapport. Occasionally, despite a therapist's best efforts to use initial sessions to build rapport, assess for coping, and build a nurturing, safe foundation for later processing, a child will come into the playroom and immediately begin revealing the details of his traumatic events. In these cases, the therapist should validate the child's experiences while gently steering the child back toward stable ground. Once a child's positive coping repertoire has been reinforced and he has acquired new skills in emotional and physiological regulation (Paule, 2009), the trauma content can be more safely addressed.

When children, for whatever reason, already have an adaptive set of coping strategies upon entering care, the treating clinician may design the treatment plan with more emphasis placed on reinforcing a child's mastery of these skills, increasing self-efficacy, and rehearsing preexisting coping. If, however, a child has a series of maladaptive coping strategies or has very little capacity to cope with stress without decompensating, the treating clinician will place much more emphasis on helping the child develop adaptive coping mechanisms before delving into any trauma-specific material.

Over the last 30 years, researchers have attempted to delineate dimensions of coping. One of the first measures was the Ways of Coping Checklist (WCC) (Folkman & Lazarus, 1980), a 68-item coping checklist that yielded a set of problem-focused and emotion-focused scales. The Ways of Coping Questionnaire (Folkman & Lazarus, 1985; Vitaliano, Russo, Carr, Maiuro, & Becker, 1985), a subsequent revision and alteration of the WCC, followed. Questions regarding psychometric shortcomings in these two measures spurred the development of a third tool, the Multi-Dimensional Coping Inventory (MCI) (Endler & Parker, 1990).

The factor analysis of this scale yielded three primary approaches to coping: task, emotion, and avoidance. The Coping Styles Questionnaire (CSQ) delineated the same three dimensions as the MCI but added an additional dimension that centered around detachment (Roger, Jarvis, & Najarian, 1993). In terms of the coping styles themselves, rational and detached coping responses clustered together, as did emotional and avoidance responses. The authors went further to suggest that the rational and detached coping styles represented adaptive coping strategies and the emotional/avoidance coping styles represented maladaptive coping strategies. Although these scales were developed for adults, we can see the parallels between these coping styles and the ways in which children cope.

Boxer et al. (2008) recently looked at how children cope with exposure to violence. Two separate studies support the hypothesis that children cope with violence in one of two broadly defined ways. In the first coping response, what they term the normalization pathway, children develop beliefs that support aggression and themselves become more aggressive. This troublesome coping response was supported by Ng-Mak (2004), who found a pattern of low emotional distress and high aggression among a subset of adolescents in the inner city. The second response pattern, what the authors term the distress pathway, is an engagement in avoidant coping. These children tend to have more emotional symptoms and maladjustment. Both pathways represent problematic coping responses. The Self-Report Coping Scale (Causey & Dubow, 1992) discriminates between approach strategies, which include seeking social support and problem solving, and avoidance strategies, which include distancing, internalizing, and externalizing. Another coping measure for children, KidCope (Spirito, Stark, & Williams, 1988; Knapp, Stark, Kurkijan, and Spirito, 1991), also breaks down coping into avoidant and approach strategies. Dempsey, Overstreet, and Moely (2000) found that cognitive distraction strategies tended to increase cognitive arousal symptoms in children exposed to violence, as did a decreased use of behavioral avoidance strategies. These findings are in line with other literature that suggests that behavioral avoidance serves a protective function with children exposed to violence (Duncan, 1996; Gonzales & Kim, 1997).

Play-based interventions provide a developmentally sensitive pathway for assessing a child's coping repertoire. Shelby (2004) has created one such intervention that anchors the assessment in the metaphor of a fruit-bearing tree. The clinician begins by drawing a tree in the center of a piece of paper. The clinician then introduces stickers of a fruit that is indigenous for the population being served. In my community, apple trees are the most common fruit-bearing tree, so I might use apple stickers in my assessments. The clinician places some apples on the tree and others on the ground. Then the clinician asks the child a question like, "What do you do when you start thinking about the bad thing that happened?" If the child gives an answer such as, "I go and hide in the woods," the clinician writes this answer next to one of the apples lying on the ground. If the child's answer is, "I go and ask my mom for a hug," the clinician writes the answer next to an apple that is still on the tree. The clinician continues to ask this question in various ways until she seems to have exhausted the coping strategies of which the child is cognizant. Each answer is accepted without judgment, so as not to stifle the child's flow of information, and recorded on the ground below the tree or on the tree itself.

Once all the coping strategies have been named, the clinician can go back and ask some questions about the tree. For example, "What will happen to the apples that stay on the tree?" The child is likely to understand that they will continue to grow and ripen. The clinician can then say, "Some of the apples that are on the ground may be picked up and taken home to eat or make into pies. What will happen to the apples that are just left on the ground for a long time?" The child is usually able to recognize that the apples that are left on the ground will rot. The clinician can then use this metaphoric distinction to parallel the outcomes of healthy coping strategies and maladaptive ones. The tree, while serving as a quick and simple information gathering tool, can also serve as a bridge to help children begin to characterize their own coping as healthy or unhealthy.

The National Child Traumatic Stress Network and the National Center for PTSD coordinated an effort to design a protocol for helping to alleviate initial post-trauma stress in disaster response situations. This protocol, labeled the *Psychological First Aid: Field Operations Guide* (National Child Traumatic Stress Network and National Center for PTSD, 2006), translated current research and best practice standards for crisis intervention into a set of eight core actions, including information on coping support and strengthening support networks. A group of play therapists from the Association for Play Therapy were involved in designing specific child-friendly, developmentally appropriate play activities to help accomplish the treatment goals delineated in the protocol. One of the main areas of our work was in designing and augmenting strategies for assessing coping and augmenting existing coping mechanisms. These activities were put together in a manual for use by teams of play therapists who provided disaster response following the tsunami in Sri Lanka (Shelby, Bond, Hall, & Tsu, 2004).

Assessing Children's Social Supports

Family Play Genograms

Traumatized children who have good social support, typically from more than one source, tend to have fewer posttraumatic symptoms and seem to recover more quickly (Bleich, Gelkopf, & Solomon, 2003; Dubow, Tisak, Causey, Hryshko, & Reid, 1991; Litz, Gray, Bryant, & Adler, 2002; Ruzek et al., 2007; Stein et al., 2003).

Therefore it is important to assess the state of a child's support systems. I begin this assessment process with the family system. A very useful intervention for assessing the child's perceived family dynamics is the Family Play Genogram (Gil, 1994, 2006). I include a family play genogram in the assessment phase of every child that I see. The child is invited to choose miniatures to represent each member of the family.

In my initial implementation of the procedure, I helped the child create a pen-and-paper version of the genogram first (McGoldrick, Gerson, & Shellenberger, 1999), and the child would place his miniatures on the paper. I have since moved to having children create their genograms in the sand tray. I find that this puts clients at ease, as children are naturally drawn to the sand. Moreover, the sand tray provides a soothing yet boundaried space in which they can arrange the miniatures. I have found that the less defined boundaries for individual figurines allow the child to add a dimension of family sculpting to the arrangement of his chosen miniatures. The distance between family members and the posturing of characters in the tray can yield rich information about how a child perceives various family members and the relationships between them. For example, a child who has positioned his miniature far away from the family is communicating something very different than the child who has positioned himself comfortably next to mom and dad. The physical distance between objects in the tray may reflect the psychological distance between various members of the family.

When the child has completed the genogram, I always invite him to create a story related to the characters that have been chosen. I encourage the child to use character names for the figures. If a child has chosen Ursula (the octopus witch from the Little Mermaid) to be his mom and a horse to be his dad, I will encourage the child to use the names "Ursula" and "horse" for the names of the characters in the story as opposed to using "mom" and "dad." The intention behind this distinction is to allow the child to continue to use the symbols and metaphors as a way of projecting psychological content. The character names allow an added dimension of removal from the self, which in turn decreases a child's defensiveness and increases the likelihood of exploring the psychological themes underlying the character choices.

The combination of a child's miniature choices and his story content can yield valuable information about which family members already provide healthy social support for the child and which do not. A case example will help illustrate. While working in an inner city school in East Nashville,

Figure 4.1   Keyon's *Family Play Genogram*

I met Keyon, a fifth-grade boy who created so much disruption in his class-room that he spent more time in the principal's office than he did engaged in academic pursuits. During an early session, I invited Keyon to create a Family Play Genogram. His Family Play Genogram appears in Figure 4.1.

After he had chosen his figures, he began to explain, without any prompt-ing on my part, why he had chosen each figure. Following is the transcript of his explanation:

Keyon holds up the joker figurine.

Keyon: Cuz he's in jail now because he beat up my mom. He's mean so I picked Joker.

Keyon holds up a Prince Charming figurine.

Keyon: This is my stepdad. Well, my real dad now. He's real nice and we play together.

Keyon holds up the figure of Eeyore.

Keyon: This is my mom because she be depressed sometimes. But we still have fun.

Keyon holds up a wrestling figure.

Keyon: This is my older brother Jared. I picked the Undertaker because he is big and strong and we wrestle.

Keyon holds up the miniature of Belle from *Beauty and the Beast*.

Keyon: This is my older sister. I picked her because she likes to dress up in dresses and she's pretty.

Keyon holds up a tiger cub.

Keyon: This is me because he's sneaky and playful.

Keyon has given me much valuable information about how he perceives various family members. He chose the Joker, a dangerous criminal from the Batman series, to represent his biological father and disclosed this man's physical violence toward Keyon's mother. He chose a heroic character, Prince Charming, for his stepdad and stated that he is "real nice" and that his stepdad plays with him. It seems that he is a social support for Keyon. Keyon chose Eeyore, the sad donkey from the Pooh series, to represent his mother and talked about her depression. These are valuable insights and begin to form a picture of his perceptions of his family members' availability and utility as support people. Once Keyon had finished explaining his choice of each character, I asked if he could make up a story about the characters:

Keyon: There was this tiger [self] that was walking through the forest and along came a man [Joker]. He had a mean grin on his face and a tricky face and he said, "I will give you food." Then he left and then he gave him some food and then he left. (*While Keyon is describing the Joker's comings and goings, he picks the figure up off the paper and moves it tentatively back and forth in the air.*) And then along came another man [Prince Charming] saying, "Are you hungry Mister or did you need something?" And the tiger said, "I wish to live with you." And he [Prince Charming] took him home. And then came the donkey. She was depressed and she needed a friend. So the tiger said, "I'll be your friend."

Again, we see the power of the play materials (Webb, 2004) and the meta-phors (Mills & Crowley, 2001) to help children articulate things for which they do not yet have adequate words. This fifth-grade boy, whose expressive language skills were on a third-grade level, could not have fully expressed in words his feelings of abandonment related to his biological father nor his idealization of his stepfather as the hero who stepped in to rescue him. He certainly could not have described the nuances of his mother's depression, the role he was currently playing as her emotional caretaker, or the respon-sibility he felt to try to make her happy. Keyon did not yet have the words to convey all these nuances of his experience, but he articulated them elo-quently through the help of the play materials.

Moreover, I was able to hone my treatment plan to include more effective utilization of Keyon's stepfather with the information gleaned from his play. The demographics of the inner city school in which I met Keyon were such that 85% of the children in that school had no consistent, reliable father figure in the home. The paucity of father figures resulted in most treatment being conducted with female caregivers. However, this client's strong posi-tive relationship with his stepfather made him a natural choice to pull into the treatment process. Additionally, I began to encourage Keyon's mom to get help for her own depression while I worked on strengthening her role as caretaker. Eventually, mom entered treatment for her own clinical issues and made significant gains.

Another example of the revealing nature of the family play genogram occurred when I worked with a 4-year-old boy named Shawn, who had been a direct witness to domestic violence for the whole of his young life. He had seen dad hurt mom over and over again. When I invited him to choose a toy to be his mother, he went to the shelves and quickly chose a woman with a cake. This relatively nurturing symbol was placed in the sand to represent his mother. When I invited him to choose a toy for himself, he went to the shelves, took a little longer selecting a figure, and finally chose a naked male baby who was disproportionately small in relation to the mother symbol. Lastly, I invited him to choose a toy to be dad. He turned toward the shelves and then turned back to me. He asked, "Can I choose more than one?" I responded that he could do whatever he needed to do, which is my standard response. He chose three separate figures. The first was a very large, aggres-sive wrestling figure. The second was a small, nonthreatening male figure. The third figure was Prince Charming. What was Shawn depicting? Shawn

Figure 4.2 Shawn's Genogram: *My Three Dads*

was showing us a rudimentary version of the domestic violence cycle. He was showing us the cycle that graduate students read about in textbooks, the cycle that is described in public service announcements (Figure 4.2).

I showed the three-dimensional genogram to Shawn's mother. She was astonished at how accurately Shawn had captured the three sides of her ex-husband. She put into words what his icons had captured, explaining that periodically her ex-husband would come home from work, usually after drinking, and beat her. After the crisis had past, dad would become remorseful and conciliatory. After the apology and the solemn pledge never to hurt mom again, he would bring her flowers, do the dishes, and generally be the embodiment of Prince Charming until the tension began to build again. At the tragically young age of 4, Shawn was an expert in the cycle of domestic violence. He just didn't have the words to adequately convey this expertise. He was, however, able to eloquently articulate the cycle in his own language, the language of play (Landreth, 1991).

In another genogram, a 9-year-old boy, after some hesitation, chose a witch as the symbol for his mother. The boy looked cautiously at me when he made this choice. When he was greeted with my acceptance of his choice, the floodgates opened and he began to talk about many of their recent interactions that had led to this perception of mom as a witch. I did some dyadic assessment following his production of the genogram and it became clear that, although she loved her son very much, there was a mismatch between this mother's natural parenting style and the child's temperament. In developing a treatment plan, I combined parent training pieces with nurturing dyadic interventions. In addition, I helped the boy to find and use appropriate words to ask for what he needed from his mother. As the family progressed in treatment, mom moved from being a life stressor for the child to being a positive social support who could help mitigate the other stressors in the child's life.

In addition to family members, a child's overall support network encompasses many other people. A child's attachment to three major socializing influences, family, school, and peer group, correlate with a child's adaptive functioning. In fact, attachment to the wrong people in each of these categories is directly related to delinquent behavior (Famiglietti, 1984). Therefore, it is important for clinicians to assess the quality of these systems in the child's environment during the initial phase of treatment.

Bronfenbrenner (1979) encouraged clinicians to employ an ecological perspective in conceptualizing the systemic influences in the lives of children. He posited four levels of systemic influence that radiate outward from the individual child in concentric circles. He labeled the circle closest to the child the microsystem. A child's microsystem includes everyone with whom the child has direct daily interaction. Parents and teachers are certainly included in this category, as are any other caregivers, neighbors, and so on. School, aftercare environments, and ongoing organized sports or extracurricular activities would also be seen as microsystemic influences.

The second level is called the mesosystem and can be understood as the interface between any two microsystems. A child's mesosystemic influences are seen as providing resiliency when individual microsystems support the values of the others. For example, if the teacher places a high value on homework and so does the parent, the child is better supported. The second characteristic of the mesosystem is how strong an interaction exists between any two microsystems. For example, if the child's primary caregiver is a room parent who frequently spends time in the school and knows her child's teachers, the child is better supported than if a parent and teacher have no direct contact with each other. The collaboration between parents and teachers is a particular dynamic that can signal success or difficulties for a child (Famiglietti, 1984).

Some traumatized children have a need for high levels of accountability between home and school. These children may lie to parents about homework or minimize the work that needs to be done. The parent is able to take charge and adequately structure the after-school environment if she is armed with accurate information from the teacher. Another mesosystemic influence that is often relevant to a traumatized child involves the quality of interaction between two households when parents live apart. Divorced coparents who communicate effectively with each other and coordinate child care, pickup, drop-off, and other logistics of the child's life in a civil and organized manner provide a healthier environment for children than do caregivers who manifest chaos or volatility in their coparenting relationship.

The third systemic level in the ecology of a child's life is the exosystem. The exosystem is composed of all the organizations, policies, and so on that have a daily influence on the child but with whom the child does not interact directly. For example, a child may never meet the governance board of his local school system but may have to wear a uniform based on the school policy set by the board. The drop-off and pickup times for the school day and the decision to offer before and after care programs can have a profound effect on a child's daily schedule and the associated stress on a child's parents. However, the child has no direct involvement in setting these policies. For children living in war-torn areas or in areas in which a natural disaster has recently occurred, breakdowns in transportation services, loss of jobs, poverty, and additional stressors can exacerbate a child's posttraumatic stress reaction, moving it from the typical range into the clinical range (Evans and Oehler-Stinnett, 2006; Layne et al., 2008; Vernberg, LaGreca, Silverman, & Prinstein, 1996).

Lastly, Bronfenbrenner talks about the effects of the macrosystem on a child. Macrosystemic issues are related to values and beliefs held by society at large. Various forms of oppression, such as institutionalized racism and sexism, have trickle-down effects in the other systems of a child's ecology. A careful assessment of a child's support systems or lack thereof includes some thoughtful analysis of how these systems contribute to risk or resiliency for a particular child.

Peers also play a critical role in a child's support network. In fact, some authors argue that peer relationships are more influential in the lives of developing children than the family system (Harris, 1998). Whereas positive peer relationships serve a protective function with traumatized children, negative peer interactions, such as bullying, can reinforce maladaptive coping, such as social withdrawal (Erath, 2007).

A child's coping responses impact the peer victimization they receive (Kochenderfer-Ladd, 2004). Children need to be equipped with specific, positive strategies for dealing with bullies (Frey, 2002; Robinson & Maines, 2008). A child who feels threatened by peers may decide that withdrawal from all relationships is the best way to protect herself, thereby cutting herself off from potential sources of encouragement and friendship.

Conversely, a child who has a strong friendship circle can use this positive peer group to mitigate other stress in his life. Craig, Pepler, and Blais (2007) administered a questionnaire to 1,852 Canadian children who ranged in age from 4 to 19 years old. One interesting finding was that no matter what strategy the child was employing, the longer the bullying persisted the less effective the students perceived their own strategies. This finding highlights the need for supportive adults to keep their finger on the social pulse of the children whom they are trying to help. An even more beneficial outcome for the child is to help him engage in his own evaluation of his peer supports. To this end, I use an instrument I call the social solar system.

The Social Solar System

First I present the client with a large black sheet of construction paper, foil star stickers, and different-colored circle stickers. The circles represent planets. I have the child choose one planet to represent herself, and this circle is placed at the center of the piece of paper. I explain that she is going to make a solar system of her social relationships. She may use stars or planets to represent different people. The peers who offer her the most support, her closest friends, will probably be placed in close proximity to her own planet. Peers with whom she experiences conflict or distance might be placed farther away. She gets to decide where everyone goes. Some children, particularly extroverted children, may put 20 stars around their planet, each representing a classmate or a member of the soccer team. Other children have a noticeable lack of stars and planets. These children tend to be socially isolated and will need help with social skills as well as other areas of difficulty. Still others can list a variety of peers, but almost all the relationships are conflictual. It is not unusual for a traumatized child to perceive that no one likes her or that everyone picks on her. Teisl and Cicchetti (2008) found that maltreated children, specifically those with a history of physical abuse, had errors in cue interpretation. Children with severe trauma histories tend to misperceive social cues and may also miscue others about what they are really wanting or needing. After the initial social solar system is complete and has been processed, the child can be invited to create a second picture of how she would like her social solar system to look. This can be used to set subgoals as the clinician and the family begin to strengthen a child's support network.

In some cases the social solar system helps parents become more intentional in targeting positive peer influences for play dates. Depending on the trauma history, parents may be hesitant to pursue social relationships. They may be afraid that their private life will be uncovered. The child may have a sexual behavior problem that understandably causes parents to be vigilant about peer interactions. However, children who have social deficits benefit tremendously by repetitions of supervised one-on-one peer interactions. Occasionally the solar system activity will uncover a bullying problem that may be exacerbating some preexisting trauma symptomatology. Sometimes the most effective intervention for a bullying situation is to remove this chronic stressor from the client's life, by helping the child to switch classrooms or, while it may sound extreme, school or aftercare environments. In these cases the parents can intervene, allowing the child to see them in a protective role.

The Community Crown

The anxiety symptoms that define many clients' trauma reactions can inhibit healthy problem-solving impulses, including those impulses that would drive children to seek out appropriate social supports. It is often helpful to assist children in designing a tangible template of the support people who are available to them in various capacities. I help children explore these dimensions of social support through an intervention called *community crown* (Goodyear-Brown, 2002). I begin with a simple paper doll chain. I invite the client to name one person who gives him hugs and kisses when he needs them. When the child supplies a name, we color in the first paper doll to look like that person and I write that person's name across the middle of the doll. I then ask the child to name someone who teaches him something. If he talks about his soccer coach, we color in the second paper doll in the chain to look like his soccer coach. I ask for the name of someone who says affirming words to him, someone who helps him with things that are hard, someone who plays with him, someone who listens to him, and someone with whom he can relax. As each of these people is identified, a cutout on the paper doll chain is colored in to represent each person. When the activity is complete, I take the two ends of the paper doll chain and staple them together. The result is a circle of support people that can be worn as a crown. The finished product is a tangible template that helps a child remember the people he can go to for help when he is in need.

Children living in postdisaster environments face the disturbing reality that many of their previous support people have vanished. When the Association for Play Therapy sent two teams of clinicians into Sri Lanka following the tsunami, one of the most profound shocks to our clinicians was the sheer number of people who had been lost to the "big water." Children who live in the inner cities of America experience the ongoing loss of support people through gang violence as a slow bleed. Children who have been physically or sexually abused have found that the people who were supposed to represent their greatest safety became their greatest danger. In all these cases, the nature of the support network may need to be revisited.

In disaster relief areas, the remaining adults can take on new supportive roles for the child. For example, a child who had historically been comforted by sitting with his grandmother and listening to her tell the stories of their ancestors lost his grandmother in the tsunami. Another elder in the village might be encouraged to take on the function of the storyteller. This sort of intentional networking can help a neighborhood begin to function as a community again after a disaster. Certainly, the child is comforted by hearing the familiar tales. However, the elder is also comforted as she recognizes her wisdom and knowledge are needed for the next generation.

The identification of supportive adult relationships can be exceptionally difficult when a child has experienced multiple caregiver disruptions. The foster care child who has bounced around from placement to placement has experienced inconsistency in her primary caregiving. Each move has been accompanied by disruptions in teachers, coaches, pastoral care providers, and daycare workers. In these cases the therapist may be one of the most stable care providers in the child's life. If a child has a denuded or often changing support network, an adaptation to the crowning community activity may be required. One modification would be to fill each of the paper dolls with a ritual that the therapist and the child share, words of affirmation the therapist speaks to the child or helpful teaching that has occurred in session. The child might write the words "You are special" in one of the paper dolls, representing the message that she consistently receives from the therapist. The phrase "Our special handshake" might be written within another paper doll to remind the child of a fun, healthy touch that she shares with the therapist.

The paper doll activity is not developmentally appropriate for adolescents. I provide a modification of this activity for older youth. The child is asked to bring in a piece of clothing. It might be a t-shirt, a hat, a scarf, a vest, or a tie.

I then provide the youth with a series of blank make-your-own-person pins. Each pin consists of a see-through plastic gingerbread cutout shape with a blank piece of paper inside that can be colored. The client creates a button to represent each of his support people and attaches these to his hat, tie, or t-shirt. Some young people like to wear them to school as a novelty. Others hang the tie on the wall like a banner and have the visual reminder of all the people they can call on for support.

Assessing School Supports

Once all the various arenas of social support have been explored, a plan can be made for augmenting the positive social supports and mitigating the influences that may put the child at risk. Sometimes an effective plan involves a fairly extreme change of environment for a child. One little boy whom I saw recently, Chad, was being bullied by children in his classroom. He went to a Catholic school and repeatedly talked about the Sister who was his teacher in negative terms. One day I invited him to choose a miniature to represent this Sister and he chose my two-headed fire-breathing dragon. The child's mother had brought him to see me because she recognized that the school environment was causing some distress. He was having what mom characterized as "hysterical, raging outbursts at home over little things." It became clear in his initial sessions that he was also experiencing panic attacks while at school. When she saw the symbol that was chosen to be the teacher, it reinforced her decision to transfer him to another school.

The family moved him to a different private school where he is now flourishing. A child spends a large part of his life in his school environment and the "goodness-of-fit" between a particular teacher and child can dramatically impact the child's sense of his own success in a given school year. A teacher who provides equal measures of structure and nurture will mitigate the manifestation of a traumatized child's symptoms in the classroom. A teacher who is low on nurture and overly strict is likely to trigger certain traumatized children. Conversely, a teacher who is highly nurturing but provides no structure in her classroom will trigger a different subset of traumatized children.

I am currently working with a 9-year-old girl named Sally who struggles with separation anxiety as an outgrowth of previous trauma. We are actively working on augmenting Sally's coping strategies and she is able to self-soothe more frequently at school. The teacher is relieved to see this change at school. However, the mother was wary of the way in which the teacher expressed her delight. According to Sally's mother, the teacher said, "She did so much better this week. She didn't need a single hug from me all week!" Although the goal of treatment is to help Sally be able to successfully leave her mother and integrate into age-appropriate environments, it is troublesome that the teacher's standard of age appropriateness for a 9 year old is that she never asks for a hug. Adults in a child's life may need training in what represents developmentally appropriate coping for children at various stages of development. Although mom and I both see Sally's occasional request for nurture as a valuable coping tool, her teacher may have a perception that any overtures of this nature are inappropriate.

Prop-Based Play Interventions that Enhance Coping

The Coping Umbrella

As we work on augmenting coping strategies, I find it helpful to use props as a way of concretizing the growth the child is experiencing. When trauma symptoms are activated, a child has less immediate access to her adaptive coping repertoire. Therefore it is beneficial to have visual and kinesthetic reminders of the coping options. One such prop that I use in relation to coping is an umbrella. The seed of this intervention germinated in a workshop I attended at which Beverly James (1989) was discussing her approach to trauma treatment. One of her handouts depicted a child holding up an umbrella. The words above the umbrella, meant to represent the rain, listed several symptoms of trauma. This metaphor of the umbrella as a protective shield against the trauma symptoms that may flood a triggered child stuck with me. I began using small multicolored umbrellas to serve as a kinesthetic touchstone to ground the therapeutic learning involved with adding coping strategies to a child's available repertoire (Goodyear-Brown 2002). When I begin to target the expansion of a client's coping repertoire, I give the child an umbrella and explain that we are going to write new skills in each panel of the umbrella as we learn and practice them. The skills help protect the child against the torrent of feelings, thoughts, or body responses that may come when he is reminded of the bad things that happened to him (Figure 4.3).

Although the child is working on learning deep breathing as a coping strategy, we use myriad play interventions to practice this skill and then write the acquired skill on one of the panels of the umbrella. Then I invite the child to role play a situation in which his trauma-related shortness of breath might be triggered. As we role play, the child holds the umbrella above his head and

Figure 4.3   The Coping Umbrella

practices his deep breathing. A fun variation of this activity is to use feathers to symbolize the trauma symptoms. The child can hold up the umbrella while the therapist has the feathers fall on top of the umbrella. In this way, the child gets the full body experience of being protected from the symptoms through his coping skills. When the umbrella panels are all filled with positive coping strategies, the client takes the umbrella home. It serves as both a transitional object representing the safety of the playroom and the person of the therapist while serving as a visual reminder of the coping options available to him. Another fun option for children is the umbrella hat (Figure 4.4).

The Coping Cake

Another intervention, the coping cake, serves as both a growing catalogue of coping strategies and a visual reminder of these techniques. I begin by giving the child a variety of thick papers in various patterns and sizes. I cut out a flat circle to serves as the bottom layer of the cake. The client then gets to layer other papers in smaller circles one on top of the bottom to represent the layers of a cake. I also cut long thin strips of paper that can serve as candles for the top of the cake. Alternatively, the cake can be made out of clay and real candles can be embedded in the top of the cake. I usually begin

Figure 4.4   The Coping Umbrella Hat

making the cake with the child when we begin to learn and practice various coping skills. After a session in which the child learns how to engage in thought-stopping behavior, we write this skill on a candle and add it to the top of the cake. Additional candles are kept and are added over the course of subsequent sessions as additional coping skills are honed (Figure 4.5).

Children's Coping Creations

Any number of metaphors can be used to help children understand the usefulness of positive coping strategies. It is not unusual for a child to offer the metaphor herself. This was the case with Missy, a 9-year-old girl who had experienced a traumatic event early in life. Some of her trauma residue was an oversensitivity to the expressions on people's faces. Her hypervigilant brain was always scanning the environment for danger. Whenever her teacher would frown or raise her voice to be heard above the noise in the classroom, Missy would feel panic rising inside her. As we began to explore these perceptions together, Missy was able to recognize that her reactions were out of proportion to the events themselves. She described her teacher's raised voice and frowning face as a flood of rain that made her feel like she might drown. I reflected her language back to her and asked if we could find anything to make her feel better when the rain fell. Missy said, "I know. A rainbow!" She eagerly began to paint a rainbow (Figure 4.6).

Figure 4.5   The Coping Cake

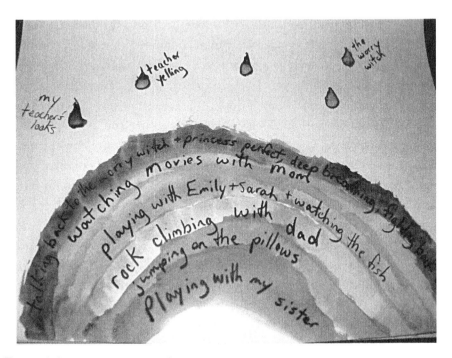

Figure 4.6   Missy's Coping Rainbow

Interestingly, all the activities that Missy listed inside the layers of her rainbow involved fun activities that she does with her mom, dad, and sister when they are together. Part of what Missy does during tense moments at school is to picture being back home in the safe haven of her family. She now compartmentalizes her anxious moments at school, puts them away, and takes them out to process with mom when she gets home from school. At the beginning of treatment, her teacher reported that Missy had daily crying spells. The teacher was also concerned because Missy would not raise her hand in class, even if she knew the answer to a question. As Missy became better able to tap the internal resiliencies that she absorbed through her family system, she became better able to put her teacher's behavior in perspective. Missy never came to embrace her teacher's communication style, but by the end of treatment she was able to tolerate the teacher without feeling the sense of panic that she had experienced earlier in the year.

The Coping Collage

As in the example of Missy and her teacher, it is not always possible to avoid unpleasant situations or stimuli. Some of the traumatized children I see have great difficulty completing tasks that are hard for them. Others become escalated as they anticipate an unpleasant event such as a flu shot or a trip to the dentist. Helping clients identify various reminders of comfort can help. What comfort object, such as a favorite toy or blanket, can the child bring with him to the stressful event? What comfort words can the child repeat that will help him soothe himself during the stressful event? Each of these questions represents various coping mechanisms that can be employed to help a child navigate a potential crisis. What enjoyable activity will happen after the stressful event? This question is aimed at helping children create a sense of a positive future. Children often benefit from focusing on future pleasurable events. Indeed, the pleasurable experiences in a child's life can often mitigate trauma responses.

One simple tool that can help children maintain a sense of positive anticipation during stressful times is the coping collage. The child is given a stack of magazines and is invited to browse through them, cutting out any pictures that remind her of her favorite things. The child is also encouraged to cut out pictures or words that anticipate future fun events. For example, if the child's birthday is coming up soon, she might cut out a picture of a birthday cake and add it to her collage. The collage is taken home and posted near

Figure 4.7 A Coping Collage

the child's bed, so that she has visual reminders of the upcoming pleasurable events as she prepares to face the impending stressful episode. Figure 4.7
shows an example of one child's coping collage. It includes pictures of tastes,
smells, activities, and places that are soothing for the child.

Coping Skill Practice Through Puppetry and Chant

The acquisition and practice of new coping skills can be augmented through
chants, puppet plays, and movement sequences. Several years ago I was
working with a group of latency-age boys, all of whom had trauma histories
and many of whom had problems of dysregulation that most often manifested
as aggressive outbursts. We first worked on helping these boys to identify the
physiological signals that their bodies gave them as clues to their own escalation. Then we developed a short list of coping strategies they could use.
We went over the list a couple of times, but the boys were thoroughly disin-
terested in the pen-and-paper exercise. They began beating their pencils on
the table in various rhythms. At first, I dismissed the behavior as disruptive.
However, as the beating continued, I decided to take advantage of the natural rhythmic flow the boys were providing. I encouraged them to create a rap
that relayed the coping skills being learned. The rap was a repetition of the

following phrase: "Stop. Calm down, take a deep breath, count to ten." The boys had so much fun creating it, they wanted to perform it for younger children in the school. The rhythm and chant helped the therapeutic content come alive in a way that was relevant to the boys.

A similar solution worked with a group of elementary-age girls who were trying to learn a positive problem-solving model. The list of problem-solving steps was turned into a song:

> Stop and think. Stop and think.
> Freeze.
> What do I want?
> Ideas, ideas, ideas.
> Is it good or bad? Is it good or bad? Is it good or bad?
> Make a choice.

The girls created a dance move to go with each line of the song. They rehearsed the song over and over. In fact, I would see them practicing the song on the playground during recess. In this way, what had been a dry, lifeless set of steps morphed into something that the girls could take on as their own. When these girls needed to apply the problem-solving steps in their daily lives, they had a higher chance of accessing the information because it had been stored in multiple forms that were meaningful to them as well as inherently fun. Any number of coping strategies can be explicated and combined with chant, song, dance, or movement as a more digestible form of skill rehearsal.

Now and Later

Children who have experienced trauma often have deficits in their problem-solving abilities. One intervention that can help traumatized children begin to come up with solutions is called "now and later." I take a standard-sized piece of paper and fold it into thirds. At the bottom of the first third, I write "Now." At the bottom of the third portion of paper, I write "Later." We choose one problem that is causing the child some current discomfort and I invite the child to draw a picture of the problem as it is right now in the first third of the paper. Then I ask the child to draw a picture of the problem "all better" in the third portion of the paper. After these two steps are completed, there is only one empty space between the other two pictures. I invite the child to think of just one step he can take toward making the problem all

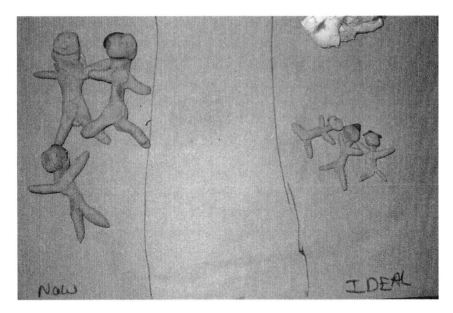

Figure 4.8   Now and Later Intervention

better and draw it in the middle panel. When a child is facing a problem, it can feel overwhelming. Approaching it in this manner breaks down the problem into manageable steps and encourages the child to take one step toward the solution. The picture in Figure 4.8 was done by a child who chose to make his pictures out of clay. In the first panel he placed himself with his peers picking on him. In the third panel he placed a sun at the top of the page and put himself between two peers at school. As we discussed the images, he explained that the solution would be to feel like an equal with his classmates. In the middle panel he will create an image to depict one step he can take toward feeling more equal with his peers.

Pretend Play as a Coping Stimulus

Sometimes the fallout of trauma includes a stunted ability to find creative solutions to the problems of daily life. There are many play materials that can stimulate a child's problem-solving abilities. Dress-up clothes, particularly those that symbolize power, such as a king's cloak and crown or a sorcerer's hat and wand, can imbue a child with a sense of power to create solutions that they don't feel in their own person. Stepping into a more powerful role can help open up possibilities for solutions for a traumatized child.

Russ (2007) posits a correlation between pretend play and advanced coping strategies. Children who are good at pretend play are also good at shifting from one coping strategy to another (Christiano & Russ, 1996). Perhaps the same mechanism that allows children to switch quickly between roles in pretend play informs their flexible use of coping options.

Subsets of Coping Addressed in Subsequent Chapters

It is the nature of humanity that we experience stress. How we cope with the stress that we experience in large part determines our daily quality of life. There are several areas in which coping can be augmented. One class of coping strategies includes soothing the physiological responses engendered by stress. Techniques such as deep breathing, biofeedback, guided imagery, and visualization can be useful additions to a child's tool box. However, both the concepts related to stress management and the acquisition of associated skills are delivered in the most developmentally appropriate way when accompanied by play. A set of play-based interventions that help children practice stress management skills is detailed in Chapter 5, *Soothing the Physiology*.

Another important form of coping for children has to do with how successful they are in accessing parental support when they need it. Information related to this form of coping will be explored in detail in Chapter 6, *Parents as Partners*. Another form of coping revolves around the manipulation of one's thought life. The skills related to identifying negative thoughts, learning to tolerate those thoughts, challenging them, and ultimately replacing them with coping thoughts make a significant difference in an older child's ability to cope with the stress of his environment. Theoretical constructs and practical interventions that help alleviate a child's cognitive stress are explicated in Chapter 11, *Addressing the Child's Thought Life*.

It is critical that clinicians assess the coping mechanisms of their child clients before beginning more intensive work on specific trauma content. Once a child's current coping has been assessed, the therapist can choose specific interventions aimed at augmenting the positive coping strategies that a child already possesses, learning and practicing new coping methods when needed, and extinguishing maladaptive coping. Laying this foundation of positive coping early in treatment mitigates any iatrogenic effects associated with later trauma processing, allowing children to feel strong enough to face their histories and move forward with newfound resiliency.

Soothing the Physiology

Helping Traumatized Children Find a State of Calm

Physiological Arousal, Dysregulation, and Trauma

One of the most troublesome consequences of childhood trauma is the resulting dysregulation that manifests in a child's physiology (Cicchetti & Curtis, 2006; Perry & Azad, 1999; Van der Kolk, 2003, 2005). Regardless of the type of trauma suffered or any one child's idiosyncratic response to the trauma, "the extreme nature of the external threat is often matched by an extreme and persisting internal activation of the neurophysiological systems mediating the stress response and their associated functions" (Perry & Azad, 1999, p. 310). Young trauma survivors often live in a state of hypervigilance. They are always scanning the environment, looking for signs of danger (Garavan, Pendergrass, Ross, Stein, & Risinger, 2001; Wright et al., 2001). Put simply, these children have a heightened physiological reactivity that makes it difficult for them to calm down.

If a child's biologically adaptive stress response mechanisms are activated consistently enough, as is the case with chronic and pervasive maltreatment, the child's neurophysiological development may be compromised (Perry & Azad, 1999; Teicher, Anderson, Polcari, Anderson, & Navalta, 2002). Early trauma, particularly cumulative exposure to stress in multiple domains, can produce lasting impairment in brain structure and function (Anda et al., 2001; Van der Kolk, 1994). When a child's stress response systems remain activated in benign environments, when the body persists in sounding the alarm throughout the day-to-day minutia of life, the system has become compromised (Pervanidou, 2008).

In this context, it is possible to have too much of a good thing. Several authors highlight the increased peripheral sympathetic nervous system activity that takes place in children with PTSD and posttraumatic symptoms (De Bellis & Thomas, 2003; Delehanty, Nugent, Christopher, & Walsh, 2005). In addition, extreme or prolonged stress can result in a host of difficulties in the body's ability to fight off sickness and disease, putting chronically traumatized children at risk for suppression of their immune systems (Sapolsky, 2004), long-term psychopathology, and physical complications (Pervanidou, 2008).

Chronically traumatized children often manifest dysregulation of the hypothalamic-pituitary-adrenal (HPA) axis, a system that is critical to our bodies' adaptive response to stress, although there is currently some controversy about the nature of this dysregulation. Studies that have measured basal cortisol levels through salivary sampling of traumatized children and nontraumatized children have yielded mixed results (Cicchetti & Rogosch, 2001), but it is clear that a differential adrenal response occurs in children who have experienced trauma versus those who have not (Carrion et al., 2002).

DeBellis et al. (1999) observed elevated levels of cortisol in maltreated children as compared with a control group. Carrion and colleagues (2002) sampled the salivary cortisol of 51 children with a history of exposure to trauma/PTSD symptoms 4 times daily for 3 consecutive days and compared these samples to those taken from a control group of 31 age- and gender-matched healthy control subjects. Their findings were consistent with De Bellis et al. (1999) in that the subjects exposed to trauma demonstrated significantly elevated cortisol levels when compared with the control group. Additionally, they found that girls with PTSD symptoms had significantly higher levels of cortisol than boys with similar PTSD symptoms.

Conversely, several other studies have found a decrease in cortisol levels after trauma. King, Mandansky, King, Fletcher, and Brewer (2001) sampled 5- to 7-year-old girls who had been sexually abused within a few months of the study's onset. These girls had significantly lower cortisol levels in comparison with the control group. Bremner et al. (2003) exposed adults diagnosed with PTSD to a cognitive challenge related to their abuse as children. They found significantly elevated cortisol levels in the PTSD population before the cognitive challenge and still significant, though decreased, elevation of cortisol during the cognitive challenge. After the cognitive challenge, the cortisol levels of the PTSD group went back down to baseline levels and were similar to those found in the control group. From this data, Bremner and his colleagues stated that there does not appear to be an impairment in cortisol response to stressors in PTSD. Two other studies failed to show the expected decrease between morning and afternoon draws of salivary cortisol levels in children with major depressive disorder (Hart, Gunnar, & Cicchetti, 1996; Kaufman, 1991).

In an attempt to shed further light on the workings of the HPA axis in traumatized children, Cicchetti and Rogosch (2001) investigated cortisol regulation in a sample of 175 maltreated school-age children and 209 non-maltreated children. No significant difference in cortisol regulation was found between the two groups. However, there were significant differences in cortisol regulation based on the form or forms of maltreatment to which a child had been exposed. Maltreated children who had experienced both physical and sexual abuse had elevated morning cortisol levels. Children with multiple forms of abuse were also more likely to show an atypical decrease between morning and afternoon cortisol levels. Additionally, a subgroup of children who had been physically abused had lower morning cortisol levels and less difference between morning and afternoon levels.

The mixed findings thus far may have to do with methodological issues, time lapse between the occurrence of the traumatic event and the cortisol sampling, the subcategory of trauma a particular subject has experienced, and the multiplicity of trauma experienced by subjects. It has been hypothesized that the nature of dysregulation may be impacted by the severity, length, and type of trauma experienced. More research is needed to better understand the exact nature of dysregulation as it occurs in the HPA axis in response to trauma.

First Things First

It is difficult to accomplish other goals of trauma treatment until a child's pathways to self-regulation and coregulation with significant others have been positively impacted. In other words, soothing the child's physiology must be addressed before other treatment goals. Cicchetti and Tucker (1994) make an argument for cortical development and organization to no longer be conceptualized as passive processes, but viewed as processes of self-organization that are steered by mechanisms of self-regulation. Perry & Azad (1999, p. 314), while articulating the cascading effects of hyperreactivity on the post-trauma sequelae of traumatized children, make this statement:

> The resulting vicious cycle of poor performance, poor self-esteem, and development of maladaptive problem-solving styles, in turn, is difficult to treat as long as the underlying physiological hyperreactivity impairs the ability to modulate anxiety, concentrate on academic or social learning tasks, and contain behavioral impulses.

Perry goes on to suggest that medication may be a necessary route toward addressing this core hyperreactivity and may help pave the way for secondary problems to be addressed through psychological intervention. Part of the treatment package includes helping the traumatized child to develop a skill set specifically focused on the self-regulation of physiological processes. This is where play-based stress management training begins. The FSPT model places the regulation of a child's neurophysiological and somatic arousal states ahead of goals that attempt to impact a child's maladaptive thoughts, provide gradual exposures to trauma content, or build coherent narrative through integration of sensory content and factual accounts of the trauma.

Many play therapy strategies can be used to help clients become more aware of their own physiological arousal and subsequently influence their body's regulatory abilities. No single intervention can magically recalibrate a child's physiology, but a multiplicity of play-based stress inoculation techniques can help children impact the state of their own arousal. Moreover, the playfulness inherent in this approach counters the toxicity of the anxiety symptoms that manifest as hyperarousal while increasing the likelihood that children will practice the stress management strategies in their home environments.

The Perceived Threat Posed by Relaxation

Clinicians must use intentionality and a titrated set of relaxation experiences when cultivating a child's ability to engage in soothing his own physiology. Therapists must have a healthy respect for the risk that the sheer act of relaxing will represent to a portion of the children we work with. The mantra "Those who risk nothing gain nothing" may motivate some clients, but others may equate relaxation with a giving over of control that feels threatening. Acknowledging up front the risk we are asking children to take when we ask them to relax may go a long way toward countering resistance. Children who are hypervigilant become accustomed to existing in a state of heightened arousal. It makes them feel prepared for any dangers that might come. It becomes their new normal. The problem is that it also makes them over-reactive to stimuli within the normal range of experience. The act of relaxing may make a child feel vulnerable to attack. It is through repetitive, progressive experiences of relaxation provided in the safe environment of the playroom that the child's equating of relaxation with danger can begin to shift.

Self-Soothing as a Form of Self-Empowerment

Teaching a child ways to calm her physiology has benefits beyond the obvious benefit of biological equilibrium. Children who have been abused either physically or sexually often carry with them a deep and sometimes unconscious belief that their bodies are not their own. After multiple experiences of their bodies being used as objects for the sexual or aggressive gratification of others, these children have trouble believing that their bodies are under their own jurisdiction. Giving a child tools to control her own physiology directly counters the lie that control is something that other people have over her and places the child squarely in charge of herself.

Prop-Based Relaxation Exercises

Punctuating the Beginning and Ending of Sessions with Relaxation

Traumatized children are soothed by routines. Therefore, it can be helpful to begin and end therapy sessions with the same activities each time they come to treatment. An activity that I was introduced to by Richard Kagan, author of *Real Life Heroes* (2007), is a great exercise to use at the start of a session. The child is given a peacock feather and is asked to balance it. The client must employ many skills in order to balance the feather. First of all, the child must tune out other distractions and find a focal point on the feather in order to gauge when it is leaning to one side or another. Second, the child must ground his body, bending his knees so that he can move fluidly to compensate for the tipping of the feather. The peacock feather is light enough and long enough that a child can balance it and thereby gain a sense of mastery over the medium. The challenge then becomes to balance the feather for longer and longer periods of time. Using an intervention like this at the beginning of each session can punctuate the transition from the other stressors and business of the child's life to the safe space and purposeful use of the playroom.

Five-Count Breathing

When I work with groups of children, we often punctuate the beginning of the group session with a five-count breathing exercise. The children breathe in for a count of five, hold their breath for a count of five, and then slowly release their breath for a count of five. Counting to five helps clients to pace their breathing and encourages intentional, controlled diaphragmatic inhalation and exhalation. Focused, diaphragmatic breathing is a useful tool for countering physiological arousal (Cyr, Culbert, & Kaiser, 2003; Gerik, 2005; Kabat-Zinn, 1990; Kabat-Zinn et al., 1992; Kajander & Peper, 1998).

Bubbles in Breath Work

Focused breathing exercises can be made more playful through the use of bubbles (Goodyear-Brown, Riviere, & Shelby, 2004; Paule, 2009). In the script I have developed for the incorporation of bubbles in deep breathing work, the therapist takes a tube of bubbles and says, "Watch what happens to the bubbles when I change my breathing. If I take a quick breath in and out [therapist demonstrates], I don't get a lot of bubbles. If I take a deep breath in and breathe out really hard, I can make a lot of little bubbles [therapist demonstrates], which can be a lot of fun. But if I take a deep breath in and I blow out really slowly—so slowly that I almost can't hear my own breathing [therapist demonstrates]—I can make a great big bubble!" After I demonstrate the concepts, clients age 3 to 18 immediately grab the bubbles and say, "Let me try!" They are often having so much fun that they don't even realize that skill rehearsal is taking place.

This simple play intervention has several therapeutic payoffs. First, bubbles are inherently engaging and fun. The bubbles are given to the child and parent along with the prescription that the child should blow three big bubbles each day. The timing of this homework can vary depending on what time in the day the child's anxiety is most strongly felt. Several years ago, I had a 5-year-old client named Zach. Zach went to a Mother's Day Out Program 2 days a week. Each school morning his anxiety would escalate on the ride to school to the point where he would throw up in the car.

I encouraged him to blow his three big bubbles in the car on the way to school to counter the escalating physiological response that accompanied his separation from mom. Mom had immediate buy-in to the intervention, as it was significantly more pleasant for her to clean up the bubble mess left in the car than the noxious substances that had been left before. This client quickly learned to control the physiological manifestation of his anxiety through this practical activity. Alternatively, a client who has nighttime anxiety might blow his bubbles just before bed. The fun of blowing bubbles counters the toxicity of the anxiety and increases the likelihood that the therapeutic homework will be completed.

Pinwheels as Focal Points

The bubble-blowing intervention gives the young child an external focal point for deep breathing, a point in space to focus on while taking diaphragmatic breaths. The idea that the child should blow out really slowly is meant to help the client achieve control over her breathing. Another prop that can function as an effective external focal point for deep-breathing practice is the pinwheel. Children are given their own pinwheels, asked to hold them close to their mouths, and blow. This is easily done for most children. They are then asked to hold the pinwheel an arm's length away and still make it rotate with their breath. This distance is more challenging and requires children to take deeper breaths. Most children tend to take shallow breaths that expand their chests and make their shoulders rise. These exercises are helpful in retraining children to take deep diaphragmatic breaths that are controlled in both their inhalation and their expulsion of air.

Clients can create their own pinwheels with kits purchased from novelty stores. When the child makes her own pinwheel, the benefits are multiplied. The creation of her own prop increases her sense of ownership of the strategy. Moreover, the make-your-own pinwheels allow for the child and therapist to personalize them with pictures and words that trigger relaxation and safety for each individual client. For example, the therapist might draw a picture of the child's favorite stuffed animal, another picture of the child's favorite book, and a third picture of the child's favorite food. When the child blows on the pinwheel, she will first see these reminders of soothing objects and then see them all blend together as the pinwheel rotates (Figure 5.1).

For sexual abuse survivors who have been traumatized in the night, anxiety is often intensified at bedtime. I give these children special glow-in-the-dark

Figure 5.1   Make Your Own Pinwheel

pinwheels. These serve the dual purpose of countering the physiological escalation at bedtime with an antithetical behavior while reminding the child of the safety of the play therapist through the transitional object of the pinwheel that has previous associations to the safety of the playroom.

Biofeedback

Biofeedback is another intervention that is helpful for children who are working on calming the physiology (Culbert, 2003; Powers et al., 2001). Intensified noradrenergic activity as manifested through increased heart rate, blood pressure, skin conductance, and heightened startle response have all been documented in clients with PTSD (O'Donnell, Hegadoren, & Coupland, 2004; Southwick et al., 1999). Clients can learn to heighten their awareness of these responses, particularly heart rate, galvanic skin response, and skin temperature. Through biofeedback, they can actually lower their own heart rate and calm their physiology. One biofeedback program discussed by Gerik (2005) has a child watch a series of visual images on a screen while hooked up to a sophisticated biofeedback monitoring system. When the child's physiology has calmed, the child is rewarded with enjoyable music or imagery on screen.

In the play therapy room, a simple stethoscope can be used routinely to help a client focus on noticing his heartbeat and reducing the number of beats per minute. This activity can be introduced to younger children as a natural outgrowth of playing with the pretend doctor's kit. After the child is comfortable with the pretend stethoscope, a working stethoscope can be introduced. Preschool-age children do this activity best if the therapist and child take turns with the stethoscope. If the child has trouble making out the heartbeats, the therapist can further structure the activity by counting the heartbeats out loud. The act of increasing one's awareness of a physiological process allows the client's body to relax. In clinical application, I have found that the child is sometimes helped by focusing exclusively on the sounds of his heartbeats while breathing slowly and deeply. In other instances, children have seemed a little awed by their own heartbeat and prefer to focus on a soothing play object or study an image from a magazine. This intense focus on an object or image outside of themselves results in a lowering of the heart rate as monitored by the therapist through the stethoscope.

Progressive Muscle Relaxation

Progressive muscle relaxation (PMR) is another physiological intervention that helps children combat anxiety (Cohen, Mannarino & Deblinger, 2006; Eisen and Kearney, 1995; Rauhala et al., 1990; Rusy & Weisman, 2000; Wolpe, 1984). PMR has also shown efficacy in pain management for a host of physiological symptoms (McCallie, Blum, & Hood, 2006). PMR can be delivered through play-based intervention. I pair the progressive muscle relaxation exercise with bubbles in an intervention called "the bubble fall." I begin the intervention by intentionally creating a relaxing atmosphere. I turn on warm lighting, put on some soothing music, and invite the child to lie down on the floor or lean back in her chair. Then I blow bubbles high up into the air. The child's only job at first is to watch the bubbles float down toward her body. Then I invite her to tense and release various muscle groups starting with the face and moving all the way down to the toes. This activity can become a normal component of sessions. After several repetitions pairing the progressive relaxation procedures with the visual images of the falling bubbles, a conditioned association is made between the two. Once the association between the image of the bubbles falling and the sensation of relaxation has been conditioned, the image can be called up in situations where the child typically experiences a stress reaction.

I used this intervention extensively with groups of children in an inner city school. The majority of children on my caseload had meltdowns on a daily basis. After we began practicing this intervention, I would see one of my clients in the hallway looking ready for a fight. His body would be rigid, his fists clenched, and his shoulders hunched. If I could catch him at that moment and help him conjure up a picture of the falling bubbles, his body would automatically begin to relax. The key is to link the conditioned somatic response to the image in the child's mind of the bubble fall. Activating the imagery activates the relaxation response. Any number of other objects could be used as the stimulus for this exercise. A ceiling fan painted with calming images or words of affirmation could serve as another point of focus to be paired with the progressive muscle tension and relaxation exercises.

Externally Grounded Guided Imagery

Positive imagery is another relaxation tool for anxious children (Cohen, Mannarino, & Deblinger, 2006; Stueck & Gloeckner, 2005). The creation of a safe place or happy place image can also be very useful as a tool for soothing the physiology. However, traumatized children may have difficulty visualizing an image internally unless it has first been created concretely. The sand tray is an excellent tool that allows the child to create a three-dimensional safe place. Art, clay, and other play creations can also be utilized in creating external images of safety that can later be internalized.

It is important to keep in mind that severely maltreated or neglected children may have no historical place of safety. In this case, the client can create an imaginary safe place. I invite the child to describe the place in some detail as he is creating it in the sand. It is important to ask questions that allow the child to integrate the sensory details of the imagined environment. Questions should target tastes, smells, sounds, and tactile experiences. The fleshing out of a safe place image can also be done through art or clay work. One preschool child made a whole forest of trees out of green and brown Play-Doh. A picture was taken of it, and the child used this picture as a bridge to solidifying her internal image of a peaceful forest (Figure 5.2).

In some cases, children may revert back to what they perceive as the safest time in their development, in utero. In the sand tray pictured in Figure 5.3, a little girl chose a clear figurine with a baby safely tucked inside her mother's womb to represent herself. Then she put the mother into a magical land with beautiful stone trees and peaceful animals. The imagery of being back in her mother's womb, safe and snug, became an important internal icon for this client as we later processed her trauma narrative.

Figure 5.2   A Peaceful Forest

Figure 5.3   Girl in Her Mother's Womb

A child may choose one particular symbol from the playroom to epito-mize safety and soothing. In the picture in Figure 5.4, a young girl who had long been separated from her mother chose a kangaroo with a baby kangaroo inside her pouch. This client was able to imagine and articulate what it felt

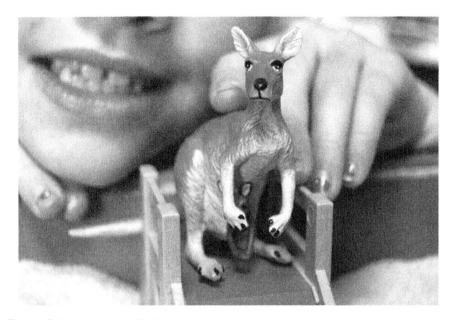

Figure 5.4 Kangaroo and Baby

like for the baby kangaroo to be safe within its mother's pouch. Later in treatment, as she began to tell her story, she often held this kangaroo figure as she
talked. It seemed to act as a grounding device, anchoring her in the here-
and-now safety of the playroom as she recounted some of the overwhelming
events of her early life.

The use of soothing visual imagery can aid a child in calming down. As
I explained in the chapter on building safety and security, many children who
have been traumatized don't have a template for safety. Therefore, visualization and guided imagery exercises should be used with caution. A careful
assessment should be made of the client's trauma history, particularly if the
trauma constituted some form of abuse. A simple invitation to close one's eyes
and relax could be a reminder of the invitations made by a perpetrator before
a sexually abusive experience. Sometimes when a child closes her eyes, all she
sees behind them are images of the trauma. This understanding has informed
my current approach, the grounding of guided imageries or visualizations
in the creation of an external representation that will become an internalized visual image. The act of creating the external representation, whether
through art, in sand, in clay, or with an arrangement of objects, grounds the
child in the here and now while serving as a bridge to internal representation.

The extra security of igniting the imagery first in three dimensions frees children to use their imaginations and create wonderful places.

In a previous chapter, I gave examples of how children with trauma histories may proceed directly to trauma imagery even when prompted to create a safe place. What follows here is an example of a child's use of story as a positive anchor for her own soothing imagery. I read the book *Where Do Balloons Go?* (Curtis, 2000), a book that stimulates the imagination, to a 7-year-old girl named Teisha. Teisha interrupted the story to give her own ideas about other silly places where the balloons might have landed. Afterwards I invited Teisha to choose a balloon (I keep a variety of balloons in different shapes and sizes in the playroom) and suggested that she create a place in the sand where her balloon could land. She worked on her tray with deep concentration for half the session and eventually signaled that she was ready to discuss her choices. What follows is a picture and explanation of her tray (Figure 5.5).

Paris: Tell us about where your balloon landed.

Teisha: My balloon landed in a fairyland and this is a place where wild horses roam free and these are guards that came to bring the king some food but then the king had a heart attack and then the doctor came and then he laid in the bed and the balloon rubbed some vapor rub on him.

Figure 5.5   Teisha's Safe Place

Therapist: So the balloon came to rub vapor rub on the king when he had
    died.

Teisha: Yes, yes, and then there's some fairy dust and he was alive.

This little girl lived in a dangerous community. She was forced to play
inside because of the indiscriminate gang violence and frequent drug deals
that went on outside her home. It is a powerful positive use of her imagination to envision herself in a place where wild horses roam free. The image
allows Teisha a momentary respite from the stressors of her restricted environment. Her creativity and imagination were given structure through the
play materials. Touching and manipulating objects while building the sand
tray world served to ground her in the here and now and reduced the likelihood of her becoming overwhelmed by trauma content while building
her safety metaphor. In addition, the variety of miniatures at her fingertips
encouraged elaboration and detail in her safe place scene.

In addition to the drama unfolding in the tray, Teisha brought several other
safety symbols within easy reach. She gathered a doctor's kit "in case someone
got hurt," a phone "to dial 9–1–1," a treasure chest to ensure that there were
more than enough resources to handle any financial need that might arise,
and a microphone to make sure that she could be heard no matter what happened around her. We were able to take all these icons and translate them
into easily accessible internal images that the client could pull up whenever
she needed to relax.

Head in the Clouds

Another exercise that helps build a client's repertoire of relaxation imagery
is called "head in the clouds" (Goodyear-Brown, 2002) and is based on a book
called Little Cloud (Carle, 1996). In the book a little cloud gets separated from
the other clouds and begins to shape itself into various forms. Little Cloud sees
a dolphin swimming in the ocean and shapes itself into the form of a dolphin.
After I read the book out loud, I give the client either whipped cream or shaving cream and offer him the invitation to shape the whipped cream into a shape
that he would take if he were a cloud. Figure 5.6 shows a picture of the kite that
a 7-year-old boy generated.

As he worked with the shaving cream, immersing his hands in the gooey
stuff, his visual imagery was kinesthetically augmented. Later, when I took
him through a visualization in which he imagined himself as a cloud floating

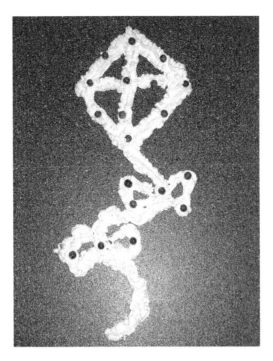

Figure 5.6   Kite Made from Whip Cream

in the sky and shifting into the shape of a kite, he had a previous full-body experience that could serve as a safety anchor for him.

Menu of Soothing Strategies

The "menu of soothing strategies" is another fun and useful stress inoculation activity designed by Shelby (Goodyear-Brown, Riviere, & Shelby, 2004). The therapist begins by introducing the child to a variety of pretend play food items. Then the child and therapist pretend that they are visiting a restaurant. The child gets to choose what he would like for an appetizer, drink, main dish, side dish, and dessert. After this the therapist creates a "menu" out of construction paper. I usually name the restaurant after the child, something like "Café Joshua." This seems to appeal to the child and increases his sense of ownership during the activity. The therapist then makes a list of all the senses and helps the child fill in the menu. Asking the child, "What is a taste that makes you feel really good?" may generate a response that runs the gambit from candy to apples.

Words can be written in the menu with school-age children. Younger children choose icons to represent their favorite tastes by drawing pictures or cutting images out of magazines. In this way, the younger child has a pictoral reminder system. Other stimuli are chosen for each sense. Children may choose "the smell of fresh cut grass" as an olfactory sense memory, the softness of a beloved teddy bear as a tactile sense memory, the sound of their baby brother laughing as an auditory sense memory, and so forth.

If the child chooses the silk from his special blanket as a texture that makes him feel calm, perhaps a square of silk can be sent to school in the child's pocket. When the child is feeling anxious, he can reach into his pocket, rub his piece of silk, and experience immediate physiological relief. Older children and teenagers often pinpoint particular music that makes them feel especially happy or calm. Because music is such a powerful modulator of affect for many children (Goldstein, 1980; Pelletier, 2004), creating associations between certain musical selections and experiences of relaxation can equip a young person to induce a relaxed state outside of treatment.

Yoga

Other modalities can be incorporated into the playroom to aid in soothing the physiology. Yoga, in combination with other relaxation strategies, such as breathing and focusing exercises and guided imagery, has been found to decrease the feelings of helplessness and the aggression that can accompany a child's response to trauma (Stueck & Gloeckner, 2005). Although there are no randomized controlled studies related to the effectiveness of yoga, a recent review of the existing literature promotes yoga as a promising intervention for stress reduction in children (Galantino, Galbavy, & Quinn, 2008). I use a book in the office called *Babar's Yoga* (Brunhoff, 2002). It's a delightful book that takes each of several yoga poses and shows Babar the elephant completing each step of the exercise. A Babar doll can be purchased with the book, and the doll can be manipulated into the yoga poses that are demonstrated in the illustrations. Children will often choose one particular pose that they like and will request this pose over and over again. The completion of a yoga pose can punctuate the beginning or ending of a therapy session and can be especially valuable at the end of a session in which difficult trauma narrative work has been done. There are several other yoga games for children on the market, any of which could be a valuable tool in helping children soothe their physiology.

Cool as a Cucumber

Another avenue for relaxation in children has to do with providing soothing touch. Various interventions related to appropriate parental touch as a mitigator for a child's stress are described in Chapter 6, *Parents as Partners*. An additional intervention, called "cool as a cucumber" (Goodyear-Brown, 2002), was cocreated by a 7-year-old girl named Carla. Carla's parents were going through a very difficult divorce while continuing to live in the same home. Carla was caught in the crossfire. She would hear them arguing every night as she was falling asleep. She carried tension in her body everywhere she went and was beginning to have a short fuse with peers at school. Together we were searching for metaphors that would help her to stay calm and cool. She tossed out the phrase "cool as a cucumber," and we designed a sensory intervention around this concept.

To begin the intervention, the therapist and the client each draw a picture of someone staying calm during a difficult situation. The therapist explains that several soothing interventions involving cucumbers will be offered to help the client get a full-body experience of relaxation. First, the client is invited to try slices of real cucumbers. This offers the child a healthy snack and some nurturing interaction with the therapist. Investigation of the cucumber slices often leads to a discussion of how the cucumber has a tender inside and a thick skin to protect the inside from getting damaged. The client is invited to place cucumber pieces or eye pads over her closed eyes. Children who deal with hyperarousal may have a difficult time allowing themselves to close their eyes and relax.

A child's desire to keep her eyes open should always be respected. However, I often see children who want the deeper experience of relaxation that comes when they are able to block out external visual stimuli, but their eyelids flutter open repeatedly, distracting them from moving into progressively deeper levels of relaxation. A child's desire to relax is often directly contradicted by her physiological state of hyperarousal. The pressure of an external weight such as an eye pad can disencumber the child from having to focus on keeping her eyes shut. After the eye pads are offered, I then offer a cucumber-scented facial mask.

The intention behind the incorporation of a facial mask is to help the child become progressively more still. A subset of children cope with anxiety by talking incessantly or becoming excessively animated. The nervous chatter and continuous facial animation keeps them from reaching a relaxed, centered place. When I apply the cucumber mask and it begins to dry on the child's face, the child consciously decreases both her verbalizations and the mobility of her face. The last component of the intervention involves massaging the hands, arms, or feet with cucumber-scented lotion.

This is a wonderful intervention to teach to parents. The whole sequence of relaxation steps can be assigned as daily homework. Especially for children who experience hyperarousal near bedtime, these relaxing rituals, provided by a safe, soothing parent, can open up new coping mechanisms. This intervention requires a large amount of trust and is therefore one that I often save for later in a treatment process. Some children may ask for all the steps of the intervention and others may just want the lotioning activities or the facial mask. Children should always be free to refuse any part of the intervention that makes them uncomfortable. For traumatized children, there is an inherent risk in relaxing their guard. However, the discomfort that a child feels at taking a relaxation risk precedes the payoff of new somatosensory learning. If the child is willing to tolerate the new experience, a form of in vivo exposure occurs. As the child chooses to take the risk, the associations that have been made in her neural networks between touch and danger may begin a process of accommodation through these new experiences.

Female clients especially enjoy the feeling of being pampered as the intervention progresses. However, I recently received correspondence from a therapist in Trinidad who used this intervention with school-age boys in an orphanage. Her anecdotal report was that the boys requested the exercise over and over again. It is easy for us to dismiss the need for nurturing touch, particularly in our young male clients, but when safety parameters, appropriate protocols, and adequate supervision are in place, these kinds of interventions can help dysregulated boys to have an experience of calm.

Positive touch serves a protective function for children. Several years ago, I had the opportunity to learn about how FBI agents are trained to recognize counterfeit money. One would think that they spend lots of time researching the various ways in which a dollar bill could be counterfeited and what to look for in a fake bill. The reality of their training is antithetical to this assumption. FBI agents spend hours and hours poring over authentic dollar bills. They familiarize themselves with the placement of the watermarks, with the look, the feel, and the smell of real money. Apparently, after being immersed in the real thing, it becomes fairly easy to spot a phony bill. This process is the same in healthy children. Children who have been raised with lots and lots of appropriate, positive touch are more likely to recognize a questionable touch as uncomfortable. Children who have been sexually abused are more in need of positive, healthy touch experiences and the corrective emotional experiences that accompany the healthy touch than any other population that I serve.

Caregivers as Soothing Agents

A traumatized child can learn that the touch of a safe parent or caregiver can be soothing. Some clinicians are skeptical about the use of touch in work with traumatized children. There are certainly cases in which touch is not appropriate. Therapists should be properly trained in touch-based interventions before using them with clients. Whenever possible, the soothing touch experiences should be facilitated by the therapist but given by a protective parent or other safe caregiver with whom the child has daily contact. Dyadic approaches to interventions that consciously utilize touch, such as Theraplay (Jernberg & Booth, 2001), facilitate positive attachments between the caregiver and the child and ensure that the child will continue to have the relational infrastructure for soothing touch experiences after the treatment relationship is ended.

Caregivers of traumatized children often need psychoeducation to better understand how to be effective soothing agents. This concept is more thoroughly addressed in Chapter 6, *Parents and Partners*, but is important enough to mention here as well. Children with trauma histories are more likely to react out of their feeling brains than out of their thinking brains. Both the reptilian parts of the brain and the limbic system are activated faster than the areas of the brain responsible for higher order reasoning when a child is stressed. For this reason, if caregivers are attempting to soothe a child by verbalizing safety messages, the brain will have a difficult time encoding the message until the physical self has been soothed. Children who have been traumatized need daily experiences of safe and soothing rituals to internalize a message of safety. I help parents design a series of rituals specific to the child in their care. These may include brushing the child's hair, rocking at bedtime, singing familiar songs while lotioning hands, sharing snacks together, swinging on a swing set together, and any number of other kinesthetic activities that rely on the structure and rituals of a significant other for the soothing to occur.

Sweet Dreams Lotion Potion

I named one such intervention the "sweet dreams lotion potion." A 5-year-old girl who was having several nightmares per night came to my office. During her initial session she explained that the dreams "get inside my head and won't go away." I wondered out loud if we could make some kind of magic helmet that she could put on before bed to help keep the thoughts out. She looked at me, sighed, and said hopelessly, "Then they would just come in through my foots." I pondered her problem. For this 5-year-old, the intrusive thoughts were a concrete threat and needed a concrete solution. This little girl needed something that could cover her from head to toe. I said, "Sounds like we need a way to keep your whole body protected from those bad dreams." She nodded her head vigorously. In response to this child's need, the sweet dreams lotion potion (Goodyear-Brown, 2005) was born.

I begin the intervention by having the parent and child sit together. I present them with a basket of lotions. The lotions have various scents and colors and are in containers of various sizes and shapes. I invite the parent and the child to explore the lotions, paying attention to scents and colors. They take turns choosing a lotion that reminds them of a happy memory or a warm, safe time. A child might choose a vanilla-scented lotion and say that it reminds her of when she and mommy baked cookies for Christmas. I usually have the parent go first, taking the lead in creating a positive narrative of previous sensory experiences. With each sense memory that is described, the parent and child squeeze some of the lotion that represents that memory into a container. The combination of memories, scents, and colors is unique to each family. At the end of the session, the parent and child stir up their lotion potion and take it home with them.

The second stage of the intervention happens at home, when the parent puts lotion on the child at bedtime. The happy memories can be verbally rehearsed again as the child is soothed by the parent's informal massage. Many hyperarousal responses are triggered by unarticulated sense memories related to traumatic events. Through this intervention the power of articulated positive sense memories is harnessed and used to combat PTSD arousal symptoms.

What follows is the transcript of a session in which a sweet dreams lotion potion is created by a mom and a 4-year-old boy named Bobby. Bobby had an experience at a summer day camp in which he was exposed to inappropriate sexual behavior in the boy's changing room. Bobby had been having nightmares consistently since he told his mom what happened.

Mom (holding up a lotion for Bobby to smell): This smells like summertime. Smell that again.

Bobby: Yeah.

Mom: This smells like sunshine and playing outside.

Bobby: No mom, it smells like spring at the lake.

Mom: Spring?

Bobby: And we were all in the pile of leaves.

Mom: Yeah—it does smell like spring at the lake. What were we doing? Tell me what we were doing there.

Bobby: We were jumping. Daddy was driving and I saw the big pile of leaves, and I said stop and I wanted to play in it and you did too. So we played and played in it.

Paris: Oh, what a great memory!

While Bobby and his mom squeeze the lotion that triggered this memory into the cup, I rehearse the narration of the memory. Bobby picks up a new lotion and smells it.

Bobby: I remember the pipe . . . smells so good!

Paris: You like the smell of the pipe smoke.

Mom: Oh, a pipe! You're thinking of Uncle Bill and his pipe. You think this smells like a pipe?

Bobby: Yeah.

Bobby attempts to squeeze the lotion out himself, but the bottle is difficult to manage. Mom puts her arms around him and helps him squeeze. She reframes the difficulty with the task in terms of how strong the lotion potion will be.

Mom: That is powerful stuff right there. That one will definitely keep all the bad dreams away. Look at that! That is some serious protection!

Paris: You know what? Monsters only like things that smell really, really bad. They don't like sweet smells at all.

Mom: Oh, I think we'll be extra safe now.

Bobby and his mom took the lotion potion home, and after a few nights of lotioning and the accompanying rehearsal of good memories, Bobby's nightmares were extinguished.

Playroom Tools as Aids
in Self-Regulation

The tools of the playroom themselves provide a way of soothing the physiology for children. Musical instruments can provide children with a way of modulating their affect as they manipulate the instruments. Randy, an 11-year-old boy who had just displayed anger for the first time in the playroom by throwing a stuffed animal across the room, cast his eyes around the play space and spontaneously picked up the child-size guitar. He strummed a very intense, chaotic, and discordant rhythm at first. After a few seconds of the intense playing, he began to pluck each string gently in an ordered, gentle rhythm. He went back and forth between these two forms of playing, the first reflecting his internal state of chaos following his display of anger and the second reflecting his attempt to self-modulate. In a few minutes, he put the guitar down and was able to calmly re-engage the therapist for the rest of the session.

The sand tray is a particularly powerful tool for helping children regain their equilibrium after they have been involved in intense trauma work. One 10-year-old boy, after a particularly difficult disclosure, abruptly moved to the sand and began to arrange soldiers and military equipment. The abrupt shift in focus signaled to me that he needed to take a break from the difficult material. The first statement after he moved to the sand was, "A sandstorm has covered up the base." The sandstorm became his chosen metaphor for communicating the internal storm of emotion that had been set off by his previous disclosure. As he worked on building his army base, he repeated, "A sandstorm has covered up the base." Then he began to chant, " . . . but we're making it OK now, we're making it OK now, do not worry, it's gonna be OK." The client's self-soothing talk paralleled his self-soothing manipulation of the sand.

Anger Management

Children with trauma-induced physiological dysregulation often have a difficult time managing their anger. These children become angry more quickly than their typically developing peers and have more difficulty channeling their anger in healthy ways. The following quotation from Aristotle (Barnes, 1984), is true of all of us, but especially true of traumatized children who manifest their dysregulation through externalizing behaviors.

> Anyone can be angry, that is easy. But to be angry with the right person and to the right degree, and at the right time and for the right

purpose and in the right way—this is not within everybody's power and is not easy. (Barnes, 1984, p.1751).

A treatment plan that includes the goal of soothing a traumatized child's physiology must often target the child's anger responses. Children who become overwhelmed by their own anger may hurt other people, property, or themselves. Clients who engage in externalizing behaviors, particularly those that involve aggression, often believe that they have no control over their anger. My clients often talk about their anger as if it is a living, breathing entity that takes them over. Indeed, many clients lack the cognitive awareness that they are experiencing anger until after their fists have hit something. Because the physiological arousal and disturbances in affect regulation can manifest in dangerous behavior, it is critical that we help children to acquire a clearly delineated set of skills to help manage their anger. The skill set includes (1) understanding one's own physiological anger cues, (2) understanding the situational cues that can ignite one's anger responses, (3) understanding one's own escalation pattern, (4) learning ways to control the physiological arousal associated with anger, and (5) practicing alternative means of communicating anger without aggression. These skills can be taught in playful ways and then practiced through play-based interventions that decrease a child's resistance to the content while helping the child feel more in control of her anger.

Anger Buttons

The intervention described below increases a client's awareness of both his physiological manifestations of anger and the situations that often trigger anger. It's called "anger buttons" (Goodyear-Brown, 2002). I usually begin the intervention by saying, "Do you ever feel like you are not in control of your anger? Someone says something or looks at you the wrong way and before you know it, you are making an angry response? I call that an anger button. Sometimes I feel like I have different buttons all over me, and all someone has to do is press that button and I blow up. Does that ever happen to you?" Once the child understands the metaphor, I draw an outline of a person. I offer the client a box of buttons. The buttons are different sizes, shapes, and colors and are made of different materials. The child gets to choose buttons and put them on the parts of the body that correspond to the parts of his own body that let him know that he is angry. The use of the props helps clients articulate both the situations that make them angry and their physiological responses (Figure 5.7).

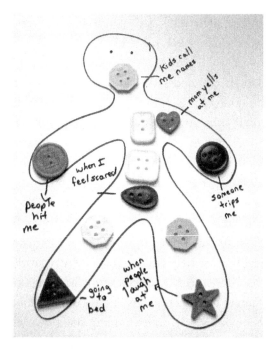

Figure 5.7   Complete Anger Buttons Activity

When this activity is completed, the child and therapist have a guide for future work around this child's anger issues. The anger buttons activity yields information that allows the clinician to intervene at the situational level and at the physiological level. After the child has identified the parts of his body where his anger tends to manifest, we can begin to find ways to control or redirect that manifestation. I usually start by giving an example. "Sometimes when I'm stuck in traffic I'll find myself gritting my teeth. When I notice my gritted teeth, I realize that I am feeling frustrated. If I don't do anything to change the pattern, the next thing I will do is start huffing and puffing and eventually I'll begin hitting the steering wheel. However, if I focus on deliberately unclenching my jaw and breathing deeply, I begin to calm down and can actually impact my own feeling of anger."

Once a client understands that his fists clench up when he is angry, he can be taught to shake out his hands and take three deep breaths when he becomes aware that his fists are clenched. When a client intentionally changes his physical manifestation of anger, he is exerting some self-control. Self-control is a constantly growing and shifting entity that requires practice and positive feedback. Positive reinforcement systems that reward clients for exercising self-control over their anger responses can be beneficial as clients are growing in this area. A loss of control is at the root of a child's experience of trauma. The development and reinforcement of self-control counters the child's sense of vulnerability. Self-control, in this context, is a way of soothing the physiology.

Understanding One's Anger Escalation Pattern

Children who have anger management problems also need help understanding their anger escalation patterns. In most cases, identifying a child's escalation pattern requires parents, teachers, and the child to become detectives. Some children give us the first sign of their escalating anger by rolling their eyes, others by sighing loudly or mumbling under their breath, and still others by tapping their feet under their desks. If we can map a child's escalation pattern, we increase our chances of intervening earlier in the climb. Early intervention in a child's accelerating anger response increases the likelihood of successfully soothing his physiology.

I use the metaphor of a volcano as a way of introducing the child to the idea of escalating layers of anger. I draw a volcano on the white board and put lines inside it. Then I tell the following story.

"One morning Johnny woke up and started getting ready for school. He was looking forward to wearing his favorite shirt and looked everywhere for it. When he realized it was in the dirty clothes hamper he was disappointed." I write *disappointed* on the bottom line of the volcano. "He finished getting dressed and went downstairs to have breakfast. He was looking forward to having a strawberry Pop-Tart, but when he opened the cabinet he found an empty box. He was really irritated that someone else had eaten the last Pop-Tart. He grumbled to himself as he ate a bowl of cereal instead." I write the word *irritated* on the next line of the volcano. "Then he grabbed his backpack and walked to the bus stop. He was excited to sit next to his friend, Mike, and tell him about the video game he played last night, but when he got on the bus, someone else was sitting next to Mike. Johnny was really annoyed." I write *annoyed* on the line above *irritated*. "Johnny was walking to his class and someone tripped him in the hallway. This made Johnny mad." I write *mad* on the line above *annoyed*. "Finally, Johnny gets to his classroom. His teacher asks everyone to get out their math homework. Johnny opens his backpack and realizes that he left his math folder at home . . . and he blows up, throwing his backpack across the room." I write the words *blow up* on the line above *mad* and draw fire and smoke shooting out of the volcano.

Then I engage the child in conversation about what happened. Usually, after I've told the whole story, the child can articulate some of the frustrating things that happened to Johnny. Moreover, clients understand how Johnny's anger built and built until Johnny exploded. We then back up and look at ways Johnny could have soothed himself or asked for help from others at each level of his anger. The therapist and client can then create a personalized volcano that maps the child's unique escalation pattern.

Blow it Up, Blow it Out

An elucidation of a child's anger escalation pattern can also be addressed using an intervention called "blow it up, blow it out" (Goodyear-Brown, 2002). This activity can be done one on one, in family therapy, or in a group milieu. I begin by showing the child a giant cardboard thermometer. We talk about what happens to the thermometer as the temperature rises. I then give the child a long skinny balloon and explain that we are going to use the balloon like a thermometer. I invite the child to choose three words that represent different intensities of anger (Figure 5.8). For example, we might choose the words *irritated*, *angry*, and *furious*. Then the child describes one situation that she responds to with irritation. She blows up the balloon to show how much irritation she feels in that situation. We take turns blowing up our balloons to various levels of anger.

Once our balloons are blown up, we get to decide how to safely get rid of the anger metaphorically captured inside them. Some children choose to pop their balloons while they verbalize one of the situations that makes them angry. Other children want to stomp on it or sit on it. Still others let it go so that it zooms around the room while it loses its air. A few children want to hold on to their balloons (and by association their anger) and take the full balloon home with them. However, even with this choice the metaphor works. As the balloon sits on a shelf at home, the air eventually seeps out, the anger dissipates, and the balloon shrivels. In all these cases, the anger is dissipated without anyone being hurt by it (see Figure 5.8).

These activities and a variety of others are done in various combinations over the course of treatment in order to help the client recognize that he can influence his own physiological responses to his environment. This burgeoning sense of control in how a client manages his anger counteracts the toxic effects of helplessness that are often induced by trauma.

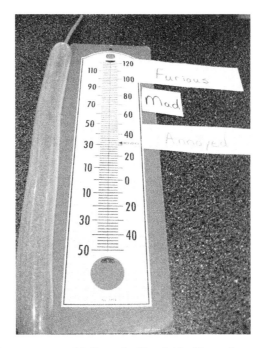

Figure 5.8   Anger Thermometer and Balloon for *Blow It Up, Blow it Out*

Conclusion

Traumatized children come to us with varying levels of physiological distress and dysregulation. Children can benefit from psychoeducation about how the body's stress systems respond. These concepts, playfully taught, can help normalize the internal experiences of dysregulated clients while giving them words and concepts to help make sense of their stress reactions. In addition, stress management skills and anger management skills can be delivered through play-based interventions that will be easily ingested by our child clients.

Although this chapter has focused mainly on interventions that can be used with individual clients to help soothe the physiology, the role of parents as coregulators of their children's physiological arousal cannot be underestimated. Interventions aimed at equipping caregivers to effectively soothe the hurting child in their care are also most effectively delivered through the vehicle of play and can be integrated into a treatment plan aimed at soothing the physiology of the traumatized child. Play-based interventions aimed at optimizing healthy coregulation aspects of the parent/child relationship are discussed in the following chapter.

CHAPTER

6

Parents as Partners

Varieties of Caregiver/Child Dyads

This chapter addresses the myriad ways in which parents serve as partners in the treatment and recovery of traumatized children. For the sake of expediency, I will use the word *parent* to encapsulate all manner of critical caregivers who may be providing the day-to-day care in the life of a traumatized child. The variety of caregiver/child dyads are as plentiful as the kinds of traumatic events that a child may have experienced. Some children have lived in a warm, nurturing family system before a sudden, discrete traumatic event, such as a car accident or a house fire, and continue to be parented by the same caregivers in the same positive manner after the event. Other children may have grown up with parents who were emotionally available and contingently responsive before a traumatic event, but may experience a different quality of caregiving after the trauma due to the parent's own stress reactions. Still other children lose one or more of the people who have been most important to them as a result of the trauma. Examples include a mother dying of breast cancer, a father killed in a violent shooting, or a grandmother who has to go into a nursing home. In these instances, some children remain in the care of a surviving parent who is experiencing increased stress due to the combination of his own grieving process and the stress of sudden and sole caretaking responsibilities.

Parenting Stress After Loss of a Coparent

Moreover, some surviving caregivers still live in war-torn or disaster-prone areas and are faced with continued exposure to the threat of harm. Often, when one parent has died, a family experiences a significant loss of income. If the deceased parent was the primary breadwinner, the remaining parent is often challenged with finding a job while providing care for the children. The quality of attunement between caregivers and their children decreases as environmental and physical stress increases. For this reason, child therapists must be aware of all the contextual and systemic issues that may be creating stress for a family. In addition to providing emotional support for parents and children, child therapists can serve as advocates for families in accessing services, working with complex systems, and helping families develop action plans for mitigating the practical stressors often associated with the loss of a caregiver.

When a parent is lost due to death, the remaining caregivers mourn the loss and often celebrate the person. Sometimes a parent is lost for periods of time due to serial incarceration, drug use, or mental illness. Remaining caregivers often have more complicated personal adjustments to the absence of a parent for any of these reasons. They may be more actively resentful of the caregiving responsibilities that have been thrust upon them. When parenting is transient or intermittently available, children and remaining caregivers have the added stressors of instability and multiple adjustments and readjustments as the parent comes and goes. An 8-year-old girl whose mother was in and out of rehabilitation programs for drug abuse confessed to me that she would rather her mom be gone entirely than have to constantly wonder if she was ever coming back. After she described her life as feeling like a ping-pong match, she said, "I'm sick of wondering if it's for real this time!" All these scenarios add layers of complexity to the child's posttraumatic adaptation.

Foster Parents

Many children are removed altogether from the only caregivers they have ever known. When the neglect or maltreatment of a child comes to the attention of the state, children are often removed abruptly from a parent's home and begin their journeys through the foster care system, an intricate bureaucracy. In some cases the urgency of the immediate danger necessitates a less than optimal initial placement, followed by another placement, and so on. Many of the children I work with have had three or four placements by the time they enter my office. I work with many foster parents and esteem them highly for their commitment to troubled youth. Foster parents agree to provide daily care and nurture, to open up their homes and their hearts, without necessarily receiving affirmation from the troubled children in their care. These parents may not see immediate or even delayed results and require a special brand of encouragement from the mental health professionals who assist them. Moreover, foster parents often need psychoeducation specific to the impact that early neglect and maltreatment have on the brain, as well as how multiple caregiving disruptions negatively impact the attachment relationship.

Adoptive Parents

Preadoptive and adoptive parents make up another category of caregivers with whom I work closely. Preadoptive parents often wrestle with how much of their hearts to give to the children in their care. I am currently working with a family in which the parents, Mr. and Mrs. Jones, sought out my services as they were in the process of domestically adopting two brothers. The two boys, ages 4 and 6, exhibited an indiscriminate attachment pattern at the time they were placed. Although they had been in the Jones household for 6 months at the time of intake, the boys showed no special preference for Mr. and Mrs. Jones. On the contrary, they showed the same level of openness with acquaintances as they did with their adoptive parents. They would run up to strangers, sit in their laps, jump into their arms, and say, "I love you." Whenever service technicians came to the house, the youngest boy always marched right up them and asked, matter-of-factly, "Are you here to take me away?" He did not appear to be distressed by the possibility, he had simply come to expect it.

Part of the reason that Mr. and Mrs. Jones decided to adopt was because they had such joy and success in raising their biological children, a 9-year-old boy and a 10-year-old girl who are, by all accounts, healthy, well-adjusted youngsters. The Joneses applied the same parenting techniques that they had used with their biological children to these preadoptive brothers with startling results. Not only did the boys not respond in expected ways, some of the Jones' strategies seemed to make things worse. I spent several sessions with them introducing them to attachment theory, trauma theory, and parenting techniques that were likely to be more beneficial than the ones they used with their biological children. These parents were truly invested in learning everything they could to help parent these children more effectively. I enjoyed watching the *Aha!* moments as the parents began to shift their paradigm. I offered them a set of attachment-based games that they could begin playing with the boys at home. We also increased the emphasis on some of the daily rituals and routines of nurture and safety that the children needed. I also taught them a modified version of parent-child interaction therapy (PCIT) to enhance their positive relationship with the children while giving them a consistent, unemotional system for daily discipline. The children began to bond with the Joneses, to prefer them to others, and to rely on their new routines. At a recent visit, Mrs. Jones reported that just that morning, when confronted with a friendly stranger, the 4-year-old had lifted his arms and asked Mrs. Jones to hold him. This was the first time that the child had demonstrated a preference for mom in relation to a stranger and the mother understood the profundity of what the child was communicating. Soon after this visit, I received a very distressed call from Mrs. Jones. The Department of Children's Services (DCS) had just called to inform them that the biological father was appealing his termination of parental rights decision. Apparently a previous caseworker did not follow the proper procedure or fill out all the correct forms, and therefore they had to start the court procedures over.

What this meant to the children was that after not seeing their biological dad for at least a year and a half, they would begin to have supervised visits with him again. The Jones family was, by degrees, shocked and frustrated by the ramifications of this decision. The Jones family was months away from the children's adoption date. They had been told when these children came into their care 1 year ago that the parental rights of both parents had been terminated. They were concerned that the children might begin to regress and that all their hard work would be for naught. Moreover, they had to face the very real possibility that if dad did everything that was required of him by the state, he might regain custody, and they might lose the two beautiful boys that they had already begun to see as their own. The parents found themselves navigating the slippery slope of trying to remain fully present in the day-to-day caregiving while feeling the need to protect themselves from the potential grief of having to give up these children. We have recently revisited some of the psychoeducation regarding brain development in order to validate the importance of their daily care decisions. Whether or not they get to be the forever parents of these boys, they understand that every positive, nurturing, attuned caregiving response that they provide the children leaves an indelible mark on the child's developing neural networks. These children will be better equipped to form enduring relationships throughout their life span because of the intentional contingently responsive care that they have received with the Jones family.

Parents as Soothing Agents/Regulators

Parents really are the first modulators of their children's stress reactions. In fact, parents have been called the psychobiological regulators of their children (Schore, 1997). From the moment of conception, the parent's own stress reactions affect the developing fetus. A neurohormonal dialogue takes place between mother and infant in utero (Borysenko & Borysenko, 1994). Intense stress reactions in the mother during gestation can have iatrogenic effects on the developing fetus. This understanding makes it necessary to redefine early intervention as a process that begins before or during pregnancy.

An infant comes out of the womb wholly reliant on others to meet its needs. The infant is hungry and his mother feeds him. The infant is wet and his mother changes him. The baby is overwrought and is held or rocked until he calms. The unpleasant sensations of hunger, cold, or isolation are all experienced by the infant as heightened states of arousal. When the baby cries, he is signaling a state of dysregulation. The attuned caregiver learns the baby's cries, meets the communicated need, and soothes the baby. The continuous dyadic regulation of affect, supported and mediated by the caregiver, sets the stage for the child's eventual autonomous regulation (Cassidy, 1994; Isabella, 1993; Sroufe, 1996). It is the millions of repetitions of this kind of caregiving pattern that help babies lay down the neural wiring for later self-soothing.

A baby's breathing rhythm often begins to match the mother's as the mother is rocking him. A baby moves from sole dependence on the caregiver for soothing to reliance on transitional objects, such as a thumb or blanket, to eventual reliance on the self. I have seen this process play out with my own children. My daughter, Madison, was nursed for the first year of her life. During that year she also learned to suck her thumb. After she was weaned, in moments of high upset, she would put one hand on my flesh and her thumb in her mouth. In this way, she regained a state of equilibrium quickly. A few months later she no longer required the physical contact with me to calm herself, but could calm herself simply by sucking her thumb. She no longer needed the immediate physical contact with her caregiver to be soothed. One explanation of her progression involves having enough repetitions of being soothed by a coregulating caregiver to internalize a mechanism for self-soothing. Acknowledging that the many, many repetitions of dyadic soothing experiences laid down between a child and his caregiver in the first few years of life play a critical role in a child's later ability to engage in self-regulation should profoundly influence our approach to treatment with children who did not receive these experiences.

Attachment Patterns and Anxiety Management

John Bowlby (1973a, 1988), Mary Main (1995), and Mary Ainsworth (1978) were pioneers on the frontier of attachment theory. Out of this research has come a series of classifications that categorize the ways in which children learn to respond to parental behavior and get their needs met. A secure attachment pattern is evidenced when a parent has been consistently available, both physically and emotionally, and contingently responsive to the infant's needs. If the child is hungry, he cries and the mother feeds him. If he is bored, he is provided with stimulation. He learns that his parent can be trusted and will meet his needs. This child sees the parent as a secure base and will freely engage in age-appropriate exploration and return to mom for comfort at times of stress or fear.

Insecure attachment patterns come in several forms. Both avoidant and ambivalent attachment styles can be conceptualized as organized attempts on the child's part to remain close in physical proximity to an attachment figure. In both cases, fear and anxiety activate the attachment system, but the child must use a roundabout method of trying to get her needs met. Avoidant infants stay away and look as if they do not need the parent. Ambivalent infants, who are uncertain of the caregiver's response, vacillate between angry, rejecting behavior and clingy behavior.

Some children who are lacking an ability to self-modulate their own arousal have been neglected or otherwise maltreated. As we expand our understanding of the role that parents are meant to play in the development of a child's competency to self-soothe, we can better understand the freeze response evidenced by many children who have received blatant maltreatment at the hands of their caregivers. According to Bowlby, the parent is biologically programmed to protect her offspring in times of crisis, in order to perpetuate the species. The offspring looks to the parent for protection. Children play and explore their environments contentedly when all is well, but when danger comes, their attachment systems are activated and they quickly return to their parents. What then of the child whose attachment system is stimulated not by an external trauma but by the caregiver herself? He has a biologically driven urge to seek out his caregiver and yet his caregiver is the source of danger. This is the double-bind in which mal-treated children find themselves. This paradox often leads to immobiliza-tion, an inability to come closer to or move away from the danger.

The expected source of comfort has become the source of greatest danger. Children have difficulty establishing a coherent system for coping with terror when it is engendered by a parent. They develop a disorganized attachment pattern. Some of the best examples of this disorganized pattern can be seen during the reunion phase of the "strange situation" experiment. When a par-ent returns to the room after a separation, the disorganized infant may begin to crawl toward mom, freeze, and then crawl into a wall. This disorganized pattern of attachment is one in which a child has been repeatedly over-whelmed with intense anxiety due to abuse or neglect. As children with any of the insecure attachment patterns discussed earlier grow into toddlers and preschoolers, many anxiety-related symptoms may emerge. The good news is that attachment patterns can be shifted over time. The bad news is that this process usually does not occur without a great deal of intentionality.

Increasing Attunement and Enhancing Positive Discipline

Several play therapy treatment models assist families in becoming more attuned to each other while enhancing positive relationship dynamics. Theraplay, a practice model grounded in attachment theory, increases attun-ement between parents and children while strengthening the parent's abil-ity to provide contingent care along four dimensions (Jernberg & Booth, 2001; Martin, Snow, & Sullivan, 2008; Munns, 2009). The four dimen-sions are defined as Structure, Nurture, Engagement, and Challenge. Each is augmented through a series of playful dyadic activities that are purpose-fully chosen and supported by a facilitator. In one study, Martin et al. (2008) administered the Marschak interaction method and found that the parent's adeptness at providing the four dimensions correlated with a child's drive for exploration and a child's regulatory capacities.

Parent-child interaction therapy (PCIT), a behavioral play therapy model, also helps build attunement between parents and children while enhanc-ing positive relationship dynamics between the parent and child. Moreover, the parent learns and practices positive behavior management skills and consistent discipline procedures that shape children's prosocial behaviors (Hembree-Kigin & McNeil, 1995). Developed by Sheila Eyberg, PCIT was originally designed for treating oppositional children and their parents (Eyberg et al., 2001). Parents who have been physically abusive with their children can be trained, through PCIT, to respond in more effective and nurturing ways (Herschell & McNeil, 2007; Urquiza & McNeil, 1996). PCIT is also gaining empirical support as an effective treatment for maltreated children in foster care settings (Timmer et al., 2006). Although there is a wealth of empirical support for the application of PCIT to both oppositional and traumatized children, PCIT is also being studied as a useful intervention for reducing separation anxiety with young children (Choate, Pincus, Eyberg, & Barlow, 2005; Pincus, Eyberg, & Choate, 2005).

Other dyadic models for treatment include child-parent relationship therapy (CPRT) (Bratton, Landreth, Kellam, & Blackard, 2006; Landreth & Bratton, 2006), a 10-week manualized filial therapy protocol; filial therapy (Guerney, 1964; Guerney, Guerney, & Andronico, 1999; VanFleet, Ryan, & Smith, 2005); and child-parent psychotherapy (Lieberman, Van Horn, & Ippen, 2005, 2006).

Another valuable model that is effective in increasing parental attunement, The Circle of Security Project, works almost exclusively with the parent, providing psychoeducation related to attachment concepts and then working psychotherapeutically with the parent in order to help the parent become more contingently responsive to the child's cues (Cooper, Hoffman, Powell, & Marvin, 2005; Hoffman, Marvin, Cooper, & Powell, 2006; Marvin, Cooper, Hoffman, & Powell, 2002; Powell, Cooper, Hoffman, & Marvin, 2007). One particularly useful exercise within the protocol illustrates a concept that they have termed "shark music." The parent is first shown a video of a beautiful path leading down to a picturesque view of the ocean. The music in the background is relaxing and the imaginary journey is a pleasant one. The parent is then shown a second video in which the images are exactly the same, but the music has been changed to evoke feelings of threat and impending danger. The second clip is meant to conceptualize the upsetting feelings that can swamp parents and keep them from contingently responding to their children. The images are identical. The situations that the parents find themselves in are identical. However, our internal response colors our approach to the situation. As parents develop a growing awareness of which of their child's cues elicit their own shark music, they can acknowledge their internal response while choosing to remain fully present to meet the child's need.

Driving the CAR

It has been established that parents are critically important in helping children regulate their affectual states. Yet often it is the manifestations of the children's dysregulation that can spike parents' own anxiety reactions, rendering them unable to respond effectively as soothing agents. Parents, in an attempt to avoid the anxious child's aversive behavior, may attempt to *cajole* the child into calming down, *argue* the child out of his anxiety, or *rescue* the child from the anxiety-producing stimuli. I teach parents the acronym CAR, created from these parenting responses:

> C = cajole
> A = argue
> R = rescue

I describe the anxious child as being headed down the road toward a meltdown. The parent can either drive the CAR or choose a strategy counter to cajoling, arguing, or rescuing. The parent and I become detectives, investigating which pattern of responding the parent uses most frequently. As awareness of their typical reactions dawn, parents can make conscious choices to respond differently to their children. Through attuned responding to children's distress, parents become psychobiological regulators of their children's developing socioemotional selves. The parent's response to a child's anxiety can make a significant impact on the prognosis for an anxious child. Preschoolers, particularly, may withdraw from activities, begin to whine and cling to the parent, or throw severe tantrums. All these behaviors can be frustrating to parents. Parents may handle the child's behavior by becoming escalated themselves, when what the child really needs is the antithesis of this. What the child really needs is to be soothed.

The SOOTHE Strategies

Through a grant from the Kennedy Center at Vanderbilt University, Linda Ashford, Patti van Eys, and I have developed a protocol for treating foster and adoptive families. The protocol combines several components of attachment-based intervention. The model, nurturing engagement for attachment repair (NEAR), uses component modules that include psychoeducation, behavioral training, relationship enhancement, and dyadic nurturing intervention as mechanisms for change. Session-to-session video feedback for parents and live coaching of skill sets enhance the treatment approach. As part of this protocol, we have designed a set of strategies that help parents respond to the anxiety symptoms of their maltreated or neglected children in ways that are often counterintuitive. The acronym SOOTHE helps parents to remember this skill set:

S = soft tone of voice, soft tone of face
O = organize the child's experience
O = offer choices or a way out
T = touch or physical proximity
H = hear what the child is needing
E = end and let go

The S in SOOTHE stands for "soft tone of voice." Children often handle their anxiety by digging in their heels and becoming intractable. Parents may respond to a child's oppositional behavior by becoming louder or more intense in their own vocalizations. However, the elevation of the parent's voice will only feed the escalation of the child's tantrum. When teaching this to parents, I often add "soft tone of face" to this description. What has been postulated about mirror neurons in the brain can potentially inform our understanding of how a parent's affectual communication is imitated by anxious children (Arden & Linford, 2009; Gallese, Keysers, & Rizzolatti, 2004; Rizzolatti, Fadiga, & Gallese, 2001). Mirror neurons, first discovered in macaque monkeys and later found in the frontal lobes of apes and humans, bypass conceptual reasoning and allow us to "directly understand the meaning of the actions and emotions of others by internally replicating them without any explicit reflective mediation" (Gallese, Keysers, & Rizzolatti, 2004, p. 396). If the parent becomes dysregulated, the child is likely to directly experience a similar intensity of dysregulation on a cellular level. If, instead, the parent deliberately speaks in a soft, nurturing (or at least neutral) tone of voice, the child can latch onto this and begin to de-escalate.

Another way of explaining this to parents is to help them see themselves as anchors. If the child tries to take control by saying "No!" as a way of handling his anxiety, the parent may be tempted to respond with her own escalation, something like, "Yes you will, young man!" This response can be equated with throwing the anchor into the boat and sinking the ship entirely. If parents can choose to lower their voices, use a soothing tone, and remain calm, they will be anchoring the child's experience beneath the current level of escalation. In a sense, parents can pull their children up to higher levels of reactivity or invite them to de-escalate through a strategy as simple as using a soft tone of voice. I also talk to parents about having a "soft tone of face." We have already discussed the variety of signals that a child may have stored in her implicit memory systems that can trigger a fight, flight, or freeze response. For some children, the immediate danger associated with a clenched jaw or pinched brow is enough to spike a child's anxiety and spark a meltdown (Pollak, Cicchetti, Klorman, & Brumaghim, 1997; Pollak & Sinha, 2002; Pollak & Tolley-Schell, 2003). Remaining neutral in our own tone, gesture, and affect gives the child the best opportunity for de-escalation.

The first O in SOOTHE stands for "Organize." The traumatized child often has difficulty sequencing information. Anxious children respond poorly to a lack of structure. Not knowing what is expected can heighten anxiety. Therefore, it is very important that the parents of traumatized children develop consistent schedules and soothing routines. Play therapists can be very useful in this regard. One activity that can help with the creation or reinforcement of a schedule is the "domino rally." Dominoes are a wonderful tool for helping families build sequential narratives of everything from trauma histories to schedules and routines. When administering the intervention, I give the family a set of dominoes in the shape of people and ask the child to stand them up one by one as the parent recites the order of events that occur in an average day. Diagnostically, this activity can help the clinician discern if the family is under- or overscheduled and to modify the schedule as needed.

Another fun way to help families concretize their schedules is to give them a blank copy of a winding board game and have them work together to fill in the routines of a given morning, afternoon, or evening (Figure 6.1).

The parents fill in the spaces one by one with the steps of the child's routine, starting at wakeup and ending at bedtime. Families can take the finished game home and "play" it again and again. There may be parts of the routine that the child has not yet learned, and repeating the succession of events through game play can provide sequential soothing for the child.

"Organize" also refers to the need to provide anxious children with help at transition times. Anxious children don't respond well to change. It can help tremendously to let them know in advance if something in their normal

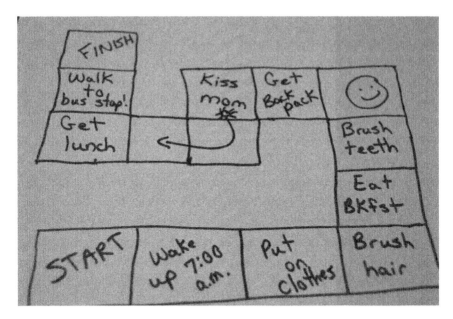

Figure 6.1   Board Game Rehearsal of Morning Routine

routine will be different on a given day. When a child's play is going to be interrupted to go to the grocery store, it can be very helpful to give the child a warning. The parent can say, "You have 5 more minutes to play, and then we are going to the store." A 2-minute warning might also be helpful.

When a traumatized child is beginning a new activity like playing soccer for the first time, advanced preparation is invaluable. Clinicians, parents, and children can brainstorm potential trouble spots together. An exercise called "brainstorm the blow-ups" is a fun way to help families be proactive in scanning the environment for anything that may spike the child's posttraumatic anxiety. I introduce a miniature volcano to the family and talk with them about times that the child may have erupted in defiance or had a meltdown because of a specific anxiety-provoking situation. I write down some situations that I believe might provoke an anxiety response in the child and put them in the volcano. One might read, "Callie will be playing on a soccer team for the first time." Each family member takes a turn pulling one out of the volcano and brainstorming specific parenting strategies that could help to relieve anxiety. Example strategies might include the following: Introduce the child to the coach before the first practice. Allow the child to go see the soccer field where she will play. Kick the ball around with mom or dad on the soccer field. Watch a movie or read a book about soccer.

The second O in SOOTHE stands for Offer. This O encompasses two concepts: offering a limited number of choices and offering a way out of a potentially debilitating anxiety reaction. Traumatized children often need a narrower range of choices in order to manage the anxiety that can arise during a decision-making process. Taking a posttraumatic child who struggles with dysregulation to the toy store and cheerfully inviting him to "pick one" might result in a total meltdown before the family has left the store.

I recently spoke with an adoptive mom who was bewildered by her newly adopted son's repeated meltdowns. I encouraged her to track the meltdowns for a couple of weeks. As we reviewed her log, it became clear that the majority of meltdowns happened in large public places that provided too many choices and too much stimulation. She relayed an incident from the week before in which she had taken her son to Wal-Mart. As he was trying to pick one kind of candy to take home, he became so dysregulated that he crawled up on a shelf, curled into a ball, and cried hysterically. The overstimulation of the environment combined with the seemingly limitless choices triggered an unmanageable anxiety response. This kind of child can be soothed by intentionally limiting the number of choices offered.

Conversely, some traumatized children compensate for their anxiety by trying to be in control of every decision. These children may have increased physiological arousal when told exactly what they have to do. This kind of child benefits from having the parent offer choices with parameters. The child who needs to drink some juice can be offered apple juice or orange juice and gets to have some control in the decision while still staying within the boundaries set by the parent.

Parents can also offer a way out if a child seems to have dug himself into an anxiety-induced hole. The following is an illustration of a mother offering a way out for her anxious child. Ryan and his mother were halfway through a dyadic assessment when Ryan's anxiety spiked. Mom picked up the card that reads, "Adult and child put lotion on each other." Mom got out two bottles of lotion and gave one to the child. She then said, "I'm going put lotion on you, and you're going to put some on me." Ryan immediately said, "No," in a petulant tone of voice and gave mom a sulky look. Mom asked, "Where would you like the lotion, on your arms or hands?" Ryan pointed to his hair. Mom said, "Well, we can't really put lotion on your hair, so how about your arms?" Ryan said, "No!" more angrily and crossed his arms over his chest. Mom accurately interpreted his response as being driven by anxiety, as opposed to sheer stubborness. Mom said, "You know, I forgot that you don't like lotion. Look, I'm rubbing it all into my arms so that there's no more on my hands. How about I just rub your back instead?" Mom then put out her hand to touch Ryan's back. He looked at her dubiously for a moment and then moved closer, turned around, and offered his back. After mom had rubbed his back for a couple of minutes, he announced, "Now I'll put lotion on you!" This mother offered her anxious child a way out of the anxiety-provoking situation while still accomplishing the task of engaging in a nurturing activity together.

The *T* in SOOTHE is meant to reaffirm the mitigating effect that a simple touch or increased physical proximity can have on anxious children. At the end of the day, for example, when a child is overwrought and exhausted, some intentional cuddling can reap a more soothing effect than words alone.

The *H* stands for "Hear" and refers to the parent's ongoing job of trying to discern what the child is in need of when she engages in anxiety-driven defiance. A child is given the direction to put on her shoes. She refuses. Most parents interpret the refusal as will-based defiance. It is possible, however, that the child may be just learning how to tie her shoes and is worried about doing it correctly and therefore wants to avoid shame or embarrassment that might accompany a failure to tie her shoes properly. If the parent *Hears* the underlying need correctly, the original command can be modified. The parent could say, "Please go get your shoes and I will help you put them on." This modified command still requires accountability but alleviates the underlying insecurity that the child is trying to avoid.

Lastly, the *E* stands for "End and let go." There are two points associated with this phrase. The first concept refers to helping the child completely de-escalate before returning to the normal activities of life. The importance of this return to baseline became clear to me in my early work at a therapeutic preschool. The program served 3- to 5-year-olds with severe emotional disturbances. They often became dysregulated and lost control of their bodies in ways that required physical restraint. On a number of occasions a child was held until his body was relatively calm and, although he may still have been grumbling, he was reintegrated into his classroom setting. What we quickly found was that the children who were not completely de-escalated would have another violent episode within the hour. Continuing to soothe and destimulate the child until he had returned to baseline was much more effective. After being fully de-escalated, clients were much more likely to tap their inner resources when the next challenging moment occurred.

The second aspect of "End and let go" has to do with the parents' reaction to a child's meltdown. Once we acknowledge that children with anxiety suffer from neurophysiological dysregulation, it becomes possible to understand how a child's meltdown may actually serve a regulatory function. Some children describe anxiety as a sense of pressure building inside their bodies and may experience relief from this pressure after an explosive episode. Parents, on the other hand, may continue to feel shell-shocked and exhausted for hours after a tantrum has occurred. The parent may understandably need some recovery time and may have difficulty being immediately responsive to the child who has just had a meltdown.

Unfortunately for the parent, it is directly after the meltdown that a child may feel most vulnerable and even ashamed of his irrational behavior. In the aftermath of the storm, reconnecting with the parent provides both immediate soothing to the child and brings a degree of repair to the parent/child relationship. Dan Siegel (2003) talks about the toxic ruptures that can occur between parents and children when upset occurs in both parties but is never processed. Therefore, while acknowledging the parents' right to their own anger and exhaustion, we ask them to let go of it and remain contingently responsive to the child after a meltdown has occurred.

Parents as Detectives

Parents are often cast in the role of detective as they are identifying both triggers for their children's trauma responses and the most helpful parenting strategies to reduce a child's distress. Parents, because of their round-the-clock involvement with their children, are in the best position to investigate trauma triggers and track escalation patterns. Once parents have received psychoeducation around how trauma affects the brain and expanded their understanding about the range of trauma triggers that a child might develop, they can become very valuable assets in mapping the idiosyncratic trauma responses of the child in their care.

Taking Baseline Data

Parents have opportunities to see their child in a whole range of settings. A parent experiences a child's reactions to wakeup rituals and the often pressured morning routines that are aimed at getting everyone ready for the day and out the door. A parent sees a child's coping strategies in relation to homework assignments, chores, bathing, grooming, eating, sleeping, and exposures to new people and new places. A parent is in a unique position to take baseline data and make observations that help map a child's trauma-related triggers. Parents can be taught a simple way of documenting a child's behaviors, antecedent events and the consequences, positive or negative, that result from the behavior. In this way parents become investigators of the unique ways in which trauma symptoms manifest in their children.

I talked at length about the amygdala alarm in the chapter on definitions and symptoms. I described one way of explaining trauma reactions to parents and children by using a toy soldier and describing a scenario in which the soldier develops a habituated response to danger in Iraq. This response is replayed automatically when he encounters similar stimuli back in the relative safety of his hometown. An exercise titled "maraca madness" helps parents to grasp the applications of these new neurophysiological under-standings to their day-to-day parenting practices.

Maraca Madness

I begin by giving the parent a set of maracas. I invite the parent to hold the maracas in her lap and gently shake them while I explain to her why I like bananas. When I am finished with my explanation, I have the par-ent repeat back some of the salient details. Then I invite the parent to hold the maracas close to her ears and shake them much harder than she did the first time while I explain why I like apples. When I am finished with this explanation, I have the parent repeat any salient details that she was able to hear. Most parents are unable to hear anything when the maracas are sounding loudly in their ears. I then compare this maraca madness with the amygdala alarm as it is triggered in the brain of a traumatized child. The parent quickly understands how their normal tendency to reason with an upset child may not be effective, as the speech may not get through the red haze of a tripped alarm system. Parents often need the help of an objective person, someone outside the family who is removed from the daily drama of the frequent upsets, to help them make connections between unintended but potentially triggering parental actions and a child's resulting tantrum. This bridge-building role can be seen in the following example. I recently did an initial intake with a couple who had only just been given the task of raising their estranged 8-year-old granddaughter, Allie. Allie's biological mother has had a drug problem for the whole of Allie's life and sent her to live with her paternal grandmother when she was 3. This grandmother was the sole caregiver for Allie for several years. Six months before Allie's first appointment, the grandmother became sick. She called her ex-husband, Allie's grandfather, who had since remarried, and asked if he could take over Allie's care. Due to some negative dynamics in the maternal grandmother and grandfather's divorce, the maternal grandfather had had almost no contact with Allie up until she came to live with him.

In the course of the first couple of months that Allie lived with her new grandparents, she was often uncontrollable. She would kick, fight, and scream over simple commands and would have unexplained panic attacks, during which she would climb under the table and shake and rock herself. The wide range of bewildering behaviors that Allie was exhibiting caused the grandparents to seek help. During the initial intake, I asked for some examples of what her stepgrandmother termed her "bizarre" behaviors. The grandmother was able to give me an example from that very morning, saying, "She did it again just this morning. I was fixing her some toast for breakfast. The toast popped up and she started to reach for it. I saw that she was going to touch the part that was still hot and burn herself, so I reached across and grabbed her arm to keep her from getting hurt. Well, you'd think I'd killed her. She screamed and cried and fell into a heap on the floor, screaming that she wanted to get it herself. She had a fit for 20 minutes over that toast."

Grandmother seemed clearly frustrated by the child's overblown reaction to her protective parenting response. Later in our conversation, both grandparents mentioned recent disclosures that Allie had made to them about being locked in a dark room by her grandmother and smacked across the face whenever she disobeyed. During our psychoeducation session, I came back to the example of Allie's meltdown as she was reaching for the toast. As I explained the neurobiology of trauma to the grandparents, I wondered out loud if she could have misperceived grandma's quick movement to grab her arm as the same kind of quick movement that used to happen when she was slapped.

Understanding dawned in the eyes of the grandmother. She became very excited about this new connection and was able to spontaneously generate a couple of other examples of how a quick movement on her part may have signaled danger for Allie. Without new conceptual understandings, parents are often left feeling like their children are simply intractable. Proper psychoeducation can engender paradigmatic shifts in the parents that generate deeper wells of compassion and re-energize them to approach the parenting process from different angles.

Is He in His Choosing Mind?

Once parents understand this piece of information, they are better equipped to discriminate between will-based noncompliance (which is often best handled through positive behavior management techniques) and a child's trauma-related decompensation. When I am working with foster or adoptive parents, I often frame the main task of parenting a traumatized child as constantly discerning when the child is in his choosing mind and when he is not. These caregivers are faced with the difficult job of learning the cues of their older charges in much the same way that a first-time parent must learn the cries of her baby. An attuned mother learns to discern the difference between the baby's hunger cry, the baby's cry of discomfort (perhaps needing to be changed or warmed), and the baby's cry to be held and stimulated.

I give an example from my own parenting to demonstrate the difference between a child who is in her choosing mind and one who is not. In the first scenario, Madison, my 3-year-old, has woken up from a good night's sleep, had her breakfast, and spent some playtime with me. When I give her the command to put on her clothes, she refuses. Because all her needs have been met and she is fresh from sleep, I am likely to interpret this "no" as will-based noncompliance. She is in her choosing mind, so I use a discipline approach that offers one choice for obedience and a not-so-fun choice for disobedience. She quickly complies and we return to playtime.

In the second scenario, it is 9 o'clock at night, past the children's bedtime, and we are coming home after a late night out. Madison hasn't eaten and she'd fallen asleep briefly in the car. When we get up to her room, I give her a gentle command to put on her pajamas and she cries, "Noooo." She is no longer in her choosing mind. She has come to the end of her internal resources for the day and is reliant on me to soothe and structure the end of the evening. If I offer the two choices at this point, I am setting her up for failure, as she no longer has the internal resources to make the best choice. Instead, I use a soft tone of voice, help her get her pajamas on, and tuck her in. The two avenues—a behavioral approach and a SOOTHE-based approach—are available to the fully trained parent. The ongoing work and discussion revolves around when and how to apply each skill set.

The question of whether or not the child is in his choosing mind at the moment of decision can dramatically impact a parent's choice of approach.

Parents as Limit-Setters

Many traumatized children demonstrate disruptive behaviors that challenge their caregivers. When children manifest early conduct problems, parent training is seen as the most promising approach to treatment (Eyberg, 1992; Kazdin, 1993). PCIT is an evidence-based treatment that changes dysfunctional parent-child interactions through didactic teaching and direct coaching in play-based and task-oriented situations. Families who completed PCIT showed significant positive changes 10 to 30 months following treatment (Boggs et al., 2004). PCIT was pioneered by Sheila Eyberg (Bell & Eyberg, 2002) and originally created for use with fairly high-functioning families with oppositional children. However, children who have been neglected, maltreated, or otherwise traumatized often respond with symptoms of externalizing behavior. For this reason, Anthony Urquiza and his colleagues at the University of California at Davis have modified PCIT and applied the model to traumatized children and their families. One of their most interesting areas of work is with maltreating parent-child dyads (Timmer, Urquiza & McBell, 2006; Timmer, Urquiza, Zebell, & McGrath, 2005; Urquiza & McNeil, 1996).

The program consists of two treatment phases, child-directed intervention (CDI) and parent-directed intervention (PDI). CDI is designed to enhance positive relationship dynamics between parents and their children. During the first phase of treatment, parents are taught positive attunement skills and practice these skills while playing with their children. Parents participate in live coaching during sessions. Interactions to be avoided during CDI include questioning, commanding, and criticizing. Interactions that are promoted and practiced during CDI include praising the child's positive behavior, reflecting appropriate talk, imitating the child's play, describing the child's positive play behaviors, and remaining enthusiastic throughout the play session. In addition to the live coaching during sessions, parents are assigned daily homework. The homework, labeled "special play time," is composed of 5 minutes of playtime each day. This allows the child a daily dose of behavioral play therapy while giving the parent daily practice in the new positive interaction skills.

Empirical evidence supports a decrease in externalizing behavior problems upon completion of CDI. Once the parents have mastered the skill set outlined in CDI, they receive didactic training in giving developmentally appropriate instructions and then practice these skills through live coaching. The next component of the program involves teaching the actual discipline procedure. Parents are trained in a step-by-step model for discipline that involves a two-choices statement, a time out as consequence, a system for releasing the child from time out in order to gain compliance with the original command given, and, in some versions of the program, a sticker chart that acts as another layer of consequence if the child is unable to successfully complete a time out.

Several dimensions of this program make it a particularly effective tool in dealing with the oppositional behaviors that often manifest in traumatized families. One very useful aspect of the program is its clear, sequential hierarchy for skill acquisition and rehearsal. Traumatized children and their families have often lived in highly chaotic environments before seeking treatment. The parenting approach at intake may be inconsistent, punitive, and highly reactive. Parents who complete treatment leave with a coherent, consistent approach to discipline. The traumatized child thrives in an environment with clear boundaries and consistent routines. A child's ability to sequence events is often put at risk through exposure to a trauma. Repetition and sequential structuring of information are both processes that are comforting and reparative for traumatized individuals. PCIT, being both sequential and repetitious, is a model that nicely fits the needs of these families.

Another valuable aspect of PCIT is its role in decreasing the heightened emotional arousal and explosive outbursts that can accompany a parental response to a child who is entrenched in negative behavior. Parents who are dealing with increased levels of stress themselves may have shortened tempers and may more easily revert to discipline tactics that attempt to dominate or control the child. Therefore, the clearly outlined step-by-step discipline procedures practiced in the PDI provide parents with a lifeline. Even the most well-intentioned parents begin to get frustrated when they have given their child a command five to ten times and it has not been completed. Typically as a parent gives a command repeatedly his tone hardens and his volume increases. PCIT teaches parents a three-step discipline model that takes out much of the wiggle room that children use to avoid compliance. The speed of consequence delivery decreases the amount of negative emotion that parents generate during discipline. In fact, many parents report that the discipline procedure in PCIT and the speed and focus with which it is administered allows them to maintain an emotional distance during the administration of consequences that they were unable to maintain before receiving treatment.

PCIT provides a play-based method for teaching necessary behavior management skills to the parents of children who have been traumatized. Additional skill sets are also necessary, and for this reason I pair PCIT training with trauma-informed psychoeducation for parents. In addition, I train parents in the SOOTHE strategies delineated earlier.

Parents as Containers

I have repeatedly referred to the therapist as being a container for the child. However, in most treatment settings the therapist is only present for 1 to 2 hours a week. The child may be generating trauma content that needs containment in settings where the parent is the primary container. It is likely that as trauma treatment progresses, a child will begin to have spontaneous memories or pieces of trauma narrative emerge that may have been suppressed earlier. Art journals and writing journals are useful tools for containment that can be used in the child's home and school environment as memories, thoughts, feelings, and impressions surface. However, nothing takes the place of having one's experience validated and held by a significant other. Therefore, if we can equip parents to be containers for their children, we can ensure a continuation of therapeutic benefit at home.

Filial Therapy

One approach to treatment that I find especially helpful in equipping parents to be containers for their children is filial therapy. Filial therapy, an approach crafted by Louise Guerney (Guerney, 1964; Guerney, Guerney, & Andronico, 1999; VanFleet, Ryan, & Smith, 2005), is an outgrowth of child-centered play therapy (Landreth, 1991) and has recently been structured into a 10-week treatment protocol (Bratton, Landreth, Kellam, & Blackard, 2006; Landreth & Bratton, 2006). Parents are taught how to engage in accurate reflection of children's behaviors and feeling states, how to set limits in the play when necessary, how to engage in role play with their child, and how to observe the thematic content that a child may communicate through his play over time.

I used this model extensively when I worked in the therapeutic preschool, particularly when a parent and child were working through reunification issues after an extended absence. I find filial therapy to be particularly help-ful in reunification cases, because the atmosphere created during the session allows for children to narrate for their parents and communicate to their parents the salient details of events that may have occurred in the life of the child while the parent was not present. In other words, filial therapy can be used as a model that helps the parent to catch up on the missed experiences of a child who has been in the care of another.

I first met 4-year-old Keyondra while I was working in the Therapeutic Preschool Program at our local community mental health center. She was liv-ing with her grandmother and came to be in the preschool after she was dis-missed from her regular daycare for intensely aggressive behavior. I did not meet Frankie, Keyondra's mom, for the first 6 months that her daughter attended the preschool. Mom was incarcerated for the first 3 months and completing a drug rehab program for the remainder of that time. After mom successfully com-pleted her rehabilitation program, she petitioned the court to regain custody of her daughter. We began a filial therapy process as part of the reunification plan. The first couple of joint sessions went well. Frankie and Keyondra were getting used to each other again and Frankie was becoming skilled in appropriately responding to her daughter's play behaviors. Frankie and I spent time together after each session discussing the play themes in which the child had engaged. The third session started off fairly innocuously. The transcript of the middle of that session follows.

Keyondra picks up a baby doll.

Frankie: You chose that baby to play with.

Keyondra starts to undress the baby doll.

Frankie: You're taking off the baby doll's clothes.
Keyondra: She's naked.
Frankie: Yep. She doesn't have any clothes on now.

Keyondra returns to the shelves to get the doctor's kit.

Frankie: Now you've got the doctor's stuff.
Keyondra: I need to find the shot.

Frankie: You're looking hard for the needle.

Keyondra: Here it is!

Frankie: You found it!

Keyondra begins to push the syringe into the vagina of the baby doll. Mom falters momentarily and then, clearly disturbed but doing her best to respond contingently to her daughter, continues to narrate what she is observing.

Frankie: You're putting the shot in the baby's private parts.

Keyondra: Yeah! It hurts. It hurts! You go over there, momma.

Frankie: You want me to walk over there?

Keyondra: Yeah—you stand against that wall.

Frankie (moving over to the wall): OK. I'm standing where you told me to.

Keyondra focuses her energy on the doll again. She continues to stab the syringe in and out of the baby's private parts:

Keyondra: It hurts. The baby doesn't like it.

Frankie has tears in her eyes but continues reflect her daughter's messages.

Frankie: The baby doesn't like how that feels.

Keyondra: Now she's gonna pee on you.

Frankie: You're pretending that she's peeing on me?

Keyondra (giggling wildly): Yeah—she's peeing on you. All the way over there! She's peeing on you! Now you're all wet!

Frankie: You got me all wet!

Keyondra moves to another toy and this play sequence ends. When mom and I sat down privately for our debriefing, I allowed her to do what she had not done with her child. I sat with her while she cried. Frankie shed many tears as she stated that she was sure something bad had happened to her baby while she was in rehab. She also feared an even worse possibility, that one of her drug buddies had sexually abused her little girl while she was high or passed out.

I too had the impression that Keyondra was using the vehicle of play to communicate some trauma content to her mother, but I was unwilling to jump to conclusions. We decided to call the grandmother and describe the play pattern that we had seen and see if this sparked any memories for the grandmother. As soon as we explained the details of the child's play, the grandmother said, "Ohhh . . . it sounds like she was showing you her trip to the doctor. A few months ago, she got a bladder infection and the nurse needed a urine sample, but Keyondra refused to pee in the cup. They ended up holding her down to catheterize her so they could get the sample that they needed."

According to the grandmother, Keyondra screamed and cried through the whole procedure and had difficulty sleeping for a couple of nights following the procedure. Because Keyondra has seemed to recover quickly, grandmother had not thought to communicate the event to mom. Obviously, Keyondra had been significantly impacted by her catheterization and needed to show mom what had happened to her in mom's absence.

Although mom was relieved that the play did not necessarily indicate a sexual abuse history, she was touched by her daughter's need to share this experience with her. Keyondra may have also been expressing anger toward the mom for not being present during the procedure by having the baby doll pee on her across the room. This is just one case example of how a child may use the playroom to invite the parent into a terrifying experience. A parent who is healthy enough to communicate in the playroom, "I see what you are showing me" in a calm, accepting way goes a long way toward building a shared narrative history with the child. This containment can be offered in a number of ways, but one of the most effective mantras designed to help parents become containers is the phrase "I am bigger, stronger, wiser, and kind." This phrase, coined by the Circle of Security Project (Cooper, Hoffman, Powell, & Marvin, 2005; Hoffman, Marvin, Cooper, & Powell, 2006; Marvin, Cooper, Hoffman, & Powell, 2002; Powell, Cooper, Marvin, Hoffman, 2007), helps parents remain focused on attitudes and behaviors that will position them as safe places for their children.

Assessing a Parent's Readiness to Contain a Child's Trauma Content

The way in which parents are incorporated into treatment must be determined on a case-by-case basis. Parents vary widely in their readiness to function as a receptacle of the child's trauma content. Treating clinicians must be actively involved in ongoing assessment of a parent's ability to function as a container for her child. Moreover, the clinician must delicately finesse the timing of dyadic sessions in which trauma content might arise. It is often helpful for the child and parent to have separate psychoeducation sessions so that information can be tailored for developmentally appropriate content. As treatment progresses, there may be other treatment goals that are most effectively pursued in individual sessions with the child or the parent.

One obvious application of this caution should be to the child's sharing of the trauma narrative with the parent. In most cases, it benefits the family for the child's narrative of the trauma to be heard by the parent and integrated into the overarching family narrative. In certain cases it can benefit a parent and child to flush out the details of a traumatic event together, to cocreate the story. In other cases, a parent's perceptions of the trauma may diverge so widely from the child's experience that the adult's verbalization of her own perceptions might feel to the child like a negation of his own truth. In cases like these, the parent may need psychoeducation about how the same traumatic event may be perceived differently by different people.

Clinicians often ask me how to know when and if a parent is ready to hear the trauma content a child has disclosed in treatment. A parent who has been able to utilize adaptive coping strategies in her own recovery will be a more available container for the child than one who is using maladaptive coping strategies, such as excessive drinking or drug use. Parents who have made sense of their own interpersonal histories, either through the help of a significant other, personal reflection, or the help of a counselor, are more available to be containers for their children than parents who have no coherence in their own narratives. This dynamic often manifests itself in cases in which the child has been referred for sexual abuse treatment and it becomes clear that the parent of that child is also a survivor of child sexual abuse. In most cases, it is safest to introduce a child's trauma narrative content to the parent in an individual session with that parent. In this way, the therapist is fully available to provide any containment necessary to process the parent's reactions while protecting the child from a sense of being overwhelmed by the parent's response.

One such dynamic presents itself when a parent is mired in her own guilt or pain and is easily flooded by the child's pain. A case example will help illustrate this point. I recently saw a 7-year-old girl named Molly. She was referred for inappropriate sexual touching with a neighbor boy who was 2 years her junior. During the initial interview, the mother seemed shamed and bewildered by her daughter's behavior. As we progressed through the intake questions, I asked if there was any previous history of inappropriate sexual behavior or sexual abuse allegations within the family. She looked at me worriedly and sighed. Then she explained that when Molly was 5 years old she had been inappropriately touched by a neighbor boy who was 2 years her senior. This older boy was being fostered by a neighbor and the neighborhood solution to the problem was to place the boy in a different foster home. Molly had no further interaction with the boy.

Mom was so distressed and embarrassed by the event that she did not talk about it with her daughter and did not pursue any counseling for her daughter at that point. As mom articulated her passivity in session, she began to face her inaction and its potential consequences and she burst into hysterical tears. I comforted her and framed treatment in terms of what we could do to move forward from here. Molly's natural reticence to talk about her traumatic experience combined with mom's impotent silence made the sexually inappropriate activity a taboo subject in their home.

When Molly came to therapy, we quickly established a sense of safety and security in the play space. She appeared eager to talk about what had happened to her 2 years ago, while less eager to talk about her own recent inappropriate behavior. Within the first few sessions, Molly used the dollhouse to act out what had happened to her. She talked about the uncomfortable touches and how she kept trying to figure out how to get away. She talked about how she said no and he didn't stop. After she described the events, I asked how old she had been at the time. When she told me, I wrote the number "five" on the dry erase board. Then I asked her how old her molester had been. When she told me, I wrote "seven" on the dry erase board. Later in the session I asked her how old she was now, and when she told me I wrote "seven" on the board. Then I asked how old the little boy was whom she had touched. When she listed the boy's age as 5 years old, I wrote this number on the board. She glanced over from running her fingers through the sand and froze. Her eyes grew large and she said, "Hey . . . it's the same!" When I asked her to elaborate, she said, "Well—I was 5 when that 7-year-old boy hurt me and now that I'm 7, I hurt a 5-year-old. It's like a pattern!"

This insight relieved her tremendously and helped counter the deep-rooted fear that she carried that she was just a bad, twisted kid. She began to see how her current behavior was related to a previous violation and much of her shame lifted. We moved forward with an integration of trauma-focused play therapy, cognitive-behavioral play therapy, and expressive arts activities.

We used eye movement desensitization and reprocessing (EMDR) adjunctively to process the negative images and sensations of the molestation.

Molly was very verbal and very creative. She constructed a trauma narrative that integrated a verbal story with drawings and sand tray images. During this time, I was also meeting separately with mom. Because of mom's emotional fragility, I gave her intentionally titrated exposures to the child's trauma content before we considered having the child share content directly with mom. As predicted, mom reacted strongly to any detail that was shared. She wept a lot and frequently became overwhelmed with guilt at the thought that her previous inaction had caused the current situation. I was able to become the container for mom's thoughts and emotions. I was able to nurture her while providing education and reassuring her that the power and tenor of her current support could help provide healing for the child.

After the mother had had several exposures to the child's trauma content via the therapist and the bulk of her emotional discharge had been contained and diluted, she was ready to receive teaching about how to respond to the child in a joint session in which the trauma content would be shared. It was fascinating to me that Molly seemed to share an understanding of mom's limitations as a container early in treatment. What follows is an excerpt from one of Molly's early sessions. She asked if she could make a story in the sand of what happened to her when she was 5. She also asked if I would videotape it. She liked to watch herself telling the story after she had recorded it on video (Figure 6.2).

Figure 6.2   Molly's Sand Tray Narrative of Her Sexual Molestation

Molly and her friend are represented by the two female figures with cakes. Behind them, she has chosen a locker to represent the closet in which the molestation occurred.

Molly kept up a running monologue as she created the tray. "It felt really bad. It felt like he was . . . it felt like he was . . . it felt kind of like . . . he was threatening us to do something. And I didn't like it at all. I . . . me and Maggie, we said, "No, that's . . . really yucky!" At this point she shrugged, stopped touching the miniatures, and just stared at the wall. "We just . . . we just didn't want to do it." Then she quickly glanced at me and asked, "Are you going to show this tape to my mom today?" When I asked for her thoughts about this, she shook her head vigorously and said, "Not today." Her thoughts mirrored mine exactly.

Asking a child to share trauma memories with a parent is asking the child to take a risk. The child is risking the parent's rejection, misunderstanding, or immobilization. This little girl may have wondered if mom would still love her after she heard the details. She may have wondered if her mother would ever see her the same way again. Her worst fear may have been that she would overwhelm mom to the point where mom could no longer care for her. Asking a child to take this risk with a parent who has not been adequately prepared to contain and appropriately reflect the trauma content can produce iatrogenic effects within the family system. The child may feel unsupported, rejected, or guilty. The parent may also feel unsupported, inadequate, or overwhelmed. Therefore, clinicians have an ethical obligation to prepare both the parent and the child for the appropriate levels of shared trauma content in the appropriate timing.

A parent can express appropriate sadness at the pain experienced by a child; in fact, this can be very therapeutic. It is when a parent becomes flooded and therefore emotionally unavailable to the child during the sharing that damage may be done. Caution was needed with Molly's mother. She needed multiple exposures to the trauma content, containment and discharge of her own emotions, and training in how to be contingently responsive to the child before we could have a conjoint session focused on the trauma narrative. Once these steps had been taken and Molly had rehearsed her narrative, the joint session provided a healing experience of containment and truth telling for both parent and child.

Allowing Room for Differences in Narrative

In other cases, parents have the internal resources and external supports that allow them to be containers for their children even while experiencing their own grief reactions. I am currently working with a family who has experienced the sudden, tragic, and accidental death of their youngest daughter. The parents, Mr. and Mrs. Smith, internationally adopted three girls after their own biological children were all teenagers. The oldest adopted daughter, Cindy, was 8 years old at the time of the accident. The two younger children, while not biological siblings, were both 5 at the time of the accident and had the kind of bond you might expect to see between twins. We will call them Mindy and Morgan.

One afternoon the girls were all playing on the swing set in the backyard. Morgan was asking her older sister Cindy to help her get onto the monkey bars. Cindy tried but was not able to lift her. At just that moment, Jack, the 17-year-old biological son, was pulling up in the driveway. Cindy suggested that Morgan get her older brother to put her on the monkey bars. Morgan ran toward the car and was hit. The injuries were fatal. The Smiths brought both Cindy and Mindy? to see me. Additionally, I saw Jack briefly for EMDR surrounding the trauma.

One of the most interesting dynamics that unfolded was that each of the three siblings involved in treatment had significantly different trauma narratives from each other. Jack, as we processed the memories of the accident using EMDR, was certain that he felt the bump of the wheels going over Morgan's body as he backed up. Cindy remembered seeing Morgan get hit by the car but did not remember anything related to the car backing over Morgan. The blood that was all over Morgan and that stained the driveway was a memory that all family members shared, except, it seemed, for Mindy. Mindy's original narrative was that she heard people screaming and ran, frightened, into the house and up the stairs to her room. In the following moments, while chaos was happening downstairs in the yard, Mindy was hiding in her bed.

The Smiths spent some time wrestling with the fact that everyone seemed to have a different story of what happened. As they began to understand the unique ways in which the brain stores trauma, and the protective processes of denial and sublimation, they began to see how each story met the needs of that particular child. The autopsy report showed no broken bones or crushed internal organs, as would have likely occurred if the car had actually run over the body. The fatality was caused by the blow to the head that she received on impact with the car or directly afterward as her head hit the ground.

The Smiths developed their own narrative of what happened and allowed space for each of their children to have their own differing stories, at least in the beginning. As Jack began to accept what had happened and had less need for self-incrimination, he was able to entertain the possibility that perhaps he did not back over his sister's body. Cindy, who had internalized the narrative that the accident was her fault because she told her sister to go get her brother, was eventually able to let go of the guilt she felt and de-emphasize that part of her narrative. Mindy had the most interesting evolution in her narrative. She spent a great deal of time establishing safety, soothing herself, and expressing intense grief over the loss of her "twin." She did not talk about the images of the trauma until much later in treatment than the other family members. Then, one day, as we were working on a memory book of Morgan, she shared new details from the day the accident happened.

She said, "I heard the screaming and I was running up to my room. My shoe got caught in the door. I was running so fast because I didn't want to get blood on my shoes." This was Mindy's first verbalization of any memory related to the blood that had pervaded the memories of the other family members. After she volunteered this new information, she was able to draw a picture that conveyed the visual image that she had kept locked inside since her sister's death (Figure 6.3).

Figure 6.3   Mindy's Image of Morgan

Everyone takes a different path to integration of their trauma experiences. We must help parents to tolerate the ambiguities that may exist as children are working it out. Parents sometimes need coaching to censor their own impressions of the trauma in order to more effectively listen to and reflect the child's impressions. When a child's perceived truth is worse than what actually happened, we will eventually have the parent correct to the truth. If the child's narrative meets his developmental needs and is not as detailed or terrible as what actually happened, we leave it alone.

Parents as Playmates

Traumatized children, particularly severely maltreated children, may have serious impairments in their ability to engage in spontaneous play behavior. The intentional time that a parent spends playing with a child can aid in relationship enhancement. Children explore, create, try on new roles, and experiment with new behaviors all through the vehicle of play. In some cases the child may harbor anger, conscious or unconscious, toward the parent. Sometimes this anger is best diffused or resolved through the vehicle of play. A case example illustrates this point.

Joanne sought out my services for her 4-year-old son Ben after a difficult divorce. Joanne reported that Ben had always been an easygoing child and described their relationship as close. She reported that since the divorce and the transitioning back and forth between mom and dad's homes, Ben had become aggressive and noncompliant with her. Joanne was bewildered and deflated when dad denied seeing any of these same behaviors at his house. I used a filial therapy model with this family. Joanne learned how to let Ben take the lead, reflect his verbalizations, track his play behaviors both verbally and physically, set limits appropriately, and engage in role play if needed. The majority of each session was dyadic time between Joanne and Ben, with time set aside at the end of each session for Joanne and I to process any thematic content that may have come up in the play session. Below are transcribed portions of the child's interactions with mom through play.

Ben pulls fence pieces out of a container.

Ben: This is what I needed.

Joanne: Yeah. That's just what you needed! You needed that fence.

Ben: Yeah. To keep out the bad guys.

Joanne: Oh. There are bad guys.

Ben: Yeah. Bad army and good army.

Joanne: There are bad and good army. How do you know the difference between the bad and the good army?

Ben: Because I just know.

Mom had received training on the importance of avoiding asking questions during play time. Questioning tends to put children on the defensive. In other cases, they just don't have an answer. In general, questions have more to do with the adult's need for information than with the child's need to give it. During our feedback time, mom laughed ruefully as we discussed his response to her question.

Joanne: You just know. OK.

Ben puts planes inside an 18-wheeler truck and places a fence around the truck.

Ben: So they'll be utech . . . putech . . .

Joanne: So they'll be protected.

Ben: Yeah! And the tank's gonna fire up! It's going to burn the bad guys up! You want me to burn the bad guys up?

Joanne: You think you should burn the bad guys up.

Ben: Yeah, because they're bad.

Clearly, Ben is wrestling with the themes of good and evil. As a 4-year-old he engages in dichotomous thinking. The divorce of his parents may be confusing in that he naturally assumes that because they fought and split up, one parent must be "good" and the other parent "bad." He continues to wrestle with this in the next session. However, in the next session he moves from the general investigation of good and bad through army figures to a staged battle between himself and his mother. Ben takes a sword and gives one to his mother.

Ben: You get the sharp sword.

Joanne: I get the sharp sword.

Ben: I'm the bad guy and you're the good guy. I'm the bad guy.

Joanne: You're the bad guy.

Ben: Yeah.

Joanne: And I'm the good guy.

Ben: Yeah.

Mom stands up and they face off for a sword fight. Ben thrusts his sword at her once and lunges but then falls down and pretends that she stabbed him with her sword.

Ben: You got me.

Mom: I got you.

Ben: You didn't stuck me through.

Joanne: But you got back up.

Ben: You didn't stuck me through.

Joanne: I didn't stick you through. I need to stick you through? Is that what the good guy does to the bad guy?

Mom plunges the sword at him playfully. Ben moves away from mom and turns his back on her, seemingly dysregulated by her play attack.

Ben turns around and whacks mom's sword with his once and then grabs her sword out of her hand, saying:

Ben: Gimme that!

Joanne: Oh, you got my sword.

Ben gives her his old sword.

Joanne: Now am I the bad guy because I have this sword?

Ben: Yeah! I'm the good guy!

Joanne: OK. You're the good guy.

Ben stabs mom with the sword and she falls to the ground, in the role of the wounded warrior. Ben is smiling and keeps the sword pressed to her as she falls. He falls with her and lands on top of her. As soon as she is playing dead, he becomes apologetic.

Ben: I'm sorry, I'm sorry.

He lays his head down on top of her, and mom chuckles and pats him on the back.

Joanne: Did you stick me through?
Ben: You was the good guy.
Joanne: I was the good guy?
Ben: Uh huh.

Mom pats his back some more.

Ben: And I was the good guy!
Joanne: You were the good guy too. We were both good guys.

Ben was able to experience, in fantasy, what it would feel like to be rid of his mother. Through this experience came a cognitive shift in which he no longer had to place her in the role of his antagonist. They could both be good. Ben's aggressive behavior decreased significantly after this session.

Conclusion

Parents play a number of critical roles in treatment. Parents are coregulators of affect and physiological arousal for their children. Parents are limit setters with their children when needed. Parents can serve as additional containers for their children's trauma content. Parents are the cocreators of coherent narrative with their children. Parents are often in the best position to gather baseline data related to a child's trauma triggers and are then in the best position to sensitively shape a child's environment in ways that will be most conducive to healing. Parents are also the first and the most enduring playmates for their children. Children can learn a host of important life lessons simply from playing with an attuned, contingently responsive caregiver.

When traumatized children and their parents enter treatment, there is often a level of distress within the system that has led to negative affect between the parent and child. When parents are being entirely honest, they will often admit at the beginning of treatment that while they still love their child, they don't really like their child at the moment. The enjoyment has gone out of the relationship. One of the primary powers of play in treating traumatized families is its ability to restore a sense of delight, delight in one another and shared delight in the family unit as a whole. A child's ability to soothe herself and a parent's ability to soothe a child are key dimensions in the work that must be done to help children heal from trauma. These dimensions are so important that they have been placed before most of the other components of the FSPT model. Although parent involvement will remain continuous throughout other aspects of treatment, such as building emotional literacy, constructing narrative, and addressing the thought life, the foundational roles of the parent are augmented early in treatment and provide the scaffolding upon which later accomplishments can be laid.

CHAPTER

7

——◆——

Emotional Literacy

"Sometimes my happy gets stuck."

T his statement made by Sally, a 9-year-old girl, as she was making a sculpture out of various colors of clay, each of which represented a different feeling state. Sally's father was beaten to death in an act of racial violence 3 months before this session. Sally explained the story of her father's death as follows. He had gone to "hang out" with a friend, who was just visiting for the weekend, in the friend's hotel room. Her dad and his friend were trying to watch a ballgame, but the people in the adjacent room were having a very loud party. Her dad eventually went and knocked on the neighbor's door and demanded that they keep it down. Five inebriated young men followed him back to his room and beat him to death.

Sally had been exhibiting extreme emotional lability, moving from intense anger and acting out to deep sadness and chronic crying spells. We decided together that it might help if we found some way to sort out her feelings. Sally was naturally drawn to the clay, and as she was exploring the colors and textures, I invited her to make something from the clay that represented her feelings. She took pieces of several different colors and flattened them into pancake-shaped circles and layered them. Sally had a dramatic flair and often asked me to videotape her while she explained her creations. She loved to watch herself on videotape after she had finished her performances. Per her pattern, Sally asked that her explanation of her clay creation be recorded. Following is the transcript of her monologue.

Sally: Now I'm making a putty thing that shows your fears, sadness and stuff. Later on in this video, we'll show you what Ms. Lovely Paris Goodyear-Brown made. The green is happy, the white you can't even see it very much but it's sad and the red—you know when there's kind of blood and sometimes you bleed when you are sad and sometimes it's kind of like attracting. Here is the mad. When you get hurt and stuff that's when you get mad and sad. And right here's the very happy. See it's going in to try to get the green out. It's because sometimes your happy gets stuck in and you don't know why . . . but this time I know why!

The manipulation of the clay helped her gain awareness of the fact that her happy was buried under anger and sadness about dad's death. Moreover, the anger and sadness were not well differentiated. After she had created her feelings ball and explained it, she began to carefully take it apart, separating each of the clay pieces into separate piles. The manipulation of the clay allowed her to begin physically differentiating her feeling states. Through this kinesthetically grounded work, she could more effectively explore and distinguish one feeling state from another.

Emotional literacy is a term that encompasses many aspects of a child's emotional life. A child's vocabulary of feelings, his ability to discriminate between individual feelings states and accurately communicate them, and his understanding of how his feelings influence and are influenced by other aspects of the self and situational factors are several components of emotional literacy. In addition to these, traumatized children often have difficulty with affect regulation (Cohen & Mannarino, 2006; Deblinger, 1996; Van der Kolk, 1996, Van der Kolk, McFarlane & Weisaeth, 1996, 2005). Each of these dimensions of emotional literacy may be impaired in traumatized children. Affect regulation strategies and a healthy understanding of emotions form a subset of the coping strategies that provide protection for clients as they are gradually exposed to the trauma content later in treatment.

In normal development, children enter the world with strong emotional responses but no words to express them. It is the job of parents and other caring adults to help children form associations between certain feeling states or behaviors and articulated feelings labels. A parent mitigates a child's understanding of feelings terminology in relation to the self. For example, when my son Sam was two years old, he would often try to build tall towers. When he couldn't make them look the way that he envisioned them in his mind, he would growl with frustration, clench his fists, and knock the rest of the tower down. I would mirror these behaviors back to him and say that he seemed frustrated. By the time Sam turned three he would ball up his fists and say "Me f'ustated!" when his buildings were not progressing according to his plan. He would not, however, knock over his work. The growth of his feelings vocabulary and his ability to use his words to express his feelings mitigated the need for a behavioral response. Part of the reason that young children tend to throw more tantrums than older children is because they don't yet have the words to express their feelings. The verbal expression of feelings, particularly when these feelings are heard and validated by a significant other, is comforting to the developing child.

A zone of proximal development exists for emotional literacy and is fostered by an attuned, nurturing parent (Vygotsky, 1977, 1967, 1978). The often denuded feelings vocabulary of maltreated and neglected children can be conceptualized as just one more facet of a parent's neglect or abuse. Conversely, children with healthy emotional development can, in the face of overwhelming or terrifying events, experience confusion and a mixing of previously discernable feeling states. Discrete feelings such as sadness, fear, and loneliness may all be rolled up in an amorphous internal knot that the child labels "angry" or "sad." Anger is a powerful feeling and children often cling to anger as a defense against the acknowledgment of underlying feelings of guilt, sadness, or terror that create a much deeper feeling of vulnerability.

Emotional Expression in Art

Children can often communicate primary feeling states more potently through their art than through their words (Gil, 2003; Loumeau-May, 2008; Malchiodi, 1998, 2008). In the drawing in Figure 7.1, a child who had recently been removed from her parents' care gives us a clear message as to her predominant feeling state.

Children often use art as an initial expression of an emotional state that is difficult to define. Exploration of the child's artistic creation can provide new levels of emotional understanding (Figure 7.2).

Eric, a 10-year-old boy referred for explosive behavior at home, drew the picture in Figure 7.2 as an initial expression of what was going on inside himself. He described a series of sensations that began with the impression that he was in a box and the walls were closing in. He went on to describe

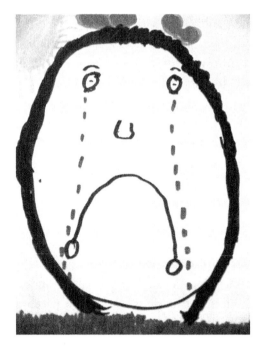

Figure 7.1 *My Sad Feelings*

Figure 7.2 *Pressure*

a sensation of weightiness in his body, "as if big boulders were being placed on top of my head." We went on to explore the situations in which he felt the most "pressured." The more we investigated his experiences, the more it became clear that Eric's primary feeling state was one related to anxiety. The outbursts that usually followed these sensations of pressure led the parents to characterize his primary feeling state as angry. However, through the exploration of his artwork, the whole family grew in their understanding of the client's deep-rooted anxiety issues. Understanding a child's primary emotional motivation can dramatically impact the choice of interventions used in treatment. Articulating Eric's underlying anxiety early in treatment allowed us to be more focused in implementing stress inoculation strategies, cognitive coping techniques, and methods for parental soothing.

The Feelings Rainbow

Children who have been traumatized need help identifying, articulating, and regulating their emotions. Clinically it is helpful to begin feelings work with a child by assessing her current range of articulated feeling states. The manipulation of colors, as they are paired with feeling states, can be a nonthreatening way to help a child explore her emotional life. An intervention called the "feelings rainbow" is a helpful tool in assessing children's color/feeling associations. I begin by giving the child a blank template of a rainbow. Together we color in all the traditional colors of a rainbow. Then I draw the child's attention to the yellow rung of the rainbow. I invite the child to match a feeling to this color.

It is helpful to have a template of feeling faces or feeling words that the child can choose from. If the child chooses happy for her color association with yellow, then I write the word *happy* in the yellow rung of the rainbow. In this way I am able to develop a client-specific template of color/feeling associations that can inform my analysis of any future artwork that the child might do for me. Several classification systems have been developed by art therapists to help us understand the use of color in children's drawings. Although these are valuable tools, I prefer to develop a template of the child's idiosyncratic pairings of colors and feelings. For example, a child might draw a picture that was full of bold red marks. It would be easy to make an assumption that the red represents passion, vitality, aggression, or, more concretely, blood in the child's drawing. However, it is possible that the child's favorite comfort object as a child was a bright red alligator that her grandmother had given her. For that particular child, red might symbolize comfort. Therefore, the child's idiosyncratic pairing of affective states with colors provides an individualized guide for the assessment of future artwork. After I have this initial template of color/feeling matches, I begin to help the child look at her internal feeling states.

Color-Your-Heart

The "color-your-heart" exercise is an intervention I designed early in my practice to help children grow in their awareness of their internal emotional life. As it has been refined, it has become a treatment tool that encourages clients to explore and quantify their feelings while associating them with specific situations. Moreover, the finished heart can yield rich information for future work while providing valuable feedback to parents. I usually complete an initial color-your-heart early in treatment. Depending on the length of treatment, additional assessments can be done at varying intervals to help assess for overall growth and change.

I begin the activity by drawing a giant outline of a heart on a blank piece of paper. I then draw a legend with five empty boxes on the bottom corner of the paper and invite the child to choose five colors. The child can choose any five colors that he wishes. Then I ask the child to pair a feeling with each of the first four colors. The four basic feeling words that we cover are *happy, sad, mad,* and *scared.* I'll ask the questions, "Which one do you want to be your happy feeling? Which one your sad? Which one your mad? Which one your scared?" Then we look together at the fifth box and a fifth color that he's chosen. I give the prompt, "What's another feeling that people feel sometimes?" If the child and I have already established a good rapport and I don't think the question will raise the child's defenses, I might ask "What's another feeling you feel a lot?" For some children, that question may be too confrontational, so I'll ask instead, "What's another feeling word you know?"

When the client offers a fifth feeling, it is often indicative of the specific emotion with which the child is currently struggling. The chosen feeling word is usually tied to the life crisis in which the child finds himself. Children who are going through the divorce of their parents often choose the word *confused* or *lonely* as this fifth feeling. Children who have a lot of externalizing behavior problems, although they've already chosen a color to represent the feeling of anger in their hearts, will offer another word in the category of anger, such as *frustrated* or *irritated*, which seems to be an indication that there are multiple levels of anger with which the child is currently grappling. Children who are referred for anxiety will often choose *nervous* or *worried* as their fifth feeling.

After we have finished the feelings template, I invite the child to color in the heart with as much of each color as might represent how much of that feeling he has in his heart. To help the child understand better, I will say, "So if you were happy all the time you might color in the whole heart yellow, but I don't really know anyone who is happy all the time. If you are only happy a little bit, you might just color in a little yellow." This explanation serves as a gentle challenge to the natural defense mechanism that leads children to over-report their positive feelings and under-report negative or troublesome feelings. The only other boundaries for the activity are that every color must be used at least once and the whole heart should be filled up.

Figures 7.3 to 7.9 demonstrate several examples of completed hearts, showing various presenting problems or symptom subsets. Figure 7.3 depicts the initial heart completed by a 5-year-old girl named Cindy who was referred to me for explosive anger outbursts. The feeling/color associations are delineated from left to right. Cindy colored the most left-hand quadrant red and named this the angry part of her heart. Next came silly, then disappointed, sad, and embarrassed. Above the embarrassed is a brown area that she named "noisy." This was interesting to me as it sounded more like

Figure 7.3 Cindy's Initial Color-Your-Heart

a description made about her by an adult than a reflection of an internal state. The little hint of yellow at the top right represented her happy part of her heart.

At the time of Cindy's intake, she was being raised by her grandparents. Her mother was selling and using drugs. Her house had become a revolving door of drug addicts and mom's boyfriends. Cindy's grandparents intervened and gained custody of Cindy. However, Cindy's younger half-siblings still lived with mom. Cindy felt rejected and confused and was acting out. I worked with the grandparents to set boundaries with the mom, to hone their discipline skills, and to form positive attachments between Cindy and each of them. Cindy and I worked on helping her express her feelings and ask for help when she was feeling overwhelmed. I also did some developmentally sensitive psychoeducation with Cindy around drug addiction as well as doing grief and loss work in relation to the loss of her mother. Helping Cindy increase her emotional vocabulary and deepen her awareness of her own feelings states were key components in the work around the loss of her mother. Figure 7.4 shows a second heart that Cindy completed 4 months into treatment.

Figure 7.4 Cindy's Second Color-Your-Heart

Incorporated in this second heart are many more feelings, including excited, bored, irritated, tired, loved, and embarrassed. Also, the top left portion of the heart is filled with yellow ink, representing a larger quantity of happiness than at the beginning of treatment. These color-your-heart templates can serve as an ongoing assessment instrument, giving the clinician a quick look at a child's current internal life. Cindy's second heart is encouraging from a treatment perspective. If the second heart had been completely filled with yellow, exclusively showing happiness, I would have entertained the possibility that she was trying to please me or defend herself against deeper, more difficult feelings. However, Cindy's perception of her own happiness had expanded while she had added new emotional vocabulary to her repertoire. The second heart reflected a higher level of sophistication in both her emotional awareness and her ability to articulate her internal feeling states.

The heart in Figure 7.5 serves as an example of how a child can move to deeper levels of emotional insight through the doing of the activity. Freddie, a 7-year-old boy referred to me for anxiety issues, chose nervous as his fifth feeling and began filling in his heart template. First he colored in his happy part. The happy color filled up of the bottom fourth of his heart. Then he

Figure 7.5 Freddie's Color-Your-Heart: *My Nervous Gets Into My Happy*

colored in the blue for nervous. As he was coloring in this next layer, his pen slipped and he made a blue squiggle into the red part that represented happy. Freddie sighed and said with some frustration, "Oh, my nervous got into my happy." Then he looked at me with his eyebrows raised as revelation dawned. He said, "Ms. Paris, that's what happens all the time!" He proceeded to put squiggles of nervous through some of the other colors of his heart as well. The kinesthetic doing of the activity revealed to Freddie some truth about his internal feeling states.

This intervention can also be useful in helping a client who is defending against negatively charged emotions to tolerate their presence and eventually accept them. Nine-year-old Mike was referred to me after his parents' divorce. Mike lived with his mother and visited his father, who had moved out of state, only 1 weekend per month. Mike would become extremely anxious before these visits. When Mike first started the color-your-heart activity, he chose the color black to represent his happy. He chose brown to be sad and blue to be mad. He scribbled black all over the heart and originally said, "I'm always happy." Instead of confronting this statement directly, I commented on the white spaces in between the black scribbles of the heart. Mike said, "I guess I should put something in the spaces." He picked up the blue and colored in one empty spot. I reflected that he had added some blue. He picked up the brown and colored in another empty spot. I reflected that he had added some brown. I deliberately stayed with reflections that were aimed at the level of the color, never attaching the feeling words that he had previously delineated (sad and mad). Mike's addition of some blue to his heart was a risk, in so far as it was an admission that he carried some sadness inside himself. If my first reflections confronted him with the sadness, Mike may have shut down completely and refused to finish the activity. Little by little, he added additional spots of brown and blue. As he became more comfortable with the emotional life that he was disclosing in his continued additions to the heart, I eventually commented, "You put a lot of happy in there at first, but the more you look at the heart the more empty places you decide to fill in with sad and mad" (Figure 7.6).

Mike looked like a kid on a mission, trying to fill in all the empty places. Finally he made a frustrated noise and asked for a new piece of paper. He divided this replacement heart in half and colored the left half blue and the right half brown. He then admitted that he felt either sad or mad almost all the time (Figure 7.7).

Figure 7.6 Mike's Color-Your-Heart With Empty Spaces Filled

Figure 7.7 Mike's Revised Color-Your-Heart

The boundaries of the activity itself helped Mike to push through to deeper levels of awareness of his true feelings. Once he had a clearer picture himself, we were able to do some treatment planning around how to alleviate some of his internal distress.

The color-your-heart creation shown in Figure 7.8 is an interesting example of the layering effect that can happen with feelings. When I originally introduced the heart activity to Billy, a 10-year-old boy who struggled with aggressive behavior, he said, "You know that our hearts are about the size of our fists." He then asked if he could make his color-your-heart template in the shape of a fist. I agreed and helped him trace his fist. He filled in his feelings and colors, starting at the top of the knuckles and working his way down to the wrist. In order, he put in happy, then sad, then angry, then scared, and then embarrassed. He colored the deepest level gray and labeled the feeling "secretive."

The layering of emotions within Billy's heart gives us valuable insight into his emotional life. He colored a layer of happiness on top of all the others. It could be that this is the emotion that he feels safest showing to others. The next layer is sadness, but this layer is very small and followed by a large quantity

Figure 7.8   Color-Your-Heart Shaped Like a Fist

of anger. Underneath the anger, which takes up a substantial amount of room, are emotions that are accompanied by a sense of vulnerability (scared and embarrassed). At the deepest part of his heart, below all the other emotions, is something that he calls secretive. The use of this descriptor raised some concern. I wondered if there might be abuse in the child's history that he was not yet willing to disclose. This hypothesis was supported several weeks later when he began telling me about the physical abuse that he had endured at the hands of his father before his parents' divorce. Putting the secret into his color-your-heart creation allowed him to experience how it felt to let someone else see the secret part. It served as a sort of initial exposure to the powerful mix of fear and relief that he felt later at bringing his secret to light.

Billy used a symbol of aggression as the shape of his heart and in so doing, communicated to me that aggression holds a place of prominence in his current coping repertoire. This client's presenting problem was a lack of affect regulation. He often ended up using his fists instead of his words to express his anger. As we began to differentiate his emotions and help him gain awareness of some of the hurts that hid under that anger, we were able to transform this image of his heart as a fist into a kaleidoscope of feelings that could be accepted and communicated appropriately.

The color-your-heart activity can also be a valuable tool in helping parents gain new insights into the emotional lives of their children. The nature of the activity allows a child to measure emotions through how much of the heart he chooses to color in with each representative color. The visual impact of the completed heart can have a powerful effect on parents, helping them to understand a side of their child of which they may have been previously unaware. Conversely, the completed image may confront caregivers with feeling states that they have not been willing or able to perceive. Therefore, it is important that clinicians use sensitivity when processing completed hearts with caregivers. After Freddie had completed the heart in which his nervous got into his happy, I was able to share it with his mother. Freddie's mother was able to make a cognitive shift in which she reframed what she had previously labeled defiance as anxiety. Her reconceptualization of Freddie's rigid and often noncompliant behavior as anxiety-driven behavior opened up a new well of compassion that allowed her to invest in a new parenting approach.

Figure 7.9 offers another example of a color-your-heart creation yielding valuable information that helped shift the parenting system. Julian, a 10-year-old boy, was referred by his parents for "extreme oppositionality."

Figure 7.9 Julian's Vengeful Heart

When we came to the part of the activity where I invite the child to add a fifth feeling, he chose two additional feelings: disturbed and revenge. From bottom to top his feelings layers are mad, sad, disturbed, happy, scared, and revenge. As we went back through the various feelings and I asked for examples of situations that engendered these feelings in him, he pinpointed dad's interactions with him again and again.

While we were processing his angry layer, he talked about getting bad reports from school. He stated that dad would whack him on the head or on the bottom when he brought home a bad report. Julian also described another time when he had made a bad choice while playing outside. Julian remembered dad roughly pushing him into the house and quoted dad as saying, "You better get in the house before I knock your block off!" As we were exploring the part of his heart that felt vengeful, Julian described yet another incident in which he had misbehaved. He quoted dad as saying angrily, "I'll deal with you later." He described a bedtime ordeal in which dad asked him questions over and over again, like "What were you thinking, son?" and "Why would you do such a thing?" Julian stated in session, "He asks me a lot of questions that I don't know the answer to. Sometimes I wish I could give him a little bit of his own medicine." Julian perceived his dad as being angry most of the time and as having little patience for his son.

If the relationship continued in this vein, the toxic ruptures (Siegel, 2003) between Julian and his father would push them so far apart that it would be difficult to find common ground. I invited the dad in for a parent session and we went over the heart in some detail. Dad was surprised and grieved to see that he was perceived in this light by his son. The visual image of a heart filled with anger, revenge, and disturbance motivated dad to reassess his parenting choices. Through family play therapy and parent training we were able to significantly decrease the level of toxicity in the relationship while increasing the number of pleasurable interactions between father and son. Clinical sensitivity is necessary when deciding how and when to present a child's color-your-heart production to parents. If a heart has material in it that is likely to be misunderstood by a parent or for which a child may receive a negative repercussion at home, such as shaming statements, lots of questions, or denial of their feelings, I may choose not to present the information to a parent. Most parents, however, welcome the new insights into their children's emotional lives.

Nonverbal Feelings Interventions

Several play-based interventions can increase emotional literacy for children and do not require much verbal investment on the child's part. Many children, latency-age boys in particular, have difficulty expressing their emotions in words. The task itself can increase their sense of vulnerability and can result in a strengthening of their defenses against exploring their feelings. Having noticed this dynamic over and over again, I designed several interventions that are low risk for the child.

Mood Music

The first of these is called "mood music" (Goodyear-Brown, 2002) and utilizes a child-size guitar or other musical instruments. I begin by explaining that music is full of feelings and that many emotions can be communicated in music without ever saying a word. I might play samples of music for the child and talk about the different feelings that the music evokes. Then I introduce the child to the guitar. Children are fascinated by musical instruments. The chance to touch and play with a guitar goes a long way toward decreasing the resistance children may feel to exploring emotions. I invite the child to pluck each of the guitar strings. We listen carefully to the sound of each and then we assign each string a feelings word. Then I tell a story while the child holds the guitar. For example, I might tell a story in which Sammy, a 7-year-old boy, is getting dressed in his brand new shirt for the first day of school. I invite the child to pluck the string that corresponds to how Sammy might be feeling. I continue the story by saying that after Sammy is dressed in his new shirt, he sits down to breakfast and accidentally spills milk on it. I stop again and invite the child to pluck the string that mirrors how Sammy might be feeling. This activity encourages the child to discriminate between various feelings as he applies them to real-life situations.

The storytelling device and the handling of the guitar make it easier for him to approach the emotional content. Moreover, the therapist can get a beginning assessment of several dimensions of a child's emotional literacy, including (1) the accuracy of a client's emotional antennae for which feelings might match which situations in the story, (2) what feelings a child comprehends the most readily, and (3) which feelings the child seems to gravitate toward as the story is being told. For example, some children might decide that Sammy was nervous or sad on his first day of school, whereas other children might decide that Sammy is happy to have a new shirt or excited about his first day of school. A child's guesses as to the feelings of the character in the story are good initial indicators for the child's own range of emotional responses. Once I have modeled the storytelling, I invite the child to switch places and let him tell a story while I pluck the strings.

Take Your Temperature

Another very simple, nonverbal feelings identification intervention is called "take your temperature." (Goodyear-Brown, 2005). I write feeling words on tongue depressors and put them in an old-fashioned doctor's bag. When working with preschool-age children, it is more developmentally appropriate to have pictures of feeling faces on the tongue depressors. I give the bag to the child and she gets to pull out all the tongue depressors that match her feelings. This intervention is especially useful at the beginning of group or family sessions, when it is advantageous to get a quick gauge of the emotional state of each person present (Figure 7.10).

Inside/Outside Feelings

Another intervention, called "inside/outside feelings," (Goodyear-Brown, 2005) begins as an internal process for the client and is then shared with the

Figure 7.10   Props for *Take Your Temperature*

therapist. I begin by giving the child a manila folder that I have cut to look like the head and shoulders of a person (Figure 7.11). I begin the intervention by talking to the child about the difference between public feelings and private feelings. All of us allow certain feelings to show when we are around other people. There are also feelings that we only let a few trusted people see, and perhaps still other feelings that we don't let anyone see. I invite the child to draw a self-portrait on the front of the manila folder. The picture should depict what other people see when they look at the client.

Once the child has completed the outward representation, I give the child a stack of magazines and invite him to cut out pictures that represent images of the feelings that he lets other people see and images of how other people see him. For example, a child who is known for being the class clown might cut out pictures of clowns, silly faces, or people laughing. The child can glue these images to the back of the folder. The child is then encouraged to cut out more pictures and words that show various aspects of the internal self and the feelings that he doesn't often let other people see.

Collage work encourages an interplay between the child's perceptions of the self, his world, mass media, and cultural icons. A picture truly is worth a thousand words, and unique aspects of a child's inner experience can be powerfully captured by the right image. The second set of images is glued

Figure 7.11   *Inside/Outside Feelings*

inside the manila folder. The therapist and client can then process the images and words with a view toward accepting all his feeling states while discerning healthy boundaries between the feelings that get shown to the whole world and feelings that are saved for trusted supports. Many children believe that certain emotions are too intense or too horrible for anyone else to see. However, it is often through showing our ugliest emotions to a trusted other and experiencing acceptance of those feelings that the feelings lose their power to control us. All these concepts can be introduced through this activity.

Sands of Time

Another nonverbal intervention, the "sands of time," targets emotional awareness and the sequencing of emotions as they coincide with certain dimensions of a child's trauma narrative. This exercise is especially helpful for children who have experienced the death of a loved one. I begin the exercise by presenting the child with containers of various colors of sand and a number of sand art bottles. Sand art bottles come in many different shapes, including crosses, hearts, suns, stars, and castles. I invite the child to choose which bottle to use. The child then pairs each of the sand colors with a feeling word. These associations are used throughout the exercise.

We start the feelings work at the beginning of the journey that ended in the loved one's death. For example, if a child lost a mother due to breast cancer, I invite the child to remember the moments in which mom first told the child that she was sick. The child would then choose a sand color and pour as much of it into the sand art bottle as she felt that feeling at the time. Whatever color she chooses will reflect the feeling state without her having to commit to it verbally. I would then verbalize the next step of the narrative. If mom started on chemo and then lost her hair, I would invite the child to choose feelings associated with these steps. The child ends up with a completed sand art creation that concretizes her emotional journey through grief. The client can keep the sand art bottle as a kind of memorial to the loved one. At each step of the process, the child gets to hear the narrative rehearsed while sequencing emotional components of the narrative through the sand. Sometimes a child's sand art creation reflects the stages of grief set forth by Elizabeth Kübler-Ross (1969). Other times, a child may only have one color of sand filling the whole bottle, reflecting a child's overwhelming feelings of sadness or anger.

Verbally Engaging Prop-Based Feelings Interventions

The previously delineated interventions allow children to warm up to emotional literacy work without having to verbalize much of their own experiences. The following interventions are more challenging for children. The challenge level is matched by the enjoyment of manipulating the props. The treatment goal, whether it be building emotional vocabulary, identifying situational cues that trigger certain feelings, or becoming aware of physiological indicators that an emotion is present, is supported by materials that are fun for children and can anchor the work. Our clients provide us with constant challenges, and many of the interventions described here are the direct result of a particular client's resistance to an area of therapeutic work. One aspect of our job as clinicians is often to design a play experience that feels "worth it" to the child—that is, worth the risk of sharing some of their inner life and allowing it to be witnessed by another.

Mood Manicure

Katie, a precocious 8-year-old client, prided herself on already knowing all this "feelings stuff." Katie's mother is a child therapist and this fact added to Katie's belief that she was ahead of the curve in terms of emotional maturity. However, Katie was having anger outbursts at school, had very few friends, and had recently experienced the traumatic divorce of her parents. She was also, at 8 years old, identifying herself as "more like a teenager than a child." I tried a color-your-heart creation with her, but even as I began to draw the heart, she rolled her eyeballs and said, "I already know all about my feelings. That's baby stuff!" I was stumped. I went home and thought about what kind of materials would spark her interest while supporting her heated assertions that she was more like a teenager than a child. I decided to try nail polish. The next time she came to treatment, I had a basketful of nail polish bottles. She went immediately to them and asked if we could use them.

I offered a game in which we would paint each other's nails. We began the game by pairing a feeling with each color of nail polish. We labeled the red polish "angry" and the blue polish "sad." The rules of the game were that we could have as many colors on each hand as we wanted, but the other person got to paint them. If I wanted one of my nails painted red, I would ask her to do it. While she was painting my nail red, I had to talk about one time that I remembered feeling angry. We played this game for the entire session. When the session was over, we both had a rainbow of colors on our hands and she had a rainbow of feelings identified and correlated to situations from her own life experience that engendered each feeling. Together we named this intervention "mood manicure" (Goodyear-Brown, 2002).

All Tangled Up

The intervention "all tangled up" (Goodyear-Brown, 2002, 2003a) offers a child a concrete tool through which to explore complex emotions. Sometimes children have difficulty differentiating one emotion from another. This phenomenon was beautifully articulated by a 4-year-old named Zoe. Zoe had been adopted from China at age 1 and had frequent rages with her adoptive mother. She came in one afternoon after a morning in which she had several tantrums. When I asked her how she was feeling, she looked up at me with big, confused eyes and said, "They're all tangled up in there." "What's all tangled up?" I asked. "My worries," she answered. This moment exemplifies the intersection at which a child's therapeutic need and metaphoric speech give birth to a new intervention. I wracked my brain for a way to take her metaphor "it's all tangled up" and give it a concrete form, so that she could untangle the emotions. She needed to externalize the worries and fears inside her in order to deal with them concretely.

I rummaged around and finally produced a ball of multicolored yarn. I said, "Sounds like your worries are all tangled up just like this ball of yarn is all tangled up." She said "Yeah!" while eagerly grabbing the yarn. Then I said, "Everyone has worries. Sometimes we have so many worries that they get all tangled up inside. It's hard to tell one from another anymore. Today we're going to untangle those worries. Let's start by pulling out one piece of yarn at a time to be each worry. Some worries may be small and some may be big. We'll cut long pieces if the worries are big and short pieces if the worries are small." She liked this idea and ran to get the scissors.

Zoe pulled out 2 feet of yarn and said, "This one's little. I worry that I might lose my TV time tonight." I wrote the worry down and attached it to the piece of yarn. Zoe articulated worry after worry and reflected the intensity of each worry in the lengths of yarn. As we neared the end of her list of worries, she let the yarn spool on the floor, yards and yards of yarn. Then she said, "I worry that my mom and dad will leave me." Here was the core worry that informed all the others. Zoe's fears of abandonment were manifesting in tantrums with her adoptive mom. I enlisted Zoe's help in tying the strands up all around the room until they looked like a three-dimensional spider web. Once we were finished, I said, "Wow, no wonder you're feeling all tangled up on the inside! These are a lot of worries. Do you think that your mom knows how many worries you have?" She said, "I don't know." I asked her if we could invite mom into the room. When mom came into the space and I explained to her what we were doing, she was overwhelmed by the visual imagery of the complexities of her daughter's worries.

In that moment, Zoe's mom made a cognitive shift to understanding her daughter's tantrums as grounded in anxiety and fears of abandonment. Mom's reframing of defiant behaviors as anxious behaviors filled up the well of compassion that had been depleted by Zoe's recent tantrums. Zoe and I enlisted mom's help in cutting down each of the worries as mom made state-ments about her constancy in Zoe's life. We cut up small pieces of the yarn to serve as a signal between Zoe and mom. When Zoe started to feel anx-ious at home, she would give mom a small piece of the yarn and this would be mom's signal to provide comfort, reassurance, and redirection if needed. This activity provided a valuable opportunity for the client to explore the dimensions of one particular feeling and communicate these dimensions to her caregiver.

Clearing it Up

Another intervention that can help clients piece apart emotions is called "clearing it up." First, I fill a clear bowl with water. I offer a set of food col-oring vials to the child. I invite the child to put drops of the food coloring into the water for each feeling. If a client has chosen blue food coloring to represent feelings of sadness, she could squeeze several drops of blue in the water. The same process would be completed for the red, yellow, and green drops. Once all the colors are mixed together in the clear water, they cre-ate a mucky brown mess. I talk with the client about how feelings that stay stuck inside and unexamined produce a confusing mucky mess much like the water. The best way to begin clearing up the confusion is to talk about these feelings with a helpful adult.

I then give the client a cup of bleach and allow him to pour small amounts of bleach into the muddy water as he talks about each of the feelings. The metaphor extends to the way in which the bleach helps clear up the water. The bowl has to be set on a shelf, because it takes awhile for the bleach to move through the water and bleach out the color. In this same way, our feel-ings have to be examined and often witnessed by a significant other before the confusion can slowly begin to be cleared away. This activity can be mod-ified and used later in treatment to work on restructuring traumagenic cogni-tions. In this modification, the food color drops represent lies the child was told by the perpetrator or false beliefs with which the client is struggling. The bleach would be poured into the water as each lie is countered and each cognitive distortion restructured.

Another aspect of the intervention that has metaphoric value is that the water, even after being cleaned by the bleach, never quite returns to trans-parency. It maintains a yellow tinge. Similarly, the emotions that have been experienced as a result of traumatic events leave us indelibly changed. The goal is to integrate the lasting changes into a positive sense of self. If the water returned exactly to the appearance it had before the trauma had been experienced, the activity might send a false message that the memories of the traumatic event could be erased. It should never be the intention of a helping professional to make a client forget that a trauma occurred or to pretend that it never happened. Rather, the purpose of the exercise is to take the emotional toxicity out of the trauma memory and to bring order and manageability to the emotions experienced.

Kinesthetic Activities that Build Emotional Literacy

Many traumatized children have difficulties with appropriate emotional expression. When they become fearful or angry the feelings can manifest in explosive behavior. Maltreated children, particularly, may have no template for effective communication or resolution of difficult feelings. They may react with quick aggression to run-ins with peers. For example, Johnny, an 8-year-old boy with a history of physical abuse, gives the wrong answer to a question in class. A fellow classmate rolls his eyes at Johnny, who reacts by immediately jumping up and punching his classmate. Johnny is removed to in-school suspension and spends the rest of the day there. The separation from peers limits the learning trials or practice that Johnny needs in order to improve his communication skills. He is given consequences but no real pathway toward change.

"I Feel" . . . Hopscotch

Play-based interventions can provide children with a path for practicing appropriate communication. One such intervention is called "'I feel' . . . hopscotch" (Goodyear-Brown, 2002). I designed the intervention after watching this dynamic repeat over and over again in the public schools. My clients would get in trouble in their classrooms and be sent to the office, receive a consequence, and usually be removed for a period of time. I went to the principal and asked that my clients be sent directly to my office after they had received whatever consequences the school meted out. When the client came to me, we would go outside and draw a hopscotch board. I would write "I" in the first hopscotch block, "feel" across the next two hopscotch blocks and leave the third square blank. I then wrote "when you" in the next hop-scotch blocks and left the final block at the top of the game empty.

During this intervention, I would lead the client back through the events that led to the altercation, and help the client articulate his feeling states along the way. With this help, the child could pinpoint the underlying affective response that influenced his choice to, as in the case described earlier, punch his classmate, and we could then craft an appropriate communication. The child then practices restating the negative communication in the "I feel" format while jumping into the corresponding hopscotch squares.

The game of hopscotch is inherently fun and well known by children. Some of my clients practiced the appropriate "I feel" communication over and over again as they jumped through the game. Children who are already familiar with hopscotch will feel a sense of competency in the physical mastery of the game. During the activity, cognitive processes are being linked with kinesthetic activity. The combination of full-body engagement and appropriate verbalizations encourages a deeper level of integration of the new skill. The new communication pattern moves from simple head knowledge to body knowledge as it is activated through physical engagement and linguistic processes.

Linking Feelings to Situations

Sticky Feelings

Children who have been traumatized often need help connecting situational triggers with specific emotions. There are many play-based methods for helping children bridge this gap. The simplest intervention, one that I call "sticky feelings," requires a laminated feelings chart and some sticky balls, which can be purchased from a variety of novelty stores. The child is given a sticky ball and invited to throw it at the chart. When the ball has stuck to one of the feeling words or faces, the child talks about a time that he felt that way. This intervention can be made more appealing to latency-age boys, who generally are not big on feelings expressions, by using glow-in-the-dark eyeballs. The lights are turned off, the client throws the eyeball, and the lights are turned back on to see where it lands. The client must then give an example of a time he felt the feeling on which the sticky eyeball landed.

"You Don't Scare Me" Spider Toss

Another play-based intervention that encourages children to share situations in which they feel afraid is called the "You don't scare me" spider toss. The props include a giant inflatable spider and a set of rings. I explain that we will take turns throwing the rings, and whenever a ring lands on one of the spider's legs, we will talk about one time that we felt afraid. The child and I stand together on one side of the room and toss the rings across the room toward the spider. The physical engagement in the task decreases the pressure a child might feel if we were sitting across a table from each other and I was asking her to share her fearful experiences with me. Moreover, we are both focused on an external focal point. This turns the activity into a joint attention task and further extends the child's comfort in sharing her experiences. Finally, the motivation to excel, to get the rings on the spider's legs, usually outweighs a child's reticence to talk about scary events. Before the game is over, the child has often come up with a whole list of experiences that have previously resulted in feelings of fear.

Conclusion

Traumatized children often need help building their emotional literacy. In this chapter I have outlined a variety of play-based interventions in pursuit of this goal. The color-your-heart, and feelings rainbow exercises are examples of assessment techniques for use in feelings work. As the case examples illustrate, the color-your-heart activity bridges the gap between assessment and intervention, in that the simple act of quantifying feeling states through color can move a child to new levels of self-awareness. Feelings can be difficult for children to discuss verbally, so a section on nonverbal feelings interventions was included. Interventions that help children to recognize situational triggers for their emotional reactions should also be part of the toolbox that well-equipped clinicians have at their disposal, and several examples are presented here.

A child's ability to articulate his emotional states, particularly those that typically escalate the child, helps lay the foundation for later trauma-processing exercises. One extension of a child's growth in the area of feelings identification is pinpointing which feelings, when activated, will need additional coping strategies to manage. For this reason, the FSPT model places the goal of increasing emotional literacy after safety has been established in the playroom, initial coping assessment has been completed, and soothing strategies (both self-directed and parent-facilitated) have been addressed. These other components of treatment equip the child with a wide range of options to safely manage the emotional life that is being targeted in this chapter. This early establishment of a shared emotional language can be used throughout the rest of treatment.

8

The Continuum of Disclosure

Something there is that doesn't love a wall,
That wants it down.

—*Robert Frost, Mending Wall*

Self-Titration of Exposure to Trauma Content

Continuum of disclosure is a phrase that I employ to describe the unfolding sequence of trauma glimpses that a child shares with us over the course of treatment. I am not using the word *disclosure* here in the traditional sense that we associate with a child's initial verbal report of maltreatment or neglect. I am using *disclosure* to encapsulate the ongoing process of revelation that often occurs between a child and therapist within the safe confines of the playroom. In some cases a child will make an initial verbal disclosure to the therapist that must be reported and handled through appropriate channels with the ultimate aim being to keep the child safe. In other cases a child's maltreatment history may be well documented, a child's disclosure of abuse may have been fully prosecuted, and the child has been made physically safe. However, the child may be experiencing symptoms of posttraumatic stress that are being exacerbated by the child's unwillingness to revisit any of the trauma content. In these cases the course toward alleviating the child's distress includes titrated exposures to the trauma content.

This chapter gives many examples of how children begin to self-titrate their exposures to trauma-based material. Children often have great difficulty articulating their trauma experiences verbally, particularly if the trauma happened prelinguistically. Moreover, the limited vocabulary of children cannot fully do justice to the richness and intensity of their experiences.

Children lean heavily on the play materials, the safety of the playroom, and the containment behaviors of the play therapist to facilitate the exposures. The glimpses a child allows into his experiences of trauma may include startling play scenarios, graphic images, disjointed sensory perceptions, irrational thoughts, and troublesome feelings. The powerful play behaviors may be accompanied by words that seem lifeless in comparison.

Early in my career I was arrested by this truth through the juxtaposition of impassively spoken words and impassioned play behaviors presented to me by a young sexual abuse survivor. Alex, a 4-year-old boy who had been repeatedly anally raped by his mother's boyfriend before his removal from her care, was referred for treatment. Unfortunately, Alex came into my office on his first day of therapy having already been told, by a case manager, that he was "coming to therapy to talk about the bad thing that happened to him." As soon as he entered the room, he volunteered, almost cheerfully, "My mommy's boyfriend put his penis in me." I reflected his verbalization with acceptance while being inwardly taken aback that he would make this verbal pronouncement to a perfect stranger in our initial meeting. Moreover, the weighty content of his words did not match the matter-of-fact, almost light-hearted nature of his delivery.

Years later, having seen many more sexually abused children, I now allow for the possibility that the ones who have already been involved with forensic interview processes or adjudications may come blithely into the room and begin to tell their stories. The problematic issue with linguistic narrative, however, is that it is often split off from a child's sensory perceptions of the event in question. Children may rehearse the same verbal narrative over and over again without gaining relief from troublesome symptoms or integrating the most difficult perceptions of their experiences. The play-cloaked glimpses that they give us throughout treatment often fill in some of these sensory details.

After Alex made this initial verbal broadcast, he immediately began playing with the kitchen materials. He stirred pots, made hot chocolate, and shared some with the therapist. After several minutes of this play progression, Alex picked up a pair of child-size egg beaters. He walked over to the animal shelf and chose a large dinosaur. He pulled the removable tail off the creature, revealing a gaping hole in the dinosaur's backside. Alex then proceeded to ram the egg beaters into the hole of this dinosaur while making grunting noises, followed by groans of distress. His earlier words had given me "just the facts, ma'am," but his intense play sequence here gave sounds to the atrocities he had endured while giving a metaphoric picture of both the viciousness of the perpetrator's act and the pain and violation experienced by the child.

In the midst of this focused play behavior, an effective therapist will offer containment to the child by communicating the messages, *"I see what you are showing me. I am strong enough to handle it, and I see how strong you are to show me."* The therapist makes no attempt to pull the content out of the metaphor and into the reality of the child's experience. Indeed, an abrupt shift from the allegorical content to the child's historical reality could have iatrogenic effects, stifling any further expressions that the child might otherwise hazard and betraying the tenuous trust being established through the therapist's unspoken agreement to respond within the scope of the play. Alex's experience was so overwhelming, the terrain so dangerous, that he could only approach it through the veil of play.

The therapist must betray no outward shock or sense of being overwhelmed by what the child has revealed, even if the therapist is feeling both these emotions at the time of the disclosure. Although authenticity is an ideal highly valued by most therapists, it must be understood that children are often overwhelmed by an adult's authentic reactions and should not have to bear the brunt of them. As counterintuitive as it may seem, our internal reactions, the reactions of our truest selves, must sometimes be tempered in order to remain contingently responsive to the child. The difficulty of providing ongoing containment for our clients is one of the main reasons that child therapists need to have good supervision, collegial support, and strong social networks. These protections help mitigate against the inappropriate use of self-disclosure with clients and the compassion fatigue that steals so many talented clinicians away from the field before their time.

No two children will express their trauma experiences in identical ways, and yet most traumatized children do have a need to try to communicate aspects of their experiences through the play materials. Each expression of their experience, each glimpse into their perceptions of the trauma, represents a risk and a trust. It requires vulnerability on the part of the child to open a window into his most personal experience. This risk taking deserves our respect and careful handling. Our response to these glimpses impacts the likelihood that the window might become a door big enough to walk through side by side with the child.

I have already alluded to the process that may occur early in treatment in which a child identifies perpetrator symbols and self-objects for containment or later manipulation. The perpetrator symbol may remain the same throughout the child's course of treatment or may be replaced multiple times with new symbols. In these cases the work may happen more thematically, with repeated battles between good and evil, or as a series of metaphors, each describing another aspect of the child's experience of the traumatic event. A child often begins his uncovering through an image, a play production, a play metaphor, or a turn of phrase stated during the play. This is part test, part challenge for the therapist. Can we handle the often horrific pictures that they must show us? If we acknowledge the risk that a child takes in uncovering a new dimension of her traumatic experience and legitimize her viewpoint, she will show us more. I see it as a great gift every time a child trusts me enough to give me a glimpse of her pain. The gift I give in return is containment. The playroom and the person of the therapist become the dumping ground for all manner of bizarre and disjointed metaphoric snapshots of the atrocities experienced by the child. If we are able to contain the content in a way that communicates, "I see what you are showing me and we're both still OK," we will most likely be rewarded with another glimpse of the trauma.

The Limitations of Spoken Language for Children

The most natural language for children is the language of play (Landreth, 1991; Schaefer & Drewes, 2009). Children learn to use words because the adults in their lives insist upon it. It is our job to socialize our children and to train them to communicate effectively with the rest of the world. One of the ways that we do this is by encouraging verbal communication. However, our ability to make linguistic sense of our world expands as our experiences and our vocabulary expand in tandem. A child who falls down will often have a grown-up say something like, "Oh, you've got a boo-boo." Then the grown-up will bandage it, kiss it, and so on.

The child learns what it feels like to skin his knee, what it looks like to have the knee skinned (perhaps there is blood), and a specific turn of phrase, "boo boo," that stands for the experience of having the skinned knee. The terminology begins to be acquired during this first exposure and is reinforced as the child watches other people have boo-boos and has more of his own that are labeled with the same words. Often by the time a child becomes a toddler, he can come crying to a parent and say "boo-boo" and adults understand his meaning and are able to offer aid. A child's vocabulary expands exponentially over time but is in large part contingent on experiences being matched with verbal descriptions. How does a child make sense of terrifying or painful events that are given no words? The child is in an even more untenable situation if the person responsible for the pain, as in the case of sexual abuse, deliberately avoids giving words to what has occurred. How much more difficult, then, does it become for a child to communicate a painful experience that was deliberately cloaked in euphemisms or overt silence?

The 4-year-old girl who is sexually molested by her father in the middle of the night has limited language to describe the painful experience. Here we must make a distinction between words that give a factual accounting of an event and language that describes the nuanced emotional reactions, the sensory impressions, and the bodily remembrances of an event. Complexities of language require a finesse that may or may not be available to children at various stages of development. The young child who is awash with terror and squeezes her eyes tight shut during the molestation will have even more difficulty articulating these subtleties. Words like *bewildered, overwhelmed, terrified, paralyzed,* and so forth are complex verbal descriptions that are not in most children's daily lexicon. However, their verbal artlessness in no way lessens the sophistication or potency of the child's internal experience. Many adults make the mistake of believing that because a child's language lacks sophistication, so does their experience. However, children who have experienced repetitive trauma scenarios, ongoing sexual abuse, for example, have a level of sophistication regarding these events that nontraumatized adults lack. Indeed, these children are more worldly-wise and perhaps world-weary than their unscathed peers. A child who has lived in domestic violence for the whole of his first seven years is more expert in the experience of domestic violence than many of the professionals who write about it.

One of my earliest exposures to this truth came from a 4-year-old boy named Timmy. Timmy had lived the whole of his young life in domestic violence. During one of our first sessions together, I invited him to complete a preschool play genogram. This activity is a modification of the family play genogram (Gil, 1994) and helps focus the child by placing a piece of treasure in the sand for each figure that needs to be chosen. As the child chooses a figure to represent each family member, he collects the treasure and gets to turn it in for a reward at the end of the session.

I began the activity by inviting Timmy to choose a toy to be mom. Without hesitation, he chose a woman with a cake, a very nurturing symbol, to be the mother. I asked him to choose a toy to be himself. He chose a tiny naked baby, perhaps reflecting the vulnerability that he feels in his home environment. Lastly I asked Timmy to choose a toy to be dad. He walked halfway to the shelves that display the miniatures. He abruptly stopped, turned, and asked "Can I choose more than one?" I answered, "You may do whatever you need to do in here," which is my standard response. He chose a giant, aggressive wrestler, a small, nondescript boy, and Prince Charming. He showed me all three phases of the domestic violence cycle as he had experienced them in the person of his father. Figure 8.1 shows the three symbols he chose to represent dad.

A 4-year-old would never have been able to say, "Ms. Paris, I have noticed this pattern in which my father loses control and becomes very violent and destructive, then he becomes remorseful, and then he is on his best behavior for awhile before it starts all over again." The prerequisite vocabulary to verbally describe his experience is not available to him. Yet he is able to eloquently articulate this cycle through the play materials and the structure of the intervention. The old adage "a picture is worth a thousand words" is especially true when capturing the inner experience of a child who has been traumatized.

Figure 8.1   Timmy's *Three Faces of Dad*

When children use words in play therapy to describe traumatic events, they are often used within the child's chosen play metaphor. James, a 3-year-old client referred for behavior that made his mom wonder if he had been sexually abused, gives us a good example of the use of disclosure language in play. When James came for his initial session, he went immediately to the dinosaurs. He chose a large dinosaur and two smaller dinosaurs and placed them in the sand tray. He began to be the voice of one of the little dinosaurs and talked about the food he ate, the games he played, and so on. After a period of time and still in the voice of the small dinosaur he said, "Dinosaurs bite me up my butt crack." This language is atypical for a child his age who is engaged in play with plastic dinosaurs. The phrase "dinosaurs bite me" was not alarming. The words "butt crack" are words that a child that age might use to describe himself or simply to get a response from an adult and were, therefore, not my focus of concern. The words "up my" did, however, raise a red flag. The use of this level of specificity in relation to the dinosaur's anus could be seen as precocious sexual knowledge.

The response to the child's play is simply to reflect what the child is saying and validate the experience of the baby dinosaur. Wondering if the baby dinosaur might be this child's chosen self-object, I stated, "I wonder how the baby dinosaur feels, being bitten up the butt crack." James replied, "Bad. It hurts." I validate the dinosaur's feelings. Although the therapist may be wondering how the play relates to the child's own experience, it is not the time to switch gears and ask a series of interrogative questions. It is enough that the baby dinosaur's experience has been seen, heard, reflected, and validated. If this is, in fact, a flash of trauma-related content or the beginning of a continuum of disclosure, the proper containment of this glimpse will afford us another. The specific turn of phrase should be recorded in the clinician's progress notes in case the child makes future elaborations.

If the metaphoric glimpse has been given through drawing, the drawing itself becomes part of the permanent record. If the child decides to use the dry erase board to show me the glimpse, I will offer to take a picture of it before erasing it. If the glimpse is through puppetry, I will ask permission to videotape the puppet play. Because these play creations represent various emotional or sensory aspects of the trauma, or nonsequential moments within a trauma history, the permanent records become a tool that has the potential to later help the child sequence the events into a more coherent trauma narrative.

It is important to get written parental permission, preferably at intake, for videotaping sessions prior to recording a child's work. Videotapes and photographs serve an additional function, beyond that of creating a permanent record for later work. These mediums allow the child to have another level of witnessing occur within the session. Once a child knows that a camcorder and camera are in the office, he often asks for play creations to be documented. The act of documenting the child's play serves as another level of witnessing. Once the child has performed his puppet play or had a picture taken of his drawing, he will often ask to see it immediately on the view screen. In this way, a child may have the benefit of an initial exposure to trauma-laden content through his original creation and an additional exposure by watching his puppet play back on the view screen or seeing his picture or sand tray displayed again.

Case Examples of the Continuum of Disclosure

Another example of the beginning of a continuum of disclosure can be seen in the case of Nakeisha. Nakeisha was a 5-year-old girl referred for treatment after removal from a home in which she had experienced maltreatment. However, the extent of the abuse was unknown. On Nakeisha's first visit to the playroom, she spent the majority of the session drawing. When I let her know that we had five minutes left before we had to end this session, she moved to the baby dolls, chose one with unkempt hair, and took her clothes off. She then moved to the puppet rack and chose my wasp puppet with its long stinger. She began stinging the baby's private parts over and over again with the wasp's stinger, saying "Owww, owww, owww." Based on my hypothesis that the baby doll was her chosen self-object and the wasp was a perpetrator symbol, I offered assistance to the baby doll by getting out the Band-Aids and showing them to Nakeisha. She eagerly accepted the proffered help and together we bandaged the parts that had been stung. Figures 8.2 and 8.3 show the bandaged doll and the wasp puppet that was used to do the stinging.

Over the course of several sessions, as we nurtured the client's self-object and made sure the wasp could no longer harm the baby, she slowly began to unfold the sexual abuse that had occurred in her previous home. Her initial aberrant play pattern represents the first step in her unique continuum of disclosure.

In another case example, Bobby, a 9-year-old boy, worked through a process of play-based disclosure over the course of several sessions. Bobby

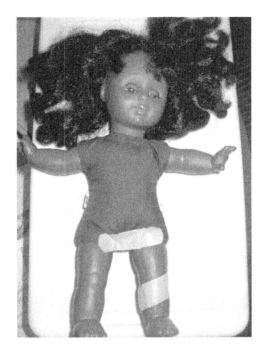

Figure 8.2 Bandaged Baby Doll

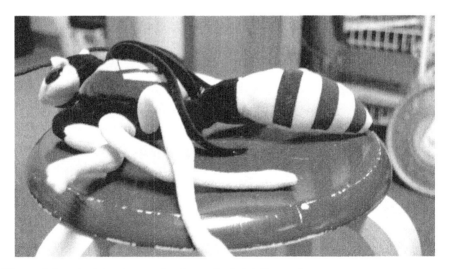

Figure 8.3 The Wasp Puppet that Stung the Baby's Private Parts

was brought to treatment by mom for extreme anger and violent behavior. Bobby's parents had been married for eight years, during which time Bobby had repeatedly witnessed dad being physically abusive to mom. At the time he entered treatment, Bobby was spending every other weekend at

Figure 8.4   Headless Man Covered with Snakes

his father's house. Mom reported a dramatic increase in his violent behavior after each visit. In addition, Bobby had great difficulty falling asleep and staying asleep for the first couple of nights back home at mom's. During Bobby's initial session, he created a sand tray (Figure 8.4).

Bobby chose the only male figure in my collection that is decapitated. He then took snakes and placed them on and around the decapitated figure. Although there was not a lot of verbal monologue accompanying the creation of his sand tray, the created image is viscerally disturbing. When Bobby returned for his next session, he immediately chose the same headless figure again and placed him facedown in the sand. Bobby then chose another aggressive-looking figure and laid him on top of the headless figure and wrapped them both in snakes (Figure 8.5).

Once Bobby had wrapped the two men in snakes, he chose a larger snake and placed it in the tray at an angle approaching the private parts of the two men (Figure 8.6).

The only other items he added to the sand tray were a mailbox and a broken-down fence. One way that children use fences in the sand is to set up boundaries between people, places, and objects. Broken-down fences may indicate broken or unhealthy boundaries between the child and a significant other. These are my own musings about the tray. They were not shared

Figure 8.5   Men Wrapped in Snakes

Figure 8.6   Larger Snake Approaching the Men's Genitals

with the child. My therapeutic response was to invite Bobby to tell me about the tray that he had created. When Bobby was done with his description, I further augmented the work by inviting him to take the perspective of one or more of the symbols in the tray, processing what it's like for that character or object in the created world. "What's it like for the headless man? How does it feel for him to have the other man on top of him?" Once the tray was fully processed, staying within the metaphors the child had chosen, we moved on to another play activity.

During the next session, Bobby chose a Power Ranger figurine. He then chose a miniature plastic weapon and shoved the weapon between the legs of the Power Ranger, horizontally (Figure 8.7). Then he removed this weapon from between the legs of the Power Ranger and inserted it into the buttocks of a police officer (Figure 8.8).

Bobby's use of the play materials was atypical in comparison to how non-traumatized 9-year-old boys play with the same materials. This penetrative use of the weapons into the figures' private parts is developmentally aberrant and as such should be given special attention, reflected in a nonjudgmental way back to the child, and documented. The acceptance of the child's play invites further disclosure.

During the next session, Bobby chose a basket and said, "This is a bed." He then chose a young male child, disrobed it, and put it in the basket.

Figure 8.7   Weapon Between Legs

He said, "The little boy is naked." Then he chose another doll, whom Bobby addressed as "He," pulled down the doll's blue jeans, and placed the doll facedown in the basket. Lastly, Bobby chose an adult male doll, pulled his pants down, and laid him facedown on top of the other doll (Figure 8.9).

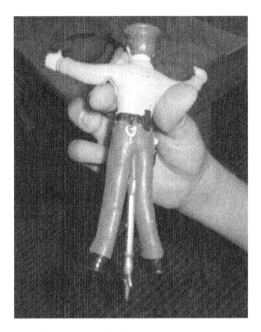

Figure 8.8   Policeman with Weapon Placed in Private Parts

Figure 8.9   Arrangement of Dolls

During the same session in which Bobby created the image in Figure 8.9 with the disrobed figures, he began to verbally disclose the sexual abuse that had occurred in his father's bed during visits. Once a child has made a verbal disclosure, it is necessary to involve the proper authorities. Often this results in a forensic interview process. Parents can become frustrated at this point and may need additional support in navigating the systems of care that we have created to keep children and families safe and accountable. Clinicians are often frustrated by the process as well.

A child who has become secure in the playroom and who has established a safe rapport with the play therapist becomes more and more comfortable and may take more and more risks, including the risk to tell, sometimes for the first time, about the bad thing that happened to him. At whatever point a verbal disclosure is made, it is the therapist's legal and ethical obligation to report this information to the Department of Children's Services. However, the child may or may not repeat the disclosures made in the safety of the playroom to the stranger who comes to interview him at his home or school. As the investigative systems involved in abuse allegations are becoming more developmentally sensitive, the interview format is being refined and sometimes expanded. The National Child Advocacy Center now has well-trained staff who can interview children in developmentally appropriate language. Moreover, the Advocacy Centers are child-friendly environments that help a child feel more at ease. Some child advocacy workers use an extended six-session interview format designed to give the child time to become comfortable in the setting. Although these new approaches to investigation increase the likelihood that children's disclosures will remain consistent across environments, it is not unusual to have a forensic interview be inconclusive because a child may not be able or willing to verbally communicate the abuse that has occurred during a single interview. In these situations the investigative case may be closed while the child continues to have a host of symptoms that require treatment. In the course of treating the symptoms, a mental health clinician may be the first person to whom a disclosure is made.

It is not possible to know, when a child enters treatment, what content will emerge in the course of therapy. However, the cleanest forensic interview is often one conducted before involvement with a play therapist. For this reason, I routinely direct families who call because their child has recently made a verbal disclosure to go through the Department of

Children's Services investigation process before entering treatment. One outgrowth of this channeling is that many of the clients I see come to me after the allegations have been founded or the case has been closed. In these cases the process of disclosure through which children move in the playroom is unencumbered by the potential agendas of others. Rather, the therapeutic progression of titrated disclosures is meant to help the child face the various aspects of the trauma, become desensitized to the painful memories, and integrate them into a positive sense of self moving forward.

Many times a child has been clear in his verbal disclosure and convincing enough to get safely away from the perpetrator. In these cases a child's physical environment has been made more secure. Unfortunately, physical safety does not translate directly into psychological safety. Some children become stuck in the intrusive symptoms of PTSD. Nightmares, flashbacks, and recurrent images torment them long after the perpetrator has been removed. The avoidance of people, places, and things related to the traumatic events is another indicator that a child has unresolved, unprocessed trauma. Extreme behavioral issues that seem rooted in the child's trauma history are another indicator that a coherent narrative has not yet been built, one that integrates both the linguistic narrative of the trauma and the somatosensory memories related to the event.

Invitations to Disclosure

The invitations to disclosure that are described next are in the service of helping a child create a coherent narrative of his trauma history. In no way are these interventions intended to supersede or replace a structured forensic interview, but rather to give permission to the child to start processing the jumble of images, thoughts, sensory impressions, and emotions connected to the trauma. It is critical that the therapist take accurate notes and avoid asking leading questions or shifting to an interview format in these cases.

Zip It

The first such directive intervention is called "zip it" (Goodyear-Brown, 2002) and is a way of giving a child permission to leave weighty information in the playroom for safekeeping until the client is ready to reveal it directly to the therapist. Many children enter the playroom with intrusive images, fears,

Figure 8.10   Ollie the Alligator Puppet

or oppressive thoughts that require an exhaustive amount of energy to keep hidden inside themselves. Children are usually unprepared to verbalize any of their troubling inner content during an initial session. However, if I can provide a container other than myself for the child, she is given an opportunity to dump some of that disturbing content in the playroom and leave it there. To this end, I keep a hand puppet named Ollie the Alligator on the puppet rack in the playroom (Figure 8.10).

Each set of his teeth are made from one side of a zipper. Through this clever craftsmanship, his mouth zips and unzips. As a child is exploring the room I may introduce him to Ollie the Alligator and explain that Ollie's job in the playroom is to chew on things for kids until kids are ready to share them with me. My explanation goes like this: "You know, a lot of times kids come in and they've got all this stuff they're thinking about, all this stuff that's sort of weighing on them, and it's kind of heavy. Sometimes kids come in here and may have secrets or troublesome thoughts or scary pictures in their heads. Kids don't usually want to talk about these things at first. But sometimes they want to put them somewhere else, outside of themselves, so they don't feel so heavy anymore. If you have something inside like that, you can draw a picture of it or write it down. Then you can put it inside Ollie's mouth and zip it up. He'll hold on to it for you until you're ready to share it with me or with someone else." I keep several smaller animals in the office whose mouths also zip and unzip, in case I have more than one client at a

Figure 8.11   Tiger Depositories

time in need of storage for a troublesome piece of information. I show all the zippable animals to the child and let him choose the vessel in which he would like to store his weighty information (Figure 8.11).

The smaller animals come in handy when I have several clients at one time who wish to leave something burdensome in the playroom. A client may draw a picture of something that's happened to him or write down something upsetting that he's experienced, fold it up, and put it inside the tiger. I tuck the tiger safely away until this client returns.

What often happens is that the act of putting the burdensome thought or event on paper externalizes it, and placing the paper in the chosen depository creates an alternative holding environment, alleviating the internal pressure that the child has been feeling. The inner significance of the subject matter that the child stores in the animal may have reached almost insurmountable proportions in the child's mind. Up until now, the child may have believed that the content was too secretive, too shaming, or too destructive to be revealed. The child's externalization of the material represents a risk. The child may feel vulnerable having the information that he has so carefully guarded up until now being "out there." When the child unveils the content and nothing catastrophic happens as a result, the child's vigilance is countered. Zip it is a stepping stone in desensitizing the child to sharing the trauma content while simultaneously allowing the client a place to leave it.

The Creep and the Creepy Crawlies

"The creep and the creepy crawlies" (Goodyear-Brown, 2002) is another intervention aimed at helping children draw near to a description of their own abuse in a nonverbal, nonthreatening way. When I have a client who has experienced abuse but is stuck in the intrusive or avoidance symptoms of PTSD, I introduce this intervention by having the child draw a self-portrait. While she is drawing, I tell a story about a time when I had a spider crawl over my foot. I tell the child that it made me feel creepy crawly. Then I talk about how certain touches can make us feel uncomfortable in that same creepy crawly way. When the child is finished with the drawing, I will ask, "Have you ever had an ant or a spider crawl on you? Have you ever had a fly or a mosquito land on you?" Most children respond with examples of their own. We then process how it felt to have the bug on their skin. I again make the comparison between this creepy crawly feeling and other uncomfortable feelings we get from creepy touches. Then I give the prompt, "Put a sticker on any part of your body (the drawing of the body) that's ever felt creepy crawly." Children who have not been traumatized might put a sticker on their self-portrait's foot and say, "That's where I got bit by an ant," or put a sticker on the self-portrait's elbow and say, "That's where a bee stung me." And that's the extent of their disclosure. The children who have been maltreated, particularly if maltreatment has been sexual in nature, will often put the spider stickers on the genital areas of the self-portrait. This action sometimes functions as a beginning point in disclosure for narrative-building purposes. A couple of examples follow.

Austin, an 11-year-old boy diagnosed with Asperger's Disorder, had been sexually abused by his 16-year-old brother for a span of 2 years. At the time that Austin entered treatment, his brother had been moved to a residential treatment program for sex offenders. However, although Austin was now physically safe, he had found no psychological or emotional safety. He had avoided any mention of the abusive events and was having extreme behavior problems. The disclosure was irrelevant for purposes of prosecution but was very important as a beginning point for his healing. The energy that Austin was investing in defending himself against recollections of the trauma was not available for use in the typical developmental processes of childhood.

On initial meeting, Austin sat in one corner of the playroom, hunched over, eyes downcast. He intermittently voiced the statement, "I don't want to talk about it," even though I was not approaching the subject in any way. He was interested in drawing and created several elaborate drawings in the course of the first session. During the second session, he was eager to create a self-portrait. When he was finished, I offered him some spider stickers and invited him to place them on any part of his portrait's body that had ever felt creepy crawly. Austin looked at me for a moment and then asked me to turn around. It was important to him that his actions not be witnessed. Once my back was turned he affixed some spider stickers to the self-portrait. He then proceeded to fold the paper in half again and again until the piece of paper was small enough to fit in the palm of his hand. Next he moved to the shelves and chose my lockbox, a wooden box with a variety of locking doors. He put the piece of paper on the floor of the lockbox and then filled it with army men, tanks, and grenades. Finally he locked all the locks and said it was OK for me to turn around now. He asked me to put the box up "very high where no one else can reach it." I did as he requested, and we did not speak of it again for the rest of that session.

A week had passed when Austin came in for his next session. He immediately looked up to the top shelf and said, "It's still there." He asked me to take it down, and he unpacked it. He then moved the piece of paper, without opening it, into a toy safe that came equipped with a combination lock. I said, "I see that you are moving the creepy-crawly paper to the safe. I just want you to know that the combination for that safe is on the bottom, so any of the other children who come in here to play could open the safe." He paused in the act of closing the safe door and, with his back turned toward me, shrugged and said offhandedly, "I know." I responded by saying, "It feels OK to you now that other people might see what you've shown on your drawing." He nodded. He had decided that the content of the paper didn't have to be a secret anymore. Austin ended his visit with the paper still stored in the safe. I removed the paper from the safe, to protect his confidentiality between visits, and put it back in the safe just before his next session. One week later, Austin marched into the playroom, went directly over to the safe, unlocked it, and handed me the paper. He said, "You can look at it now." By degrees, his self-titrated progression of unveiling had desensitized him to the

Figure 8.12 Austin's *Creepy Crawlies*

shame produced by the content of the paper. The picture he had drawn and the spiders he had placed can be seen in Figure 8.12.

Soon after Austin decided to show me his picture, we were able to begin verbally and kinesthetically processing the sexual abuse that he had experienced at the hands of his brother. The kinesthetic act of moving the evidence of the abuse, step by self-guided step, from maximum security locations within the playroom to minimum security locations and finally into the hands of the therapist allowed Austin to overcome the shame that had previously kept him immobilized.

Three-Dimensional Creepy Crawly

The self-portrait and the spider stickers are effective kinesthetic props for older children. Younger children can absorb the metaphor that equates spiders to creepy touches, but they may need to manipulate the metaphoric content in three-dimensional form. For example, I attempted this intervention with a 4-year-old boy named Chris. He drew a scribble on the paper and stuck the spider stickers to the furniture. Given his developmental level I should have been prepared for the incoherence of his response and

I shrugged it off as a failed intervention. However, some part of the metaphor resonated with Chris.

The next week when he came into the playroom, he chose an African-American baby doll and undressed it. He got out the doctor's kit and began to "fix" the baby. It is a typical play pattern for traumatized children to choose a self-object and then try to fix it, so I was responding to his play with supportive, nondirective responses. Abruptly, Chris left the baby doll and went to my shelves. He chose a large, grotesque rubber spider and brought it back to the baby doll. He placed the spider on the exposed private part of the baby doll and said, "Ms. Paris, take a picture" (Figure 8.13).

I immediately remembered our attempted paper and sticker version of the creep and the creepy crawly from the last session. I hypothesized that he was giving me the three-dimensional version of his own experience of creepy touching. Once again, this was not the appropriate time to ask if anyone had ever touched him in a way that made him feel creepy crawly. I simply contained what he was showing me and took the picture as he requested. Chris smiled and then he did something that I have never had a client do before or

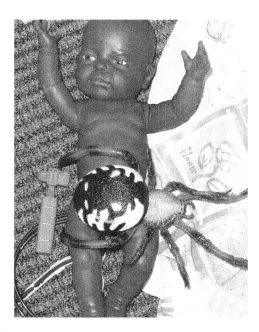

Figure 8.13   Chris's *Creepy Crawly*

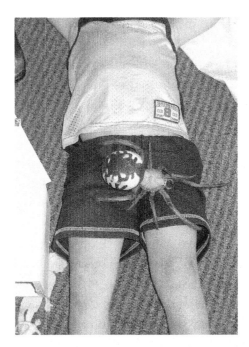

Figure 8.14   Chris Puts the Spider on Himself

since. He laid down on the floor, put the rubber spider on top of his clothes in the vicinity of his own private parts, and said "Ms. Paris, take a picture" (Figure 8.14).

If Chris's behavior had crossed a sexually inappropriate boundary—if, for example, he had taken his pants or underwear down—I would have calmly set appropriate limits. However, his extremely atypical play behavior was another test, another challenge of containment. "Can you handle what I am showing you?" I told him that I thought it would be a good idea if mom was present while the picture was being taken. After preparing her privately, I helped her to be another container for him as we documented his use of the toys. Chris came into his next session asking to see the pictures again. After I showed them to him, he set about creating a sand tray. In the tray there was a little boy in a bathtub, covered in sand (which he explained was water) up to his neck (Figure 8.15).

Chris said, "The boy's in trouble. Something bad is happening in the bathtub."

After I expressed my concern for the boy in the bathtub, Chris chose rescue vehicles and placed them in the scene. This play behavior represented

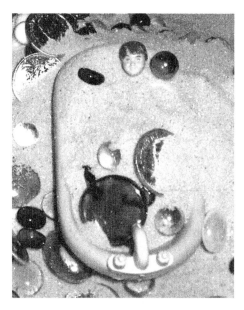

Figure 8.15   Boy in Bathwater up to His Neck

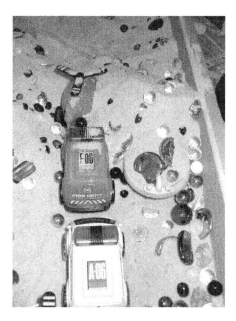

Figure 8.16   Rescue Vehicles Alongside the Boy in the Bathtub

a clear shift from previous play, in that it was Chris's first attempt to get help for a character in a play scene. After he had placed the rescue vehicles alongside the bathtub, we explored how it might feel for the boy in the tub to know that people were coming to rescue him. Chris smiled and said that it probably felt pretty good (Figure 8.16).

One week later Chris told me about the sexually abusive acts that he had endured at the hands of his father. The majority of his abuse had occurred during bath time. This continuum of disclosure was a series of self-titrated exposures delivered through Chris' metaphoric images. My communications of "I see what you are showing me and I can contain it" in response to each measure of trauma content were the authorization Chris needed to show me more.

Therapeutic Storytelling Devices

Storytelling devices are another powerful way of loosening the choke hold that trauma symptoms may have on a child. Therapeutic stories can normalize a child's experience while sending hopeful messages that a way out of their current dilemma exists. One such hopeful narrative is a wonderful story called *The Very Quiet Cricket* (Carle, 1990). The hero of the story is a very quiet cricket who keeps trying to communicate with various bugs that come across his path. Each page of the book ends with the phrase "He rubbed his wings together, but nothing happened. Not a sound." The next page shows the cricket's predicament the next day, when he again wants to talk to another creature, so "He rubbed his wings together, but nothing happened. Not a sound." The cricket experiences failure over and over again, and the repetitions of the words set the reader up to expect the same outcome on future pages. However, at the end of the book, the cricket comes across another very quiet cricket and he rubs his wings together one more time. The reader turns the page in anticipation and hears, through a built-in mechanism in the book, the sound of a cricket chirping.

The metaphor is rich. It's about finding one's voice. It is not a far stretch from a cricket that can't make noise to a child who can't talk about what happened to him. The plight of a child who wants to tell but can't is normalized. A child who is keeping a self- or other-enforced silence will identify with the quiet cricket. Equally important is the hopeful message embedded in the tale. In the story the cricket keeps trying to communicate effectively, even in the face of multiple failed attempts. This provides hope for the child and a subconscious message that someday the child will be able to break the silence. The possible endings of the story can be expanded by offering a cricket puppet to the child after the story has been read. The prompt from the therapist could be, "Pretend you are the cricket. What would you most want to say once you had learned how to talk?" Whether or not the content produced by the child is immediately relevant to her situation, she gets the experience of making the cricket talk. This adds a kinesthetic dimension to the child's understanding of the cricket's breakthrough.

Many beautiful therapeutic stories can be used in the service of our traumatized clients. Compendiums of therapeutic stories are available for busy clinicians who may want to augment a client's current treatment with a therapeutic storytelling metaphor (Burns, 2005; Davis, 1990). Child therapists can also learn to create therapeutic stories to meet the unique needs of their clients by following a simple, straightforward format. A protagonist is chosen first, a character with whom the client can identify. This character must then face a challenge of some kind, a crisis that must be resolved. Often a helping figure is introduced into the story and aids the hero in overcoming whatever obstacle is keeping him from his goal. Lastly, the hero's success is celebrated by a community of witnesses. Within these basic parameters, any number of rich metaphors can become part of a child's healing narrative journey. The power of metaphor in therapeutic storytelling is more fully explicated by several gifted professionals (Cattanach, 2002, 2008; Mills & Crowley, 2001).

I have added to these offerings through a therapeutic story titled *Gabby the Gecko* (Goodyear-Brown, 2003b). It is an amalgamation of the experiences of the many sexually abused children who have come through my playroom over the years. The book centers on a young gecko girl named Gabby. She gabs with girls and babbles with the boys. She is strong and healthy and trusting. She represents the innocent self-confidence that was present in many children we see before they were traumatized (Figure 8.17).

Figure 8.17   Gabby Gabs with the Girls

One day a character named Wiley the Wizard Lizard comes to town to give a fireworks demonstration. Everyone gets a job except Gabby, and when he offers to let her accompany him back to his home to get a forgotten firework, she eagerly accepts. When they get to his house, he does some "bad magic" on her. This bad magic is deliberately undefined in the story. The two-page spread that follows the bad magic is written in white lettering on a deep black background. No pictures appear on these pages. Rather, the writing describes some of the sensory impressions that a child might have while experiencing a traumatic event. Gabby's tummy hurts. She feels like she is stuck in molasses. The traumatized child is likely to resonate with one or more of the sensory experiences described. Afterward, Wiley puts a spell on Gabby's lips so that she can't tell anyone what has happened (Figure 8.18).

This part of the story evolved directly from the repeated scenarios played out by my child clients who have survived sexual abuse. Over and over again they create stories in which their lips are locked and despite the internal pressure of the secret to get out, the external pressure is more powerful. The external pressure can come from a number of sources. Many children have been overtly threatened by their perpetrators. The threat may be the promise of harm coming to the child if she tells. The threat may be the promise of harm coming to a beloved parent or sibling if the child tells. A perpetrator may implant the sometimes more devastating fear in the child that a beloved parent will no longer

Figure 8.18   Wiley Casts His Spell on Gabby's Mouth

love the child or will even be actively disgusted with the child once that parent knows about the sexual acts. Sometimes the child is promised tangible rewards for keeping the secret or gets intangible rewards, like undivided adult attention or the feeling that she is special. In other cases the shame and sense of dirtiness experienced by the child is enough to keep the child quiet. The shame itself acts as a massive weight and serves to seal the child's lips.

After the spell has been cast, Gabby returns home but is not acting normally. Her parents assume that she is going through a phase. Soon she meets another young girl who recognizes Gabby's pain because she had a similar experience. She encourages Gabby to go back into the woods to find help. Gabby gathers up her courage and returns to the woods. In the woods she comes to the home of Carey the Kangaroo (Figure 8.19).

Gabby says, "I can't tell you what happened." Carey accepts her silence and invites her to dig in the garden. Together they walk to the edge of a lake that adjoins Carey's garden. Gabby begins to dig in the dirt. As she digs she begins to cry. The deeper she digs the more she cries. This part of the story is my way of describing the process that happens almost magically over and over again in the playroom. A child who is unable to tell begins to play in the sand, or work with the other expressive materials. I join the child in this activity. The act of being involved in the same soothing yet kinesthetic activity loosens the hold of the silence. The experience of being side by

Figure 8.19   Carey the Kangaroo

side, heads together over a play activity allows the child to feel supported, as opposed to confronted. The story of what happened seems less awful. As the therapist and child build mountains in the sand together, the child's own mountains seem less insurmountable. This process continues until the story of the abuse begins to flow out of the child.

In Gabby's story, her tears fall into the lake and activate the Telling Tree. The Telling Tree bubbles up through the surface and Gabby picks a magical blossom from the tree, rubs it against her lips, and they are magically unlocked. She tells Carey what happened, and then she runs home and tells her family what happened. Wiley the Wizard Lizard is rounded up and banished from the town, never to return. In the final pages, Gabby breaks the magician's wand over her knee as her family and friends cheer in the background.

This story came from the children. As such, it holds a special place in my heart. When I go to speak at sexual abuse and maltreatment conferences, clinicians who have read Gabby the Gecko to some of their locked-up clients have been gracious enough to share the results with me. Clients have been empowered, verbal disclosures have been made, and the metaphors from Gabby have become part of other children's healing journeys. I am grateful to all the children who contributed to the creation of Gabby every time I hear that this story has brought a new level of freedom to a child.

Conclusion

A child's continuum of disclosure is the journey taken in the playroom, the telling of the trauma narrative through the medium of play. During a child's process of disclosure, I first give permission for the child to display disjointed and often disturbing images, sensations, and verbalizations through their engagement with the play materials. Second, I witness the displays and validate the child's experiences. Last, I make sure there is a permanent record of the display. Later in treatment the child and I revisit the self-titrated glimpses of trauma narrative and attempt to sequence them or otherwise provide structure for the narrative. This work will be covered in subsequent chapters.

Throughout this chapter, you have seen the journeys of many children through their continuums of disclosure. The nature of a child's unveiling is unique to the individual, often cloaked in the metaphors of play and may or may not include words. It is not our job to interpret the metaphors so much as it is to witness them and experience them together with the child. The metaphoric witnessing invites the child to take the next step on the journey of revelation.

9

Experiential Mastery Play:
A Form of Gradual Exposure

*E*xperiential mastery play (EMP) is an umbrella term that is meant to capture the variety of ways in which children, through prop-based gradual exposure, begin to work through their immobilizing fears and desensitize their trauma content. This may begin to occur under the child's self-direction or may require directive assistance on the part of the therapist. Children choose symbols and create scenarios that allow them to safely approach a mastery experience in relation to disturbing subject matter. Sometimes children engage in this process spontaneously. Other times children are mired in patterns of stagnant posttraumatic play. This repetitive, stuck play often requires more directive invitations by the therapist to approach the process of play-based gradual exposure that can, with attunement and patience on the part of the therapist, lead to resolution of the traumatic material. Gil (2006) calls this process trauma-focused play therapy (TF-PT) and lists specific therapist interventions, including the purposeful selection of toys that serve as literal symbols of the trauma. The therapist then encourages the child's interaction with these toys in ways that foster energized emotional and psychological movement to advance the resolution of posttraumatic play in children.

Gradual exposure is a crucial component of trauma focused cognitive behavioral therapy (TF-CBT)(Cohen, Deblinger, Mannarino, & Steer, 2004; Cohen, Mannarino, & Deblinger, 2006), a much-researched and valuable intervention model for treating traumatized children. One recent study contends that imaginal exposure is the primary mechanism through which people experience resolution of their PTSD symptoms. Johnson and Lubin (2006) compared prolonged exposure, EMDR, and the counting method in 51 women who had experienced multiple traumas. The researchers found a significant symptom reduction in all three groups but negligible differences between methods. They go on to posit that imaginal exposure may be the necessary and sufficient component of PTSD treatment. However, young children have limitations in their cognitive capacities for internal manipulation of symbols. These limitations, taken together with posttraumatic avoidance symptoms, limit the usefulness of imaginal exposure with the youngest children. Therefore, concretizing the in vivo exposures in the form of the three-dimensional materials of the playroom, as happens in EMP, utilizes the child's natural bent toward play to achieve the same goal in a developmentally sensitive manner.

This chapter includes examples of child-directed experiential mastery play as well as case examples in which I facilitate an increased experience of mastery through (1) carefully chosen questions, (2) encouragement of active engagement with or disposal of a perpetrator symbol, (3) the kinesthetic manipulation of an art or sand creation, or (4) a direct invitation to dispose of the troublesome content in a way that is meaningful to the child.

One such directive intervention, the experiential mastery technique (Shelby, 1997), encourages the client to draw a picture of the scary content, talk about the emotions connected to the content, and then choose a way to manipulate the drawing that helps the client feel empowered in relation to the content. Gil (2006) describes an adaptation of this technique that involves the use and manipulation of sand tray miniatures.

Still other children will find other forms of expression, containment, and manipulation more appealing based on an individualized combination of age, developmental stage, gender, history, personality, and play style. For a subset of children, the sequence of experiential mastery play follows a similar format. Children choose perpetrator symbols and self-objects, and in the playroom environment find the unique opportunity to be in the same room with the perpetrator in fantasy while retaining all the power in the relationship.

The definition of trauma has at its core a loss of control, a disempowerment. When a baby comes out of the womb she coos up at her mother, and her mother coos back at her. Through the many repetitions of this reciprocal interaction she learns that she can impact the world. A healthy developing child experiences a burgeoning sense of self-efficacy. As she masters new tasks and receives affirmation from her caregivers, she feels competent. She can, through either signaling or aversive behavior, get caregivers to respond in need-meeting ways. The contingent responsiveness of a child's environment is empowering. Trauma strips away this sense of power and control. Traumatic experiences erode a child's burgeoning sense of competency. Traumatized children often feel vulnerable, raw, and very, very small. When the trauma has involved abuse, the child may perceive herself as tiny and inconsequential, while the perpetrator is perceived as a huge, often immovable force.

Long after a child becomes physically safe from a perpetrator, the child may still experience the perpetrator as the single most influential adult in his life. The child may carry a lurking vigilance and may expect that, despite the protestations of caring adults, the perpetrator will find him and put him back in his powerless position. Maltreated children are easily flooded by the possibility of coming face to face with their monsters again. Seeing a picture of the perpetrator or hearing the perpetrator's voice can cause panic or momentary immobilization in the child.

The symbols of threat that clients choose often include, but are not limited to, the toys in the playroom that represent dangerous creatures, dangerous characters, or dangerous circumstances. Favorite symbols in my playroom include the two-headed dragons. These symbols give powerful expression to the sense of duality that these children communicate when they reference their perpetrators. The dynamic of duality is particularly noticeable with preschool-age clients who engage in dichotomous thinking. These children have difficulty keeping two disparate characteristics in mind at the same time. Therefore, when mom is nurturing and kind, the child perceives her as "good mommy." When she is mean or yells at the child, she becomes "mean mommy." Abusive adults are often understood as manifesting at least two distinct personalities. Sometimes the grownup embodies the caring adult who can be fun and friendly, who may buy gifts or treats for the child, who may listen to the child and make the child feel special. At other times, this person may seem to morph into a monster in the child's imagination as the grownup calls the child names, hits him, hurts him, or touches him in sexually inappropriate ways. The two-headed dragon conveys this impression of two personalities in one person.

Another powerful symbol for the perpetrator is Two-Face from Batman. I found my Two-Face figure at a flea market for 25 cents, but he is worth much more than this to the children who have caged and manipulated him in the playroom. One half of his body shows an attractive man in a tuxedo. The other half shows a scary-looking man with a twisted face. Jill, a 3½-year-old girl, endured ritual satanic abuse until she was removed from this environment and placed with a nurturing relative. She was fascinated, during her initial session, with the Two-Face figure. She turned him over and over in her hands and eventually said the name of her perpetrator. Once she had chosen him as her perpetrator symbol, she put him in the sand tray laying flat on his back. She went over to the shelves and chose a small snake. Jill's caregiver reported that snakes had been used in the same rituals in which she was sexually abused.

Apparently, Jill was terrified of snakes. Approaching the miniaturized play snakes in her own timing and for her chosen purpose within the safe confines of the playroom allowed her to experience a beginning sense of mastery over the feared creatures, a sort of in vivo exposure. Moreover, Jill chose to place the snake in the sand tray near the private parts of Two Face (Figure 9.1).

Jill was able to turn the terror around and point it at the perpetrator, adjusting the balance of power in her favor. This is a form of experiential mastery play. Jill's presenting symptoms included frequent nightmares, clinging to her caregiver, and occasional panic attacks, particularly when she was in public. She would see someone who resembled the leader of the abusive sect, become paralyzed with fear, and wet her pants. Trauma reminders or other exposures to trauma content were completely overwhelming for her, and her primary coping strategy had become avoidance. A directive intervention might have encouraged Jill to keep the perpetrator in mind or review the

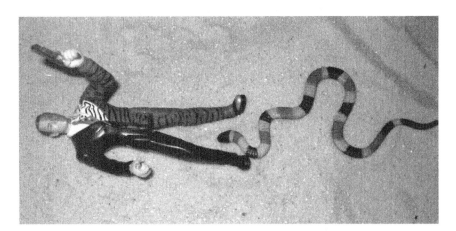

Figure 9.1   Two-Face with Snake Approaching

details of her experiences. However, her self-directed choice of a plaything to represent the perpetrator and her subsequent self-directed manipulation of this symbol gave her a manageable exposure to the trauma content, while rewarding her with full command of how her chosen symbol is dealt with. The dimensions of power are turned on their head in the playroom and she is able to have full control over how he is handled. Indeed, roles are reversed on a number of levels. In relation to Two-Face, Jill is disproportionately bigger and stronger. As an automaton, he is helpless to defend himself and completely at the mercy of her use of him in play. She calls the shots. The figurine must submit and accept his fate.

Furthermore, he must stay immobilized in whatever final position she chooses for him. This final positioning is an external construction that children create, usually in response to my prompt that the session is coming to an end. At the end of Jill's session, I gave her a five-minute warning. She took Two-Face out of the sand and put him into the jail and locked it. She was rewarded by another mastery experience as she chose his method of containment. He must stay locked up where he can't hurt anyone until she returns to deal with him again (Figure 9.2).

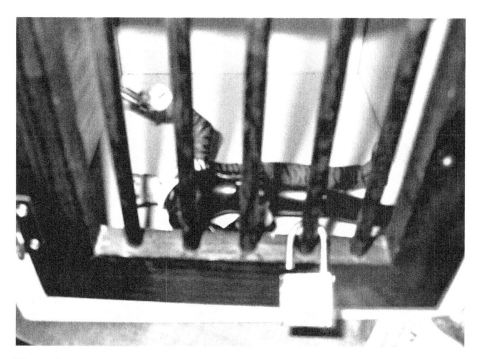

Figure 9.2   Two-Face Perpetrator Symbol Behind Bars

As she looks at it and absorbs the dynamics of his entrapment, this experience can become a permanently encoded internal image of power or control. Another way to describe the process would be as one of wish fulfillment through fantasy. Obviously, the actual perpetrator is so distressing to Jill that she becomes paralyzed with fear when confronted with any actual reminders of him. She will most probably not have the opportunity to influence any long-term consequences that may be visited upon him outside the playroom, but within the walls of the playroom she is the final arbiter of his fate.

As children become bolder in relationship to their perpetrator symbols, they may trade them in for larger symbols. Sally, a 5-year-old client, eventually chose my Screamer toy to stand in for the janitor who had sexually molested her in her preschool. The Screamer is battery operated and makes screaming noises when turned on. The first time Sally put the switch in the on position, she was unnerved by the screaming sound he made and quickly turned it off (Figure 9.3).

Then she turned to me and grinned. Sally sprang up, went and got my jump rope, and began to tie him up with it (Figure 9.4).

Next she found my ball-and-chain and put it on his foot (Figure 9.5).

When she was satisfied that he was completely immobilized, Sally flipped his switch back to the on position and listened to his screaming. After she listened to him for a minute or so, she asked if I would help her find a way to

Figure 9.3 Sally's Perpetrator Symbol: *The Screamer*

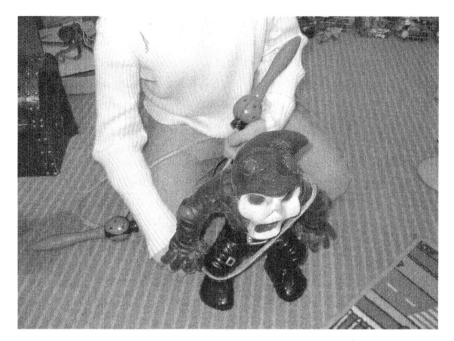

Figure 9.4 Sally Containing *The Screamer*

Figure 9.5 *The Screamer* Fully Bound

slide him onto the baseball bat and hold him suspended in the air, so that she could chop at him with a plastic sword. I was happy to oblige. As he swung suspended from the bat as a perpetrator piñata, she hit him over and over again. I wondered out loud if she could speak to him while she was using the sword. She began to say things like, "I hate you," "You're a bad man," "Why did you do it?" and "Now you see how it feels!"

The pairing of words with actions allowed for a powerful catharsis of anger. When Sally was done beating up the Screamer, she took a deep breath and seemed altogether more settled. Her experiential mastery play took the form of full-body kinesthetic aggression against the perpetrator symbol. Through her physical domination of the symbol, she achieved a role reversal between her helpless self and her abuser while experiencing her body as powerful once again.

When I share this case material in workshops, I am occasionally asked if this aggression toward the symbol in the playroom could translate to actual aggression toward the perpetrator outside of the play arena. The terror and immobilization engendered by reminders of the perpetrator make it unlikely that the child would approach the perpetrator in reality. It is only through the play that children begin the process of coming to grips with the consequences of their perpetration, their own emotional and relational responses to it, and have some empowerment through wish fulfillment.

The question of whether or not to allow aggression in the playroom is one that is the focus of much controversy (Drewes, 2008). When I am working with clients who were referred for externalizing issues, including aggression, I steer children away from physical displays of anger and spend more time augmenting coping and working toward affect regulation. For children who already exhibit self-control deficits, allowing for or encouraging aggressive activity in the playroom can exacerbate a child's difficulties.

The problem with unfocused aggression is that it is positively reinforcing. It feels good to hit things. When I began practicing, all my encounters with children happened in a fully equipped CCPT playroom. Some children would enter the playroom and be immediately drawn to the bop bag. They would hit the bop bag over and over again. I would reflect their aggression without judgment and label any affect that was being communicated. In my experience, children would become more escalated and more dysregulated the more they hit the bop bag. It was as if the anger was reverberating within the child as opposed to being expelled. So I began inviting children to pair words of some sort with their actions. A child might say, "You are a liar!" or "I don't have to do what you say anymore!" This is the approach that I now employ with traumatized children in relation to their perpetrator symbols. If a child is physically aggressing against a perpetrator symbol, I invite the child to match verbalizations with the kinesthetic engagement. This focused pairing of cognition with physical activity provides for a cathartic release that leaves children calm and settled.

Therapist as Role Play Partner in Experiential Mastery Play

The next time Sally came in she asked me to be the bad guy in her fantasy play. I said I would be happy to be the bad guy if she told me what to do. She was delighted to boss me around. The transcript of that session follows:

Sally: OK. You put on this hat.

Paris: OK. I'm putting it on.

Sally: You're the bad wizard who lives in a castle. You have me trapped in your dungeon.

Paris: So you want me to play the bad wizard and you will be my prisoner.

Sally puts handcuffs on herself and arranges a series of dragon puppets in a semi-circle around herself (Figure 9.6).

Figure 9.6   Sally in Her Self-Prepared Dungeon

Sally: Yeah. This is my dungeon room. You sit over in that chair. Tell me to be quiet.

Paris (in a character voice): Be quiet, little girl.

Sally (in a pseudo-scared voice): Yes, sir.

Sally (in a side whisper): Now tell me to make you dinner.

Paris (in the voice of an old wizard): Little girl, I'm hungry. You make my dinner!

Sally steps out of role, grins, and whispers to me.

Sally: I'm gonna put poison in it and kill you.

Paris: Oh, you're thinking up clever ways to get rid of the bad guy.

Sally: OK. Now eat the food and pretend to die.

Returning to the role play, I pretend to eat the food.

Paris (in the voice of an old wizard): This is delicious! But wait . . . what's happening? You poisoned me! I'm dying.

I pretend to choke and then to die.

Sally: Now I can get out!

Sally repeated this play theme week after week for several sessions. Each time she would give me the role of the "bad wizard in the castle."

Each time she would design her own cell in the dungeon and put the handcuffs on herself. Each time she would find a way to kill the bad wizard. One time she had me pretend to fall asleep and she snuck the phone into her prison cell, called 9–1–1, and the police came and got the wizard. During another session she commanded me to look out the window, snuck up behind me, and attached a fake grenade to my wizard's cloak. It goes without saying that I blew up. Sally needed the live interaction to fulfill her fantasy subjugation of her perpetrator. She needed to solve the problem of how to escape him, so she staged the problem over and over again and challenged herself to come up with new solutions each time. By the time therapy ended, Sally had engaged in a series of self-directed experiential mastery play exercises and had come up with a plethora of ways to rid herself of the perpetrator.

Whenever a client asks me to play the bad guy, my safety antennae goes up. It can be very useful for a child to be able to perform their experiential mastery play in the living, breathing three-dimensional relationship of self and therapist. One must be careful, however, that the lines of pretend play are clear. Moreover, a play therapist must immediately step out of role and set a limit on behavior that might endanger either the therapist or the client. For example, if the child instructs the therapist to engage in an action that crosses appropriate physical boundaries, the therapist must stop the play and redirect. A child might attempt to reenact some of the abuse that has occurred. A little girl who has been sexually abused may ask the therapist to take off her clothes. If a child asks me to perform an action in the role of the bad guy that is inappropriate, I calmly step out of role and explain to the child that the most important rule in the playroom is that everyone stays safe. Following the child's direction would not be safe for her and therefore we have to find another way to play. Usually clients accept the limit and move directly back into the role play with a different action. If a child became physically violent in the midst of a role play, the therapist would also need to step out of the role and set the limit. Although the interruption may be frustrating for the child, the child ultimately experiences the therapist as keeping the playroom safe for everyone.

Helpers in Experiential Mastery Play

A different manifestation of experiential mastery play occurs when a child enlists a helping symbol to fight the perpetrator for him. Sometimes the child feels inadequate, even in the fantasy world he has created, to defeat his demons himself. In this case, he may choose a magical symbol or someone who represents a helping figure in his own experience. The case of Michael, a 10-year-old boy with significant maltreatment history, illustrates this dynamic.

Michael experienced a range of atrocities while in the care of his biological mother. A friend of the family eventually got wind of the abuse and called DCS. They immediately removed Michael from his home and placed him with a foster mom, whom he calls "Momma Kathy," who is now in the process of adopting him. The biological mother continued to pursue the child and threatened to kidnap Michael and kill the foster mother. The foster mom protected the child in every way she could. Moreover, she agreed to take on this very troubled, violent boy and care for him over the long haul. At the time that Michael entered treatment it had already been a long haul. Michael had been on medication for many years and experienced chronic dysregulation. On one occasion, he took a shovel and smashed in the back windows of Momma Kathy's car. He had been through a series of therapists. He had been dismissed from each one after he lost control in their offices. After he had been seeing me for a couple of months, he asked if I was going to "fire" him from therapy like the other counselors.

Michael has been in treatment with me for a year and a half now and due to his complex trauma history he will continue to need supportive services for awhile. As of this writing, he is now a month away from being officially adopted by his foster mother. On one of Michael's most recent visits, Momma Kathy described a meltdown that had just occurred. They had stopped for a quick lunch on the way to treatment. Michael had ordered a piece of pizza and Momma Kathy had ordered a sandwich. His pizza was blackened on the bottom and he was convinced that there was something wrong with it. Mom tried to explain to him that sometimes the pizza gets a little burned on the bottom but it's fine to eat it. Michael responded by throwing her sandwich on the floor and kicking it across the room.

In our session, I brought up the incident. As Michael's relationship abilities are growing, so is his conscience. He felt remorse, a fairly new emotion for him, over his actions. Moreover, he seemed puzzled by his own reaction. We decided to be detectives. We built a narrative of the most recent times when he had lost control and done something hurtful. Then we rehearsed Momma Kathy's responses. She stuck with him whether he made good choices or bad choices. I highlighted how Momma Kathy had chosen him and that this was a forever choice. We began to talk about his biological mom and made a list of how Momma Kathy is different from his birthmother.

As we rehearsed the patterns of his behavior, Michael recognized that his volatility and difficulty in trusting others was tied to the maltreatment he received at the hands of his biological mother. Michael articulated his new revelation by saying, "It's like she controls my todays even though she is my yesterday." I was astonished at both the eloquence and the simple truth of this statement. Through narrative building and rehearsal of life

Figure 9.7   Biological Mom Enclosed by Fences

events, Michael was able to draw two new cognitive connections. The first connection was that his current meltdown behaviors were tied directly to biological mom's early treatment of him. The second connection was that Momma Kathy was the complete antithesis of his biological mom and could be trusted. This was an important step for Michael, but the head knowledge itself was not going to be enough. Once he recognized his biological mom's continued influence in his decision making, he needed to separate himself from her in some tangible way. He chose the Bride of Frankenstein figure and said "This is my first momma." Then he put her in a corner of the sand tray and separated her from the rest of the tray by enclosing her in several layers of fencing material (Figure 9.7).

His experiential mastery play first takes the form of containment. Notice that one fence does not provide enough of a boundary to Michael. He surrounds her with two layers of fencing. This double layer of containment provides Michael with enough sense of safety for him to begin to approach the problem of what to do with his birth mom. He has been grappling with conceptual information about her in the first half of the session and now needs to grapple with her kinesthetically. He chooses first to bury her (Figure 9.8).

He exerts his power over the symbol of his biological mother through this burial. Through this action sequence, he effectively makes her disappear and absorbs the sense of what this feels like. Somehow, this is not enough for

Figure 9.8   Michael Buries his Biological Mom

Michael. He digs her back up and holds her in his hand for a minute, staring intently at her. Next, he puts a bridge in the sand tray. The use of bridges in sand tray work may represent transitions made or a journey between two different sets of life experiences. After wrapping her in layers of fence, he moves the Bride of Frankenstein onto the bridge. He then chooses the figurine of the girl in white, whose hands are folded in prayer, to represent Momma Kathy and places her directly in front of the biological mom figure on the bridge (Figure 9.9).

He chose a little girl dressed in white with hands lifted in prayer to represent his adoptive mother. He talked about how she was like an angel, the way she had swooped in and committed to being his forever mom. I commented that it looked like the moms were in a face-off on the bridge. Michael nodded and smiled. He stared intently at the two figures for a moment and then said, "I need to change something." He took the praying girl figure out of the sand and replaced her with Wonder Woman. Michael said, "There. Now she can kick her butt." He needed a more powerful symbol to represent Momma Kathy in order to ensure her victory over the biological mom (Figure 9.10).

As Michael contemplated the original figures that he'd placed on the bridge, he seemed to realize that there was a disparity in power. Initially, he had focused on his adoptive mom's goodness and chosen the sweet

Figure 9.9   The Stand-Off between the Two Mothers

Figure 9.10   Wonder Woman and Biological Mother Face Off

symbol of innocence. However, as he absorbed the scene, he felt the need to more fully represent her as his strong protector, hence the switch to Wonder Woman. The timeline that we had created earlier in the session of Michael's meltdowns and Momma Kathy's responses had highlighted her strength and

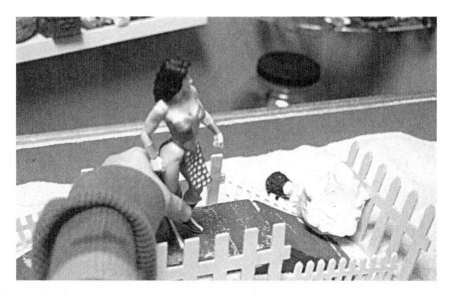

Figure 9.11   Wonder Woman Kicks the Biological Mom Off the Bridge

staying power in Michael's mind. His symbolic shift from a sweet, innocent symbol of goodness (the praying girl) to a strong, powerful and mature symbol of goodness (Wonder Woman) added visual and kinesthetic dimensions of this new knowledge to his cognitive awareness. Wonder Woman remains a symbol of goodness, but she is a defender of the weak and is powerful enough to defeat evil. She has enough power to overcome the biological mom, to move her out of the way so that the path forward is uncluttered. He begins to envision an outcome in which his forever mom provides a forever kind of protection from his birth mother. Michael tests out this possibility experientially by having Wonder Woman kick the Bride of Frankenstein off of the bridge (Figure 9.11).

Michael begins to psychologically open himself to the possibility that his adoptive mom can keep him safe from his birth mom. The kinesthetic learning that occurs through Michael's experiential mastery play reinforces his growing belief that there is a way out. Moreover, Michael receives experiential satisfaction from knocking the biological mom off the bridge. He is empowered by his play. Experiential mastery play often takes the form of wish fulfillment. In Michael's play, his wish for a protector powerful enough to defeat the nemesis of his birth mom was fulfilled.

In the following case example, Tracy, an 11-year-old girl who was sexually molested by an uncle, generates her own brand of wish fulfillment.

Tracy came in for a session during the week of her perpetrator's trial. Her videotaped testimony was being shown in court, so Tracy did not have to go through the court proceedings. Although most of the grownups involved with the case saw her lack of involvement in the court proceedings as protection, she saw it as an injustice. She wanted to be involved in deciding his punishment. Tracy picked up the giant wizard puppet as soon as she entered the room and put it on her hand. She began to tell me, in the wizard's voice, how unjust it was that she couldn't mete out his punishment.

Tracy: I'm calling my molester Mr. Dummy. What I don't think is really fair is I've gone through all this but I don't get any say-so about it. Isn't that weird? I mean like a say-so about his punishment.

Paris: Well, Mr. Wizard, what would you like his punishment to be if you could choose anything in the whole world?

Tracy (grinning widely): Well . . . if I could have three punishments for him that I would want to have happen to him, then I would want him to go to jail for 10 years or maybe 15 or even 30 years, and he loves to eat. He has a pretty big belly and so I would like him to have to stand up in one little chair and we're eating all this good, yummy food and he has to stand for 3 hours while we watch a movie and eat the food. And if he moves or stumbles or even talks he will spend 1 more year in jail. And I would like him to have to do whatever I told him to do. He would have to buy me anything I wanted him to but I wouldn't want him to take me anywhere. No way. Cuz I would be forced to punch him right here!

Tracy punches an imaginary character.

Paris: Oh. Punch the dummy.

Tracy: Yeah! Punch the dummy! Punch the dummy! Hold on one second. I'm gonna get something to punch! I'm mad!

Tracy goes and gets a big teddy bear to represent her uncle. She also gets a magician's wand.

Tracy: Bibbity bobbity boo.

Tracy thinks about what she will turn him into while she has the wizard puppet stroke his beard like he is thinking.

Tracy: I know! He can be a big beanbag.

Tracy has the wizard hit the teddy bear.

Paris: So beanbags are for beating up on, huh? Can you have the wizard talk to him while he's hitting him?

I ask her to pair verbalizations with movement in order to connect her cognitive processing to her physiological release, thereby allowing for a more focused channeling of emotion.

Tracy: Yeah. You make me so mad! And you are going to pay! One more good hit.

She knocks the bear off the couch. Tracy begins to stomp on him.

Tracy: Yeah! Stomp on him! Stomp on him! This is great!

Tracy pretends that the teddy bear grabs her.

Tracy: Help! Ms. Paris, he's got me!

I speak directly to the teddy bear, aligning with the client against her perpetrator symbol, while dragging him away from her.

Paris: You come over here! You get on the floor!

I grab him and hold him still while Tracy giggles and continues to stomp on him.

Tracy's experiential mastery play took the form of physically aggressing against her perpetrator symbol. As I joined with her in the physical subjugation of her perpetrator, her mastery play was augmented. She asked for another level of experience, that of being rescued from the perpetrator, when she cried out to the therapist while pretending that the perpetrator had grabbed her. She overtly asked for help within the role play and I was able to set verbal and physical limits with the symbol. Tracy's alignment with me against her perpetrator allowed her another level of mastery play. She "mastered" the task of asking for help when she needed it and was immediately rewarded with the experience of being rescued within the play.

Cleansing Rituals as Experiential Mastery Play

An initial discussion of cleansing rituals can be found in Chapter 3 on augmenting safety and security in the playroom. That discussion is expanded upon here. Cleansing rituals form another subset of play themes within the realm of experiential mastery play. Children who have endured physical abuse or sexual molestation or who have been involved in the gore of interpersonal or intrapersonal violence often feel tainted by the tactile stuff of the trauma. Sometimes they may feel like they can't get free of the distressing substances to which they were exposed. Blood, semen, feces, or other body fluids leave an indelible impression on a traumatized child. The associated physical sensations, smells, tastes, and other sensory memories may flood the child without notice. The child may do everything within his power to avoid materials that would serve as triggering reminders of the noxious substances. In the playroom, the finger paints, clay, wet sand, Play-Doh, and glue are only a few of the items that have the potential to remind traumatized children of sensory experiences that they may wish to avoid. However, once safety has been established in the playroom, children are often willing to approach experiences of these substances with the supportive presence of the play therapist. The child's eventual handling of these substances can serve as exposures to sensory content related to the trauma. With ongoing handling of the expressive arts materials, the toxicity associated with the traumagenic sense memories can be desensitized.

Clara, the 8-year-old-girl with a history of complex trauma, whose desensitization work was discussed briefly in Chapter 1, was brought to treatment by her adoptive mom. She had spent the first four years of her life in the care of her father. She had been chronically physically and sexually abused by both her father and her father's friend during this time. She was forced to perform fellatio on both men as well as on her younger brother. She and her brother were also photographed in sexual positions with each other. We began our work by building a sense of safety and security in the playroom. She chose figures to be her father and his friend and locked them up. She actively avoided any mention of her past experiences for the first couple of months of treatment.

Clara liked art and often made books out of construction paper and crayons or markers. She generally stayed away from any of the more kinesthetically activating materials. Then one afternoon she entered the playroom and went straight over to the glue. She began to squeeze it until it pooled on a piece of paper. As she squeezed, she said "I don't want to touch it." I validated her feelings and noted that she continued to use the material even though she didn't like it. I stated, "If and when you're ready to touch the sticky stuff, you'll know." After she had made an enormous glob of it on the paper, she put the glue down and began to run her fingers through the sticky stuff. She said, "It's so sticky and yucky--and I don't like it." I again reflected her verbalization and augmented her sense of power and control by reminding her, "In here, you are in charge of the sticky stuff." She responded with a grin and continued to push the glue around the paper with her fingers, until it had reached every edge of the paper. I wondered out loud if the sticky stuff reminded her of anything and she instantly said, "Bill and Bob," her two abusers. I told her how brave she was to touch the sticky stuff even though it reminded her of some scary times. Once she had the glue arranged just as she wished, she said, "I'm ready to wash it off now." We went to the bathroom and cleaned up. When we came back, she asked me to put her glue creation up to dry so that she could show it to her new mom later. This play sequence is an example of a child's self-directed gradual exposure to a trauma reminder.

Children who have been traumatized will often choose a self-object, a figurine or other play object, to represent the self and then begin to use the object in ways that are either metaphorically or literally similar to the ways in which they themselves were misused. Once they have demonstrated their mistreatment by inflicting something similar on the self-object, they will often fix or cleanse the object in some way. The self-object undergoes a metaphorical and/or literal set of repairs. For example, a child who has had stitches might choose a stuffed animal, make a rip in the fabric, and then sew it back up.

Children often enter the playroom, choose a baby doll to represent the self, and present the baby doll to the therapist with an imaginary injury. In these cases, a child may be asking for the therapist's active assistance in fixing the baby doll other childern may choose to begin the reparative processs

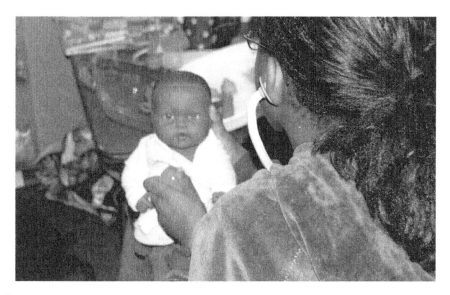

Figure 9.12   Child "Fixing" Her Self-Object

alone. Doctors' kits are a much-used tool and should be readily available to children in the playroom (Figure 9.12).

The case of 5-year-old Layla gives us several examples of these thematic cleansing and fixing rituals. My initial impressions of Layla were formed when I went out to the lobby of the community mental health center where I worked to meet her. Her mother, whom I had met with alone previously, had Layla's two older brothers with her in the lobby. These boys, ages 7 and 9, were chasing Layla around the lobby. When they caught her, they hit her or pulled her hair and then danced away in delight. Mom sat and watched with vacant eyes and occasionally said, "Stop that" in a half-hearted tone of voice. I introduced myself to Layla and invited her to come and play in my room. She took my hand and started to walk down the hall with me. When we had arrived at my office door her brothers came tearing down the hallway, threatening to get her again. Layla had a look of terror on her face and I responded by getting physically in between her and her brothers and quickly closing and locking the door. Then I told her that the playroom was her special place and that her brothers would not be allowed in.

Instead of going over to the toys, Layla sat right down on my couch and began to tremble. Her story poured out of her. She said, "My brothers get on me and hurt me." At first I thought she was just talking about their aggression, but it became clear by the end of this first session that her brothers were also sexually inappropriate with her. I made the call to DCS. Layla had a forensic interview and was immediately removed from mom's care and placed in a foster home. Layla continued to see me for play therapy and the foster mom and I worked together on parenting and attachment issues.

Her first few sessions were filled with experiential mastery play that involved both of us being hurt and then fixed up. Layla would pretend that she got shot by a bad guy. She'd bring me the doctor's kit and have me get the bullet out and sew up the wound. She brought me a stack of Band-Aids and bandages. For one whole session, she made up scenario after scenario in which she got hurt and I had to bandage her. Then it was my turn to be hurt and she would bandage me. Layla insisted that we keep our bandages on until her foster mother could see them. As we walked down the long hall to the lobby, more than one person gasped in shock and asked if we were all right. Covered from head-to-toe in bandages we looked like we had been through a war. Layla's internal repair process was accompanied by a great deal of external repair.

Soon after Layla went to live in a foster home, she began to create a painting at the end of each session. The first time she did this, she chose every color of paint and brought them to the art table. She carefully scooped out some of each color and placed the scoops on a piece of construction paper, forming a makeshift palette. Then she looked at me and carefully smeared all the colors into the middle of the page, stirring them together with her fingers until they formed a brown, feces-like paste. She spread the paste to the very edges of the paper, covering the whole surface in the thick brown paint. Then she tunneled her fingers through the paint from one end of the paper to the other. What follows is our discussion of her painting.

Paris: Tell me about your painting.

Layla: It's a road.

Paris: Where is the road going?

Layla: Nowhere.

Paris: What can you see along the road?

Layla: Nothing.

Paris: Who is on the road?

Layla: No one.

Paris: Seems like a pretty lonely road.

Layla: Yeah.

Layla took what were, separately, beautiful colors, mixed them all together into a mucky brown mess, and used the muck to create a desolate landscape. Layla's road was a powerful metaphor that wove itself through the rest of our treatment. At the end of each session she performed this same ritual of gathering her colors, smearing them together, and generating another brown painting. Eventually she told me that her older brothers had smeared feces on her on several occasions. Her sense of being dirtied and defiled was overwhelming.

She engaged in several forms of experiential mastery play aimed at restoring an internal picture of herself as clean again. In her early sessions, she would look carefully at the princess costumes. She would touch them reverently but wouldn't try them on. Even when given an invitation to try them on, she avoided them. After several sessions, she asked for my help in putting one on. I saw this as a breakthrough. Layla was willing to risk the possibility that she could be as beautiful as a princess. After she was all dressed up, she went to the sandbox, held her princess skirt like a basket, and dumped all the sand into her skirt. She turned around and looked at me solemnly while she smeared the sand up and down all over her dress. It seemed that Layla was communicating her internal belief that no matter what she did to beautify her external appearance, she would still be dirty.

She repeated this play pattern for a couple of sessions. I reflected that no matter how much she dressed up, she seemed to still get really, really dirty and that this seemed to make her feel very sad. I then let her know that the good thing about dirt is that it can be washed off. Next session, she came into the office and immediately put her hand into the big Rubbermaid bin that I kept full of water. Most children used this bin to pretend to wash dishes or to wash baby dolls. She asked me if the water was clean. I told her that I had just changed out the water that morning. She said, "Good. I'm going to take a bath." I thought she was going to pretend to take a bath, but before I had time to react, she had stepped into the bin, fully clothed, and sat down.

I quickly realized that instead of choosing a self-object to use for cleansing rituals, she was using herself. Layla needed a full-body experience of being washed clean in the playroom. She asked for pretend soap and pretended to wash herself. When she stood up, soaking wet, in the tub and announced that she needed fresh clothes, I told her I would find some. I explained to her that I would need to get another adult to supervise while we changed her out of her wet clothes and into clean, dry clothes in order to make sure that everyone's bodies stayed safe all the time. I went to get the foster mother, who immediately understood the metaphor and Layla's attempts to get clean from the abuse inflicted on her by her brothers. We agreed that the foster mom would just bring a change of clothes with her to Layla's next few sessions in case she needed them. For the next several weeks, Layla would walk in and announce that we needed fresh water in the bin. We would drag it outside, dump it, clean it, and fill it with fresh water. We would drag it back into the office. She would step into the tub fully clothed, take her pretend bath, and then her foster mother and I would supervise her change into fresh clothes together. One day Layla came in and said, "No more baths." At the end of this session, she made another brown finger painting of a road. The picture looked almost identical to her first painting, but when I explored her painting with her, her narrative was dramatically different.

Paris: Tell me about your painting.

Layla: It's a road.

Paris: Where is the road going?

Layla: To town.

Paris: What can you see along the road?

Layla: Oh, there are beautiful flowers along the road and a bunny rabbit jumping.

Paris: Who is on the road?

Layla: I am. And you.

Paris: What is at the end of the road?

Layla: There's a really neat fountain and it has water and it's pretty. We're going there.

Layla's metaphor for her internal landscape was shifting. No longer did she see herself and her future as a barren wasteland. Life and movement were beginning to infuse her painting. The road was leading to a beautiful place, full of promise. The water that had been such a vehicle of cleansing in the playroom was transformed into a beautiful fountain at the end of her journey.

The experiential play pattern of fully immersing herself in the water gave Layla the feeling of being cleansed that allowed her to move forward. This example illustrates a key dimension of experiential mastery play: *children often need to experience the feeling of the truth in addition to the telling of the truth*. Clinicians and well-meaning parents expend lots of words telling traumatized children that they are safe, that they are clean, that what happened is not their fault. These are words, and as such, they offer one avenue for a child to absorb the truth. However, because children are kinesthetically wired for learning, their absorption of new truths happens more potently through physical experience. For Layla the feeling of the water and the participation of the therapist in her pretend bathing routine created internal shifts that would not have occurred if I had simply told her that she didn't need to feel dirty.

Layla's case illustrates the use of art as a gauge for and reflection of her internal movement. The expressive arts can also be the main medium through which experiential mastery play happens. Andy, a 4-year-old boy who had been anally raped repeatedly by mom's boyfriend, used a scribble as his main instrument of mastery play. Apparently, Andy and his brother had been made to sleep in the bed with mom and her boyfriend "Unca Dave" and were used as sex toys. Although Andy was now physically safe from this man, Unca Dave had reached mammoth proportions in Andy's imagination. He had difficulty falling asleep in his new home and woke nightly from nightmares of monsters entering his bed. Andy still saw himself as helpless and trapped with no way of fighting back. Although the situation had changed, his perception of the situation had not.

I asked Andy if he could draw a picture of Unca Dave. I gave him a very large piece of paper. He drew a giant scribble. When I asked him to tell me about his picture, he explained that it was a picture of him, his mom, his brother, and Unca Dave in the bed. He stared intently at the scribble that was Unca Dave and then brought the marker down hard on that spot, leaving a dot on the paper. I said, "It looks like you did something to Unca Dave." Andy stared up at me while he got his head around the idea that he could manipulate Unca Dave's scribble on the paper. As understanding dawned, Andy's eyes lit up and he grinned. He deliberately made another hard mark on the scribble. I asked what he had done that time. Andy said, "I kicked him." I said, "I see where you kicked him. I'll mark the places where you do stuff to Unca Dave, so we can remember later." Thus ensued 30 minutes of

Andy coming up with more and more imaginative ways of manipulating Unca Dave's image. At the end of the session we had a giant piece of paper covered in scribbles. The development of Andy's artistic finesse was limited both by his chronological age and by his trauma history. The scribble was the clearest definition he could give to the form of his perpetrator and to the form of his retaliation. My help in narrating and writing down what each new scribble meant helped augment the meaning-making potential of Andy's primitive art. Andy's foster mom reported a dramatic reduction in his nightmares after this session. The next time Andy came for treatment, he immediately asked to see his scribble picture again and wanted me to read out loud what each of the scribbles meant. This became a ritual that marked the beginning of the next several sessions with Andy.

Stacy, a 7-year-old girl who was struggling to make sense of her removal from mom's care due to mom's drug addiction, talked about one particular memory that kept bothering her. She remembered coming home from school one day very hungry and thirsty. Her mother was lying down on the couch and Stacy ran over to her and asked for some Kool-Aid. Her mom did not respond to her. Stacy kept repeating the question, over and over again, until her mom finally mumbled to her that she should make it herself. She remembered feeling nervous about doing this "grownup" job. Stacy got down the big glass pitcher, filled it with water, and poured some powder into it. She stirred it up with a spoon and got out a cup. She remembered feeling proud that she could do it all by herself. Stacy picked up the pitcher and tried to tilt it to the correct angle to pour some into her glass. The pitcher was heavier than she expected. It slipped from her hands and crashed onto the floor. Stacy expected her mother to jump off the couch and yell at her for making a mess. However, her mom barely moved. Once again, Stacy went and shook her mother, explaining in a louder and louder voice that there was glass and Kool-Aid all over the kitchen.

She finally roused mom enough to have mom mumble, "Clean it up." Stacy remembers soaking up the red Kool-Aid with paper towels and sweeping up the glass with a broom. She told me that the whole time that she was cleaning up, she felt alone. She instinctively knew that this was the kind of thing a mom should be doing and she was terrified of stepping on glass or cutting her hand as she scooped up the pieces. Soon after this episode, Stacy's dad gained custody of her and her brother. At the time I began seeing her, she had not seen her mother for almost 6 months. Her mother had been in two rehabilitation programs and had not completed either one. Stacy exhibited burgeoning signs of depression and anxiety. She was referred after making several comments that threatened self-harm. Stacy had turned the anger at her mother inward and was slowly withering.

After Stacy had built a sense of safety and security in the playroom, we began some psychoeducation around drug addiction. As Stacy was learning about drugs and addiction, she had an epiphany in which she shifted the blame away from herself and squarely onto the drugs themselves. During one session, we were playing with clay while we were talking about the drugs. Stacy decided that she wanted to make pretend drugs out of the clay. As she was shaping the clay, her affect began to change. Her face became angry and she began to punch the Play-Doh aggressively. The transcript of what happened follows:

Paris: You're punching those drugs really hard. In here you can do whatever you want to those drugs.

Stacy picks up a sword and begins to stab at the drugs.

Paris: Can you use some words while you're using the sword?
Stacy: I hate drugs. I hate drugs because they are so stupid.
Paris: Yeah! Do it one more time as loud as you can.

Stacy continues to stab at the drugs with the sword while she talks.

Stacy: I hate drugs because they are so stupid.
Paris: Yeah! How do you feel now?
Stacy (smiling really big): Good!
Paris (laughing): Sometimes it's really fun just to get some of that mad out.
Stacy (returning to her focused destruction of the drugs): Because I hate them and I hate them and I hate them because they did too much stuff to my mom. Now my mom is gone, gone, gone, gone, gone.

Each of the repetitions of "gone" is accompanied by a sword-blow to the drugs.

Paris: Yeah. And that makes you very mad. Let me see your maddest face.

Stacy makes a mad face.

Paris: Whoa. That's a good mad face.

Stacy returns to intently stabbing the drugs.

Paris: You are killing those drugs. You are really beating up on those drugs. They're not in charge of you.
Stacy: I'm in charge of them!

This is the crux of experiential mastery play. In play, Stacy is empowered to have control over the drugs that she cannot control outside the playroom.

Paris: Yes, you are.
Stacy: Bad drugs.

Stacy suddenly sits back and holds the sword against her chest like a teddy bear. She looks at the therapist forlornly.

Stacy: I hate them.
Paris: I hate them too.

Stacy's focus shifts at this point. After she expends some of the anger that she has directed against herself by focusing the anger on the drugs themselves, she moves into a place of grieving the loss of her mother to the drugs. The rest of our session is spent exploring this new affective content.

Conclusion

This chapter has demonstrated the myriad ways in which EMP facilitates a client's approach to troublesome trauma content. The gradual exposure process, aided by the natural draw that play holds for children, results in desensitization to immobilizing fears, distressing sensory impressions, and troublesome thoughts. Additionally, EMP provides a forum in which children can begin to generate adaptive solutions to problems, experience a sense of power in relation to the previously disempowering content, and gain a sense of mastery in relation to traumatic incidents. The gradual removal of toxicity from the content prepares the child for sequencing events and building coherent trauma narratives. Both these processes are explicated in the following chapter.

CHAPTER

10

Trauma Narrative Work

Truth is more of a stranger than fiction.
—*Mark Twain, Notebook, 1898*

Each of us has an internal drive to make sense of our lives. Oftentimes, this sense-making is pursued through storytelling. As we continually craft our life narratives, embellishing certain details, letting go of others and ultimately building coherence, we begin to understand ourselves and our experiences more fully. When our stories depict the joyful events in our lives, they get more enjoyable with each telling. When our stories depict the terrifying events in our lives, the effect of the narration is counterintuitive. Instead of exacerbating the fear, the repeated telling of an integrated trauma narrative desensitizes us to the distress. In other words, the terror loses its intensity with each telling. However, posttraumatic children often actively avoid discussion of their traumatic events. Children can be threatened by the potential flooding they may experience if they tell the stories about the bad thing that happened to them. In their minds the story has the power to drown them. For this reason, a child's trauma narrative may evolve in snippets and snapshots, through play and the expressive arts, as opposed to being delivered in one session as a fully detailed accounting.

It is through titrated doses of exposure to trauma content that children have the greatest likelihood of persevering through the crafting of an entire narrative. Integrating play into trauma narrative work allows a client to approach the trauma through exposures that are mitigated by the child's control over the play materials. The dose of exposure to the trauma narrative can be self-titrated by the child as he manipulates the play objects. A child's natural drive to make sense of the world around him through the medium of play wars with his avoidance of trauma reminders. Capitalizing on the child's natural inclinations allows the client a gentler approach to the trauma content.

The kinesthetic manipulation of the play materials by the child is inherently soothing and counters the toxicity of the traumatic events that are being narrated. The manipulation of objects also grounds the client in the here and now and decreases the likelihood of the child becoming dissociative while revisiting content related to the trauma. Additionally, certain dimensions of a child's experience may be communicated more potently through a play metaphor or an experiential product than through verbal or written narrative alone. For example, drawing and painting provide powerful outlets for a child to communicate a visually overwhelming detail of a traumatic event or some horrific image for which he has no words. In these cases, the drawing of a picture may serve as a child's first witnessed exposure to the trauma content. The case of three siblings illustrates this point.

Keshon, a 4-year-old male child, along with his twin 3-year-old siblings, watched their dad bludgeon their mom with a clothing iron until she was unconscious. The event was so frightening and the children were so young that they had very few words to articulate what they had seen. The oldest could say, "Daddy hit mommy with an iron." This simple statement of fact could not sufficiently convey the look or smell of the blood or the sickening sounds of metal sinking into flesh. Many times the verbal fluency that children lack is a frustration to themselves and those around them. However, children can compensate for their linguistic limitations through their art. Keshon was seen first and separately from his siblings. During his first session, he spontaneously generated the drawing in Figure 10.1.

When I asked Keshon to talk about his drawing, he kept saying, "He wasn't being safe. He wasn't being safe." This phrase was repeated, almost like a chant. When I drew Keshon's attention to the lines he made on mom's face, he said, "That's tears, like when you cry. She was cryin' and hollerin'." When I asked him what words she was using, he said, "She was yellin' help." Keshon asked me to write the word in a bubble coming out of her mouth and I obliged him. Then Keshon picked up his pen again and just stared at his picture. I said, "It looks like you're deciding what else you might draw." Keshon said, "I need to draw the iron but I can't." He asked me to draw it, and he brought me a toy iron as a guide.

After I drew the iron to his satisfaction, he went and got the purple Play-Doh and stuck some on the drawn iron. He was not using his words to

Figure 10.1   Keshon's Drawing of His Mom after Her Attack

describe the horrific image of blood and brain matter on the iron, but he was approaching the reality of the sensory memories through carefully calibrated additions to his picture. Finally he added the two red slashing marks on the right side of the paper and said, "There was blood on her pillow."

This 4-year-old had a whole series of grotesque and disjointed images in his mind. The prompt, "Draw a picture of what happened," gently confronts the child with the task of beginning to bring disparate elements together to make a coherent snapshot. Using the picture as an anchor, Keshon was able to show me what happened and then give verbal elaboration to his mom's tears, the brain matter on the clothing iron, and the blood on mom's pillow. When I showed the picture to mom, she was shocked to see that he remembered so much of what happened. Mom was unaware that he had been in the room. The attack took place 2 months before Keshon's drawing, and in all that time he had not discussed any of his traumatic imagery with his mom. This is not unusual.

In the wake of a traumatic event, children intuitively understand that the ghastly imagery they carry around on the inside of themselves could overwhelm their caregivers. In this case, Keshon already perceived his mother as fragile and in need of care. Keshon might put his own survival at risk if he floods his mother, his only remaining caregiver, with the nightmares in his head, so he keeps them hidden deep inside.

Illustrations are helpful in many ways. The drawing paper serves as a screen onto which internal horrors can be externalized. The externalization of the images through art becomes the first set of exposures and the jumping off point for subsequent desensitization to the trauma content. The act of creating a coherent drawing requires a child to begin sequencing details related to the traumatic event, an exercise that can be supported by the therapist who explores the drawing with the child.

When Keshon finished his session, his 3-year-old sister Keandra came into the playroom. Keandra was exhibiting a host of classic posttraumatic symptoms and kept her eyes lowered and her shoulders hunched for the first part of the session. When I introduced her to the expressive arts materials and invited her to draw a picture of her family doing something together (a kinetic family drawing), she brightened considerably. Figure 10.2 shows the picture she drew.

Figure 10.2   Keandra's KFD and Blood Trail

Notice the figure on the far right and the trail of red dots coming from that figure's head. Mom had previously described a trail of blood left in the apartment as she struggled to get away from her attackers' advances. The act of drawing a trail of blood is the child's self-measured exposure to the trauma content. In order to draw it, Keandra has to intentionally focus on the visual image of the trauma that she carries inside herself. She was unable to talk about the picture in this session. The inclusion of the blood trail was the full dose of trauma content that she could handle in this first exposure. We spent the rest of the time making things out of clay.

Keandra's twin brother Josue came in next for his session. Josue bounded around the room, moving quickly from one toy to another. Then he announced that he was going to draw a picture of his mother. He drew an outline of her head and torso in black and then filled her body with bright red color, pressing the marker energetically against the paper as he moved the marker back and forth. Notice the same blood trail dripping down the side of his picture (Figure 10.3).

Clearly, a pattern emerges across the art drawn by each of the three siblings. Each approaches the visceral stuff of the trauma, the blood and the

Figure 10.3   Josue's Mom and the Trail of Blood

gore, through drawing. The family lived in low-income government housing. After the attack occurred, mom asked to be moved to another house. Her request was refused. Concerned friends and family cleaned up the blood as best they could, but some bloodstains remained on the carpet, trailing from the bedroom to the living room. Once the children's internal picture of the blood trail was externalized through the drawings, the children could weave this new, concrete visual detail into the evolving narrative of the trauma.

Integrating Hemispheric Content

Current conceptualizations of hemispheric activity in the brain can help inform our understanding of the need for integration of various kinds of experience in trauma narrative work. The left hemisphere of the brain is responsible for logical, linear, and linguistic encoding of experience. The left hemisphere helps us structure the verbal narrative of events in our lives. The right hemisphere of the brain is more visual-spatial in nature. It encodes tone, affect, and other nonverbal body language communications. The right hemisphere encodes the gestalt of an event. The left hemisphere will tell you that the police officer who arrived on the scene was named Mr. John, but the right hemisphere will translate how you feel about him.

This hemispheric division of labor is important in trauma processing on many levels. The presentation that I see most often in my office is that of an adolescent who can give me the whole laundry list of terrible things that have happened to her. This list is delivered in a manner devoid of any emotional expression. These teenagers have developed a linear, linguistic, and often factually accurate accounting of the traumatizing events in their lives. However, these accounts are removed from their affective experiences of those life-shaping events. Their narratives are bereft of any sensory content. It is likely in these cases that the somatosensory memories and emotional experiences attached to these traumatic events have been split off and stored elsewhere in the brain. By definition, these stories lack internal coherence. Siegel (2003, p. 15) posits the solution in this way: "To have a coherent story, the drive of the left to tell a logical story must draw on the information from the right. If there is a blockage, as occurs in PTSD, then the narrative may be incoherent."

The corpus callosum, the band of neural tissue that runs in between the left and right hemispheres of the brain, helps the two hemispheres of the brain talk to each other. It functions as a sort of neural highway between the two hemispheres. However, children who have maltreatment histories often have developmental impairment in the corpus callosum (Arden & Linford, 2009; Siegel, 2003). The lack of myelination in the corpus callosum limits the usefulness of this structure in transferring information across the two hemispheres (Schore, 2003; Teicher, 2002). In other words, children who have lived through chronic maltreatment may have neurophysiological deficits in critical brain structures that limit the brain's ability to integrate all aspects of trauma memories. Therefore, the pursuit of integration of disparate elements of trauma content into a coherent narrative may require assistance and intentionality by the helping professional.

Andrea's Case

The case of Andrea illustrates this phenomenon. Andrea was a tall, strikingly beautiful 17-year-old girl referred by her mother for "out-of-control, rebellious behavior." I met with the mother alone first and asked for a full family history. Andrea had been domestically adopted at the age of 2. Little was known about her biological family, except that Andrea was removed due to neglect. She was a happy little girl, but as she hit puberty, according to her mother, she became unmanageable. At the time that mom sought treatment, Andrea was running away from home, being verbally abusive to mom and dad, and threatening self-harm.

The first moments of Andrea's first session were typical of a teenager who involuntarily enters treatment. She sat across from me with her arms folded and her legs crossed, kicking up the heel of her foot and smacking her gum as loudly as possible, daring me to speak. I said, "It must suck to be here." She snorted, glared, and said "Yeah." That one word was a start. My next foray was, "Who's making you come here anyway?" She rolled her eyeballs and said, "My mom." Two-word answers meant she was warming up, so I approached her frankly, saying, "Look. Your mom and dad have one idea about why they are bringing you to see me. However, at 17 years old, you are almost an adult and I imagine you have your own ideas about what's making you unhappy. Now, we can spend the time talking about boys and fashion and stuff like that or you can tell me what's bothering you."

Andrea sighed and stopped kicking her foot. Her face became blank and she said, "Well, when I was 2-years-old I was adopted. I started preschool when I was 3. I was sexually abused by my dad from 6-years-old until I was 9-years-old.

When I started fourth grade nobody liked me." She went on and on, hitting the highlights of her laundry list from ages 2 to 17.

Mom had not mentioned any sexually concerning activity even though it was specifically addressed during the intake, so this disclosure was news to me. When she took a breath, I asked her if she could go back and tell me more about what happened between the ages of 6 and 9. She rolled her eyeballs and began to kick her foot again. Andrea described a trip to the doctor when she was 9 years old. At the doctor's appointment she was diagnosed with a urinary tract infection. On the way home, her mom asked her, "Has anyone ever touched you on your private parts?" Andrea said, "Only daddy." When they got home, mom called dad and asked him to come home from work.

Mom put Andrea on one side of the kitchen table and had dad sit on the other side of the kitchen table. Mom confronted dad with Andrea's allegation. He broke down in tears and confessed that he had sexually abused their little girl. Mom asked Andrea, "Do you want him to leave?" Andrea said, "Yes." Mom started to cry and Andrea said, "No, that's OK." Dad promised that he would never do it again and agreed to get help. He went to one personal ministry session at church. The family never talked about it again and never sought any additional help for the dad or for Andrea. No reports were made to the Department of Children's Services. Andrea had been suffocating her rage at both dad's behavior and mom's inaction for 8 years by the time she came in for treatment.

The other dynamic at play in this family was that Andrea was the first adopted child of many. Several younger adopted siblings lived in the home at the time of Andrea's disclosure. I explained to Andrea that I would have to get some other systems involved to make sure that everyone in the home was safe. Andrea said, "Good!" and smiled with satisfaction at finally having the seriousness of her violations validated. I then explained that I was going to talk with mom and tell her the steps I would be taking. When mom came into the room, I started the conversation by saying, "You know, I have seen many adolescent girls who have issues with their fathers, but I have never seen one who carries this level of animosity toward her father. Can you think of any reason why she might have such negative feelings toward him?" Mom sighed, folded her hands in her lap, and said quietly, "Well, I was hoping we wouldn't have to get into this."

This quote from Andrea's mother exemplifies the pathology of a nonprotective parent. This mom was horrified when she originally found out about the dad's behavior. However, she rationalized that she had an obligation to all her adopted children and needed the dad's financial and emotional help to raise them. She convinced herself both that Andrea's abuse had ended at age 9 and that none of the other children in the house could potentially become victims. Her rationalization cost the family dearly. I explained to mom that I was going to make the report and why. She became very fearful. We addressed her fears directly and I empathized with her current distress. Then I explained how the lack of intervention years earlier was directly related to her daughter's current out-of control behavior. It was fascinating to watch mom's process as she began to understand the impact of her inaction years ago.

The way in which a therapist handles the need to make a report to DCS has a significant impact on an evolving relationship with a family. There are certainly clear-cut cases in which the child's safety would be jeopardized by making the parents aware of the child's disclosure. However, as often as possible, I let caregivers know when I am going to make a report to DCS. Laying out both my obligation to report and my hopes for the family's healing can mitigate a family's termination from treatment. Staying with a parent through his or her initial reaction to the news can go a long way toward salvaging the trust relationship. Sometimes parents become very angry with me for what they see as a betrayal. However, once I become the container for the parents' anger and show, by my ability to hear their distress, that I can handle their emotions while holding firm to my duty to report, they often move to feelings of guilt or shame. This often leads the parents to new levels of self-awareness and opens the door for future work in correcting distortions that led to their nonprotective parenting choices.

In Andrea's case, the report was made to DCS later that same night. The speed with which DCS intervened was surprising. DCS representatives arrived at each of the children's schools the following afternoon. All the children were removed from the home and placed in foster care that same day. Each of the children was referred for assessment. Mom, having felt supported through the reporting process, asked me to complete the assessments on the other children. The assessments yielded disclosures of similar sexual molestation from two of the other adopted siblings.

Andrea's euphoria at suddenly being seen, heard, and taken seriously was immediately replaced with intense guilt at the way in which her disclosure seemed to tear the family apart. Mom's failure to report the abuse when it should have been reported set Andrea up for additional trauma. If dad's misconduct had been reported when Andrea was 9, she would have received help, and the meaning she would have made of the whole experience would have included an understanding that one of her authority figures had kept her safe. As a typically developing teen, Andrea would have been grappling with the power of being on the cusp of adulthood and all the choices that entails. As a teenager whose mom chose loyalty to a sick husband over her daughter's need for protection and the chance to heal, Andrea spent her adolescent energy coping with the power of the secret and the rage she felt at being betrayed. When she finally had both the opportunity and the courage to tell, her worst fears were realized and all her siblings were placed in different foster homes.

This young lady's healing process was an extended one. The complexities of the case, the time lapse, and the swift response once the secret was unveiled made it difficult for Andrea to make coherent sense of the events in narrative form. The current traumas, including the loss of all her siblings and the blame that she placed squarely on her own shoulders for telling, superseded the original traumatic events. The sexual abuse narrative was hard to craft, in part because it happened years earlier and in part because the burden of the current situation muddied the waters of her memory.

In treatment, Andrea was drawn to the sand tray again and again. The sand tray is the place where many children and adolescents begin to grapple with their trauma narratives. The sand tray functions much like a TV screen, creating a boundaried space where the child and therapist can watch a story unfold. Often children will choose miniatures to represent important players in their own history. When this occurs, I usually encourage the child to tell the story in narrative form. That is, we often give the figures character names, as opposed to labeling them as mom, dad, and self. This depersonalization tactic affords a psychological level of removal for clients that allows them to describe the traumatic events in a less guarded fashion.

When Andrea was ready to begin to tell her story, she found that she wanted to tell it in three dimensions. The directive that I gave her was simply, "Put the trauma in the tray." She took her time choosing the tools she needed to represent her abuse. A picture of her finished tray can be seen in Figure 10.4.

What follows is the transcript of our joint exploration of her finished sand tray.

Figure 10.4   Andrea's Sexual Abuse Sand Tray

Paris: So this is your world while it was happening. Why don't you take me through this world, step-by-step, and show me what's in it?

Andrea points to the wizard.

Andrea: This is my dad.

Andrea points to the crown.

Andrea: And this is his little, or his big circle of power that he has over me at that time and that's me because I feel trapped. So that's why I have a little spiderweb thing over me.

Therapist points to the figure under the spiderweb.

Paris: And that's a little bitty baby?

Andrea: Yeah, that's what I felt like. I felt tiny. And this arrow is how my heart was feeling then. Like I had just been stabbed [Figure 10.5].

Andrea: And this is me imagining trying to get away.

Figure 10.5   Baby Under Spiderweb

Paris: So you were imagining getting away while it was happening?

Andrea: Yeah and not being able to because I knew that I wouldn't . . . or that I couldn't.

Paris: Because what would happen?

Andrea: Well . . . because of course he would tame me.

At this point Andrea paled visibly and she began to shake. Her affect became blunted, and I was concerned that she was beginning to dissociate. I decided to combine humor with an attempt to ground her in the here and now by refocusing on the figurines in the tray. I pointed to the guards she had posted on the left side of the tray.

Paris: These are some big, bad dudes.

Andrea laughed and made eye contact with me. Then she smiled.

Andrea: Well, that's what it felt like.

Paris: You felt like you had no way out?

Andrea: Uh huh.

After establishing connection again between the two of us, I return her attention to the tray. In this next layer of processing, I help Andrea to notice the details and expand on the experiences of various characters within the tray.

Paris: So let's go through it again and this time I want you to talk about them for who they are in this sand tray. Let's start with this wizard. What does the world look like from his perspective? What's it like to be the wizard in this world?

Andrea: Well, I guess he's probably cackling because he knows he has all the power. I mean, he doesn't think anything can go wrong because how's anybody gonna find out?

Paris: Look at his body position in the sand. What does it seem to be saying in relation to the others—particularly to the little baby?

It is important for the therapist to pay attention to how the client physically handles the characters in the tray while the world is being built and during any verbal processing. As I drew attention to how she had positioned the wizard in the sand, she picked him up with two fingers and forcibly turned him so that he would be looking directly at the baby covered with the web. She then turned him back to his original position without speaking and left him there.

Andrea: That he's conquered me.

Paris: It feels like he's conquered you. So what are his hands saying up in the air like that? One of them is . . . is that a fist ?

At this point, both Andrea and I are down at the side of the tray looking at the wizard from all angles.

Andrea: He's thinking, "I have it all!"

Paris: Where is he looking? Is he looking at the little baby?

Andrea: No . . . no.

At this point, Andrea began to cry big silent tears. We stared at the sand tray with our heads together while she mourned the fact that her father had never really seen her as his precious daughter, only as an object to be used.

Later, I shared with Andrea my observation that she had moved the wizard into a position where he was forced to look directly at the baby but that she quickly put him back the way he had been originally. She made the connections herself, talking about how much she wanted to believe that he saw her for herself. I encouraged Andrea to journal any thoughts or feelings that arose after we processed the sand tray. When Andrea came in for her next session she had already begun to see her out-of-control behavior as more and more desperate attempts to get her dad to really see her. Andrea felt safest approaching her trauma by projecting it into the tray. The metaphor of a vulnerable baby trapped under spiderwebs gives rich content for sensory processing. Right hemisphere perceptions are tapped and can be integrated into the linguistic narrative of the events themselves.

Erin's Developing Story

Another example of narrative building can be seen in the case of a 7-year-old girl named Erin whose parents were going through a messy divorce. Over the 2 years prior to the divorce, Erin's dad had developed a drug habit. While feeding his habit he lost his job, ran up a tremendous amount of debt, and went to jail. Erin's mom filed for divorce. When dad got out of prison, he broke into Erin's house in the middle of the night and stole some computer equipment to pawn for drug money. At the time of Erin's intake her dad was back in jail and the divorce had been final for 6 months. Erin was beginning to act out in her classroom and was being unusually defiant with mom at home.

During Erin's first session, I invited her to create a family play genogram. She chose puppets to be each of her family members and put them in the sand tray. Erin made dad a police officer and mom a beautiful princess. She chose a unicorn for herself. The family she created was the family of her fantasies, in which everyone lived happily ever after (Figure 10.6).

I wondered if perhaps Erin was stuck in denial and unable to accept the fact that her parents were divorced. I was concerned that her grieving process and her eventual acceptance of the changes in her family could be stunted by remaining in denial. I invited her to draw a picture of her family "divorced" and she said, "I'll draw a picture of when we got married!" (Figure 10.7).

Erin drew herself on the left, her dad in the middle, and her mom in her wedding veil on the right. It is worth noting that Erin and her mother were both dressed in red, with black shadowing the bottom edges of their clothes.

Figure 10.6 Erin's Fantasy Family

This is when me+my dad+my mom got married.

Figure 10.7 Erin's Drawing: *My Family gets Married*

Dad was drawn completely in black, perhaps connoting the child's dangerous associations with her father. Erin asked me to write a statement on the side of the picture that said, "This is when me and my dad and my mom got married." The next couple of sessions were spent doing some psychoeducation around divorce. We read *Dinosaurs Divorce* (Brown & Brown, 1988). We also read *I Don't Want to Talk About It* (Ransom, 2000), a book designed for children who are psychologically defending themselves against the truth of their parents' divorce. When we finished reading this book, Erin began to cry and said that she didn't want her parents to get divorced. Then she verbalized for the first time that her dad was in jail. I validated her feelings of distress and acknowledged the truth of her dad's incarceration. The following week mom brought in a picture that Erin had drawn at home but wanted to bring to the playroom (Figure 10.8).

Erin drew big smiling faces on all three family members and encased them in a rainbow. She drew a family of three birds flying together in the center of the picture. However, she drew mom and dad on opposite sides of the page now, with Erin in the middle. She also drew multicolored lines on

Figure 10.8   Erin's Picture of Her Dad in Jail Clothes

dad's clothes and described his outfit as "jail clothes." The small changes in her artistic creations mirrored the changes in Erin's internal narrative. Manifesting her changing narrative in visual images allowed her to tentatively test how the new truths felt and, simultaneously, see how they were perceived by significant others. After she showed me the picture and pointed out dad's jail clothes, she played with other things. When it was time to go, she said, "I want to send this picture to my dad. Will you write something on it?" I said I would be happy to. She had me write the words, "Your child is almost dead."

During the next session I met with mom, who reported that Erin's aggressive behavior was decreasing at home and that her anger was seeming to focus more clearly on her father and his choices. Erin had asked her mother if she could go visit dad in jail, and mom wanted my recommendation about whether or not this would be good for Erin. The next time that Erin came for treatment, I asked her how she envisioned her father's surroundings when she imagined him in jail. She had seen the Disney movie *Aladdin*, and in her mind's eye she pictured him as emaciated and in chains, being fed only bread and water. I told mom that a trip to visit dad would help correct some cognitive distortions that were increasing Erin's distress over her dad's situation.

Erin went to visit dad over the weekend and returned for her next session with a big smile on her face. She immediately began to tell me all about her visit to see dad. She described his living quarters with her eyes twinkling. "He even has his own sink and his own potty. He gets to play basketball outside sometimes." Then she drew the picture you see in Figure 10.9.

Notice that dad is in his jail cell. Erin and mom are standing outside the jail. Erin offered, "This is me and mom visiting dad." I commented on the brown marks on everyone's face. Erin said, "Those are tears. Everyone's crying because we're not together." Erin's internal narrative had finally caught up with her family's current reality. In this way, children can use art to help shift and expand their internal narratives.

Brian's Case

I have given examples of how art and sand can be employed to help children articulate and refine their trauma narratives. Puppets are another play therapy medium that has powerful applications to helping children structure coherent narratives. Both hand puppets and finger puppets can be employed in this work. Children in the early stages of treatment may prefer the finger

Figure 10.9   Erin's Dad in Jail

puppets because they are smaller and more manageable. They can be manipulated to tell a story without becoming overwhelming. Very young children have difficulty making distinctions between what is real and what is pretend. Therefore they may be overwhelmed by hand puppets. As the therapist manipulates a scary or aggressive hand puppet, the child may believe that it has come to life and be frightened. However, friendly puppet characters can be effectively used with even these youngest children.

One strategy for incorporating puppets in trauma narrative work is to simply invite the child to create a puppet play that tells the story of what happened. Latency-age children are especially intrigued by this task. Brian, a 9-year-old boy who had a traumatic reaction to a new medication, provides a case illustration. Brian had been diagnosed with attention deficit hyperactivity disorder, bipolar disorder, and oppositional defiant disorder before entering treatment with me. Brian had already seen a series of therapists for counseling and a series of doctors for medications. Mom called me to schedule an emergency session after a crisis. Mom reported that Brian had been on a new psychotropic medication for 1 week when his jaw locked up and he couldn't move it. Brian and his mother were both terrified, and mom rushed him to the emergency room. The doctor on duty prescribed Benadryl, and within a couple of hours Brian's jaw relaxed, but the event was clearly traumatic for both parent and child.

Brian was obviously dysregulated when he entered the playroom. As a child with attentional difficulties, he had previously exhibited some distractibility in the playroom, but on this day posttraumatic anxiety exacerbated his hyperactivity. He bounced around picking up play materials and putting them down again. He had difficulty organizing his play. Brian mentioned the "freaky doctors" in passing but steered away from discussion of his traumatic experience. I wondered how I could help to organize his experience and build a scaffold on which he could eventually process the terrifying trip to the emergency room. I said, "Your mom told me what happened this weekend, after you had started your new medicine. I'm wondering how that felt to you. I'm remembering that you've been on a few different medicines already—" Brian interrupted me by rolling his eyes and saying, "A few. Ha! You mean a bunch!" I reflected his perception that he had been on a bunch of medicines.

Then I said, "You know, I see a lot of kids who've been on meds. Some are younger than you and don't know much about how the medications work or how they can make kids feel. I think if you could tell your story it might help some of them. Do you think you could make a puppet play about the medicine?" Brian perked up at this and eagerly set about choosing the characters for his play. He decided to use only finger puppets. Brian chose a flamingo for himself, a blue jay for his mother, and a black bat for the doctor. The transcript of his play follows:

Flamingo: Hello. I am Mr. Flamingo Dude.

Blue Jay: Hello. I am Mr. Flamingo Dude's mother. Mr. Flamingo Dude is quite
    hyperactive as you can clearly see.

Brian makes the flamingo puppet bounce around all over the place.

Flamingo: Yahah-yah-yahh. Woo-hoo! Wee-heee!

Blue Jay: Do not do that, Mr. Flamingo Dude.

Brian (narrating): So the next day the mother said we're going to visit a doctor.

Blue Jay: Mr. Flamingo Dude, you must see a therapist!

Flamingo: Ahhhh! What's a therapist?

Blue Jay: It's a person.

Flamingo: Oh. People aren't that bad.

Flamingo and Blue Jay walk to a therapy appointment.

Bat 1: Hello, I will be your therapist today.

Flamingo: You look just like a bat, you freak.

Brian makes the flamingo puppet hit the bat.

Bat 1: Now let's settle down. Oh, isn't that nice. See, don't you feel a lot bet-ter? Now where were we? I want to give you something called a pill. And here it is.

Flamingo: Looks more like a stupid retard.

Bat 1: Oh, is that so?

Flamingo: Yes, that is so!

Bat 1: Well, I'm gonna shove it down your mouth. Don't worry. This won't hurt a bit.

Flamingo: Ahhhhhhh! Stop!

Bat 1: There. Don't you feel better?

Flamingo: Woo! I'm glad that's over with. I'm gonna poop on you.

Brian has the flamingo poop on the bat.

Bat 1: Now out you go.

The bat kicks Flamingo Dude out of the office.

Flamingo: Hey! Stop! What are you doing? This stinks!

Blue Jay: Just be patient, Mr. Flamingo Dude!

As Brian has been playing out his dismissal from the therapist's office his voice has become high and shrill, giving me a hint of his growing anxiety.

I need to help Brian manage his rising anxiety so that he can complete the narrative that he is building. Instead of drawing attention to the anxiety itself, which Brian would probably deny, I help him manage a physiological symptom of the anxiety. I ask him if he can use a deeper voice and slow the flow of his words so that his story can be clearly understood on the videotape. My prompt served a practical purpose and was therefore easily received by Brian. The primary purpose of the prompt was to deliberately draw his focus back to his physiological reactivity and offer him a simple way to consciously control the anxiety response. Brian took a deep breath and consciously lowered the pitch of his voice.

Brian: The next day . . .

Bat 2: Hello.

Flamingo: I don't like you. You suck. Die retard die!

Flamingo hits the bat again. It is clear from this reenactment that Brian has strong feelings of anger toward the helping professionals whom he has visited.

Bat 2: Help!

Bat knocks flamingo and Blue Jay out of the office.

Blue Jay: Be patient, Mr. Flamingo Dude.

Brian: And day after day they got booted out.

Brian is showing us his perception that he was rejected from each of the offices he visited. Flamingo and Blue Jay enter the new office.

Bat 3: Hello, my name is doctor. Hold on. This is called a pill. I'm going to shove it down your mouth. This won't hurt a bit.

Flamingo: Wahhh! Wahhhhhhh! I feel terrible.

Flamingo screams and makes vomiting noises.

Paris: Oh, he's throwing it up. And he looks like he is shaking.

Brian nods in agreement.

Brian: The next day . . .

Blue Jay: We're switching doctors, son.

Flamingo: Oh no, not again!

Flamingo and Blue Jay walk to a new office.

Bat 4: Hello, my name is doctor.

Flamingo: Oh, I know exactly what you're gonna say: "My name is doctor. Hold on a minute. Here's a pill. I'm just gonna shove it in your mouth. This won't hurt a bit."

Bat 4: Oh well, you're exactly right.

Flamingo: Yes! And then I'm gonna start throwing it up. And this is just gonna keep on happening and we're gonna keep on switching doctors and none of them is going to work!

Brian makes all the characters start physically fighting and makes accompanying fight noises. Eventually the bat is thrown down.

Paris: The doctor dies?

Brian: Yes. And none of the doctors ever worked and the mommy was satisfied.

This statement ended Brian's puppet play. When the play was over, Brian asked to see it played back on the LCD screen of the video recorder. Videotaping puppet plays and other dramatic productions can be invaluable in constructing coherent narratives. The child first gets the kinesthetic experience of creating the story by using the play materials. Then the child can watch it back as many times as needed. The viewing of the video serves as rehearsal of the trauma narrative in the same way that a caregiver's telling and retelling of a story over time helps the child sequence events.

Danielle's Case

Trauma reenactment is more easily approached by children in the arena of play than solely in the verbal arena. The truth of this statement was confirmed to me again in a recent case. A respected colleague called to refer a young girl named Danielle whose mother had recently been murdered. Danielle's mother was murdered in their home while the girl slept. Mom and dad had a volatile and domestically violent relationship for most of Danielle's life. The children were initially seen by my colleague, who attempted to engage with Danielle. She made very little eye contact with this colleague and when the therapist asked questions, Danielle shut down further and further, eventually turning her back entirely and refusing to speak. My colleague referred Danielle for play therapy, believing that another medium would be needed to help this client approach the traumatic events.

Before I met with the child I met with Danielle's new and fairly bewildered guardians. Mr. and Mrs. Jones had been caring for this young girl since the death of her mother 2 weeks earlier. Danielle had only a passing relationship with this couple before her mother's death as they were distant friends of the family. They were confused by Danielle's reaction to her mother's death. They reported that when they told her that her mother had been killed, she cried for 2 or 3 minutes and had not shed a tear since. She flinched away from being touched and kept to herself at home and at school.

Mr. and Mrs. Jones reported that in the 2 weeks they had cared for her, Danielle never asked about how her mom was killed. She never asked about her father or if she could go live with him. When they took her to the first counseling center, everyone was very compassionate. Danielle leaned over to Mrs. Jones and said, "It's creepy here. Everyone is too nice." This informed me about the wariness with which Danielle approached people and her instant distrust of kindness. To counter this mistrust, I chose to take a very matter-of-fact approach with Danielle during her first visit. I invited Danielle into the playroom and immediately turned slightly away from her to clean out the sand tray. I hoped that this sideways approach and my seeming preoccupation with shelving the sand tray toys would put her at ease. Below is the transcript of those first few moments of the session.

Paris: My name is Ms. Paris. This is your special time in the playroom. In here you can do almost anything you want to do as long as we both stay safe. Mr. and Mrs. Jones told me about your mom's death. I want you to know that in here you get to decide when and if you tell me about that. They also told me that your parents fought a lot. I see lots of kids whose parents fight. They tell me about all kinds of scary things they saw. We call them the crazies. I'm betting you've seen your fair share of the crazies.

Danielle nods and rolls her eyes.

Danielle: Yeah.

She watches me put things on the shelves and then comes over to join me. As she returns objects to the shelf, she makes the following disclosure.

Danielle: Dad threw a TV out the window once.

Paris: You remember that he threw a TV out the window. That's a great example of a crazy.

Danielle: She threw hot soup at him—a whole pot of hot soup or pasta . . . something.

Paris: Sounds scary.

Danielle: I told them to stop because it scared my little brother.

Paris: I bet.

Danielle: And it scared me. Then there was the time . . .

Paris: You know what. It sounds like you've had a lot of crazy things happen. I'm going to make a list of the crazies because it helps me keep track of them.

I move to the table by her chair. I write the phrase "The Crazies" at the top of a blank piece of paper. Then I repeat each thing she's told me slowly as I write it down. The list and the repetition are both tools that I employ to help her organize the episodic snatches of violence and chaos tumbling around inside her. They also serve as exposures to the trauma content. She bends over the paper with her head close to mine, examining the words giving form to her history. I repeat the list one more time.

Danielle (contemplating the list): The high-speed chase.

Danielle is clearly remembering another disturbing event, one that I had not been told about during the intake. I remain nonchalant and write it down as a matter of course.

Paris: OK. I'll add that. The high-speed chase.

Danielle: My little sister was in the car.

Danielle's demeanor changes. She takes a breath and launches into a very fast-paced account of how dad came to the house, where he parked in the driveway, what he said, how his face looked, and so forth. It is as if a floodgate has opened and Danielle is now eager to share her experiences. Her breathing becomes shallow and she looks as if she is becoming overwhelmed with the memory.

Paris: Sounds like you remember a whole lot about that chase and you want me to see what you saw. You can show me in the sand tray if it would help make the picture in your head more clear.

Danielle: Can I use the cars and everything?

Danielle moves over to the sand tray.

Danielle: I need a police car—oh, here's one. Actually, I need two. One came in the driveway and one kept going after my dad. I need a house too.

Danielle begins to carefully recreate the scene in front of her house the day that dad took off with her baby sister.

Danielle: Dad took off his shoe and started banging on her window. Mom screamed and got out. Dad grabbed my baby sister and got in his car. He tried to get us to go with him.

Paris: He wanted you to get in the car too.

Danielle: He screamed at us to get in the car, but mom was yelling for us to go to the neighbor's yard and we did. He gave up and got in the car with sissy.

Paris: So he got in his car.

Danielle: Yeah. Then he slammed into mom's car.

Paris: He hit mom's car. What was that like?

Danielle: It was so loud and it smashed the back.

Paris: So, he hit her car. Then what happened?

Danielle: He had a knife.

Danielle begins to breathe shallowly again. Again, I interrupt the narrative and back up a step, clarifying the last detail. I am intentionally slowing down the telling of the narrative and trying to help her make sequential sense of events while grounding her in the here and now of the toys.

Paris: Wait a sec. I'm confused. I thought he was in the car.

Danielle: Mom was trying to call the police on her cell phone. He ran over with the knife. Dad was trying to pop out the battery.

Paris: Oh, OK. So he was trying to take the battery out of the phone with the knife.

Danielle: Yeah. He got it out. Then he drove off with sissy. She's just 1 year old.

Paris: Sounds like it was scary to watch him drive off with your little sister.

Danielle drives the car down the driveway she'd made in the sand.

Danielle: Yeah. I didn't know where they were going.

Paris: So dad pulled out.

Danielle: Yeah. The police were just pulling up and mom pointed at dad's car and the police chased after him. They clocked him doing 80. He was going 80 miles fast with sissy in the car. The police slowed down so he wouldn't go so fast.

Paris: The police wanted to keep your sister safe.

Danielle: Yeah. They tracked him on his GPS. They got him at a hotel.

Paris: So they got him. And sissy?

Danielle: She was OK.

Danielle abruptly breaks away from the sand tray, picks up a smooth rock shaped like a pyramid, and begins to examine it. I shift my attention to the rock.

Paris: You found my rock!

Danielle is repeating a pattern that I see over and over again with children who are telling the story of their traumatic events. They will work in a very focused way on simultaneously showing and telling me what happened. When the memory or affect gets too intense, they break away from it by physically distancing themselves from the current processing. They often move across the room, suddenly fascinated by a toy that had previously gone unnoticed. This is a coping mechanism and as such should be respected by the play therapist. In adult treatment, when processing becomes overwhelming, a client will signal the therapist by reverting to small talk. It is the wise therapist who tracks with the client. In child therapy I immediately switch tracks with the child, becoming equally interested in whatever is currently capturing her attention.

The dance between trauma content and safe, soothing play can take many configurations. The most important dynamic to remember is that the therapist is a partner in the dance and needs to move fluidly between the trauma process and more grounding play behavior. The breakaway moments allow the child to perform an internal recalibration that equips the child to eventually return to the trauma content. The therapist's own desire to know more can get in the way of being an effective partner in the dance and must be guarded against.

After a few minutes, Danielle puts down the pyramid and picks up a tree made from beautiful stones. While our heads are together admiring the stone tree, she returns to trauma processing.

Danielle: We don't know what happened.
Paris: You don't know yet.
Danielle: They think she got murdered by someone.

It is clear that she has overheard the adults talking. I remember her guardians saying that she has not asked any questions about how her mom died.

Paris: Oh, they think that she was murdered.
Danielle: It was a really heavy couch.

Here we see another example of how children will give disjointed pieces of information.

Paris: You're remembering a couch.

Danielle: Well, the couch was up against the closet door in our room. We were sleeping in mom's room because she likes our bed better for her back.

Paris: I'm confused. If you weren't in your room, how do you know the couch was up against the closet?

Danielle: I could see the closet from the hallway. The couch was tipped. I thought maybe mom was in there.

Paris: You thought she might be inside the closet.

Danielle: Yeah. It's a big heavy couch with a rollout bed. Dad couldn't tip it—it's too heavy for him.

Paris: So you're thinking that your dad couldn't have moved it.

Danielle: Yeah. I don't think he killed her.

Danielle once again breaks away from the sand tray to play with some magnets. I join her in this activity and we do not return to the sand for the rest of the session. Danielle clearly wanted to tell someone about what she had seen. It was exhausting for her to keep all her perceptions and images inside, but she needed the sharing to be grounded in the materials of childhood. She titrated her own doses of trauma content and gave herself breaks when needed. My job is to contain, reflect, and validate what she is showing me. Secondarily, my job is to move with her toward and away from the trauma content as she provides signals for what she needs.

In Danielle's case, she began to process a specific traumatic event during our initial session. As I mentioned in a previous chapter, the safest progression of treatment for traumatized children places the development of relaxation skills and stress management competencies before trauma processing. However, a child may spontaneously begin to create trauma narrative in the midst of the therapist's attempt to build safety and security within the playroom. Allie's case, mentioned briefly in Chapter 6, illustrates this point.

Allie was an 8-year-old girl who was placed in the home of her paternal grandparents 6 months before treatment began. Allie was neglected and maltreated by her biological mother and was originally put in the care of her maternal grandmother when she was 3 years old. She remained in this placement until her grandmother became too sick to care for her. Since she had been with her paternal grandparents, who had agreed to become her new guardians, she had made allegations against the maternal grandmother. Allie alleged that the maternal grandmother locked her in dark rooms and slapped her when she misbehaved. On Allie's third visit to the playroom, she chose the smallest jail in my office and put it in the sand tray. She chose a figurine of a blonde-haired, blue-eyed baby holding a bottle. I wondered silently if this symbol was going to become her chosen self-object. She then began a play pattern that I would characterize as an attempt to build safety and security in the playroom by actively enlisting the therapist's help in taking care of the figurine.

Allie: The little baby girl has to go to jail!

Paris: Oh no! The baby girl is being put in jail!

Allie (turning to look with exasperation at the therapist): Well, are you just gonna sit there?

Paris: You want me to help.

Allie nods and gives the therapist a figurine of a strong man. She is requesting more active alignment from me.

Allie (pretending to be the baby): Help me!

Paris (as strong man): I'll help you, baby girl. You shouldn't be in jail. You need new parents to take care of you.

I open the jail and put the baby girl in the strong man's arms (Figure 10.10).

The next week Allie returned and immediately asked for the big jail to be placed in the sand tray. She chose lots of little horses and put them in the jail. Allie chose the same baby girl that we rescued last week and put her in front of all the horses in the largest jail. (Figure 10.11).

Allie: I want rescuing.

Paris: You want to be rescued.

Allie: Not yet. I'm not ready yet.

Paris: You'll let me know when you're ready for rescuing.

Allie: Momma . . . not my new momma, my first momma. She put me in jail.

Paris: She put you in jail?

Figure 10.10   Strong Man Saves the Baby Girl

Figure 10.11   Baby Girl in Jail

Allie: I threw my toys and yelled. She called the police. She was gonna put me in jail.

Paris: I wonder if that felt scary . . . to be a little girl and to think you were going to jail.

Allie stares hard at the little girl inside the jail cell and nods vigorously.

Allie: Maybe I need one more jail.

She moves toward the shelves, notices a water toy, and picks it up.

Allie: It's got a dolphin inside!
Paris (mirroring the child's delight): You found the dolphin toy!

The dolphin toy gives Allie a necessary break from the trauma content. The game is one in which the child presses a button to flip rings up through the water in an attempt to hook them on the dolphin's nose. I have purposefully place similar toys throughout the playroom with the understanding that children will use them as a form of self-regulation. It is vital that the therapist flexibly follows the child's shifts from trauma processing to play that provides a safe, noncommittal anchor in the space. Therapists must understand that the breaks between trauma processing moments are as important as the processing itself. Non–trauma-focused play breaks serve as power naps for children. They allow children to titrate their doses of exposure to the traumatic material. Exploratory, noncommittal, and mastery-oriented play soothes the child and reaffirms the child's sense of competency. When the child returns to trauma processing, it is often with a clearer focus or a new piece of information. Sometimes the child returns from the breather through a different sensory door. A child may have been giving a linear narrative previous to the break but approaches the work again by talking about a sound he heard or something that he smelled while the bad thing was happening.

Allie sticks her tongue between her teeth and focuses on pumping the rings up to the top of the water tank. She finally gets one ring onto the dolphin's nose and I cheer. She smiles, puts down the dolphin, picks up the second jail, and returns to the tray and the trauma processing.

Ending the Session

Another important consideration in play-based trauma narrative work is how the play materials are left at the end of a given session. When a child is actively working through a trauma narrative process, the play therapist must build in time at the end of the session for the child to close down the processing. Most children have learned to cope with their trauma histories by developing a range of defense mechanisms. Although some of these strategies may not be optimal, they serve a protective function at the time the child enters treatment. The child's defense mechanisms must be respected. Through the course of a play therapy session, we create an environment where the defensive walls can come down. The client and therapist can together begin to peek over and around them. However, the child must be given time to put the walls back before returning to daily life. I often see families in which the relationship between a child and his current caregiver is strained. A given child may have to return home to an overwhelmed, underattuned caregiver. This child must have the necessary coping mechanisms back in place when he enters the lobby and takes this caregiver's hand to return home.

The process of ending a session can begin with a statement that lets the child know how much time is left in the playroom. I suggest giving the child at least a 5-minute warning. Many children prefer to end the playtime by having perpetrator symbols contained and self-objects nurtured. In Allie's case, when I gave her the 5-minute warning she became very focused. She got down to the serious business of being rescued. She ran out to the lobby and got her "new momma" and brought her into the playroom. Allie told her new momma exactly how she was to get the baby girl out of the jail. After mom had followed her instructions and was holding the figurine, Allie took it from her. She shifted the baby doll from a sitting position to a lying down position. Then she spoke to me.

Allie: Ms. Paris, you put her in the stroller. Just be sure she's lying down.
Paris: You want the baby to rest. She's out of jail and now she can safely rest in this stroller until you come back again.
Allie: Yeah, she can sleep in there and she's got all her horse friends around.
Paris: She must feel very safe in her stroller. The baby girl can relax because there are others who are watching out for her [Figure 10.12].

Allie is able to leave the playroom knowing that her self-object is safely tucked in until she returns.

Figure 10.12   Baby Girl Safely Resting between Sessions

Directive Interventions

There are times when a child's trauma processing happens spontaneously. The metaphors are potent and easily mined by the therapist/child team. The dyadic dance moves fluidly back and forth between trauma content and revitalizing play. However, some children are stuck in avoidance symptoms that require a more directive invitation from the therapist. The parameters of a specific intervention can add just the right level of structure to a child's trauma processing. For example, a variation of the creep and the creepy crawly exercise can be used to help a child structure her first sequenced look at her abuse. The completed creepy crawly drawing of a 10-year-old girl named Libby serves as an example.

Libby was sexually molested by an extended family member. Her aunt eventually noticed a change in her demeanor and asked what was wrong. Libby disclosed that her uncle had sexually abused her. Her aunt responded to Libby's disclosures with support and Libby's mom and dad immediately limited all contact with the alleged perpetrator. The perpetrator was prosecuted and already serving jail time when the family sought counseling for Libby.

During the initial investigation, Libby had given very specific information about the sexual acts to which she had been subjected. However, her parents had noticed a slow withdrawal since then. They reported that she had become sullen and rebellious. She no longer smiled, and she avoided all reminders of her abuse. She refused to even drive near the neighborhood where her uncle had lived. After establishing safety in the playroom, completing emotional literacy activities, and training her in stress inoculation strategies, I introduced the idea of trauma processing. I normalized avoidance symptoms as a response to trauma. I compared the pressure that Libby was exerting to repress all her trauma content to the pressure that builds up in a volcano. This analogy seemed to resonate with her. I said, "Sometimes it's hard to remember the bad things that happened. It can be scary to remember, so kids will try not to think about it. Sometimes this works well and children are able to play with their friends, do their school work, and get along with their parents. Sometimes, however, the 'I'm not going to think about it' approach backfires. It can take so much energy to not think about the bad stuff that there's no energy left for being a kid. The good news is that there's a way to let the pressure out slowly—so that you don't have to blow up like a volcano. You and I will let the pressure out together, a little at a time. You tell me when you want to stop."

Then I explained the creep and the creepy crawly activity. I let her know that we'd only do as much as she wanted to do that day. We developed a signal she could use to let me know when she wanted or needed to stop.

This activity provides a nonverbal but powerfully evocative way of showing the bad touches that happened without having to verbally articulate them. Libby moved forward without hesitation, affixing several different insect stickers to her drawing (Figure 10.13). Libby affixed a spider sticker to her left ear, another to her chest, and a third to her vaginal area. Then she surprised me by putting an ant sticker on her forehead. Lastly, she chose a ladybug sticker and placed it next to the spider sticker on her chest. She was making powerful communications without ever opening her mouth. She moved her picture toward me. I noticed out loud that she had put a spider sticker on her ear.

Paris: I see that you put one on your ear.

Libby (looking at the paper): He used to suck on my ear. It felt really gross.

Paris: So he would suck on your ear. Did this happen before or after the other stuff?

Libby: Before he licked me down there.

Figure 10.13   Libby's *Creepy Crawly* Picture

This is the first step in my attempt to come alongside Libby and help her sequence the trauma narrative. What happened first? What happened next? Walking a child through the step-by-step events of a previously avoided memory helps in the process of building a coherent narrative.

Paris: OK. So he would suck on your ear before he did other things.

Leaving the hard things unspoken gives them extra power. Restating the trauma content in a matter-of-fact manner helps take the power out of what has seemed so large in silence. Hearing the bad stuff said out loud by the therapist acts as a form of exposure and desensitizes the child to the traumatic content while helping the child rehearse the sequenced story. The enslavement to the pattern of avoidance begins to be shaken. The child who has been mastered by the fear begins to get mastery of the trauma content.

Once a linguistic narrative has been outlined, other sensory dimensions of the trauma can be explored. Several passes can be made at the same piece of trauma content with a view toward integrating additional somatosensory

Figure 10.14 Libby's Perpetrator Puppet

content. In Libby's case, I offered her a set of interchangeable puppet parts and invited her to create a puppet to represent her uncle (Figure 10.14).

Notice the two tufts of hair that Libby placed on either side of the puppet's head. When I invited Libby to talk about the puppet, she offered this explanation of the hair:

Libby: He had a big bald spot. Sometimes, when he was doing stuff down there, I would stare at it.

She had previously told me about her uncle performing oral sex on her. I synthesize this new information into the parts of her story that Libby has already shared, helping her weave this new perspective into the trauma narrative.

Paris: So, while he was licking you down there, you were looking at his bald spot.
Libby: Yeah. I get a little creeped out whenever I see guys like that.

The simple addition of a prop allowed Libby to access and give voice to a part of her trauma memory that was not available for integration on our first pass at the trauma narrative. Moreover, it helped us identify a previously unpronounced trauma reminder. Libby was having panicky feelings whenever she was around a balding man but only mentioned this in the course of completing this activity. Libby had attached a mustache to her puppet. She had not drawn a mustache on him before. I remembered from our previous drawing activity that her uncle's pattern was to suck on her ear before other sexual activity. The puppet's mustache became the bridge to integrate sense memories related to the tickly wet feel of the mustache on her ear. The repeated passes at the trauma content through multiple play materials can help traumatized children access and integrate various pieces of sensory information into the linguistic narrative of what happened.

Interventions Aimed at Integrating Somatosensory Memories

Putting the Pieces Back Together

I have created a few playful interventions that are specifically designed to access the sense memories related to trauma. The first of these involves the use of puzzles (Goodyear-Brown, 2005). I keep two wooden puzzles in the office. One is a close-up of a little girl's face and the other is a close-up of a little boy's face. Each puzzle consists of a larger face piece and smaller pieces for the eyes, ears, nose, and mouth. In the playroom I empty the smaller pieces into a brown bag. The child draws a piece out of the bag without looking and shares a sense memory related to the trauma about whichever part they chose. If the child draws the nose piece from the bag, I ask him to tell me one thing that he smelled during the trauma. Then he gets to put that piece in the puzzle (Figure 10.15).

When the face is complete, with all the pieces inserted, the whole person can be recognized. The fitting of the pieces together within the puzzle parallels the integration work that is happening inside the child as somatosensory memories are intentionally accessed and assimilated into the child's internal narrative.

Monster Ears

Another intervention, called "monster ears" (Goodyear-Brown, 2005), helps children to make sense of the sounds that they heard during a traumatic event. Years ago I came across a pair of large rubber ears at a costume shop. Knowing that they would appeal to latency-age boys especially, I designed an interven-

Figure 10.15   Face Puzzle for *Putting the Pieces Together Again*

tion targeted at auditory memory integration. The exercise has proven especially useful with auditory memories related to a child's experience of domestic
violence. Children who have lived in domestic violence have often "witnessed"
the violence from underneath a table, around a corner, or huddled under a blanket. I have had many clients make the following admission: "They thought I
was asleep, but I actually climbed out of my bed and was right behind the living
room wall listening to them screaming and yelling at each other." Figure 10.16
depicts a client hiding behind a couch while listening to her parents fight.

These children perceive a series of sounds without any actual visual reality to ground them in. Sometimes when they put on the monster ears and
focus on a particular memory, they remember the words of heated arguments.
Other times they remember the sounds of smashing glass, sickening thuds,
terrifying screams, or soft sobs. Sometimes children tell me that the most
frightening sound they heard was the deafening silence after a violent argument. Children take these auditory memories and very naturally begin to create a visual narrative of events that will make sense of the sounds they heard.

When I am using the intervention, the child puts on the ears and giggles
while admiring himself in the mirror. I first ask him to identify the sounds he

Figure 10.16   Girl Hiding Behind Couch

heard during the traumatic event. I write these down, usually on sticky notes, because they are not likely to come out in sequenced order on the child's first attempt. Every sound that they remember gets written down. Then we stick all the notes to the wall and I help the child put the sounds in order according to when they occurred. Finally, I ask the child what he thinks happened based on what he heard. Whether or not the child is willing to share his internal images, he has usually already created a series of pictures that coincide with the sounds. Often, the story is worse than what actually happened.

One little girl described the sound of breaking glass followed by mom's weeping. When I asked her what she thought had happened, she shared a visual narrative that she had pieced together from the sounds. As she huddled on the staircase she heard the glass break and she heard mom start to cry. She peeked her head around into the kitchen as far as she could and she saw a pool of dark red liquid. She had made sense of these disparate pieces of information by deciding that dad had thrown a glass at mom, cut her face, and made her bleed. She believed that what she had seen was mom's blood in a pool on the floor. The image haunted her.

When I shared the girl's memory with her mom, mom seemed bewildered at first and then her face cleared. Mom explained that she and dad had indeed been having a fight, but that she had thrown the wine bottle in anger and the pool was one of red wine. My guideline for shifting these kinds of constructed memories is identical to the one employed in deciding whether or not the little girl discussed earlier should visit dad in jail. If the truth is less horrible than the story that has been created, we enlist the parent's help in correcting to the truth. In this case, I invited the mom into the room and had her explain what happened to her daughter. Once the pool of red liquid had been redefined as a red wine stain, the visual image lost its potency and the child was no longer bothered by the picture in her head. Moreover, when she remembered the crashing sound, the image of mom throwing the bottle replaced her more troublesome image of mom with a blood-streaked face.

See No Evil, Hear No Evil

A third intervention aimed at helping children integrate other sensory aspects of their traumatic experiences into the linear narrative involves the use of several monkey figurines (Goodyear-Brown, 2005). The three figurines that I use for this activity are See No Evil, Hear No Evil, and Speak No Evil. I put the three monkeys in the sand tray and explain the history of the monkeys (Figure 10.17).

Then I ask the child, "What's one thing that you wish you hadn't had to see when your bad thing happened?" The client may verbalize the answer or may choose to draw a picture and slip it underneath that monkey figurine in

Figure 10.17   See No Evil, Hear No Evil, Speak No Evil

the sand. When we get to the second monkey, I ask, "What's one thing that you wish you didn't have to hear?" Finally, I ask the child "What's one thing that you wish you didn't have to say during the trauma?" Sometimes this activity generates very poignant answers. I asked a 7-year-old boy recently what he wished he hadn't had to say during the bad thing that happened to him. His mother was drug-addicted and often described herself as feeling sick. He described standing beside the couch where she had lain face down all day. He asked over and over again, "Can you make dinner? I'm hungry." His request got louder and louder as he tried to make her get up. She didn't stir, but he felt guilty for raising his voice to his "sick" mother.

Google Eyes

The last intervention that I regularly use to help clients sequence visual images of traumatic events involves the craft eyes that are often used in children's art projects. I begin by hiding a handful of these eyes, in the sand tray. The child is invited to search for the eyes, and whenever she finds one, she describes the next thing she saw during the traumatic event. This game is another in which the questions are sequenced by the therapist. What was the first thing you saw? What did you see next? Some children may benefit from the additional structure of a chart. As part of this modification, each craft eye is glued onto the left side of a piece of paper as it is found. Beside each craft eye, the therapist writes the factual description of what the child saw first, second, third, and so on. Whenever I make lists with clients, I verbalize what I am writing down as I am doing the scripting. This allows for the child to hear the narrative rehearsed in verbal form while seeing it written down in a sequenced way.

Conclusion

The myriad case examples presented in this chapter showcase the variety of ways in which children tell the story of what happened. Each child finds a way of relating to her trauma content. A fraction of children approach the narrative head on, giving verbal details of the trauma as early as the first session. Many more clients begin to approach the trauma through their art and play creations. They offer veiled glimpses of their inner truths, abrupt snapshots of horrific images, and metaphoric conveyances of their posttraumatic perceptions. They dance toward the trauma content and then away again, grounding themselves repeatedly in the soothing tools of childhood. It requires patience, practice, and careful attunement on the part of the therapist to partner a child in this dance and lead her toward an integrated narrative.

In some cases, children are able to give a factual accounting of their traumatic events but remain mired in posttraumatic symptoms. In order to cope, these children may have split off affectual and sensory impressions related to the trauma and compartmentalized them separately from the verbal story. In these cases, more directive intervention may be required by the therapist to aid the child in integrating all the aspects of the trauma. The series of directive interventions listed here are aimed at helping children find the sensory information that is stored separately from the linguistic account of the trauma and weave the pieces together into a coherent narrative. The overarching goal of this work is to gift the child with a story that includes the gestalt of the child's experience, while relieving the toxicity of the memories. Often in the crafting of trauma narratives, remaining cognitive distortions are revealed. Strategies for helping children explore, and when necessary shift or reconstruct these cognitions, are addressed in the next chapter.

11

Addressing the Child's Thought Life

There is nothing good or bad, but thinking makes it so.
—*William Shakespeare*, Hamlet

This chapter comes chronologically after many other treatment goals; not to denigrate its importance or to even imply that thought life work starts after all the rest, but rather to punctuate that any remaining false attributions or faulty cognitions should be addressed before the child's termination from treatment. It is worth reiterating that many of the treatment goals delineated in this text often overlap and may even change priority over the course of treatment. Certainly, cognitive distortions can be addressed at whatever point they arise. However, I find that the cognitive distortions are often not easily accessible during the initial phases of treatment. The process of pinpointing maladaptive thought patterns is often one of excavation. Cognitive distortions, particularly false attributions related to the cause of the traumatic event, can engender deep anxiety and low self-esteem and must be approached with care.

Moreover, this chapter is placed directly after the chapter on trauma narrative work, because it is often through the narrative process that trauma-genic thoughts and irrational beliefs surface. Once the thoughts are laid bare, the child can learn to tolerate them, challenge them, restructure, and replace them. In children, the process of dealing with the thought life is greatly aided by play-based interventions that encourage the child to externalize specific thoughts and then kinesthetically manipulate them until the child feels like he is in control of his thought life and it is not in control of him.

A foundation of safety, trust, and respect must exist before implementing play-based interventions aimed at addressing the thought life. The child must first feel safe with the therapist and understand that her beliefs will not be judged or mocked. The stress management activities addressed in Chapter 5, Soothing the Physiology, give the child tools for handling the increased anxiety that often arises as a child confronts irrational thoughts and negative self-talk and is therefore part of the foundation that should be laid before addressing the thought life.

Emotional literacy training helps clients to more accurately identify and cope with the feelings engendered by various maladaptive thoughts. Finally, it is often through the child's telling of the story of what happened (as discussed in Chapter 8, The Continuum of Disclosure, and Chapter 10, Trauma Narrative Work) that the faulty cognitions begin to be revealed. A patient clinician will record the cognitive distortions as they become apparent and address each one as the child is being taught the skills for handling troublesome thoughts.

Addressing a child's faulty attributions and cognitive distortions related to the trauma are a necessary component in the alleviation of a child's posttraumatic symptoms. Cognitive-behavioral therapy, a widely endorsed treatment for reducing posttraumatic symptoms (Chambless & Ollendick, 2001), has at its core the theoretical construct that our thoughts are inextricably linked to our actions and our emotions. Aaron Beck (1976) pioneered the idea that thoughts influence our behavior and our feelings.

Extrapolated from this triangulation is the hope that by intentionally changing our thinking we can change our behavior and our feelings. A natural extension of this hypothesis is that positively changing the thought life will positively impact both our feelings and our behaviors. A solid empirical base now exists for the effectiveness of cognitive-behavioral therapy in work with posttraumatic children (Cohen, Deblinger, Mannarino, & Steer, 2004; Cohen, Mannarino, & Deblinger, 2006; Friedberg & McClure, 2002; Knell, 1993, 1998). I conceptualize my work around a child's thought life in cognitive-behavioral terms but integrate the therapeutic powers of play in the delivery of those concepts. Young children, in particular, have difficulty accessing and articulating their thoughts and are better equipped to do so when the exploration of thoughts is paired with kinesthetic activity or expressive endeavors such as sand and art creations.

Play-Based Interventions in Psychoeducation

The first goal of play-based intervention in relation to thought life is psycho-educational. We must help the child understand the interplay among thoughts, feelings, and actions. To begin this process of explanation, I draw a large triangle on the dry erase board and label each of the three points with one of the following words: *Thoughts, Feelings, Actions.* I then offer the child a magnetic building set. These magnetized lengths and balls come in various shapes and colors and are a wonderful prop for helping children create their own three-dimensional triangles. We choose specific scenarios and build our own triangles out of magnetic pieces. We articulate the thought, feeling, and resulting action engendered by each situation. I often give the following example.

Sally walks into the lunchroom at school and sees two of her closest friends. Their heads are together and they are whispering. She immediately thinks, *They're talking about me.* I then ask the client how Sally is going to *feel* in response to this thought. The client produces feeling words such as *upset, angry,* and *betrayed.* When I ask what Sally is likely to *do* next, the client predicts that she will either intentionally avoid her friends, or walk up to them in a confrontational manner and accuse them of gossiping about her.

Once we have built a magnetic triangle to stand for the thought-feeling-action pattern, I change the story. I ask the child to press the rewind button in his head. Sally walks into the lunchroom at school and sees two of her closest friends. Their heads are together and they are whispering. She thinks, *I wonder what they're talking about?* I ask the client to guess how Sally will *feel* if this is her thought. The client produces words like *curious* and *interested.* When I ask what Sally is likely to *do,* the client predicts that she will approach her friends and join the conversation. In each scene the actual event Sally observes is exactly the same. In both cases her friends have their heads together and are whispering. Her self-talk in each case leads to a significantly different behavioral choice. Once children have this basic understanding of how the triangles work, we can use them over and over again in treatment for various situations.

Shelby & Berk (2009) describe another intervention involving dominoes that can help convey the idea of the interdependence of thoughts, feelings, and actions. Dominoes are placed in a circle and knocked over, each impacting the next until they have all fallen down. Then labels are attached to three separate dominoes at equidistant points around the circle. Each label says "thought," "feeling," or "behavior," and the child knocks them over again, noting the inter-relatedness of the three dimensions. A musical triangle can provide another interesting prop to help anchor the psychoeducation related to the cognitive triad.

A child's thought life can provide several paths toward healing. A child's false attributions that attempt to answer the question "Why did this terrible thing happen?" can be identified and countered. False attributions engender difficult emotions such as guilt and shame. As the false attributions are eradicated, the child's struggle with guilt and shame diminishes. A child who is dealing with anxiety symptoms as a response to trauma can identify his anxious thoughts, learn strategies for stopping these thoughts, and consciously replace them with positively restructured self-talk.

The child who struggles with depression can benefit from being introduced to the kinds of irrational thoughts that contribute to depression. Dual states of hopelessness and helplessness are perpetuated by distorted thoughts. We must offer alternate cognitions for a child that expand the anxious, depressed, or otherwise distorted worldview in which the child may be mired. The child therapist must hold a deep belief that the troublesome thoughts can be changed. In fact, the therapist often functions as the container of hope for the client until the client gains the courage to begin to hope for himself.

Fighting False Attributions

Traumatized children often rehearse a set of false attributions about why a particular trauma happened to them. A little boy is convinced that his dad died in a car accident because he yelled at his dad before school that morning. A teenage girl is convinced that she caused her mother's death because she asked mom to leave work and bring her something at school. In the teenager's mind, if she hadn't selfishly insisted that mom bring something to her school, her mother would still be alive.

Child survivors of sexual abuse have a range of faulty attributions, some of which may have been directly implanted by their perpetrators. A sexually abusive dad tells his daughter that what happened to her was because she wore sexy pajamas to bed. A teenage girl is told by the boy who raped her that if she didn't flirt so much, he wouldn't have been so tempted. As hollow as these blame-shifting statements may sound to other people, children who are the recipients of these messages often believe them and take false responsibility for the abuse. One of the jobs of a trauma therapist is to challenge these false attributions.

The Why Chain

One activity that I use to accomplish this goal is called the "why chain." The child and I begin the activity by cutting out a series of question marks in a multitude of colors. I then invite the child to talk about, without censoring herself, any reason she can think of that the abuse may have happened. The goal is to get every possible attribution that the child might be entertaining out onto paper so that we can analyze them one at a time. As each reason is written on a question mark, they are hooked together to form a chain. This initial phase of the intervention is meant to resemble a brainstorming session in which no judgment is made about the ideas presented. Once the chain is complete, we take each of the attributions in turn and assess whether or not this is the real reason that the abuse happened.

Any reason that places responsibility for the abuse in the child or in the child's behavior is countered with psychoeducation. As each reason is read and disproved, the child gets to tear that question mark into tiny pieces. As the methodical deconstruction of each reason continues, the pile of multicolored pieces of paper grows. Once all the false attributions have been challenged, the only true reason that remains is that the perpetrator chose to do it. I will write the question, "Whose fault was it?" at the top of a large piece of paper. If the perpetrator was a male, we then write the word *HIS* in oversized bubble letters. If the perpetrator was a female, we write the word *HERS* underneath the question. The child gets to glue the rainbow of torn question mark pieces into the bubble letters, creating a mosaic effect while reinforcing the correct placement of responsibility for the abuse.

Blameberry Pie

Another useful intervention for challenging false attributions is called "blameberry pie" and was designed by Janine Shelby (Goodyear-Brown, Riviere, & Shelby, 2004). The props for the intervention include blank strips of paper and several empty pie tins. The child is invited to exhaust their list of attributions by writing each one on a strip of paper. As the strips are written on, each strip of paper is balled up and becomes a berry for the blameberry pie. Initially all the berries are jumbled up in the same pie tin.

One by one the berries are unraveled, read, and discussed. A teenage girl who believes she was raped because she skipped school the day that she was assaulted needs to have that attribution challenged. One way to do this is to ask questions that help the client reflect on a wider range of experiences. A script might go like this:

Clinician: Have you skipped school before?

Teenager: Yes.

Clinician: Did anything bad happen the other time that you skipped school?

Teenager: No.

Clinician: Do you know any other kids who have skipped school?

Teenager: Yes.

Clinician: Did this happen to them while they were skipping?

Teenager: Not that I know of.

Clinician: So does it make sense that the reason you were raped was because you skipped school?

Teenager: I guess not.

At this point, other pie tins might be employed. One might be labeled "skip-ping school" and serve as another topic of conversation or area of interven-tion, but is separated from the reason that the abuse happened. When the intervention is finished, the only berry that should remain in the blameberry pie tin is the one that reads "Because he did it."

Identifying the Adaptive and Maladaptive Thoughts

Attaching cognitive distortions to props or physically engaging activities allows the child to manipulate otherwise elusive thoughts in three dimen-sions. Generating a list of the cognitive distortions is the first step. I begin by drawing a big circle on a piece of paper to represent a brain. Then I draw sev-eral compartments inside the brain. As the child verbalizes the troublesome thoughts, I write each one down in a compartment of the brain. Once the brain has been filled in, we give the brain a name. Some of the labels that children have used are the Sick Brain, the Worried Brain, the Sad Brain, and so on. We put a second piece of paper on top of this brain, trace the outline of the compartments and then begin to craft replacement statements that will be meaningful weapons for the child. We label this second brain the Healthy Brain, the Well Brain, or the Happy Brain.

One important caveat about replacement statements is that they are not necessarily the opposite of the cognitive distortion. For example, a child who makes Cs and Ds in school will not benefit from replacing the negative self-talk statement "I am stupid" with "I am brilliant" because the replacement statement is not an accurate representation of reality. It is an attempt to overcompensate for the negative belief, but because it lacks truth it cannot be owned by the child. Replacement statements must be meaningful to the child who will use them. For the child who makes Cs and Ds in most subjects but Bs in math, his counter to the thought "I am stupid" might be "I'm good at math" or "I'm good at other things." Again, the most important dynamic of a strong replacement statement is that the child can believe it and claim ownership of it.

Containment, Thought Stopping, and Cognitive Restructuring

Once cognitive distortions have been articulated, the dual processes of thought stopping and thought replacement are vastly aided through the focused handling of props. There are many play-based methods for practicing thought stopping and thought replacement. If a child feels he is having racing thoughts and/or describes an impression that his thoughts are overtaking him, it can help to make a containment device. For example, Eva, who had been sexually molested by an older cousin, kept having one particular troublesome thought in relation to her abuse. We wrote the thought down together and she sealed it on every edge with tape. Then she chose the box pictured in Figure 11.1, put the paper inside, and sealed the edges of the box with tape.

During the next session, she unwrapped the box and cut open the sealed paper on which the negative thought was written. She said that the thought had not bothered her all week, but that she needed to "get rid of it once and for all." We went outside and burned it up in the parking lot. This particular thought did not trouble her any longer. Another child continued to have intrusive thoughts following an episode in which he had witnessed interpersonal violence. He created the "bad thoughts jail" (Figure 11.2). He put all the intrusive thoughts into the box, and over the course of the next few sessions we took out each thought individually and created an appropriate counter statement. Finally, he practiced each replacement statement over and over again until they were automatic.

Figure 11.1   A Thought Containment Box

Figure 11.2   The Bad Thoughts Jail

Lose the Bruise

My favorite intervention in this vein is called "lose the bruise" (Goodyear-Brown, 2005). I begin by helping the client identify negative self-talk statements or lies that she was told by perpetrators. We talk about how these lies morphed into cognitive distortions over time. We make a brain picture that displays cognitions like, "It's all your fault!" "You are worthless." and "You are dirty." Once these cognitions have been identified, we generate the replacement statements that will boss back these thoughts. We display this second brain in a prominent place in the room. I have a handful of kickballs that I purchased through a novelty store. They have faces on them and Band-Aids and bruises. They look like little people who have been kicked around. I explain to the client that these beat-up balls represent the negative thoughts that repeat over and over again inside her head. If we can't find ways to stop these hurtful thoughts, they will leave bruises on the inside. Then I invite the child to choose a shield and a sword from my collection. I explain that I will throw the bruised balls in her direction while I say one of the negative cognitions out loud. The child's job is to block each ball as she verbalizes a replacement statement from the list we generated earlier.

Train the Truck

The sand tray can also be used to practice thought stopping. An intervention that I use called "train the truck" can be useful for school-age boys who love all manner of moving vehicles. In this intervention the therapist invites the child to choose a truck to be himself. The therapist makes two intersecting roads in the sand. At the intersection, two roads have stop signs and two do not. We compare a negative thought that repeats over and over again to a truck going down the same road again and again, crashing repeatedly into the same danger. The therapist then helps the client to identify an irrational worry thought, like, "I'll never be safe!" and has the child move the truck down the road while saying these words. We also choose a symbol to represent the feeling state or behavior that ends up being the outgrowth of the negative self-talk. Perhaps the child feels all stirred up on the inside after he has listened to the negative thought for awhile. A miniature tornado can be put at the end of the road in the sand tray. As the child moves the truck down the same path over and over again, the truck repeatedly gets swept up into the tornado.

The therapist then puts the truck back in its starting place and gives the child miniature stop signs to put at the intersection. Client and therapist can brainstorm some of the positive outcomes of choosing a different route, create symbols to represent these better outcomes in the sand, and place them at the ends of the side streets. The child then chooses a replacement statement like "I can get through this" or "I am stronger than my fear." The therapist verbalizes the negative self-talk while the child drives the truck. However, as soon as the truck reaches the stop sign, the therapist must stop. This time the child has other choices and can turn left or right while repeating some of his replacement cognitions. Boys, particularly, will do this over and over again, motivated in part by the inherently fun kinesthetic activity and familiar toys. The child receives powerful reinforcement through the combination of kinesthetic change (moving the truck in a different direction) and the repeated verbalizations.

The important part of the intervention is that the child has kinesthetic involvement in stopping his Worried Brain from speaking the worried thoughts over and over again. Children can make individual stop signs and practice holding them up to stop the Worried Brain cognitions. The stop sign can serve as both a transitional object from the safety and empowerment of the playroom to the child's home or school environment and as a reminder of the therapeutic intervention being practiced. Once the child has developed an awareness of the troublesome thoughts and has kinesthetically practiced silencing those thoughts, the newly crafted replacement thoughts can be freely rehearsed.

Old Hat, New Hat

Another play-based intervention, "old hat, new hat," offers a way for children to pair their irrational thoughts with a prop and their replacement thoughts with another prop and then practice switching back and forth between them (Goodyear-Brown, 2005). Blank baseball caps are a great way to help children practice switching between their worried thoughts and new, helpful thoughts. The therapist presents two unadorned canvas baseball caps of different colors. The previously identified negative thoughts are written on various sections of the hat, and the child is encouraged to decorate the brim of the hat with pictures or symbols that show how the troublesome thoughts make the child feel.

The second hat is adorned with the statements that detail the client's restructured cognitions. Once the hats are complete, they are used to help the client differentiate the behavioral responses that might result from each set of cognitions. Children who are 7 years of age or older will often wear the hats themselves. I give the child a real-life scenario and we role play the child's response to it, tying his response to whichever set of cognitions he has on his head. For example, I might say, "Let's imagine that you got home from school a little while ago, you had a snack and got to play outside for awhile, and now it's time to do your homework. You sit down at the table." Once I have set the scene, I have the child verbalize one of the negative thoughts that is on his hat. The child might say, "I'm never going to finish all this!" I then ask the child how this thought makes him feel and what it makes him want to do. The child's reply to this question might be that he wants to leave the table or that he wants to rush through his work and get it done. The thought that he'll never finish might make him sit frozen with his pencil suspended above his paper or look out the window and daydream about what he would be doing if he didn't have to do homework.

The child is then invited to switch hats and puts on the one with the replacement cognitions listed. We repeat the same scenario, but this time the child verbalizes one of the thoughts from his new hat, something like, "I can do this!" I ask the child how this statement makes him feel and what his resulting action might be. The child's answer is usually that he will start his work quickly and finish it faster than if he were thinking discouraging thoughts (Figure 11.3).

A modification of this activity makes it accessible to preschoolers. Preschool-age children are fascinated by puppets and storytelling. This population can gain a first exposure to how thoughts influence actions by watching a puppet wear the different hats and make different behavioral choices depending on which

Figure 11.3 *Old Thoughts/New Thoughts* hats

hat the puppet is wearing. As the child watches a puppet behave one way in response to one set of thoughts and another way in response to another set of thoughts, he can begin to make a connection between thoughts and actions. The child gets to change the puppet's hat and then watches as the puppet reacts differently to the same scenarios because he is wearing the hat with the helpful thoughts. The child can then wear the hats and practice saying some of the positive replacement statements out loud.

Punching Holes in that Theory

Another intervention that allows child clients to manipulate a troublesome thought through the manipulation of a prop is called "punching holes in that theory" (Goodyear-Brown, 2005). This intervention was created to combat both irrational thoughts and the lies that children have been told by their perpetrators. A child survivor, even one who is now physically safe, can still feel controlled and manipulated by the lying voice of the perpetrator. The tapes that play in the minds of traumatized children can be hard to stop. An insidious process occurs when a grownup makes a negative comment about a child to the child. The grownup says, "You're stupid." The child who hears this several times will internalize the meaning and morph the language into the phrase, "I'm stupid." There is now internal ownership and the negative self-talk has become a new truth that will inform that child's future approach to the world. The first step in confronting the new truths as owned lies is often psychoeducation around the dynamics of trauma and abuse. From this education, a set of countering cognitions can be generated.

To begin the activity, a salient lie that the perpetrator told the child is defined and written on a piece of paper (Figure 11.4). The therapist introduces a hole-punching set with cutters of many different shapes. The child systematically punches holes in the written words of the negative thought while verbalizing a counterthought or restructured cognition. The child gets the verbal practice while having the kinesthetic experience of destroying the irrational thought.

Figure 11.4 shows the lie that an 8-year-old girl was told by a teenage boy. Interestingly, the perpetrator did not further explain what would happen to her once he told, but the threat of "I'll tell" from an older boy was enough to cow this child. The threat coerced her into participating in uncomfortable touching games. In session the little girl repeated the words that the perpetrator said to her as I wrote the words on a large piece of paper. I offered her my set of holepunches, which she eagerly explored.

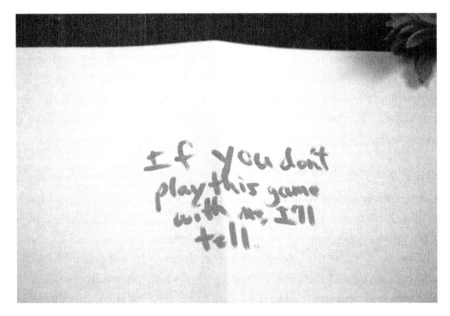

Figure 11.4   The Perpetrator's Lie in Writing

She spent a great deal of time punching holes the lie while she spoke the truths that countered this lie. She also enjoyed talking back to her abuser while she punched the holes. She used all the words that she had fantasized about saying to him during the molestation. In addition to the power of her words, she had the visual satisfaction of watching the lie disappear little by little as she punched holes in it. By the end of the activity, all traces of the lie were gone and in their place was an interesting new pattern that the child had crafted (Figure 11.5).

Extinguish the Flame

Another full-body engagement activity that helps clients confront and counter negative thoughts is called "extinguish the flame" (Goodyear-Brown, 2005). I pull out a toy fire extinguisher and fireman dress-up clothes and offer them to the child. Some clients prefer the small, handheld play fire extinguisher and others prefer the backpack fire extinguisher that comes with a hose. The backpack model squirts a significant amount of water with each pump, so it is not for the faint of heart. The child gets to squirt water onto the white board while I talk about how certain thoughts can make us feel bad. I wonder out loud what it would feel like to be able to get rid of

Figure 11.5 The Lie All Gone

a thought that is perpetually bothersome. In the same way that firefighters can put out a fire before it destroys everything, we can learn to snuff out our negative thoughts before they can make us feel miserable.

I then help the child to identify one negative thought that has been bothering him recently. If this activity is one in a series of activities aimed at helping the child feel a sense of mastery over these negative thoughts while practicing thought replacement, I may refer back to a list of negative cognitions that was generated earlier. I write the identified thought down on the white board and draw flames around it. With younger children it may be more effective to draw a picture that represents the thought than to write the thought itself. Next, we talk about some of the feelings and actions that are the outgrowths of this thought. The child is invited to extinguish the negative thought by spraying it with water as he counters it verbally with a replacement statement. By degrees the writing fades from the board and the child feels a sense of empowerment.

Augmenting Positive Self-Talk

When a traumatized child has played the tapes of negative self-talk over and over again, the child's developing self-esteem is damaged. The therapeutic change process is the same with this form of negative self-talk as with others. First the child must identify the negative self-talk statements, generate meaningful, self-affirming counterstatements, and then practice halting the negative self-talk and replacing it with the positive self-talk. The right props can be the means to helping children achieve these therapeutic ends.

Repairing Self-Esteem

The intervention "repairing self-esteem" (Goodyear-Brown, 2002) uses simple materials and is easily implemented. The child is given a paper cutout of a gingerbread person. The therapist helps the child articulate his negative self-talk statements. Each statement is written down on one of the body parts of the cutout. One negative statement can be written on each arm, each leg, and so on. Once this record of the negative self-talk has been recorded on the gingerbread cutout, the child is given the figure and invited to rip the cutout into pieces as he says each of the negative self-talk statements out loud. The therapist then talks about how the repetitions of hurtful self-talk can literally tear us down (Figure 11.6).

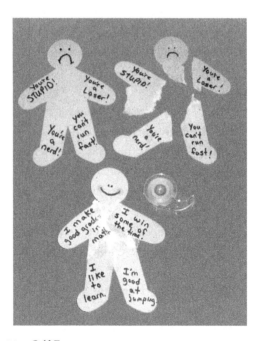

Figure 11.6 Repairing Self-Esteem

Once the cutout is in pieces, the pieces are turned over. For each negative self-talk statement, a positive one is generated and written on the back of the body part that carries the first unhelpful statement. Once all the positive self-talk statements have been written down, the child is encouraged to try saying each one out loud as they tape the person back together. The therapist highlights that repeating the helpful self-talk can build the client up again.

The "Good-At" Game

The "good-at game" is a prop-based intervention that provides another way for children to rehearse their positive self-talk in session. I begin by inviting the child to choose a tub of Play-Doh and I choose one as well. I fashion my Play-Doh into a container with a top and encourage the child to fashion something similar. Then I take a handful of gems, coins, and other pretty baubles from the treasure chest and fill the Play-Doh container with them. The child follows suit with his own container. The lid is placed on the container and I draw a face on it. I ask the child if she can tell what is inside the Play-Doh just by looking at the outside. Because this is impossible, most children say no.

I explain, "Let's pretend that this is a person filled with beautiful things, but no one can see them unless he opens himself up and shows them. I'm going to pretend this is me." I take the top off the container. "I'm going to tell you one thing that I'm good at for each of the jewels inside my container." I then proceed to make a list of the things I am good at, starting each sentence with, "I am good at . . . " as I move each of the jewels. I am careful to model some statements that the child can also make, like "I am a good friend" or "I am good at listening." Once I have modeled the activity, the child gets an opportunity to share her inner jewels. Children sometimes need prompting to start each sentence with, "I am good at . . . ", but this articulation turns every statement into positive self-talk. Children remain engaged in the activity because the manipulation of the jewels grounds them in the work. Even clients who have serious attentional issues will stick with this play-based intervention because of the draw of the materials, generating lists of 10 to 20 things they are good at. I write their list down while they are reciting them, and they can take it home as a visual reminder of all the areas in which they excel.

Enforcing a Child's Sense of Competency

Another part of treatment must include helping the child to reestablish a sense of competency and self-worth. Activities that highlight a child's strengths can aid in this endeavor. A child who has a natural talent for art will experience a sense of competence as this medium is used in therapy. A child who is good at building towers will experience a sense of competence as he builds in the playroom. The very use of play materials to which the child is naturally drawn helps to build a child's self-confidence. If we revisit the idea that trauma includes a stripping away of power and control, one can easily understand how a traumatized child might question her own competency to meet the challenges of her posttrauma world. Interventions that activate new competencies as well as interventions that help a child rehearse her pretrauma competencies can reinforce a client's sense of self-efficacy.

The "I Can Mobile"

One activity that helps the client to rehearse her pretrauma competencies is the "I can mobile" (Goodyear-Brown, 2002). To begin the activity, the child is given an assortment of empty, clean soda cans, string, and a clothes hanger. The child is encouraged to tie strings of various lengths through the pop-tops of the soda cans and then attach these to the clothes hanger. The end result is a mobile of cans. The child then draws pictures that represent various pretrauma competencies that the child still performs with proficiency. Some examples include riding a bike, drawing animals, shooting a basketball, and giving hugs. These pictures are cut out and wrapped around the individual cans that constitute the bulk of the mobile. Whenever possible, caregivers should be included in the building of the mobile, as they may be able to pinpoint competencies that the child may not think of on her own. Once the mobile is complete, it is sent home and hung above the child's bed. The mobile provides daily visual reminders of the child's proficiency in various areas (Figure 11.7).

Children do sometimes lose, for a time, a competency they had developed before a trauma. An ability to hold one's urine and feces until they can be relieved in a proper place is one example. A subset of traumatized children experience regression in this area. Children who had good sleep hygiene habits and went to sleep quickly in their own beds may revert, for a time, to sleeping with their parents again. Particularly for these children,

Figure 11.7   The *I Can* Mobile

the rehearsal of their continued competency in other areas of development is reassuring. The future return of any competencies lost through regression can be foreshadowed as this intervention is completed. The therapist and child can choose two or three additional cans and wrap blank paper around each can. These can be left at the therapist's office or taken home. As new competencies emerge, the remaining cans can be decorated and added to the mobile in celebration of the child's emerging competencies.

Another way to promote a child's sense of competence is to put him in the role of "expert." This goal can be accomplished in a variety of ways. In my office, we often switch roles and the child gets to be the therapist. In preparation for this activity, the child is given a play phone and the therapist has another play phone. The therapist calls in pretending to be various people. The use of silly voices can make the whole intervention more playful. Children seem to respond best when the pretend caller is younger than himself or herself. The therapist might ask questions related to a skill that the child has mastered. The therapist could call in to ask for specifics on skateboarding, building Bionicles, or the storyline of the child's favorite book. Later in therapy, after the child has worked on his cognitive distortions, has learned how to engage in thought stopping and thought replacement, and has received psychoeducation that normalizes his responses to the specific trauma that he has survived, the pretend callers can ask questions that allow the child to share his expert knowledge related to these areas.

Randy Wrestles with a Core Belief

Sometimes older children and adolescents are able to pinpoint the cognitive distortion, but it is wrapped in so much shame that they have difficulty saying it out loud or writing it down. The client may believe that giving verbal or written weight to the false belief will give it more power. Randy, a 10-year-old boy referred for depression, is a powerful example of this. Randy's grandmother accompanied him to the first visit. She explained that Randy was sent to live with his grandparents because his mother "couldn't control him." Randy's two younger siblings continue to reside with their mother. During the initial phase of treatment, Randy refused to talk about his mother and refused to talk about any of the thoughts that were bothering him. He would sit slumped in a chair in my office with his eyes downcast. Randy's grandmother had a rather severe demeanor, believed strongly that Randy needed more discipline, and made no spontaneously affectionate or positive statements about Randy.

One afternoon grandmother asked if she could speak with me before I met with Randy. She was very angry over a particular misbehavior from the prior week. After validating her frustration over his behavior, I asked if he had displayed any positive behavior over the course of the week. The grandmother said, "Absolutely not. The boy is a little hellion!" I was thrown by grandmother's complete inability to see anything positive in her grandson. Once she had left the office and Randy had sat down, I asked, "Is she always like that?" Perhaps this was not the most professional opening to the session, but Randy grinned and seemed to appreciate my authentic bewilderment at grandmother's attitude toward him. He rolled his eyes and said, "Yeah!" I asked, "What do you hear when she goes on and on like that? I mean, bottom line, what do you hear?" Randy did not hesitate. He said, "That I'm a mistake." He allowed me to hear his core belief articulated. We talked about the things that mom and dad used to say to him. We talked about the statements that his teachers make to him. All these communications reinforced the belief that he was a mistake and that the world would be better off if he had never been born.

Now that he had verbalized this core negative belief we could begin to fight it. I asked him if he could try out the statement, "I am not a mistake." He nodded. However, he proceeded to come up with multiple excuses for why he couldn't say it out loud. I decided to change tactics. I wondered if getting his body moving, getting him kinesthetically involved in play behavior, would loosen his tongue and decrease his inhibitions. He put on the black Zorro-type mask that he always wore when we began to play and dressed himself with a sword and a play gun. Randy chose a sword for me and we began a mighty battle. Interestingly, Randy needed no prompting to conscientiously keep the swordplay at a speed and distance that kept us both safe. I never needed to set a limit with him. After a couple of minutes of Randy showing me his fancy ninja moves, I gave this prompt:

Paris: Tell me "I'm not a mistake."

Randy (quickly while smiling): I'm not a missnake.

Paris: Tell me loud.

Randy: I'm not a missnake.

Paris: Mistake.

Randy (laughing loudly): I'm not a missnake.

Paris (laughing also): You're not a missnake? No, you're not a missnake either, but you are also not a mistake.

At this point I recognize the defense mechanism that Randy is using as he transforms the cognitive counterstatement into an assertion that he is not a snake. I wonder if I can gain some ground if we focus the counterstatement on the people who helped to engender his false belief.

Paris: Pretend like I'm all those people who have ever said you were a mistake—

Randy (interrupting quickly): Then I'd end up hitting you instead of the sword.

It is telling that this boy who is painted by his grandmother as purposely destructive is working hard to make sure that he does not take any anger out inappropriately on the therapist. He is warning me about how much rage is associated with this core belief that he is a mistake. It would be harmful to the therapeutic relationship if I allow him to become aggressive toward me, so I take his warning seriously and find another option for him. I pull out a giant stuffed dog from under the table.

Paris: Well, let's pretend that this dog is all those people.

Randy: I'm not gonna say it out loud but once.

He is still bargaining. The potency of saying the potential new truth "I am not a mistake" out loud is scary for him. Even though his current core belief is troublesome and negatively informs his behavioral choices and his general approach to the world, there is risk involved in verbally trying out a truth that would contradict it.

Paris: Okay.

Randy: I've already said it out loud once.

Paris: Say it out loud once while you hit it.

Randy (while hitting the stuffed animal): I'm not a missnake.

I do not comment on his repetition of the misstatement, but Randy makes a frustrated growling sound low in his throat.

Paris: Can I help you?

Randy: It would be better if he was standing up. In a chair.

Paris: Sure. We can stand it up in a chair. Do you want to do it by yourself or do you want me to help?

Randy: It's okay.

Randy sets the dog up in the chair by himself, beginning to take ownership for what is to come.

Paris: Okay. Talk to it.

Randy (while hitting the dog with the sword): I'm not a missnake.

Paris (deciding to confront the misstatement more directly this time): Whoa. *Missnake* is not the word. *Mistake.*

Randy: I can't say it right. I keep saying *missnake.*

Paris: Maybe it's because part of you still thinks you are a mistake. So I want you to say "I am not a—"

Randy (interrupting the therapist in a loud voice): I am not a mistake!

As he says the words, they seem to loosen something in him. He begins to beat up the dog with his sword. Randy throws the dog across the room. It lands on top of a flexible play tent and caves in the top of it.

Paris: Whew. You threw it all the way across the room.

Randy: Sorry.

Paris: There it went. That's okay.

Randy tries to pick up the dog and fix the tent.

Paris: It's all right. You can leave it if you need to.

Randy seems adrift here. He moves without focus away from the toys and toward my desk. He pulls his mask away from his face and lets it slap back into place. He delivers the next words while carefully avoiding eye contact with the therapist.

Randy: Told ya I'd end up hitting you.

Randy seems embarrassed by his actions. Showing me the intensity of anger that is associated with his core belief has left him feeling vulnerable. His perception may be so colored by his own anger that he believes he has hurt me, but it is more likely that he fears he has overwhelmed me or scared me with the intensity of his emotion. In a way, he has shown me what he considers to be one of the worst dimensions of himself. Either way, I choose to correct his distorted view of what happened.

Paris: You didn't end up hitting me. I'm not hurt. Nothing in the room is hurt.

Randy: Well, if I—well, if it was you I would have ended up hitting you.

Paris: I'm glad you decided to use something else.

Randy: I warned you and you took the warning.

Randy moves over to the sand tray and begins to run his hands through the sand. This is a strategy that children often use to calm themselves after their play behavior has resulted in an internal escalation. Randy begins to put cars in the sand tray and covers them with sand. I quickly switch gears, joining him by the sand tray and reflecting this new play behavior.

Randy: Okay everybody. Identity time.

He takes off the black ninja mask he has worn throughout session and looks straight into camera. There is an incredible power in his unmasking. It is the first time he has allowed the camera to see his bare face in the course of treatment.

Randy: Now you can see my real face.

Paris: Now we get to see your real face. We get to really know that you are not a mistake.

One important detail in this case is that Randy has chosen to put on a black mask every time he has come to the playroom and worn it for the entirety of the session on each occasion. He has also asked that swordfights and other play vignettes be videotaped along the way, but he always kept the mask on for these tapings. After throwing the stuffed dog across the room, he freezes, momentarily paralyzed by the fear that he has overwhelmed the therapist. He tells the therapist, "I told you I'd hurt you" when in actuality no one was hurt and no property was damaged. He turns away from the therapist, pulls the mask away from his face quickly, and lets go of it, so that it stings his face with a small slap. He appears to be punishing himself for showing his anger to the therapist. I reassure him that I am unscathed. I give clear messages that I have not been overwhelmed by his anger and that our relationship is intact.

He moves directly to the sand tray and begins to soothe himself by running his fingers through the sand. As understanding dawns that he has been able to show a new piece of himself to the therapist and not damage the relationship, he decides to lift his mask and let the camera see his real face. His words, "identity time," spoken as he lifted his mask, were telling and powerful. Randy showed the intensity of his anger and his worst self-talk and was still accepted by the therapist. He was able to give up a layer of protection and show an uncovered dimension of the self in the playroom. As he shares this more vulnerable part of himself with the therapist, he begins to accept it within himself.

The restructured cognition "I am not a mistake" paired with his physicality actively challenges the existing core of his identity and opens up room to believe that he is not a mistake. In Randy's case, he approached his negative core belief most easily through physical engagement. Randy never put the mask back on after this session.

Conclusion

Children who have been traumatized often experience negative fallout in the cognitive arena. Children can create false attributions in an attempt to explain why the bad thing happened to them. Children can engage in negative self-talk that may lead, if unchecked, to self-blame, negative self-esteem, and maladaptive coping strategies, such as self-injurious behavior, aggression toward peers or parents, and withdrawal from others.

Children can be taught how cognitions, emotions, and behaviors influence each other. Moreover, children can be given skills that help them identify maladaptive thoughts, stop those thoughts, and replace them with restructured cognitions. Whereas adults can manipulate their thoughts internally, children benefit greatly from the use of play-based methods to delineate the thoughts that are problematic and to externalize them. Once the thoughts have been externalized, the child can playfully manipulate them. This playful manipulation brings with it a sense of mastery that aids the child's recovery even as the child is practicing thought stopping and thought replacement strategies. The practice of positive self-talk and the rehearsal of competencies are both augmented through play-based interventions such as the ones mentioned in this chapter. It is my hope that the case examples and interventions articulated here will provide practical techniques for helping children grapple effectively with posttraumatic cognitive distortions.

12

Making Positive Meaning of the Post-Trauma Self

"And I, I took the road less traveled by, and that has made all the difference."

—*Robert Frost*

The Wise Old Soul

There is a brand of wisdom that is only won through painful experiences. Children who have had intensely painful or terrifying experiences may manifest developmental delays in some areas while showing an astonishing depth of insight in others. Child survivors of neglect and chronic maltreatment may face structural changes in their neurophysiology that set them apart from typically developing peers. These changes can impact learning, memory, affect regulation, and a host of other developmental arenas. These young people may have a harder time learning to read, accurately interpreting the nonverbal language of others, keeping a lid on their tempers, and building a coherent narrative. In these ways their development has been compromised by their traumatic experiences.

However, there is another dimension of the self of a traumatized child that we may be fortunate enough to encounter in the playroom. I have taken to calling this part of the hurt child the Wise Old Soul. Wisdom beyond a child's years, including surprising verbal eloquence or depth of insight, are occasionally glimpsed in the playroom. This phenomenon is unique to the traumatized children with whom I work. The relationship among the play therapist, the client, and the play materials affords an exceptional milieu for the wizened aspects of the child to come forth. The use of metaphor that is inherent in the play therapy process and the metareflective language that the therapist uses is picked up and amplified by the most intuitive parts of the traumatized child. A child may be physically engaged in zooming a car through the sand while a very sophisticated understanding of his trauma experience is being verbalized. At times it seems that the medium of play engages the childlike parts of the self in a developmentally appropriate way and leaves the Wise Old Soul dimension of the child free to communicate.

In Chapter 9, Experiential Mastery Play, I described 9-year-old Michael staging a war between a symbol that represents the mom who hurt him and his new adoptive mother. His child self is caught up in the manipulation of the symbols and the preoccupation with war and battle. I comment on how the Bride of Frankenstein (his symbol for his biological mom) keeps popping back up when it seems that she has been defeated. While his child self is occupied with the play, his Wise Old Soul hears the metacommunication and responds, saying, "It's like she controls my todays even though she is my yesterday." I sat in awe of his ability to articulate the core dilemma of his life, with a sophistication that is often lacking in some of our adult clients. From there we were able to talk very briefly about how his early experiences still colored his approach to the daily stresses of life.

He returned, after this discussion, to telling gross jokes involving burping and farting and the Wise Old Soul was put away again. These nuggets of wisdom cannot be demanded; they can only be treasured as they are given. Nor can they be produced by the child on cue. Instead, it is through the ongoing metaphoric communication that the child's inner poetic wisdom is most effectively tapped. Part of the play therapist's role throughout the course of treatment is to recognize these gems of understanding when they surface, validate and reflect this dimension of the child, and accurately record the voice of the Wise Old Soul when it is accessed. These communications can be revisited and reflected upon further during the termination phase of treatment.

Determining When the Child is Ready for Graduation

One of the most important aspects of a therapist's job is structuring a meaningful goodbye at the end of treatment. Many people talk about the goodbye process as a termination. Although I use this word with the parents, I almost always present the goodbye process to the child as one of graduation.

This phrasing encourages a sense of accomplishment in the child and mitigates the feelings of loss that must still be intentionally addressed but that might otherwise become pervasive. One of the most common questions I am asked during training is how to know when a child or family is ready to graduate from treatment. There is no one definitive answer to this question.

A host of variables must be factored into this decision, and ultimately clinical judgment must be relied upon. The goal of trauma treatment is never to help the child forget the traumatic events through which he has lived. Although most of us at some point harbor a secret desire to somehow forget the painful experiences through which we have lived, we cannot escape the truth that we would no longer be ourselves if they were erased. Forgetting is certainly not the goal. However, less painful remembering would be one way to conceptualize a positive treatment outcome. Put another way, by the end of treatment, the client can tolerate the trauma content without it being overwhelming. The emotional toxicity of the trauma has been siphoned off, leaving the child with a history that can be folded into a positive sense of self and future. A more complete checklist to use in determining if a child is ready for termination includes a review of the treatment goals and to what extent the goals have been successfully accomplished. The positive outcomes one hopes to see are as follows:

1. An increase in emotional literacy
2. A decrease in physiological reactivity
3. A coherent narrative of the trauma
4. An effective restructuring of distorted cognitions
5. An increase in the client's ability to access and be soothed by social supports, primarily caregivers
6. An increase in utilization of healthy coping skills
7. Most importantly, a restored sense of safety, at least in relationship to certain people and places

In addition to these dimensions, successful resolution of posttraumatic play can also be an indicator of a child's readiness to graduate. When children first come to treatment, after safety has been established, they are often intensely focused on reenacting their trauma experiences, working them out through the processes described in this book. At some point in the treatment continuum, a child's play becomes less activated, less focused on resolution of trauma issues, and more developmentally typical. The child who has been eagerly containing and manipulating a perpetrator symbol slowly shifts his interest toward more developmentally typical play. As a child moves toward healing, his play looks more age appropriate. The child engages in play for the pleasure it brings and loses the emotional intensity that was present earlier in treatment.

Sometimes the child, who originally did not wish to leave the playroom, will begin to ask how much longer he has to keep coming. He may express interest in joining a soccer team or taking an art class. He may simply want more time to play outside after school. I usually see this as a positive sign, one that indicates that the child's developmental energy, once preoccupied by his trauma reactions, is being channeled back into the normal tasks of childhood.

When Treatment Is Not Progressing

However, a treatment plan can be followed to the letter without any true heart change occurring, without any moments of epiphany or insight for the child. Sometimes this happens because the child is not yet safe in his home environment. A child who is still using the bulk of his developmental energy to keep a secret or to survive ongoing but undisclosed maltreatment will not progress in a meaningful way through the steps of treatment. When there seems to be a sense of superficiality to the work, the possibility must be entertained that the child's maltreatment is ongoing. It is possible that the child is being forced to keep an unhealthy secret. The focus of treatment often shifts at this point to building a sense of safety and security in the playroom in order to provide an environment in which a child feels free to tell the secret. The therapist can make open-ended invitations to disclosure through the play materials. Psychoeducation around when it is appropriate to keep a secret and when it is appropriate to tell a secret can also be undertaken.

At other times, progress may have stalled because the treatment is not being delivered in a developmentally sensitive manner. Six-year-olds do not respond as well to pen and paper activities as to concepts wrapped in a kinesthetic package. An 8-year-old may have a large vocabulary but be unable to follow the abstract language being used by a therapist. When treatment feels mired, it is useful to take a fresh look at the child's developmental level and preferred activities and recalibrate interventions to be easily ingested by the child.

When treatment feels stuck, another hypothesis is that the child needs more time and attention paid to a treatment goal that falls earlier in the continuum of treatment. For example, a child may have developed an initial sense of safety and security in the playroom and increased his emotional literacy skills but seems stuck in a trauma narrative process. It may be that the child needs the therapist to spend more time equipping the child with individual and dyadic strategies to manage the child's physiological anxiety, which may be overwhelming the child as he approaches the content of the traumatic incident. The FSPT model allows the flexibility for children to skip goals they have already mastered, to spend longer in pursuit of a certain objective, and to revisit any goal that needs augmentation during the treatment process.

Goals of Termination

Once a child has accomplished the treatment goals listed earlier and both the child and her caregivers are reporting a reduction in troublesome symptoms, it is time to begin the termination process. The goal of termination is twofold. The first goal is to help the child take a step back from all the psychoeducational activities, goal-directed play-based intervention, and metaphorical play content to cull out the most meaningful moments and integrate this new knowledge into a positive sense of self. I have heard people describe traumatized children as "damaged goods" or "broken." It may be true that particular beliefs or coping patterns resulting from traumagenic experiences may be dysfunctional and that certain relationships or aspects of the self need mending. Indeed, these are the reasons that therapy is often sought. However, once these coping strategies, faulty beliefs, and relationships have been positively impacted, therapy should end with a celebration of the child and the making of a meaningful goodbye.

Celebrating the Child

I have watched children work hard in treatment and heal. A miraculous, if clichéd, thing happens. In the same way that a broken bone, once healed, is stronger at the point of the break than it was before the break occurred, many of these children leave treatment stronger than they were before the trauma happened. By stronger, I mean wiser, more relationally savvy, and if not wholly restored to neurophysiological balance, at least more aware of how to soothe themselves and receive soothing from others than they were before. The child has often engaged in hard, even grueling work to resolve their trauma reactions. The hard work should be celebrated and the child's gains in treatment should be concretized.

Making a Meaningful Goodbye

The second goal is to make a meaningful goodbye with the therapist. I use the word *make* because it is a more active verb than *have* and better expresses the creative intentionality that is needed to help a child and therapist to take their leave of one another in a way that will have lasting positive implications. Many clinicians face their strongest counter-transference reactions during the termination phase of treatment. If a relationship has been meaningful, it is often painful to say goodbye. Our natural inclination as a species is to avoid pain. Therefore, most of us avoid saying goodbye in a definitive way, a way that acknowledges the finality of that particular season of relationship. We say, "See you soon" when we leave people who we may not see again. Child clinicians are human and therefore as susceptible as others to the desire to avoid the painful goodbye with clients who have become important to us.

Early in my professional life I began providing clinical consultation for the teachers in a therapeutic preschool program. When we found a teacher who was bright, compassionate with the children, and full of therapeutic promise, the likelihood was high that she would stay with the program for a year or two and then return to school to pursue further training. Part of my job was to help these teachers say goodbye to the children in their care (usually classrooms of 10–12 children) in a way that was meaningful. The teacher and I would meet and go over a variety of interventions to use throughout the month before the teacher's departure to set up a meaningful goodbye. Time and time again, the interventions were not used. Teachers would say that the activities were forgotten or crowded out by other events in the school day. Without continued encouragement, teachers would wait until the week of their departure to tell the children that they were leaving. A party, complete with cupcakes, would be held on the teacher's last day, and this was often the extent of the leave-taking process.

As I pondered this pattern, it occurred to me that the teachers might be avoiding the meaningful goodbye because, simply put, it felt bad. I tested this hypothesis in individual supervision. When confronted with a tendency to avoid termination rituals, several of the teachers volunteered that they felt guilty, as if they were abandoning the children who needed them. Children are vulnerable creatures. They look to the adults around them to guide and take care of them. A compassionate teacher, realizing the need to move on for professional reasons, might feel a sense of guilt that she is leaving the children with whom she has forged bonds. During this transition time, supervision around termination procedures dealt with the removal of any false responsibility the teachers might be carrying in relation to the children while shifting their conceptualization of "the goodbye" from an abandonment of the children to a potential gift that they could give them.

The majority of chronically traumatized children have experienced multiple caregiver disruptions with no narrative woven around the goodbye, no meaning made of the partings. In some cases, a mother goes to drug rehab and the child is told "she's gone for a while." Later she shows back up and life resumes without any processing of her absence. A father is incarcerated. Mom does not mention him while he is gone. One day he returns, his reinsertion as abrupt as his departure, and life picks up where it left off. Children who have experienced multiple disjointed goodbyes have great difficulty developing a coherent life narrative. They begin to expect that people will come and go at random. They may anticipate a caregiver's possible removal at the beginning of a new relationship and protect themselves from forming any depth of attachment. This confluence of events in a child's life can lead to an indiscriminant attachment pattern and lifelong difficulties with interpersonal relationships.

A preadoptive mother was very disturbed during a recent visit to my office. She described a moment from earlier in the week. She and her 4-year-old preadoptive son, who had been in her care for almost a year, were playing in the front yard. While they were playing, the lawnmower repairman pulled up to the curb. The child played nearby as the mother explained to the man what needed fixing on their lawnmower. After a few minutes the 4-year-old tugged on the repairman's sleeve and said, "Are you here to take me away?" Mom was rocked to the core to see how, even after a year in her care, he still harbored the expectation that he would be moved again without warning.

Goodbyes can be painful. In most cases, the more important the relationship, the more painful the final goodbye will be. As clinicians, we can hope that a goodbye will involve a bit of sadness, as this reflects the importance of the relationship built and the work accomplished in treatment. It is OK for the clinician to feel sad while simultaneously celebrating the client's growing independence. It's permissible for the client to miss the therapist at the same time that he is eager to graduate from treatment. When saying goodbye to a client, I am intentional in my attempt to give the child an internal representation of myself that he can access when he needs to call up a picture of me. To this end, the child and I take turns closing our eyes and describing each other. I close my eyes and playfully describe the child's hair color, eye color, smile, and so on. Then I invite the client to close his eyes and describe me. Sometimes the child has to open his eyes to check what color my eyes are.

The child often draws a picture of us together. The parent may take a digital picture of the child and I for the child to keep. Once the child has an internal representation of how I look, I invite the child to remember particular words, phrases, or other interactions that are unique to this relationship. For example, a mantra that the child and I practiced together might become an important part of our relational narrative. Perhaps the child and I engaged in a routine of checking for boo-boos at the beginning of each session. This routine might become part of our remembered history. Words such as "You're a survivor" or "You are stronger than your fear" might be words that the child associates with the treatment process and the person of the therapist.

How Long Should a Termination Process Be?

Another question that clinicians often ask relates to the proper length of time to allot for a termination process. If the therapy has been short term and related to one specific traumatic event, termination may have been talked about since the first session. For more complex cases, where it is difficult to project the exact length of time that treatment might take, I suggest allowing four sessions from the time when the clinician lets the child know that they are moving toward graduation to the time at which the child actually graduates. However, many situations arise that make it difficult for this to occur.

Some clinicians find themselves in the position of having to terminate abruptly. Therapist factors for abrupt termination may include the sudden loss of a job, an unexpected shift in job duties or job sites, and emergent health issues. Client factors influencing abrupt termination may include a felt lack of attunement with the therapist, a sudden family move due to a job shift or divorce, the sudden move of a child from one foster home to another, financial strain that causes a client to withdraw, problems with transportation, lack of a perceived need for continued services, or other life stressors. One of the most challenging situations arises when a child has achieved symptom reduction and the parent is unconvinced of the benefits of termination. It is then incumbent upon the therapist to give the parent a thorough rationale for the need for at least one or two termination sessions in order to concretize the gains made in treatment.

Tools for Remembering

Remembering tools such as memory books and memory boxes are excellent aids in helping a child structure a narrative of her treatment process while she is preparing to say goodbye. I keep a variety of colored card stock, patterned papers, and gift boxes in my office for just this purpose. Children who are preparing for graduation choose one of these. If the child chooses to make a book, she can choose the color of paper for front and back. She can choose the hole-punch shapes to form the holes. She can choose the ribbon or brads to bind the book. If the termination activities have begun 4 weeks before the final session, the time spent on the book can be spread out over the remaining time, with one or two pages completed on each remaining visit. The therapist can prompt the child to draw a picture of her first day in the playroom and any feelings she had or experiences that she remembers from that day. In subsequent sessions, the child may be prompted to draw pictures for any of the following: the child's favorite activity, the activity that was most difficult emotionally, a funny moment from treatment, his favorite toy, or something important that he learned.

The memory box can function in the same way. For her final creation, Carrie, a 9-year-old girl who was completing a course of treatment for sexual abuse, chose a plain white box with a see-through window in the top. I invited her to draw pictures on the outside of the box that represented soothing, safe images from treatment. Inside the box she placed props and drawings that would help her remember the parts of treatment that were most important to her.

Inside the box she placed one miniature maraca. This reminded her of the lessons she had learned about the warning signals that her own body gives her when she is uncomfortable or feeling unsafe. It also reminded her to pay attention to the warning signals when they come. She took a piece of

Figure 12.1   Carrie's Memory Box

pipe cleaner and shaped it into a circle and used it to represent her personal space. This helped her remember the hula-hoop metaphor we had used when working on boundaries and personal space issues. She drew a picture of a big muscle and said, "This shows how strong I've gotten." She drew the statement, "I don't always have to be nice." Initially Carrie had thought that the "nice" thing to do was to allow the perpetrator, an older boy, to please himself, even at her expense. During her graduation session, she said adamantly, "I won't make that mistake again!" She also included a little ball in her box. This helped her remember the diaphragmatic breathing exercises that we did as part of relaxation training before constructing her trauma narrative. We would each place a ball on our bellies and watch it rise and fall as we took deep breaths. Carrie particularly enjoyed this activity and thought it would be a simple one to keep using at home after treatment ended. During her graduation session, Carrie showed her memory box and its contents to her parents and explained each item's significance. The box became a final transitional object from the playroom to Carrie's home environment and a marker of all the work that had been done in treatment.

In addition to the remembering tools and the internalization of the therapist and the therapist's affirming words, each child gets to choose a stone from the treasure chest as a keepsake to help him remember his time in the playroom. Revisiting the idea that children are tactile creatures, the stone becomes an anchor to help ground the child's memories of the playroom while also serving as a final transitional object from the child's safe place in the playroom to his other life arenas.

The Child's Goodbye

I have described some of the intentional steps that clinicians can take to make a goodbye meaningful. In addition, once children understand that graduation is imminent, children will engage in spontaneous play sequences as part of saying goodbye. In some cases, a child may engage in a previously unseen behavior during the termination phase of treatment. For example, a 4-year-old named Mary acted out some of her disappointment at having to say goodbye in the following play sequence.

Mary came in for her second to last session. I reminded her that we had today to play and one more visit after today and then we would say goodbye. She immediately walked over to the play phones. She kept one and gave one to the therapist. She instructed the therapist to wait by the phone for her call. Mary dialed numbers and made a *brrrring, brrrring* noise to represent the telephone ringing. When I picked up the telephone and said hello, she banged hers down and said angrily, "It's broken." This play pattern was repeated several times in this session. I was able to reflect and validate her anger at not having the continued open line of communication with the therapist. Mary processed her anger at the severing of the therapeutic relationship through the play sequence. Throughout treatment the therapist had used the tools of witnessing, validating, containing, and reflecting to create an environment in which the child's trauma history could be resolved. In this same way, the therapist must witness, validate, contain, and reflect the child's reactions regarding termination in order for the child to push through to acceptance of the impending separation. Mary came in for her final session with a sense of acceptance and did not replay the broken phone sequence in our final session together.

Jillian, a 5-year-old girl referred for sexual abuse treatment, engaged in a new behavior in her final session. As she entered the playroom, I reminded her that this was the last session we would have together. She paused and then moved purposefully toward a toy watering can, a toy that she had never used before, and asked to go fill it up. When we returned from the water fountain, she carefully poured the water into the one plant that I kept in the office. As I reflected on this parting gesture, I realized that she wanted to give me a gift. She wanted to do something that took care of the playroom. Perhaps she also wanted to contribute to the health of something that would continue to grow in the playroom after she left it. Either way, she felt the need to make, in the course of her play, a parting gesture that she had not made over the course of treatment.

One final example involves a 7-year-old girl named Keisha, who during her final session also chose a toy she had never touched before. Keisha chose a pretend camera and spent the bulk of the session directing me into various poses. She took pictures of me Playing in the sand, reading a bibliotherapy book out loud, and taking care of a baby doll. Then she gave me the camera; she recreated a couple of her favorite moments from treatment and had me take pretend pictures of her. The camera seemed to be an aid that helped her focus on and remember with deeper clarity moments within the playroom that she wanted to be able to call up later.

Directive Interventions

I use a series of interventions with children to help them integrate the trauma content into a positive sense of self. As the final step in completing a trauma narrative, I invite the child to participate in an intervention that I call "before, during, and after." This activity can be done using sand trays, art products, puppets, collage, or independent miniatures. The following examples show the children's use of several of these mediums.

Betsy, a 10-year-old girl who was sexually molested by an uncle for a year, created a set of sand trays depicted in Figures 12.2 to 12.6. First I invited her to create a sand tray that portrayed her or her life before her uncle started hurting her (Figure 12.2).

The blond-haired, blue-eyed girl in the back center of the sand tray is Betsy's self-object. She is surrounded by friends, family, and pets. Her description of her life before her abuse included an extended social network and a chaotic but happy home. Once we had processed this tray, I asked her to create a second tray that showed me how her life was different during the abuse (Figure 12.3).

At the far end of the tray is a two-headed monster blocking her mother and father from being able to get to her. Her mother is at the far right end

Figure 12.2 Betsy's *Before the Trauma* Tray

Figure 12.3 Betsy's *During the Trauma* Tray

Figure 12.4   Betsy's Sense of Imprisonment During the Abuse

of the tray and is staring at the jail in which her daughter is trapped. Betsy stated about the mother, "She didn't really see what was going on." There is a lion in the middle of the tray. Finally, a bare-chested strongman is facing the jail. The child explained that although her dad was really strong, the lion was in his way so that he couldn't see what was happening either. Figure 12.4 is a close-up photograph of the girl.

She put herself inside a wooden jail and placed the jail outside the boundaries of the sand tray that contained her family. In addition, she put a miniature ball and chain around her feet inside the jail and put a lock on the outside of the jail. Her felt layers of entrapment and isolation are eloquently expressed in her choice of materials. She chose the burly man in suspenders to be her perpetrator symbol and placed him just outside her jail cell, guarding her. She also chose a young boy to represent a friend who did notice a change in her behavior over the course of that year and kept asking her what was wrong. Although she had not been able to tell him, she appreciated his perseverance and the fact that he knew her well enough to notice a change in her. She has him holding onto the bars, looking in but ineffectual in his attempts to release her from prison. As we processed this

Figure 12.5 Betsy's *After I Told* Tray: Her Release From Prison

tray, she talked about her sense of being imprisoned during the year that the abuse was occurring. She felt like she had no way out. Her perpetrator was always watching, and he had convinced her that if she told anyone, something bad would happen to her or her family. After we had processed this tray, I asked her to create another tray that showed me what her life has been like since she told her secret (Figure 12.5).

In this tray, the door of the jail is flung wide open. She is standing on top of the jail, holding her friend's hand. Her father is standing behind the two of them, watching over her. She described the incredible sense of freedom that she'd felt since she told her secret. She also used this tray to depict what happened to her perpetrator (Figure 12.6).

Notice that she transferred the ball and chain from herself to her perpetrator. She also arranged to have her mother and other family members, as well as pets, picking the perpetrator up and carrying him into the jail cell. This is a powerful image of justice served and became an important image for this young lady as she moved forward to reclaim her childhood. The before, during, and after here took her from a time when she experienced safety and

Figure 12.6   Betsy's Perpetrator Being Put in Jail

love in the crucible of her family, through the year of abuse, and out the other side to a new reality in which she is free and supported by loved ones and the perpetrator is imprisoned.

In another example of this before, during, and after intervention, another sexually abused child chose puppets to create her series of images (Figures 12.7–12.9).

The prop used in this activity is a set of puppets that includes two blank hand puppets and many facial parts, hands, legs, and hair that can be attached to the blank puppet with Velcro. This allows the child a great deal of versatility in designing the puppet that best expresses her internal state. Figure 12.7 shows the puppet creation that represents her life before the trauma occurred. The eyes are wide open and looking ahead. A full smile has been chosen for the mouth. She talked about how much fun she had with her friends before she was hurt. She described the simple pleasure of curling up on her bed with her dog. Once we processed this puppet, I asked her to change it in some way that would show what it was like for her during the abuse (Figure 12.8).

Figure 12.7 Before the Abuse

Figure 12.8 During the Abuse

One of the main changes that this child made was to the eyes. She covered the first pair of eyes with the pair of bloodshot eyes pictured in Figure 12.8. This is an eloquent nonverbal articulation of the exhausting hypervigilance this child experienced while the abuse was occurring. She never knew when it was going to happen, and she described herself as always watching for signs that he was going to come to her bed again. Another change that she made to the puppet was to turn the nose pointing upward. Lastly, she switched out the full smile for this gap-toothed smile. As we processed her choices for the puppet, she talked about the strain she felt having to smile and act like everything was all right when she was hurting so badly on the inside.

I then invited her to change the puppet to show me what it was like for her now that she was safe again (Figure 12.9).

The first thing she did was take away the bloodshot eyes. She no longer had to wonder if he might come in the night. She also didn't have to wonder if her secret would be found out or worry about what the repercussions would be. She could relax her vigilant stance. She also turned the nose facing downward again. Finally, she took the gap-toothed smile and turned it

Figure 12.9   After the Abuse Puppet

upside down. As we processed the changes she had made to her puppet, she said that she felt sad a lot now, thinking about what he had done to her. She described her growing awareness that she was just beginning to realize all that had been stolen from her. While the abuse was occurring, all her energy was focused on keeping the secret and surviving the nighttime visits. Now that she was safe, she was beginning to grieve the loss of her innocence.

Jackie, a 15-year-old girl with a sexual abuse history, created one sand tray that she split into three parts. She then chose one symbol to put in each part of the tray to represent, respectively, the before, during, and after parts of her own experience (Figure 12.10).

Paris: Give me a couple of words that describe the before object.

Jackie: Innocent, not harmed, confident, feel like I can do anything.

Paris: Her eyes are wide open and she's got cute little ponytails.

Jackie: Yeah.

Paris: She seems very, very loveable.

I am affirming the pretrauma self through the description of the symbol.

Paris: Tell me about this one.

Figure 12.10   Jackie's Before, During and After Sand Tray

I point to the second symbol, the one that she has chosen to represent her experience while the abuse was happening.

Jackie: Crying for help, scared.

Paris: Crying for help and scared. This one is actually made from a different material than the rest of the stuff you chose.

When helping a child process a sand tray, I often notice out loud various characteristics of the objects that are chosen. The client will often recognize another part of her own experience that is expressed in an aspect of the symbol that the young person had not previously explored. Jackie's middle symbol, the stone wolf, is unique in that it is the only item in the tray made from stone.

Paris: Wonder what it's made of?

Jackie: I don't know. It's hard and it reminds me of my—my heart hardened.

Paris: So your heart felt hard.

Jackie: Yeah.

Paris: This one is the after symbol, but right after, when it was still a secret in your family. Tell me about her.

Jackie: Her arms are out, like "Why did it happen to her?"

Paris: So she's asking why?

Jackie: Um hum.

Paris: She's got the word *fly* written on her hat.

Jackie: (laughing): Cuz she's a fly girl!

Paris: Uh huh.

Jackie: Fly away from everything.

Paris: Tell me about her face. You can't see her eyes.

Jackie: Uh uh.

Paris: I wonder what that's like for her.

Jackie: It's like she kinda wants to hide, like she's ashamed of what happened.

Paris: Um hum . . . but she's still a cool girl.

Jackie (grinning at therapist): Right!

Jackie's before, during, and after intervention required an extra step. Her molestation had occurred when she was significantly younger, but she had just recently disclosed it. This resulted in consequences for the dad and upheaval within her family system. I invited her to choose a fourth symbol to represent her current experience and she chose a lioness.

Paris: This last one is for after you told me the secret and the police got involved and dad was removed for a while and you guys were in counseling. So tell me about what you chose.

Jackie: I'm like—I found out that it wasn't my fault and that I have my whole life to live and everything and that I shouldn't blame myself for it.

Paris: Tell me a couple of descriptors of this animal.

Jackie: Wild . . . and courageous.

Jackie had transformed her self-image from a scared, frozen, helpless victim into something resembling a wild and courageous lion. For her, the final encapsulation of the traumatic experience had to include a before, during, after, and now. In her case the abuse had stopped suddenly years before, but the secret was still not told until she entered treatment. She needed a symbol to represent the time between when the abuse stopped and when she revealed the secret. Many variations of this activity can be used, depending on the dynamics of the child's trauma and recovery process.

The last case example that illustrates the potential uses of the before, during, and after technique showcases the drawings of Andy, an 11-year-old boy whose mother died of acquired immune deficiency syndrome (AIDS) when he was 10. During our first session, it became clear that he had little narrative of the events surrounding his mother's death. He lived with his maternal grandmother and had visited mom in the hospital a couple of times early in her illness. Instead of being told that his mother had died, he overheard that she had died weeks after her death, when his grandmother was talking with another relative. He had no idea how long it had been since her death. He had no idea about the disposition of her body. In our first session together, he said, "I don't even know if she was buried or cremated." Apparently the maternal grandmother was experiencing so much of her own pain that she could not discuss Andy's mother with him.

When I met with the grandmother, she expressed guilt over not being able to help him make sense of it all and was eager for me to meet with her grandson. In the beginning of treatment, Andy would ask questions about what happened and we would fill in the gaps of his narrative together. We did many closure rituals together. Andy made a figure of his mother out of clay. He chose and decorated a box to be the coffin. He made a cross out of popsicle sticks and string. Then we chose a spot in a beautiful park and buried her by some of her favorite flowers. Once we had done the bulk of his closure rituals, I invited him to draw a picture of how his mom looked before she got sick (Figure 12.11).

Notice that she is a large figure, taking up the bulk of the paper. Notice also the ragged edge of her skirt. This family lived in poverty and Andy described with admiration all the jobs that mom worked to make sure they had enough to eat. He described her as happy when she was with him. He also described her as being absent a lot. Once we had processed his picture of how he remembered his mom before she got sick, I asked him to draw a picture of what she looked like while she was sick (Figure 12.12).

Figure 12.11   Andy's Drawing: *Before Mom Got Sick*

Figure 12.12   Andy's Drawing: *While Mom Was Sick*

Mom's body is proportionately smaller in this picture than in his previous drawing. Andy stated, "She got little," a child's description of the slow emaciation that can happen as a person dies. Notice that her facial features are difficult to differentiate from one another. He talked about the bruising on her face and the tubes running in and out. He said her face was "messed up a little." Her hair is also changed from Andy's previous drawing. When I asked him about this, he said, "She couldn't get her hair done, so it was nappy." The same ragged edge is present on mom's skirt. He talked about his last visit to her hospital room and how she had been in some pain and unable to talk very well. He reported that the picture that rushed into his mind whenever he thought about his mother was her distorted image during that final hospital visit.

Part of the impetus to create an after image, in this case, was to give Andy a replacement image, one that might bring some comfort. Once we had fully processed the picture of how she looked during her illness, I invited Andy to draw a picture of the way he saw her now (Figure 12.13).

He imagines her inside the pearly gates of heaven. Her image is once again transformed. Her hair is perfectly done and she no longer has a ragged edge to her skirt. Andy talked about how God cleaned her up and gave her

Figure 12.13   Andy's Drawing: *Now That She's in Heaven*

new, beautiful clothes. She also has wings. More importantly, she is smiling. Andy described his belief that she is up in heaven watching over him. In this case, the after picture is one that brings great comfort to Andy.

For Andy, the combination of closure rituals and narrative building through the before, during, and after technique helped him to say a meaningful goodbye. He was able to earn a sense of closure through the belated rituals. When a child has lost a loved one, especially one as critically important to him as a mother or father, it is our job to help create a meaningful goodbye in relation to the lost parent. If a parent has died, the other parent may be so overwhelmed with his own grief that he is unable to support the client through the grief process. Certainly in this case, the grandmother was so deeply entrenched in her own grief at the loss of her daughter that she was unable to provide the kind of support that Andy needed to fully process the trauma. For Andy to integrate the trauma of the loss of his mother into a positive sense of self, he needed markers in the sand, moments of meaningful leave-taking. He also needed accurate information about how she died and what had been done with her body. In this case, the therapist plays multiple roles of providing information, structuring the goodbye, building coherent narrative, and supporting the child in his grief.

It is important to explore the clients' beliefs about what happens to a person's body, soul, and spirit after death. Some clients may have no clearly articulated convictions about death and the afterlife. Others will have a clarified set of beliefs about the afterlife or lack of it. Bibliotherapy can aid in this discussion. The book *When Dinosaurs Die* (Brown, 1996) gives a good psychoeducational overview of several aspects of death, including exposure to several points of view about what happens to a person after death. More and more, the realm of psychology is embracing the realm of the spiritual as an important aspect of the whole self and one that cannot be separated from psychological issues. A child's beliefs about what happens to a person after death will have an impact on how treatment is structured.

The child who believes that what happens after death is a positive experience will often have an easier adjustment to the loved one's death than will the child who believes that what happens after death is a negative experience or a void of nothingness. Some of the most difficult cases that I have dealt with involve the death of a loved one through suicide. I have worked with several families who hold the belief that a person who takes their own life is doomed to an eternity separated from God. Normal grief over the loss of a parent or sibling is complicated by this concern that the person is now in a bad place.

In these cases, the before, during, and after technique may more usefully be focused on the survivors. For children and adolescents who have lost a parent to suicide, I focus the after portion of the exercise on the forever gifts that the deceased gave to them. An adolescent whose mother committed suicide struggled with lots of anger at her mother's decision to leave her. It was only when we shifted the focus of treatment to honoring the forever gifts that her mother had given her that she began to heal. We spent time exploring the lessons that she had learned from her mom, lessons about how to live and lessons that taught her about which parts of historical family patterns she could choose not to repeat. She talked about the gifts of mom's hugs and smiles, the gifts of mom's positive words of affirmation to her and the forever gift of having chosen to give birth to her.

In Figure 12.14, an 8-year-old girl whose younger sister was killed in a terrible accident creates a drawing to represent the forever gifts that her sister left to her.

The gifts her sister gave her included things like her sweet little voice and her funny faces. Another way to structure this drawing activity is to cut out a

Figure 12.14   Sister's Forever Gifts

heart from construction paper and cut many doors into the heart. Allow the child to glue the heart with many doors onto a piece of white paper. Through guided conversation the therapist can help the child fill in the space behind each door with a gift that the lost parent or sibling gave to the child. This activity encourages the integration of positive interactions with the deceased into a positive sense of self.

Parents as Partners

The importance of parents as partners was discussed in an earlier chapter. Caregivers are as important in the integration of trauma content into a positive sense of self as they are in the accomplishment of any other treatment goal. During the termination phase of treatment, parents can aid their children in developing a positive post-trauma identity. Moreover, parents themselves need closure to the treatment process.

Wisdom Feathers

One activity that can aid in this endeavor is called "wisdom feathers" (Goodyear-Brown, 2002). I invite the family to work together to create an owl out of clay. Once the owl is finished, complete with googly craft eyes,

I introduce a variety of feathers to the family. Some of the feathers are real and some are brightly colored and synthetic. Some are big and some are small. We talk about the metaphor of the wise old owl that has seen much of life. I compare the post-trauma family to this wise old owl. Each family member has learned new things, grown, and evolved in the course of recovering from the traumatic events. They have weathered the storm and each family member is now wiser than he or she was before.

Each member of the family chooses a feather that best symbolizes one piece of wisdom he or she has gained through the trauma recovery process. They take turns articulating important pieces of knowledge that they have gained while adding a feather to the owl's clay body. The family is given more feathers to take home and is encouraged to continue adding feathers as they recognize new pieces of wisdom, knowledge, or growth that have been either a direct or an indirect result of their healing.

Termination Takeaways

Another activity that I offer to families during the final phase of treatment is called "termination takeaways" (Goodyear-Brown, 2005). I lay out a variety of boxes that resemble Chinese takeout boxes. Some are big and some are small. Some have bold colors on them, some have hearts, and some are plain. All of them can be decorated with positive affirmations or symbols of the work done in treatment. I ask the child if she has seen one of these boxes before. Usually, the child quickly identifies the boxes as the kind used to take leftovers home from a restaurant. I explain that these boxes are to help the family take home important ideas or images from the playroom. Each family member is given several strips of paper and asked to write or draw important ideas or memories from treatment. Family members take turns verbalizing what is written on their strips of paper as each strip of paper is added to the takeaway box (Figure 12.15). Another fun variation of this activity would be to have the family generate the statements and then bake them into wisdom cookies. These cookies could then be given to the family as a goodbye present.

Bandage Banners

"Bandage banners" (Goodyear-Brown, 2005), (another graduation activity, is an intervention that can be particularly meaningful for children. In the

Figure 12.15 Termination Take-Aways

office I keep a large, silly-looking mummy. When a child first comes in, if he is interested in the mummy, I may use the bandaged figure as an opening for discussing the need to cover wounds and let them heal. The child is invited to talk about whatever hurts or wounds may have been inflicted as a result of the trauma she experienced. I wrap the child in a bandage for each hurt that we discuss and write a list of the hurts as we go. At the end of treatment we revisit the mummy. I get the bandages back out, we wrap the child, and then we unwrap the bandages as we talk about how the child has healed. The child is given a bandage to decorate. We write a mantra such as, "I am a survivor" on the bandage and transform it into a banner that can be displayed in the child's room.

Pats on the Back

Another termination activity that can be done with the whole family or individually is called "pats on the back" (Goodyear-Brown, 2005). I begin by introducing a variety of cutout handprints to the child. I have tiny foam handprints and larger stenciled handprints. One nice variation of this intervention involves tracing the handprints of each family member present, cutting these out, and using the actual family member's handprints to become the pats on the child's back. The child's body can be outlined on butcher paper or a smaller cut-out template of a person can be used. We then explore different ways in which family members are proud of the identified client for weathering the storm of the trauma and coming out the other side. Each affirmation is written on a handprint and glued to the back of the client's self-portrait. The focus of the affirmations can begin with the child but then move to each family member and the roles they played in the child's healing journey. These can be taken home as a keepsake reminder of the child's accomplishments and the family's healing journey.

Graduation Hats

Another keepsake that can also be created before the final session is a graduation hat. I buy cardboard graduation hats that can be individually decorated. Around the band of the hat, we write the treatment goals that the child has completed. On the top, the parents and I take turns writing positive affirmation statements (Figure 12.16).

Figure 12.16 Graduation Hat with Affirmations

The Final Session

Once all the preparations have been made, the final session becomes a purposeful celebration, complete with meaningful rituals. The child and I collaborate on the guest list for the final session. In most cases the caregivers are invited. Caregivers are asked to write a letter that talks about the hard work the child has completed, any positive transformation that the caregiver has witnessed, and any words of encouragement they want to offer. In advance of this last session, the child has created his own award certificates or thank you notes for the caregivers, noting the unique ways in which the parents supported the client through his treatment. The child puts on the graduation hat while the parents read their letters and then the child presents his creations to them. The child can then keep the hat as another reminder of his hard work.

I also create a Certificate of Graduation that includes the child's full name and his final date of treatment. I write my signature at the bottom, then the child signs the bottom, and finally the caregivers sign the document. I present the certificate with some pomp and circumstance while the parents smile and the child giggles. I bring a special food item that the child had chosen in advance and we all share the snack together. As a closing gesture, the child gets to choose a stone or jewel from the treasure chest that has been used at various points in the treatment process to take home with him. The stone serves as a final transitional object from the memories of the playroom to their home environment.

Conclusion

It is critical that the hard work that a child and family have completed be properly punctuated at the end of treatment. Celebration rituals may differ from family to family and from culture to culture, but in every case the gains made during a trauma recovery process should be concretized and honored. Once the toxicity of the traumatic event has been siphoned off, a narrative constructed, and any other troublesome symptoms alleviated, some time should be spent helping the child create a sense of future, looking at how the traumatic event can be folded into an ultimately positive sense of self.

Some of the children we treat do not get, for any number of logistical reasons, an intentional meaningful goodbye with the therapist. It is in these cases that the words quoted at the beginning of this chapter bring the most hope: "And I, I took the road less traveled by, and that has made all the difference." The time spent in the playroom can become that road less traveled for the child, a unique set of experiences in a place set apart strictly for the child's healing journey. The child may also experience a unique and healing relationship with the play therapist that is different than any she has experienced before. It is my belief that this set of experiences can run parallel in the child's mind and body to any others, providing another road that the child may traverse when she is able. In other words, we, the clinicians providing services for these children, offer the child "the road less traveled by." To that end our involvement can make a significant, positive difference in the lives of the children we treat.

References

Ainsworth, M. S., Blehar, M. C., Walters, E., & Wall, S. (1978). *Patterns of attachment: A psychological study of the strange situation*. Oxford, England: Erlbaum.

American Psychiatric Association. (2000). *Diagnostic and statistical manual of mental disorders*, 4th ed. (text revision DSM IV-TR). Washington, DC: American Psychiatric Association.

Anda, R. F., Felitti, V. J., Bremner, J. D., Walker, J. D., Whitfield, C., Perry, B. D., Dube, S. R., & Giles, W. H. (2006). The enduring effects of abuse and related adverse experiences in childhood: A convergence of evidence from neurobiology and epidemiology. *European Archives of Psychiatry and Clinical Neuroscience*, 256, 174–186.

Arden, J. B., & Linford, L. (2009). *Brain-based therapy with children and adolescents: evidence-based treatment for everyday practice*. New Jersey: John Wiley & Sons.

Asarnow, J. R., Tompson, M. C., & Berk, M. S. (2005). Adolescent depression: Family focused treatment strategies. In W. Pinsof and J. Lebow (Eds.), *Family psychology: The art of the science* (pp. 425–450). New York: Oxford University Press.

Axline, V. M. (1947). *Play therapy: The inner dynamics of childhood*. Boston: Houghton-Mifflin.

Baggerly, J. (2006). Preparing play therapists for disaster response: Principles and practices. *International Journal of Play Therapy, 15*, pp. 59–81.

Barnes, J. (Ed.). (1984). *The complete works of Aristotle: The revised oxford translation*. 2 vols. Princeton, NJ: Princeton University Press.

Beck, A. T. (1975). *Cognitive therapy and the emotional disorders*. NY: International Universities Press.

Beck, A. T., Shaw, B. F., & Emery, G. (1979). *Cognitive therapy of depression*. New York: Guilford Press.

Beck, A. T., Emery, G., & Greenberg, R. L. (2005). *Anxiety disorders and phobias: A cognitive perspective*. New York: Basic Books.

Beck, J. S. (1995). *Cognitive therapy: Basics and beyond*. New York: Guilford.

Beck, J. S, Rush, A. J., Shaw, B. F., & Emery, G. (1979). *Cognitive therapy of depression*. Sussex, England: Wiley & Sons, Ltd.

Beck, A. T., (1972). *Depression: Causes and treatment*. Philadelphia: University of Pennsylvania Press.

Bell,S. , & Eyberg, S. M. (2002). Parent-child interaction therapy. In L. VandeCreek, S. Knapp, & T. L . Jackson (Eds.), *Innovations in clinical practice: A sourcebook* (Vol. 20). Sarasota, FL: Professional Resource Press.

Boxer, P., Morris, A. S., Terranova, A. M., Kithakye, M., Savoy, S. C., & McFaul, A. F. (2008). Coping with exposure to violence: relationship to emotional symptoms and aggression in three urban samples. *Journal of Child and Family Studies, 17*, 881–893.

Bowlby, J. (1973). *Attachment and loss: Vol. 1. Attachment*. New York: Basic Books. ;

Bowlby, J. (1988). *A secure base*. New York: Basic Books.

Bleich, A., Gelkopf, M., & Solomon, Z. (2003). Exposure to terrorism, stress-related mental health symptoms, and coping behaviors among a nationally representative sample in Israel. *Journal of the American Medical Association, 290*, 612–620.

Boggs, S. R., Eyberg, S. M., Edwards, D. L., Rayfield, A., Jacobs, J., Bagner, D., & Hood, K. K. (2004). Outcomes of parent-child interaction therapy: A comparison of treatment completers and study dropouts one to three years later. *Child and Family Behaivor Therapy, Vol 26*, 1–22.

Borysenko, J., & Borysenko, M. (1994). *The power of the mind to heal*. Carson, CA: The Hay House, Inc.

Bratton, S., Ray, D., Rhine, T., & Jones, L. (2005). The efficacy of play therapy with children: A meta-analytic review of the outcome research. *Professional Psychology: Research and Practice, 36*, 376–390.

Bratton, S., Landreth, G., Kellam, T., Blackard, S. (2006). *Child parent relationship therapy (CPRT) treatment manual: A 10 session filial therapy model for training parents*. New York: Taylor & Francis.

Bremner, J. D., Vythilingham, M., Vermetten, E., Adil, J., Khan, S., Nazeer, A., Afzal, N., McGlashan, T., Elzinga, B., Anderson, G. M., Heninger, G., Southwick, S. M., & Charney, D. S. (2003). Cortisol response to a cognitive stress challenge in posttraumatic stress disorder (PTSD) related to childhood abuse. *Psychoneuroendocrinology, 28*, 733–750.

Brestan, E., & Eyberg, S. (1998). Effective psychosocial treatments of conduct-disordered children and adolescents: 29 years, 82 studies, and 5272 kids. *Journal of Clinical Child Psychology, 27*, 180–189.

Briere, J., & Scott, C. (2006). *Principles of trauma therapy: A guide to symptoms, evaluation, and treatment*. Thousand Oaks, CA: Sage Publications.

Bronfenbrenner, U. (1979). *The ecology of human development: Experiments by nature and design*. Cambridge, MA: Harvard University Press.

Brown, L. K., & Brown, M. (1988). *Dinosaurs divorce: A guide for changing families.* Boston: Little Brown & Co.

Brunhoff, Laurent de. (2002). *Babar yoga.* New York: Harry N. Abrams, Inc.

Burns, G. W. (2005). *101 Healing stories for kids and teens: Using metaphors in therapy.* New Jersey: John Wiley and Sons.

Carle, Eric. (1990). *The very quiet cricket.* New York: Philomel Books.

Carle, Eric. (1996). *Little cloud.* New York: Philomel Books.

Carrion, V., Weems, C. F., Ray, R. D., Glaser, B., Hessl, D., & Reiss, A. (2002). Diurnal salivary cortisol in pediatric posttraumatic stress disorder. *Biological Psychiatry, 51*, 575–582.

Cassidy, J. (1994). Emotion regulation: Influences of attachment relationships. In N. Fox (Ed.), *The development of emotion regulation. Monographs of the Society of Research in Child Development, 59*, 228–249.

Cassidy, J., & Shaver, P. R. (1999). *Handbook of attachment: Theory, research, and clinical applications.* New York: Guilford Press.

Cattanach, A. (2008). *Narrative approaches in play with children.* London: Jessica Kingsley Publishers.

Cattanach, A. (2002). *The story so far: Play therapy narratives.* London: Jessica Kingsley Publishers.

Causey, D. L., & Dubow, E. F. (1992). Development of a self-report coping measure for elementary school children. *Journal of Clinical Psychology, 2*, 47–59.

Cicchetti, D., & Tucker, D. (1994). Development and self-regulatory structures of the mind. *Development and Psychopathology, 6*, 533–549.

Cicchetti, D., & Rogosch, F. A. (2001). Diverse patterns of neuroendocrine activity in maltreated children. *Development and Psychopathology, 13*, 677–693.

Cicchetti, D., & Curtis, J. (2006). The developing brain and neural plasticity: Implications for normality, psychopathology, and resilience. In D. Cicchetti and D. Cohen (Eds), *Handbook of developmental psychopathology* (2nd ed., pp. 2–64). Hoboken, NJ: John Wiley & Sons.

Christiano, B., & Russ, S. (1996). Play as a predictor of coping and distress in children during an invasive dental procedure. *Journal of Clinical Child Psychology, 25*, 130–138.

Chambless, D. L., & Ollendick, T. H. (2001). Empirically supported psychological interventions: Controversies and evidence. *Annual Review of Psychology, 52*, 685–716.

Choate, M. L., Pincus, D. B., Eyberg, S. M., & Barlow, D. H. (2005). Parent-child interaction therapy for treatment of separation anxiety disorder in young children: A pilot study. *Cognitive and Behavioral Practice, 12*, pp. 126–135.

Cohen, J. A., Deblinger, E., Mannarino, A. P., & Steer, R. (2004). A multi-site, randomized, controlled trial for children with sex abuse-related PTSD symptoms. *Journal of the American Academy of Child and Adolescent Psychiatry, 42*, 393–402.

Cohen, J., Mannarino, A., and Deblinger, E. (2006). *Treating trauma and traumatic grief in children and adolescents*. New York: Guilford Press.

Constantino, M. J., Castonguay, L. G., and Schut A. J. (2000). The working alliance: A flagship for the scientist-practitioner model in psychotherapy. In E. S. Tryon (Ed.), *Counseling based on process research: Applying what we know* (pp. 81–131). Needham Heights, MA: Allyn & Bacon.

Cooper, G., Hoffman, K., Powell, B., & Marvin, B. (2005). The circle of security intervention: Differential diagnosis and differential treatment. In L. J. Berlin, Y. Ziv, L. Amaya-Jackson, M. T. Greenberg (Eds), *Enhancing early attachments* (pp. 127–151). New York: The Guilford Press.

Craig, W., Pepler, D., Blais, J. (2007). Responding to bullying: What works. *School Psychology International, 28*, 465–477.

Culbert, T. (2003). Integrative approaches in pediatrics: Biofeedback in the context of complementary/alternative medicine. *Biofeedback, 31*, 4–8.

Curtis, Jamie Lee. (2000). *Where do balloons go? An uplifting mystery*. New York: Harper Collins.

Cyr, L. R., Culbert, T., & Kaiser, P. (2003). Helping children with stress and anxiety: An integrative medicine approach. *Biofeedback, 31*, 12–17.

Davis, Nancy. (1990). *Therapeutic stories that teach and heal*. Burke, VA: Self-published.

Davis, M., & Whalen, P. J. (2001). The amygdala: Vigilance and emotion. *Molecular Psychiatry, 6*, 13–34.

De Bellis, M. D., Chrousos, G. P., Dorn, L. D., Burke, L., Helmers, K., Kling, M. A., et. al. (1994). Hypothalamic-pituitary-adrenal axis dysregulation in sexually abused girls. *Journal of Clinical Endocrinology and Metabolism, 78*, 249–255.

De Bellis, M. D., Leffer, L., Trickett, P. K., & Putnam, F. W. (1994). Urinary catecholamine excretion in sexually abuse girls. *Journal of the American Academy of Child and Adolescent Psychiatry, 22*, 320–327.

De Bellis, M. D., & Putnam, F. W. (1994). The psychobiology of childhood maltreatment. *Child and Adolescent Psychiatric Clinics of North America, 3*, 663–678.

De Bellis, M. D., Birmaher, B, Keshavan, M. S., Eccard, C. H., Boring, A. M., et al. (1999). Developmental traumatology: I. Biological stress systems. *Biological Psychiatry, 45*, 1259–1270.

De Bellis, M. D., Keshavan, M., Clark, D. B., Casey, B. J., Giedd, J., Boring, A. M., Frustraci, K., & Ryan, N. D. (1999). Developmental traumatology Part II: Characteristics of trauma and psychiatric symptoms and adverse brain development in maltreated children and adolescents with PTSD. *Biological Psychiatry, 45*, 1271–1284.

De Bellis, M. D., & Thomas, L. A. (2003). Biological findings of posttraumatic stress disorder and child maltreatment. *Current Psychiatry Reports, 5*, 108–117.

Deblinger, E., Lippmann, J., & Steer, R. (1996). Sexually abused children suffering posttraumatic stess symptoms: Initial treatment outcome findings. *Child Maltreatment, 1*, 310–321.

Delahanty, D. L., Nugent, N. R., Christopher, N. C., & Walsh, M. (2005). Initial urinary epinephrine and cortisol levels predict acute PTSD symptoms in child trauma victims. *Psychoneuroendocrinology, 30*, 121–128.

Dempsey, M., Overstreet, S., & Moely, B. (2000). "Approach" and "Avoidance" coping and PTSD symptoms in inner-city youth. *Current Psychology, 19*, 28–45.

DiMario, F., & Emery, E. S. (1987). The natural history of night terrors. *Clinical Pediatrics, 26*, 505–511.

Drewes, A. A. (2008). Bobo revisited: What the research says. *International Journal of Play Therapy, 17*, 52–65.

Dubow, E. F., Tisak, J., Causey, D., Hryshko, A., & Reid, G. (1991). A two-year longitudinal study of stressful life events, social support, and social problem solving skills: Contributions to children's behavioral and academic adjustment. *Child Development, 62*, 583–599.

Duncan, D. F. (1996). Growing up under the gun: Children and adolescents coping with violent neighborhoods. *Journal of Primary Prevention, 16*, 343–356.

Duncan, S., & Barrett, L. F., (2007). Affect is a form of cognition: A neurobiological analysis. *Cognition and Emotion, 21*,1184–1211.

Durand, V. M., & Mindell, J. A. (1999). Behavioral intervention for childhood sleep terrors. *Behavior Therapy, 30*, 705–715.

Durlak, J. A., Fuhrman, T., Lampman, C. (1991). Effectiveness of cognitive-behavior therapy for maladapting children: A meta-analysis. *Psychology Bulletin, 110*, 204–214.

Eisen, A. R., & Kearney, C. A. (1995) *Practitioners guide to treating fear and anxiety in children and adolescents: A cognitive behavioral approach.* New Jersey: Jason Aronson.

Endler, N. S., & Parker, J. D. (1990). Multidimensional assessment of coping: A critical evaluation. *Journal of Personality and Social Psychology, 58*, 844–854.

Erikson, E. (1950). *Childhood and Society.* New York: Norton & Company.

Erath, S. A., Flanagan, K. S., & Bierman, K. L. (2007). Social anxiety and peer relations in early adolescence: Behavioral and cognitive factors. *Journal of Abnormal Child Psychology, 35*, 405–416.

Evans, L. G., & Oehler-Stinnett, J. (2006). Structure and prevalence of PTSD symptomatology in children who have experienced a severe tornado. *Psychology in the Schools, 43*, 283–295.

Eyberg, S. M. (1992). Parent and teacher behavior inventories for the assessment of conduct problem behaviors. In L. VandeCreek, S. Knapp, & T. L. Jackson (Eds.), *Innovations in clinical practice: A sourcebook* (Vol. 11). Sarasota, FL: Professional Resource Press.

Eyberg, S. M. (1993). Consumer satisfaction measures for assessing parent training programs. In L. VandeCreek, S. Knapp, & T. L. Jackson (Eds.), *Innovations in clinical practice: A source book* (Vol. 12). Sarasota, FL: Professional Resource Press.

Eyberg, S. M. ,Funderburk, B. W. ,Hembree-Kigin, T., McNeil,C. B. ,Querido, J. ,&

Hood, K. K. (2001). Parent-child interaction therapy with behavior problem children: One and two year maintenance of treatment effects in the family, *Child & Family Behavior Therapy, 23*, 1–20.

Eyberg S. (2004). The PCIT Story. Part one: The conceptual foundation of PCIT, *Parent-Child Interaction Newsletter, 1,* 1–2.

Famiglietti, J. F. (1984). Delinquency prevention: Four developmentally oriented strategies. *Social Work in Education.* 6, 259–273.

Felix, E., Bond, D., & Shelby, J. (2006). Coping with disaster: Psychosocial interventions for children in international disaster relief. In C. Schaefer & H. Kaduson (Eds.), *Contemporary play therapy: theory, research, and practice* (pp. 307–329). New York

Fleming, N. D., & Mills, C. (1992), Not another inventory, rather a catalyst for reflection. *to improve the academy, 11,* 137–155.

Folkman & Lazarus, R. S. (1980). An analysis of coping in a middle-aged community sample. *Journal of Health and Social Behavior, 21,* 219–239.

Folkman, S., & Lazarus, R. S. (1985). If it changes it must be a process: A study of emotion and coping during three stages of a college examination. *Journal of Personality and Social Psychology, 48,* 150–170.

Frey, D. (2002). *Play therapy solutions for bullies and victims.* Dayton, OH: Mandala Publishing.

Friedberg, R. D., & McClure, J. M. (2002). *Clinical practice of cognitive therapy with children and adolescents: The nuts and bolts.* New York: Guilford Press.

Galantino, M. L., Galbavy, R., & Quinn, L. (2008). Therapeutic effects of yoga for children: A systematic review of the literature. *Pediatric Physical Therapy, 20,* 66–80.

Gallese, V., Keysers, C., & Rizzolatti, G. (2004). A unifying view of the basis of social cognition. *Trends in Cognitive Sciences, 8,* 396–403.

Galvaby, R. J. (2003). Juvenile delinquency: Peer influences, gender differences and prevention. *Journal of Prevention & Intervention in the Community, 25,* 65–78.

Garavan, H., Pendergrass, J. C., Ross, T. J., Stein, E. A., & Risinger, R. C. (2001). Amygdala response to both positively and negatively valenced stimuli. *Neuro report, 12,* 2779–2783.

Garbarino, J. (1992). *Children and Families in the Social Environment,* 2nd ed. New York: Aldine De Gruyter.

Gardner, (1993). *Multiple intelligences: The theory in practice.* New York: Basic Books.

Gerik, s. (2005). Pain management in children: Developmental considerations and mind-body therapies. *Southern Medical Journal*, 98, 295–302.

Gil, E. (1994). *Play in family therapy*. New York: Guilford Press.

Gil, E. (2003). Art and play therapy with sexually abused children. In C. A. Malchiodi (Ed.), *Handbook of art therapy* (pp. 152–166). New York: Guilford Press.

Gil, E. (2006). *Helping abused and traumatized children: Integrating directive and nondirective approaches*. New York: Guilford Press.

Goldstein, A. (1980). Thrills in response to music and other stimuli. *Physiological Psychology*, 8, 126–129.

Goleman, D. (1995). *Emotional intelligence: Why it can matter more than IQ*. New York: Bantam Books.

Gonzales, N. A., & Kim, L. S. (1997). Stress and coping in an ethnic minority context: Children's cultural ecologies. In S. A. Wolchik and I. N. Sandler (Eds.), *Handbook for children's coping: Linking theory and intervention* (pp. 481–511). New York: Plenum.

Goodyear-Brown, P. (2001) "Postcards in Motion", "The Preschool Play Geno-Game", and "The Good-At Playdoh Figures". In H. G. Kaduson., & C. E. Schaefer (eds). *101 More favorite play therapy techniques, Volume 2*. New Jersey: Jason Aronson, Inc.

Goodyear-Brown, P. (2002). *Digging for buried treasure: 52 prop-based play therapy interventions for treating the problems of childhood*. Nashville: Sundog, Ltd.

Goodyear-Brown, P. (2003a). "I'm Sick of Eggs" and "All Tangled Up". In H. G. Kaduson, & C. E. Schaefer, (eds), *101 More favorite play therapy techniques*, Volume 3. New Jersey: Jason Aronson, Inc.

Goodyear-Brown, P. (2003b). *Gabby the Gecko*. Nashville: Sundog, Ltd.

Goodyear-Brown, P., Riviere, S., & Shelby, J. (2004). *10 Peas in a pod*. DVD.

Goodyear-Brown, P. (2005). *Digging for Buried Treasure 2: 52 more prop-based play therapy interventions for treating the problems of childhood*. Nashville: Sundog, Ltd.

Goodyear-Brown, P. (2007). *You are my speedbump*. APT Magazine, March 2007.

Goodyear-Brown, P. (2009). Theraplay approaches for children with autism spectrum disorders. In E. Munns (Ed.) *Applications of theraplay with families and groups*. (pp.). Rowman Littlefield.

Goodyear-Brown, P. (in press). Play therapy with anxious preschoolers. In C. Schaefer (Ed), *Play therapy with preschoolers*. Washington, DC: American Psychological Association.

Gordon, J., King, N. J., Gullone, E., Mursi, P., & Ollendick, T. H. (2007). Treatment of children's nighttime fears: The need for a modern randomized controlled trial. *Clinical Psychology Review*, 27, 98–113.

Gravea, J., & Blissett, J. (2004). Is cognitive behavior therapy developmentally appropriate for young children? A critical review of the evidence? Clinical Psychology Review, 24, 399–420.

Guerney, L. (1964). Filial Therapy: Description and rationale. Journal of Consulting Psychology, 28, 304–310.

Guerney, B. G. Jr., Guerney, L., & Andronico, M. (1999). Filial therapy. In C. Schaefer (Ed), The therapeutic use of child's play (pp. 553–566). Northvale, NJ: Jason Aronson.

Haley, D. W., & Stansbury, K. (2003). Infant stress and parent responsiveness: Regulation of physiology and behavior during still-face and reunion. Child Development, 74, 1534–1546.

Harris, J. (1998). The nurture assumption: Why children turn out the way they do. New York: Free Press.

Hart, J., Gunnar, M., & Cicchetti, D. (1996). Altered neuroendocrine activity in maltreated children related to depression. Development and Psychopathology, 8, 201–214.

Hembree-Kigin, T., & McNeil, C. B. (1995). Parent child interaction therapy. New York: Plenum.

Herschell, A. D., & McNeil, C. B. (2007). Parent-child interaction therapy with physically abusive families. In J. M. Briesmeister & C. E. Schaefer. (Eds), Handbook of parent training: Helping parents prevent and solve problem behaviors (3rd ed.). New Jersey: John Wiley & Sons.

Hiscock, H. (2008). The child who will not sleep. Pediatrics and Child Health, 18, 250–251.

Hoffman, K. T., Marvin, R. S., & Cooper, G., & Powell, B. (2006). Changing toddlers' and preschoolers' attachment classifications: The circle of security intervention. Journal of Consulting and Clinical Psychology, 74(6), 1017–1026.

Holmbeck, G. N., Greenley, R. N., & Franks, E. A. (2003). Developmental issues and considerations in research and practice. In A. E. Kazdin & J. R. Weisz (Eds.), Evidence-based psychotherapies for children and adolescents (pp. 21–41). New York: Guilford.

Isabella, R. (1993). "Origins of attachment: Maternal interactive behavior across the first year. " Child Development, 64, 605–621.

James, B. (1989). Treating traumatized children: new insights and clinical intervention. New York: The Free Press.

Jernberg, A., & Booth, P. (2001). Theraplay. San Francisco: Jossey-Bass Publishers.

Johnson, D., & Lubin, H. (2006). The counting method: Applying the rule of parsimony to the treatment of posttraumatic stress disorder. Traumatology, 12, 83–99.

Kabat-Zinn, J. (1990). Full catastrophe living: using the wisdom of your body and mind to face pain, stress and illness. New York: Delta.

Kabat-Zinn, J., Massion, A. O., Kristeller, J., Peterson, L. G., Gletcher, K. E., Pbert, L., Lenderking, W. R., & Santorelli, S. F. (1992). The effectiveness of a mediation-based stress reduction program in the treatment of anxiety disorders. *American Journal of Psychiatry, 149*, 936–943.

Kabat-Zinn, J. (2005). *Coming to our senses: Healing ourselves and the world through mindfulness.* New York: Hyperion.

Kaduson, H., Cangelosi, D., & Schaefer, C. (1997). *The playing cure: Individualized play therapy for specific childhood problems.* Northvale, NJ: Jason Aronson.

Kagan, R. (2007). *Real life Heroes: A life storybook for children* (2nd ed.). New York: The Haworth Press.

Kajander, R., & Peper, E. (1998). Teaching diaphragmatic breathing to children. *Biofeedback, 26*, 14–17.

Kaufman, J. (1991). Depressive disorders in maltreated children. *Journal of the American Adacemy of Child and Adolescent Psychiatry, 30*, 257–265.

Kazdin, A. E. (1993). Treatment of conduct disorder: Progress and directions in psychotherapy research. *Development and Psychopathology, 5*, 277–310.

Kimball, W., Nelson, W. M., & Politano, P. M. (1993). The role of developmental variables in cognitive-behavioral interventions with children. In A. J. Finch, W. M. Nelson, & E. S. Ott (Eds.), *Cognitive-behavioral procedures with children and adolescents: A practical guide* (pp. 25–66). Needham Heights, MA: Allyn & Bacon.

King, J. A., Mandansky, D., King, S. M., Fletcher, K. E., & Brewer, J. (2001). Early sexual abuse and low cortisol. *Psychiatry & Clinical Neurosciences, 55*, 71–74.

Knapp, L. G., Stark, L. J., Kurkijan, J. A., and Spirito, A. (1991). Assessing coping in children and adolescents: Research and practice. *Educational Psychology Review, 3*, 309–334.

Knell, S. M. (1993). *Cognitive-behavioral play therapy.* Northvale, NJ: Jason Aronson.

Knell, S. M. (1998). Cognitive-behavioral play therapy. *Journal of Clinical Child Psychology, 27*, 28–33.

Kochenderfer-Ladd, B. (2004). Peer victimization: The role of emotions in adaptive and maladaptive coping. *Social Development, 13*, 329–349.

Kubler-Ross, E. (1969). *On death and dying.* New York: Macmillan.

Landreth, G. L. (1991). *Play therapy: The art of the relationship.* Muncie, IN: Accelerated Development.

Landreth, G. L. (1993). Self-expressive communication. In C. E. Schaefer (Ed.), *The therapeutic powers of play* (pp 41–63). Northvale, NJ: Jason Aronson.

Landreth, G. L., & Bratton, S. C. (2006). *Child parent relationship therapy: A 10-session filial therapy model.* New York: Taylor & Francis Group.

Layne, C. M., Saltzman, W. R., Poppleton, L., Burlingame, G. M., Pasalic, A., Durakovic, E., Music, M., Campara, N., Dapo N., Arslanagic, B., Steinberg, A.

M., Pynoos, R. S. (2008). Effectiveness of a school-based group psychotherapy program for war-exposed adolescents: A randomized controlled trial. *Journal of the American Academy of Child and Adolescent Psychiatry, 47*, 1048–1062.

Leiberman, A. F., Van Horn, P., & Ippen, C. G. (2005). Toward evidence-based treatment: Child-parent psychotherapy with preschoolers exposed to marital violence. *Journal of the American Academy of Child and Adolescent Psychiatry, 44*, 1241–1248.

Leiberman, A. F., Van Horn, P., & Ippen, C. G. (2006). Child-parent psychotherapy: 6-month follow-up of a randomized control trial. *Journal of the American Academy of Child and Adolescent Psychiatry, 45*, 913–918.

Litz, B. T., Gray, M. J., Bryant, R. A., & Adler, A. B. (2002). Early intervention for trauma: Current status and future directions. *Clinical Psychology: Science and Practice, 9*, 112–134.

Loumeau-May, L. V. (2008). Grieving in the public eye: Art therapy with children who lost parents in the world trade center attacks. In C. A. Malchiodi (Ed.), *Creative interventions with traumatized children* (pp. 81–111). New York: Guilford Press.

Main, M. (1995). Attachment: Overview, with implications for clinical social work. In S. Goldberg, R. Muir, & J. Kerr (Eds.), *Attachment theory: Social developmental and clinical perspectives*, pp. 407–474. Hillsdale, NJ: Analytic Press.

Malchiodi, C. (1998). *Understanding children's drawings*. New York: Guilford Press.

Malchiodi, C. (2003). Effective practice with traumatized children: Ethics, evidence, and cultural sensitivity. In C. Malchiodi (Ed.), *Creative interventions with traumatized children*. New York: Guilford Press.

Martin, D. J., Garske, J. P., & Davis, M. K. (2000). Relation of the therapeutic alliance with outcome and other variables: A meta-analytic review. *Journal of Consulting and Clinical Psychology, 68*, 438–450.

Martin, E. E., Snow, M. S., & Sullivan, K. (2008). Patterns of relating between mothers and preschool-aged children using the Marschak Interaction Method Rating System. *Early Child Development and Care, 178*, 305–314.

Marvin, R. S., Cooper, G., Hoffman, K., & Powell, B. (2002). The circle of security project: Attachment-based intervention with caregiver-preschool child dyads. *Attachment and Human Development, 1*, 107–124.

McCallie, M., Blum, C., & Hood, C. (2006). Progressive muscle relaxation. *Journal of Human Behavior in the Social Environment, 13*, 51–66.

McGoldrick, M., Gerson, R., & Shellenberger, S. (1999). *Genograms: Assessment and intervention*. New York: Norton and Company.

Mills, J. C., & Crowley, R. J. (2001). *Therapeutic Metaphors for Children and the Child Within*. Philadelphia: Brunner/Mazel.

Mindell, J. A. (1993). Sleep disorders in children. *Health Psychology, 12*, 151–162.

Moore, G. A., & Calkins, S. D. (2004). Infants' vagal regulation in the still-face paradigm is related to dyadic coordination of mother-infant interaction. *Developmental Psychology, 40*, 1068–1080.

Munns, E. (2009). Applications of family and group theraplay. Jason Aronson, Inc.

Muris, P., Merckelbach, H., Ollendick, T. H., King, N. J., & Bogie, N. (2001). Children's nighttime fears: Parent-child ratings of frequency, content, origins, coping behaviors and severity. *Behaviour Research and Therapy, 39*, 13–28.

National Child Traumatic Stress Network and National Center for PTSD (2005). Psychological first aid: Field operations guid (2nd Edition). http:/www. ncptsd. va. gov/pfa/PFA. html.

Nebrosky, R. J. (2003). A clinical model for the comprehensive treatment of trauma using an affect experiencing-attachment Theory approach. In M. F. Solomon, & D. Siegel (Eds.), *Healing Trauma: attachment, mind, body, and brain.* New York: Norton & Co.

Ng-Mak, D. S., Salzinger, S., Feldman, R., & Stueve, C. A. (2004). Pathological adaptation to community violence among inner-city youth. *American Journal of Orthopsychiatry, 74*, 196–208.

Nielsen, T., & Levin, R. (2007). Nightmares: A new neurocognitive model. *Sleep Medicine Reviews, 11*, 295–310.

Newman, R. (2008). Adaptive and nonadaptive help seeking with peer harassment: An integrative perspective of coping and self-regulation. *Educational Psychologist, 43*, 1–15.

Norton, C. C., & Norton, B. E. (2002). *Reaching children through play therapy: An experiential approach.* White Apple Press.

O'Donnell, T. O., Hegadoren, K. M., & Coupland, N. C. (2004). Noradrenergic mechanisms in the pathophysiology of post-traumatic stress disorder. *Neuropsychobiology, 50*, 273–283.

Parkinson, F. (2000). *Post-trauma stress: A personal guide to reduce the long-term effects and hidden emotional damage caused by violence and disaster.* Tucson, AZ: Fisher Books.

Paule, S. T. (2009). Play therapy techniques for affect regulation. In A. Drewes (Ed.), *Blending play therapy with cognitive behavioral therapy: Evidence-based and other effective treatments and techniques* (pp. 353–372). New Jersey: John Wiley & Sons.

Pelletier, C. L. (2004). The effect of music on decreasing arousal due to stress: A meta-analysis. *Journal of Music Therapy, 41*, 192–214.

Pervanidou, P. (2008). Biology of post-traumatic stress disorder in childhood and adolescence. *Journal of Neuroendicronology, 20*, 632–638.

Perry, B., Pollard, R., Blakely, T., Baker, W., & Vigilante, D. (1995). Childhood trauma, the neurobiological adaptation and 'use-dependent' development of the brain: How "states become traits". *Infant Mental Health Journal, 16*, 271–291.

Perry, B. D., & Azad, I. (1999). Posttraumatic stress disorders in chidren and adolescents. *Current Opinion in Pediatrics, 11*, 310–316.

Phelps, A. J., Forbes, D., & Creamer, M. (2008). Understanding posttramatic nightmares: An empirical and conceptual review. *Clinical Psychology Review, 28*, 338–355.

Piaget, J. (1954). *The construction of reality in the child.* Translated by Margaret Cook. New York: Basic Books, Inc.

Pincus, D. B., Eyberg, S. M., & Choate, M. L. (2005). Adapting parent-child interaction therapy for young children with separation anxiety disorder. *Education and Treatment of Children, 28*, 163–181.

Pollak, S. D., & Tolley-Schell, S. A. (2003). Selective attention to facial emotion. *Journal of Abnormal Psychology, 112*, 323–338.

Pollak, S. D., Cicchetti, D., Klorman, R., & Brumaghim, J. T. (1997). Cognitive brain event-related potentials and emotion processing in maltreated children. *Child Development, 68*, 773–787.

Pollak, S. D., & Sinha, P. (2002). Effects of early experience on children's recognition of facial displays of emotion. *Developmental Psychology, 38*, 784–791.

Powell, B., Cooper, G., Hoffman, K., & Marvin, R. (2007). The circle of security project: A case study—"It hurts to give that which you did not receive". In D. Oppenheim, & D. Goldsmith (Eds.), *Attachment theory in clinical work with children: Bridging the gap between research and practice* (pp. 172–202). New York: Guilford Press.

Powers, S., Mitchell, M., Byars, K., Bentti, A., Lecates, S., & Hershey, A. (2001). A pilot study of one-session biofeedback training in pediatric headache. *Neurology, 56*, 133.

Ransom, J. F. (2000). *I don't want to talk about it.* Magination Press.

Rauhala, E., Alho, H., Hanninen, O., et al. (1990). Relaxation training combined with increased physical activity lowers the physiological activation in community home boys. *International Journal of Psychophysiology, 10*, 63–68.

Ray, D., Bratton, S., Rhine, T., & Jones, L. (2001). The effectiveness of play therapy: Responding to the critics. *International Journal of Play Therapy, 10*, 85–108.

Ray, D. C. (2006). Evidence-Based play therapy. In C. E. Schaefer & H. G. Kaduson (Eds.), *Contemporary play therapy: Theory, research and practice* (pp. 136–157). New York: Guilford.

Read, J., Perry, B. D., Moskowitz, A., & Connolly, J. (2001). The contribution of early traumatic events to schizophrenia in some patients: A traumagenic neurodevelopmental model. *Psychiatry: Interpersonal and Biological Processes, 64*, 319–345.

Reinecke, M., Dattilio, F., & Freeman, A. (Eds.). (2003). *Cognitive therapy with children and adolescents: A Casebook for clinical practice* (2nd ed.). New York: Guilford Press.

Rizzolatti, G., Fadiga, L., & Gallese, V. (2001). Neuorphysiological mechanisms underlying understanding and imitation. *Nature Reviews Neuroscience, 2,* 66–70.

Robinson, G., & Maines, B. (2008). *Bullying: A complete guide to the support group method.* Thousand Oaks, CA: Sage Publications.

Roger, D., Jarvis, G., & Najarian, B. (1993). Detachment and coping: The construction and validation of a new scale for measuring coping strategies. *Personal and individual Differences.* Vol. 15, 619–626.

Rothschild, B. (2000). *The body remembers: The psychophysiology of trauma and trauma treatment.* New York: Norton and Company.

Russ, S. W. (2007). Pretend Play: A resource for children who are coping with stress and managing anxiety. *NYS Psychologist, XIX, 5,* 13–17.

Rusy, L., & Weisman, S. (2000). Complementary therapies for acute pediatric pain management. *Pediatric Clinics of North America, 47,* 589–599.

Ruzek, J. I., Brymer, M. J., Jacobs, A. K., Layne, C. M., Vernberg, E. M., & Watson, P. J. Psychological first aid. *Journal of Mental Health Counseling, 29,* 17–49.

Sadeh, A. (2005). Cognitive behavioral treatment for childhood sleep disorders. *Clinical Psychology Review, 25,* 612–628.

Sapolsky, R. M. (2004). *Why zebras don't get ulcers.* 3rd edition. New York: Henry Holt and Company.

Schaefer, C. E. (1993). *The therapeutic powers of play.* Northvale, NJ: Jason Aronson.

Schaefer, C. E., & Drewes, A. A. (2009). Therapeutic powers of play and play therapy. In A. A. Drewes (Ed.), *Blending play therapy with cognitive behavioral therapy: Evidence-based and other effective treatments and techniques* (pp. 3–15). New Jersey: John Wiley and Sons.

Schore, A. (1997). Early organization of the nonlinear right brain and development of the predisposition to psychiatric disorders. *Development and Psychopathology, 9,* 595–631.

Schore, A. (1998). The experience-dependent maturation of an evaluative system in the cortex. In K. Pribram (Ed.), *Brain and values: Is a biological science of values possible* (pp. 337–358). Mahwah, NJ: Erlbaum.

Schore, A. (2003). Early relational trauma, disorganized attachment, and the development of a predisposition to violence. In M. F. Solomon, & D. Siegel (Eds.), *Healing Trauma: attachment, mind, body, and brain* (pp. 107–167). New York: Norton & Company.

Schredl, M. (2009). Nightmares. *Encyclopedia of Neuroscience.* 1145–1150.

Schulte,D., & Eifert, G. H. (2002). What to do when manuals fail? The dual model of psychotherapy. *Clinical Psychology: Science and Practice, 9,* 312–328.

Schwartz, S., & Andrasik. (2003). *Biofeedback, third Edition: A practitioner's guide.* New York: Guilford Press.

Segal, Z. V., Williams, M. G., & Teasdale, J. D. (2002). *Mindfulness-based cognitive therapy for depression: A new approach to preventing relapse.* New York: Guilford Press.

Shapiro, F. (1995). *Eye movement desensitization and reprocessing: Basic principles, protocols and procedures.* New York: Guilford Press.

Shapiro, F., & Maxfield, L. (2003). EMDR and information processing in psychotherapy treatment: personal developmental and global implications. In M. F. Solomon, & D. Siegel (Eds.), *Healing trauma: Attachment, mind, body, and brain* (pp. 196–220). New York: Norton & Company.

Shelby, J. S. (1997). Rubble, disruption, and tears: Helping young survivors of natural disaster (pp. 143–169). In H. Kaduson , D. M. Cangelosi, & C. E. Schaefer (Eds). *The playing cure: Individualized play therapy for specific childhood problems.* Lanham, MD: Jason Aronson.

Shelby, J. S., & Felix, E. D. (1997). Rubble, disruption, and tears: Helping young survivors of natural disaster. In H. Kaduson, D. Cangelosi, & C. Schaefer (Eds.), *The Playing Cure* (pp. 143–170). Northvale, NJ: Aronson.

Shelby, J. S., Bond, D., Hall, S., & Hsu, C. (2004). *Enhancing coping among young tsunami survivors.* Los Angeles: Authors.

Shelby, J. S., & Berk, M. S. (2009). Play therapy, pedagogy and CBT: An argument for interdisciplinary synthesis. In A. A. Drewes (Ed.), *Blending play therapy with cognitive behavioral therapy: Evidence-based and other effective treatments and techniques* (pp. 17–40). New Jersey: John Wiley and Sons.

Shelby, J. S., & Felix, E. D. (2005). Posttraumatic play therapy: The need for an integrated model of directive and nondirective approaches. In L. Reddy, T. M. Files-Hall, & C. E. Schaefer (Eds.), *Empirically based play Interventions for children* (pp. 79–103). Washington, DC: American Psychological Association.

Siegel, D. (2003). An Interpersonal Neurobiology of Psychotherapy: The Developing Mind and the resolution of trauma. In M. F. Solomon & D. J. Siegel (Eds.), *Healing trauma: Attachment, mind, body and brain.* New York: Norton and Company.

Siegel, D., & Hartzell, M. (2003). *Parenting from the inside out: How a deeper self-understanding can help you raise children who thrive.* New York: Penguin/Putnam.

Solomon, M. F., & Siegel, D. J. (2003). *Healing trauma: Attachment, mind,body, and brain.* New York: Norton and Company.

Southwick, S. M., Bremner, J. D., Rasmusson, A., Morgan, C. A., Arnsten, A., & Charney, D. S. (1999). Role of norepinephrine in the pathophysiology and treatment of posttraumatic stress disorder. *Biological Psychiatry, 46,* 1192–1204.

Spirito, A., Stark, L. J., & Williams, C. (1988). Development of a brief checklist to assess coping in pediatric patients. *Journal of Pediatric Psychology, 13,* 555–574.

Sroufe, L. A. (1996). *Emotional development: The organization of emotional life in the early years.* New York: Cambridge University Press.

Stein, B. D., Tanielian, T. L., Vaiana, M. E., Rhodes, H. J., & Burnam, M. A. (2003). The role of schools in meeting community needs during bioterrorism. *Biosecurity and bioterrorism: Biodefense strategy, practice, and science, 1,* 273–281.

Stueck, M., & Gloeckner, N. (2005). Yoga for children in the mirror of science: working spectrum and practice fields of the training of relaxation with elements of yoga for children. *Early Child Dev Care, 175,* 371–377.

Teicher, M. (2002). Scars that won't heal: The neurobiology of child abuse. *Scientific American, 286,* 68–75.

Teicher, M. H., Anderson, S. L., Polcari, A., Anderson, C. M., & Navalta, C. P. (2002). Developmental neurobiology of childhood stress and trauma. *Psychiatric Clinics of North American, 25,* 397–426.

Teisl, M., & Ciccheti, D. (2008). Physical abuse, cognitive and emotional processes, and aggressive/disruptive behavior problems. *Social Development, 17,* 1–23.

Terr, L. (1990). *Too scared to cry: Psychic trauma in childhood.* New York: Harper & Row Publishers.

Timmer, S. G., Urquiza, A. J., & Zebell, N. (2006). Challenging foster-caregiver-maltreated child relationships: The effectiveness of parent-child interaction therapy. *Children and Youth Services Review, 28,* 1–19.

Timmer, S. G., Urquiza, A. J., Zebell, N., & McGrath, J. M. (2005). Parent-child interaction therapy: Application to maltreating parent-child dyads. *Child Abuse & Neglect, 29,* 825–842.

Timmer, S. G., Urquiza, A. J., Herschell, A. D., McGrath, J. M., Zebell, N. M., Porter, A. L., & Vargas, E. C. (2006). Parent-child interaction therapy: Applications of an empirically supported treatment to maltreated children in Foster Care. *Child Welfare Journal, 85,* 919–939.

Tronick, E. Z., Als, H., Adamson, L., Wise, S., & Brazelton, B. (1978). The infant's response to entrapment between contradictory messages in face-to-face interaction. *Journal of the American Academy of Child Psychiatry, 1,* 1–13.

Tronick, E. Z. (1989). Emotions and emotional communciation in infants. *American Psychologist, 44,* 112–119.

Tronick, E. Z., & Cohn, J. F. (1989). Infant-mother face-to-face interaction: Age and gender differences in coordination and the occurrence of miscoordination. *Child Development, 60,* 85–92.

Urquiza, A., & Mc, Neail, C. B. (1996). Parent-Child Interaction Therapy: An Intensive Dyadic Intervention for Physically Abusive Families. *Child Maltreatment, 1,* 134–144.

Urquiza, A. J., Zebell, N. M., & Blacker, D. (2009). Innovation and integration: Parent-child interaction therapy as play therapy. In A. Drewes (Ed.), *Blending play therapy with cognitive behavioral therapy: Evidence-based and other effective treatments and techniques* (pp. 199–218).

van der Kolk, B. A. (2003). The neurobiology of childhood trauma and abuse. Child and Adolescent Psychiatric Clinics of North America, *12*, 293–317.

van der Kolk, B. A. (1994). *The body keeps the score.* Harvard Review

van der Kolk, B. A., McFarlane, A. C., & Weisaeth, L. (1996). *Traumatic stress: The effects of overwhelming experiences on mind, body, and society.* New York: Guilford Press.

van der Kolk, B. A. (2003). The neurobiology of childhood trauma and abuse. *Child and Adolescent Psychiatric Clinics of North America, 2,* 293–317.

van der Kolk, B. A. (2005). Developemental trauma disorder: Towards a rational diagnosis for children with complex trauma histories. *Psychiatric Annals, 35,* 401–408.

VanFleet, R., Ryan, S. D., & Smith, S. (2005). Filial therapy: A critical review. In L. Reddy, T. Files-Hall, & C. E. Schaefer (Eds), *Empirically-based play interventions* (pp. 241–264). Washington, DC: American Psychological Association.

Van Horn, P. J., & Lieberman, A. F. (2006). Using play in child-parent psychotherapy to treat trauma. In J. L. Luby (Ed.), *Handbook of Preschool Mental Health: Development, Disorders, and Treatment* (pp. 372–387). New York: Guilford Press.

Vernberg, E. M., LaGreca, A. M., Silverman, W. K., & Prinstein, M. J. (1996). Prediction of post-traumatic stress symptoms in children after hurrican Andrew. *Journal of Abnormal Psychology, 105*(2), 237–248.

Vitaliano, P. P., Russo, J., Carr, J. E., Maiuro, R. D., & Becker, J. (1985). The ways of coping checklist: Revision and psychometric properties. *Multivariate Behavioral Research, 20,* 3–26.

Vygotsky, L. S. (1967). Play and its role in the mental development of the child. *Soviet Psychology, 5,* 6–18.

Vygotsky, L. S. (1978). *Mind in society: The development of higher psychological processes.* Cambridge, MA: Harvard University Press.

Webb, N. B. (Ed.) (2004). *Mass trauma and violence. Helping families and children cope.* New York: Guilford Press.

Weisz, J. R., Southam-Gerow, M. A., & McCarty, C. A. (2001). Control-related beliefs and depressive symptoms in clinic-referred children and adolescents: Developmental differences and model specificity. *Journal of Abnormal Psychology, 110,* 97–109.

Weisz, J. R., Weiss, B., Han, S. S., Granger, D. G., & Morton, T. (1995). Effects of psychotherapy with children and adolescents revisited: A meta-analysis of treatment outcome studies. *Psychological Bulletin, 177,* 450–468.

Wolpe, J. (1958). *Psychotherapy by reciprocal inhibition*. Stanford, CA: Stanford University Press.

Wolpe, Joseph. (1984). Deconditioning and ad hoc uses of relaxation: An overview. *Journal of Behavior Therapy and Experimental Psychiatry, 15*, 299–304.

Wright, C. I., Fisher, H., Whalen, P. J., McInerney, S. C., Shin, L. M., and Rauch, S. L. (2001). Differential prefrontal cortex and amygdala habituation to repeatedly presented emotional stimuli. *Neuro Report, 12*, 379–383.

Ziegler, D. (2002). *Traumatic experiences and the brain: A handbook for understanding and treating those traumatized as children*. Phoenix, AZ: Acacia Publishing.

Author Index

Subject Index